SPACE
to
THINK

SPACE

to

THINK

Ten Years of the *Dublin Review of Books*

drb | ESSAYS | *Volume 1*

Space to Think by *Dublin Review of Books*

© *Dublin Review of Books* 2016

For the purposes of copyright, all essays are the property of the authors.

ISBN 978-0-9954586-2-8

Printed in Spain by GraphyCems
Typeset in Garamond Pro
Designed by Niall McCormack

10 9 8 7 6 5 4 3 2 1

The *Dublin Review of Books* receives financial assistance
from the Arts Council / An Chomhairle Ealaíon

The *Dublin Review of Books*
17 D'Olier St
Dublin 2
Ireland

www.drb.ie
info@drb.ie
@dubreviewbooks

In memory of Brian Earls

1947–2013

Preface   *xv*

Introduction   *xvii*

People

The Irish Literary Tradition

Poetry

Ireland: Culture and Society

Novels and Novelists

Europe and Beyond

War and Revolution

Contemporary Controversies

In the Post

Notes on Contributors

Preface

THE *Dublin Review of Books* is a free online journal of ideas available at www.drb.ie. The journal has been running for ten years, the pilot issue having been published in the winter of 2006. Currently, a complete issue of the *drb* is published every month, with two email newsletters issued to our subscribers in the course of each month. Some material is added between issues. Free subscription is available through our website. The present volume is a selection of essays drawn from our first ten years. The editors would like to thank Matthew Parkinson-Bennett, Niall McCormack and Robert Towers for their assistance in preparing this volume for publication.

Introduction

IF A society is healthy it thinks about itself. We know that the future and what it may hold are, in the nature of things, uncertain, but we also know that present and future are open to human intervention, and certainly open to discussion. With awareness of what is and what has been, a culture can influence its own future, or at least answer questions it will face with some element of self-knowledge.

To say a society can shape its future is perhaps to make too large a claim. What is possible is to achieve an element of understanding – derived from the interplay of thinking, argument, debate and appreciation – which will illuminate and explain but which will, happily, always fall short of finality, an illusion which supports all sorts of dogmatism, and worse, puts a stop to inquiry. The past will always be difficult, the present and the future mercurial. If it were otherwise we would be living a dull existence in a dull world.

In practice, the type of thinking we have dealt with in the *Dublin Review of Books* involves considering what has passed as much as the present, and we have talked as much about art and literature as society. It also involves looking outwards. Ireland in the twenty-first century is a society distinct in itself but it is also, and much more so than some larger societies, one which is engaged with and integrated in a greater and more extensive world. For the Irish, as in varying degrees for other nationalities, thinking about one's culture ultimately and necessarily involves thinking also about the cultures of other peoples. While the degree of engagement may vary, other cultures, especially European cultures, are us. This has long been the case by virtue of our history as part of the Western world, but it is now even more so the case, given the nature of the transformation of Irish society in recent decades.

It is thinking and writing around concerns of this sort that the *Dublin Review of Books* was founded to publish. Our contributors have typically written on questions that emerge from reflection on the arguments and content of particular books. Essays we publish might comprise a detailed appreciation of the work of a particular novelist or poet, or a carefully developed argument in response to a complex – or just as often a straightforward – historical question, or they might form a treatment of some issue in the human or hard sciences. The style might be serious or light and the reading experience might be enlightening or fun or compelling, or all of these. But in all cases the *Dublin Review of Books* provides its contributors with the freedom to develop an argument; it provides them with the *space to think*, the space to develop their ideas.

The review also sees itself as taking a position against the cultural fragmentation which can follow from specialisation. Specialisation is necessary and unavoidable but the high hedges around individual specialisations are not. A healthy intellectual culture is not one comprised of a multiple patchwork with the activities under way in each patch largely hidden from all the others and the world in general. We have sought to publish the work of authors whose prose is accessible and free from specialist terminology; in this way an expert in a particular area can communicate a great deal to interested non-specialists.

In eighteenth century Ireland the pamphlet was the chief means by which ideas were elaborated and debated. In the nineteenth century that role fell mainly to the great journals of the time, such as *The Dublin University Magazine* and *The Nation*. That pattern continued into the twentieth century with journals such as *The Irish Review*, *The Bell* and *The Crane Bag*. There were many others, often excellent but sometimes less well-known or less remembered, which were also concerned with the broad question of what

Irish society was and where it was going. This is the tradition in which the *Dublin Review of Books* sees itself.

Some of the questions which interest us are regularly examined too in other media, such as books and newspapers. We do not have a unique claim on any subject, nor have we discovered any new subjects. However, newspapers and books have limitations associated with their individual forms. In establishing the *Dublin Review of Books* we felt there was a need for a journal that in its detailed long-form treatment of subjects would fall somewhere between a book and a newspaper. It was hoped to establish a journal which would offer continuing stimulation and pleasure to readers through publication of considered essays and other material that would touch on a broad intellectual range in each issue.

We are, of course, aware that the type of journal we publish is not the only worthwhile kind available today. Other journals, for example those devoted primarily to creative writing and *belles lettres*, also have a long history in Ireland. Indeed this category is currently undergoing an exciting and expansive phase to the cultural benefit of all. Journals such as the *London Review of Books* and *The New York Review of Books* are obviously models and they have indeed inspired us, particularly in their range and in the quality of their editing and of the writing they publish. It is certainly no harm for us to be reminded that material of the highest standard is available and regularly enjoyed in these journals by readers who also read the *drb*. Both these journals are similar to us in that they are firmly lodged in the culture of the cities and countries in which they are published but also look out to the world as a place not just of ancillary interest but vital to their own cultural health.

The similarities should not be overstated, however. The main difference is in the size of the countries from which the three journals emerge. *The New York Review*, though undoubtedly in many respects a labour of love, is commercially viable; it comes from a country with a population of 320 million, which also happens to be the most powerful in the world, making many people around the globe interested in the concerns of its intelligentsia. The excellent *London Review of Books* on the other hand comes from a smaller country and has a smaller circulation but is fortunate in being the beneficiary of enlightened philanthropy. Both journals publish and distribute an elegant print edition.

Prosperity has brought great benefits to Ireland and also a prioritising in the business world of commercial values, and this has included a professionalising of distribution channels, which in turn affects the circulation potential of small-run journals. The same channels deliver the best of international English-language journals, such as the reviews mentioned, which in practice means that nothing which does not have the highest production standards will circulate beyond a tiny audience.

The consolidation of chains in retailing, the contraction of independent booksellers and newsagents and the increasing role of supermarkets in selling print material have reduced the number of outlets willing to deal with independent distributors. These factors make distribution difficult for any journal which does not strive for and achieve broad appeal. These are the conditions facing anyone who might consider starting a journal. Like everyone else, we felt we would have to cut our cloth according to our measure.

The solution we settled on was to publish online, a decision which allowed for independent worldwide distribution and freedom from print bills. This, along with Arts Council support and a willingness of the editors and those contributors who enjoyed a salary to contribute on a pro bono basis, rendered the project viable. Within its own terms it has been a success.

Individual essays published in the *drb* are read or downloaded by numbers which vary widely but can be as high as 15,000 individuals. Each issue is distributed free to over 6,000 people and is available to anyone with access to the web. International websites such as Arts and Letters Daily, Eurozine and Poetry Daily frequently pick up items from the *drb* and as a result of this exposure items first published by us have been republished by other journals and in other languages, including Italian, Spanish, Ukrainian and Slovenian. As a result, the circulation and readership figures we enjoy are much greater than those achieved by traditional print-based literary journals published in Ireland. Essays continue to be read years after their original publication. No essay ever completely ceases to circulate. The readership, which is international, divides into three roughly equal segments, a third in Ireland, a third in North America and a third elsewhere.

This modest but definite success has been gratifying, particularly in light of the previously unimagined mass of information now instantly available and capable of absorbing time which might otherwise be available for reading.

Another problem here, and one worth noting, is that the information which crowds out reflective thought is quite different from comprehension. Information is not an alternative to thought. It is good, but if the term "information society" means a society dominated by information unleavened by a strong current of analysis and discussion then it is not so good.

Our view is that a culture which replaces analysis, argument and understanding with information is a culture in difficulty. We see the *drb* as contributing in a small way to tilting the balance a little from the dominance of information and if we have been in any degree successful it is because certain initial assumptions proved accurate.

A key assumption behind the founding of the *drb* was that there was a population in Ireland and elsewhere which would welcome such a journal and read it. We also instinctively felt that writers of ability and insight would contribute. The steady readership has confirmed the first assumption and since we began ten years ago over 360 writers, interested in developing and disseminating their ideas, have contributed, many on numerous occasions. Without the willing involvement of these talented writers the *drb* would not have survived ten years and would not be looking forward to publishing into the future. Clearly the appetite for ideas among both writers and readers persists despite the changes noted.

The *drb* is published online for the reasons we have outlined. It has nothing to do with any disenchantment with the world of print – our preference would be to publish in both forms. Up to quite recently those involved in the world of print used to wake up every morning to read or hear another obituary of their enterprise. It was as if the printed book and those who worked with it were the twenty-first century equivalent of the handloom weavers, hopelessly caught on the wrong side of progress and destined for extinction. But like some other famous literary deaths this one was announced prematurely. It turns out that the printed book has unique qualities, especially in relation to key cognitive processes, and is here to stay. Perhaps more importantly, people just like print and books.

The purpose of the present anthology is to celebrate in printed form our first ten years. We are offering established readers of the *drb* and others a selection of essays in a number of categories, including some from our "In the Post" section, which draws on a miscellany of shorter items written by the editors over the years. The main content is the essays, which in the view of the editors are all excellent. They do not necessarily however include all of the very best we have published: size excluded some fine but very lengthy essays from this anthology. We are thinking particularly, but not solely, of the several very fine explorations by the late Brian Earls of oral culture in Ireland and the world view of the pre-Famine peasantry. There was also the necessity of filling the particular categories that were chosen, which themselves represent a balance of the subject areas in which we have published. It is hoped to make this publication an annual one which will draw on the previous year's essays and also on the range of good writing published over our first ten years and not yet celebrated in print.

Maurice Earls
Enda O'Doherty

OCTOBER 2016

People

The distinguished filmmaker Brian Desmond Hurst came from a working class Belfast background that in later life he found little pleasure in recalling, constructing for himself in its place an Irish republican and Catholic identity. His Catholicism, however, seemed to have little effect on his bohemian homosexual lifestyle, which he maintained well into old age. ÉAMON Ó CLÉIRIGH *finds that Hurst was lucky in his biographer, Christopher Robbins, who has saved a most unusual life from time's oblivion and in the process written a book that is extremely funny.*

CATRIONA CROWE *reviews a biography of Laetitia Pilkington, an eighteenth century writer who was a friend of Swift, who treated her as an intelligent doll, playing tricks on her, pinching her, smacking her, quizzing her on her knowledge of literature and expecting her to listen to him for hours on end.*

WT Stead was one of the pioneers of investigative journalism and exposed the evils of child prostitution in Victorian England. JOHN HORGAN *salutes a biography written with an energy, flair and fair-mindedness that must have been difficult to maintain in the face of its subject's bewildering eccentricity and megalomania, and a moral compass that did not always point to true north.*

The historian Hugh Trevor-Roper was immensely talented but some who knew him wondered why one so young and gifted spent so much time hating people. ÉAMON Ó CLÉIRIGH *finds Adam Sisman's biography wide-ranging, acute and convincing.*

Charles O'Conor was an eighteenth century scholar who was an authoritative voice of Gaelic-rooted Ireland and a cultural mediator between native and Ascendancy Ireland. He was also, writes FERGUS O'FERRALL, *a full participant in the European Enlightenment, who annotated his copy of Montesquieu in Irish.*

ENDA O'DOHERTY *finds that while George Orwell's political writing was of the highest order, his political judgment, with the exception of his central insight into the nature of Stalinist communism, was often flawed and self-deluding. Indeed, if he'd taken to betting on the basis of his political forecasts he would have been bankrupt many times over.*

Angel of the North

The Empress of Ireland: Chronicle of an Unusual Friendship by Christopher Robbins
Simon & Schuster UK | 400 pp | ISBN: 978-0743220729

ONE WEEKDAY morning sometime in the 1970s, the distinguished filmmaker Brian Desmond Hurst made his way shortly after opening time into the Turk's Head in Belgravia. The pub, which was his regular, was empty save for three labourers from a nearby building site, who were seated over pints of Guinness. The drinkers observed the newcomer, a tall, distinguished man in his early eighties, with pale blue, ageless eyes and a shock of white flowing hair. He was dressed in a Savile Row jacket of antique cut, grey flannels, chocolate brown suede shoes and with an emerald green tie set against a white shirt.

The three men were in no doubt what to make of this apparition. "Fucking old queen," one of them commented. The elderly party affected not to hear and proceeded to the bar, where he placed his usual breakfast order of half a glass of fresh orange juice topped up with champagne. He then turned to his fellow drinkers, instructing the barman: "Please ask those three gentlemen if they would like a drink." The labourers accepted and, when fresh pints had been drawn, each in turn raised his glass to his lips, murmuring somewhat shamefacedly: "Cheers mate!" "Your very good health," Hurst replied, raising his glass in their direction. "And by the way, gentlemen," he added, pausing long enough to oblige them to look at him, "I am *not* an old queen. *I am the Empress of Ireland.*"

Apart from the barman, and the homophobic trio, this scene was witnessed by Christopher Robbins, who more than two decades later was to become Hurst's biographer. The author, then a young journalist and apprentice writer, had been drawn into Hurst's orbit as a potential scriptwriter for a film based on events leading up to the birth of Christ. The film, which was to be called *Darkness Before Dawn*, reflected the concerns of its intending director who, although of Belfast Protestant background, had become, apparently as early as the 1920s, a devout if eccentric Catholic.

Over an extended period Robbins worked with Hurst on the script, provided an audience for his musings on its theological implications and visited potential locations as far away as Malta, before realising that the old man had no intention of ever making the film. This proved to be the case; there was nothing to be gained professionally from the relationship, and, as Hurst was broke, the handsome scriptwriter's fees Robbins had been promised proved as illusory as the film. By this stage it was too late, as he was already bewitched by Hurst's endless stories and by his admission into the strangely magical world his new friend inhabited. For a young heterosexual this proved to be an unusual place, made up of eccentric neighbours, theatre folk, young men of religious convictions, aristocrats, policemen, blackmailers, sly procurers, feral rent boys and assorted waifs and strays.

Robbins proved to be a good listener and careful observer, who provides an amusing and informative portrait of a corner of late bohemian London. The milieu in question, presided over by the ageing BDH, might be characterised as gay-artistic with occasional visitors – such as Siobhan McKenna – from more normal places. Although lower in creative vitality, it recalls the Soho world of Francis Bacon as described in Daniel Farson's *Never a Normal Man* or Anthony Cronin's evocation in *Dead as Doornails* of the doomed lives of the two Roberts, Colquhoun and MacBryde, also acted out against a Soho background. Apart from an undoubted eccentricity, inevitable perhaps in milieus from which women are absent, all three settings were linked by the shared centrality of alcohol.

In gay terms the world which Christopher Robbins entered was utterly out of date, indeed by the 1970s almost archaic. Gay liberation had arrived and the young were elsewhere, in bars in Earl's Court, discos in Islington and Notting Hill and holidays in Mykonos. This was not for Robbins's host who, by the time the author met him, was an old man and not about to change the habits and associates of a lifetime. Hurst's Belgravia can best be seen as a fragment of earlier blendings of bohemia and sexual heterodoxy, dating back to the 1930s if not earlier. Nowhere is this line of descent more evident than in its deeply English linkage of homosexual desire and social class. At an early stage in their friendship, when he may have felt some signposting was required, Hurst remarked to his biographer: "Some people have asked me over the years whether I'm bisexual. In fact I'm trisexual. The Army, the Navy and the Household Cavalry."

This might be seen as a translation into commercial terms of the world of longing which animates AE Housman's *A Shropshire Lad*, EM Forster's *Maurice* and JR Ackerly's *My Father and Myself*. What resulted may in part have been opportunism, as working class young men were more available than those of other classes. Nonetheless, for these late Victorians and Edwardians, as for their successors until as late as the 1950s, it seems to have been part of the yin and yang of desire that lover and beloved should come from different social backgrounds. One consequence of the availability of mass travel in the 1960s was that the gay need for differentiation could assume forms other than social class. This, however, was too late for BDH, who well into old age continued to be sexually active with traditional partners. Something of the flavour of these transactions, and of their immense quaintness, is suggested at one point by Hurst's request to the author: "Run out and buy a half-dozen bottles of Newcastle Brown, will you Christopher? Terry's coming round and the corporal gets most upset if there's only champagne to drink."

In common with Boswell, who met Doctor Johnson when the great man was in late middle age, it was Robbins's fate to meet his subject when much of his life was already over. One result is that parts of the life which are of immense interest can only be glimpsed through the medium of BDH's fragmentary and at times unreliable reminiscences. One of the most surprising aspects of that life was how central, in the strangest of ways, Ireland proved to be. One suspects that Christopher Robbins found this aspect of Hurst's biography a little puzzling, yet the Republican Catholic persona constructed by this scion of the Protestant Belfast working class was clearly of immense, if uncertain, importance to him. A variety of factors seems to have gone into the young Hurst's reimagining of himself in terms that those among whom he grew up would certainly have found puzzling and possibly offensive. Of these the most obvious was a family history of immense emotional bleakness, set against a background of sectarian rancour and grizzly shipyard violence. The young BDH was clearly in flight from a world that he later found little pleasure in recalling and about which he lied, or at least constructed consoling fictions. But on the face of it there would seem little reason for the flight to have ended up emotionally south of the border.

As a young man BDH served with the Royal Irish Rifles in Gallipoli, where he witnessed the horrors of that terrible campaign and came near to death from dysentery. My reading of *The Empress of Ireland* is that in some obscure way whose ultimate dynamics remain elusive, the groundwork for Hurst's Irish identification was laid amid the squalor and suffering of the Gallipoli trenches. The experience seems to have been profound, almost sacramental, as, in a landscape peopled by the ghosts of former comrades, he came to experience Ireland as a hope and consolation. This benign vision was mediated by fellow soldiers, one of whom used to sing the old ballads of Ulster such as "My Lagan Love", in a "beautiful tenor voice with all of Ulster in it". The singer was also a narrator, who "knew all the old Irish legends and told us about the children of Lir, the Irish prince and princesses, who were changed by enchantment into black and white swans and doomed to fly forever over stormy Lough Foyle". Ireland was present in the intimacies of death, as when a dysentery-stricken Australian soldier, seeing the harp on his badge, addressed Hurst as "Pat". BDH did what he could to clean the young man and then, carrying him through the dead and dying, placed him in the shade, where he too died. The narrative continues:

A group of some twenty Turkish prisoners stood nearby under guard, and as he helped the stretcher-bearers cover the dead Australian with a ground sheet, one of them gestured for permission to cross over to them. A guard nodded. The prisoner broke off a piece of wild thyme and laid it in the hands of the dead man. 'Then the Welshman said "Let us pray for him." The three of us knelt down. The Welshman said the Lord's Prayer in Welsh, and the Connaught Ranger in Irish. I had no Irish, so I said it in English. They carried him away to Australian headquarters for burial at night. As I watched him go I thought of the lines by Yeats: "And he had known at last some tenderness / Before earth took him to her stony care.'"

A strong pan-Irish identification seems to have been in place by the time BDH was evacuated from Gallipoli to hospital in Cairo. It was there he learned of the 1916 rising when "an Irish nurse, Sister McNulty, came rushing up to me and said: 'Oh Brian, they're shooting us down in Dublin.'" It seems plain that both BDH and Sister McNulty regarded him as included in that "us". It was from this perspective that he witnessed English troops stationed in Cairo, who themselves had not seen combat, turning on Irish veterans of Gallipoli when news of the Rising came through. His own sympathies were with the insurgents; among the stories he told Christopher Robbins was how before his execution James Connolly was asked to forgive the members of the firing squad. In Hurst's retelling Connolly replied: "I forgive all brave men everywhere who do their duty." There is a certain ecumenism in the remark he attributes to Connolly, suggesting that his own Irish patriotism was to be a fairly broad church.

WB Yeats is an unexpected presence at the edge of Hurst's memories of Gallipoli. His account of the singing of Irish ballads in the trenches included later being told by Yeats, almost as if the poet was providing a retrospective validation of Hurst's own emotions, that "My Lagan Love" was the oldest song in Ireland. Yeats reappears at the death of the young Australian, when Hurst's quotation from "The Man who Dreamed of Faeryland" is clearly experienced as an implied equivalent to reciting the Our Father in Irish. I infer that, like the young Londoner Alfred Willmore, who at about the same time was embarking on an ambitious self-transformation into Mícheál Mac Liammóir, BDH had been drawn into the powerful gravitational field of WB Yeats.

For Hurst, as an art student immediately after the war, there seems to have been some cross-fertilisation or mutual reinforcement between the prestige of modernism, conversion to Catholicism and an imaginative commitment to Ireland. This found its embodiment in a portrait of St Bridget in the style of Modigliani, which BDH painted during those years and which remained with him until his death. In conventional account, as evidenced in George Orwell's rancorous comment that in the twenties one heard endlessly that so-

and-so had been received into the Church, before the fashion shifted in the thirties to membership of the Communist Party, conversion to Catholicism (or Anglo-Catholicism) was fashionable in postwar artistic circles. One suspects that Orwell would have found Hurst's combination of Catholicism with *New Statesman* orthodoxy on political issues particularly unbearable. Hurst was not, however, overserious about his commitments, and when asked by Vanessa Redgrave what cause he felt strongly enough to march for, replied: "That would depend on the weather." It is an answer which nicely suggests the role of camp as dissolvent of solemnity and as goy equivalent of Jewish irony. Orwell might even have approved.

Other factors may have influenced Hurst's Irish and Catholic identifications. A generation earlier Forrest Reid had withdrawn from what he took to be the narrowness of Belfast's commercial middle class into a world of lightly coded homosexual pastoral. Where BDH was concerned, Southern Ireland might be seen as his version of pastoral. Certainly, in terms of attitudes to homosexuality, differences between post-independence Ireland and residually Protestant England were not to the discredit of the former. No doubt the Ireland of those years was an uncomfortable enough place to be gay but, out of some combination of charity, dislike of calling things by their proper name and the desire to avoid causing pain to others a qualified and euphemistic tolerance was extended. There was no equivalent on this side of the Irish Sea of the ferocious assault on the gay community during the years when David Maxwell Fyfe was British home secretary, which resulted in the suicide of the mathematician Alan Turing and sent such diverse spirits as Rupert Croft-Cooke and Peter Wildeblood to jail.

A unionist friend whom I asked if he had come across *The Empress of Ireland* replied that he had glanced into it but that its subject seemed to dislike his own people so much he hadn't bothered to proceed further. This seems a bit hard. Certainly the shape which Hurst gave to his life involved a rejection in all kinds of ways of Protestant working class Belfast. This, however, did not extend to his family nor, when the chips were down, was there any question of not rallying to the flag. Following the pattern established during the First World War, during World War II he once again put his talents at Britain's service. The documentary films he made for the Ministry of Information during those years are described as "concerned not with action and derring-do but with the cold courage of men in hopeless situations, and the tenderness that soldiers have for one another amidst brutality and death". Among his wartime films was *Letter from Ulster*, designed to counter rumours that US troops in Northern Ireland were behaving like an army of occupation.

Contemplating all of this, Christopher Robbins puzzles over, without resolving, the problem of how BDH could fight for Britain while supporting Irish independence and sympathising in his films with those condemned for misplaced loyalties. It may well be that the question is misdirected and that Hurst's contradictions are not resolvable as he allowed himself the luxury of inconsistency. He certainly permitted himself a degree of flexibility and was fond of quoting a remark of his father's that the Orange marchers on July 12th were the Irish celebrating "the defeat of themselves by themselves".

The Ireland Hurst embraced was not the poor, narrow-minded and self-engrossed state which conducted its business south of the border, but an imaginary, almost Platonic realm, constructed out of literature, music and the resources of language. He does not seem to have endangered his dream by frequent visits to the place. The only occasion on which the author accompanied BDH to Ireland was passed among the eccentric inhabitants of a big house near Kinsale. Otherwise his Irishness flourished at a distance, most notably in Hollywood, where it formed the basis of his friendship with John Ford. The latter, we learn, "was delighted to meet somebody from Ireland who wasn't either a policeman or a domestic servant", while something of the social insecurity and longing for refinement of the emigrant Irish can be glimpsed in Ford's announcement, when introducing Hurst to Sam Goldwyn: "Brian speaks French."

Hurst learned his trade working as an assistant to Ford, his screen debut being as an extra in his last silent film, an Irish story called *Hangman's House*. (Other Irish echoes, sometimes of an unexpected kind, were at hand. While in Hawaii with Ford, BDH met the immensely wealthy lesbian heiress "Joe" Carstairs. When aged sixteen Joe had an affair with Dolly Wilde, who claimed to be possessed by the spirit of her uncle, Oscar.) Whatever the chemistry between Hurst and Ford, the relationship seems to have been profound, with the director addressing BDH as "cousin" while Hurst described Ford as "my most valued and loved friend on this planet". Late in life he travelled to Los Angeles to bid farewell to the director, who had six months to live. He found

Ford in bed drinking Guinness and with a big box of cigars on his lap. The dying man asked his visitor to sing "The Rose of Tralee" and, although Brian's voice was a poor one, he croaked out the song. Ford's death some months later hit Hurst hard. He told his biographer: "It is impossible for me to accept that this great genius is ended by dissolution. I am certain that angels watch over him in other dimensions."

For Irish readers, apart from its contribution to the universal pleasure of laughter, Christopher Robbins's account of BDH's career is likely to elicit responses of a somewhat more piquant kind. Over several decades he was an extremely active filmmaker, with over thirty films to his credit. His Irish obsessions were reflected both in his repertoire and in unachieved projects; one of his late films was *The Playboy of the Western World*, starring Siobhan McKenna as Pegeen Mike and with music by Seán Ó Riada, while it had always been his ambition to make a film of *The Shadow of a Gunman*. Where filmmaking was concerned, Hurst's good will towards Ireland was, potentially at least, of a practical kind. It was in this context that his only recorded encounter with official Ireland took place. This occurred when he flew to Dublin to seek support from Seán Lemass, then minister for industry and commerce, for his ambitious plans to launch an Irish film industry. Hurst was prepared to break his contract with Rank, accept the resulting loss of income and come to live in Ireland if the necessary, comparatively modest, funding could be put in place. The interview got off to a bad start:

> 'Which part of Ireland do you come from, Mr Desmond Hurst?' the minister asked.
> 'Northern Ireland.'
> The minister looked at the aide sitting beside him. 'Mr Desmond Hurst means, of course, the Six Counties.'
> 'No, Mr Lemass, I do not mean the Six Counties. I mean what is now and has always been the dominating province in Irish affairs – Ulster.'

Not surprisingly Irish government support was not forthcoming and Hurst's plans came to nothing. The anecdote is a depressing one, which almost seems designed as yet another piece of confirmatory evidence for the thesis advanced in Tom Garvin's *Postponing the Future*. Independent Ireland seems to have had an almost active desire not to possess a film industry. Brian Hurst's desire to help was neither a caprice nor a piece of self-interest. Christopher Robbins's account of his life is marked by regular connections between its subject's commitment to Ireland and his career as a filmmaker. Given his track record, ability to raise funds and immense good will, any industry minister with his wits about him would have seen him as a resource to be used in the creation of a local film industry.

As we have seen, like others of a homoerotic bent, from Gerard Manley Hopkins to Oscar Wilde, BDH converted to Catholicism. One suspects that there was some connection between his sexual disposition and his religious convictions and that, like his Irish identification, conversion was a way of creating space. He certainly seems to have taken his Catholicism seriously. He had a confessor from Brompton Oratory, a special devotion to St Thérèse, whom he had seen in a vision and to whose home in Lisieux he made regular pilgrimages, and favourite churches all over London. He was also fond of the church of Saint Multose in Kinsale.

His religious commitments are most delightfully on display at a meeting, which took place some time in the 1970s, with a well-known Norwegian avant-garde theatre director, who had read the screenplay of *Darkness Before Dawn* and agreed to comment. As the visitor, who was in London to put on a piece of revolutionary gay theatre, was a man of drearily puritan disposition and hostile to form on ideological grounds, and as BDH's aesthetic was both traditional and gorgeous, the meeting was ill-omened. The breaking point came when Sven objected, with "a nasal fart of contempt", to the relevance of the subject and the presence of angels in the script. As Brian believed in the historicity of the Bible and the reality of angels, this was not the best approach. The meeting ended with a tirade from the outraged old man defending his angels ("Magnificent angels on high, seen from a great distance against a heavenly cloud formation") and his own non-combative homosexuality ("And, I might add, when it comes to homosexual politics, homosexual nomenclature, or good old-fashioned homosexual screwing, I do not need any lectures from you.")

Hurst's Catholicism does not appear to have had any impact on his sexual life, which remained enthusiastic until well into old age. When questioned regarding this apparent anomaly, his apologia ranged from the routine to the profound. In the former mode he commented: "The pronouncements of

God's minions are subject to fashion and politics – Jesus preached love and forgiveness, and never condemns or comments on sexual love between men … And even if this natural state were a sin – which I have never believed to be the case, and have therefore never felt any guilt – Jesus had a soft spot for sinners." To this he added the more sober thought that "a soul finds Hell through acts of unkindness and cruelty, not sexual peccadilloes". He was also capable of a strain of wildly heterodox biblical commentary, as when he told his biographer:

> The French say, *Croquez le pomme!* Bite the apple! Not *Grignottez le pomme*, or *Pas de pomme pour moi, merci*. Adam was not the first sinner, but the first man to take up the challenge of life. The first hero. And it was what God wanted. Adam took Great Big Smacking Bites from the apple of the tree of life, and it tasted so good he ate the core as well.

It seems plain that, like other Catholics of his generation who, as a result of disposition or circumstances, led lives which were incompatible with areas of the Church's moral teaching, BDH found some way of reconciling an irregular sexuality with participation in the sacramental life of the church. One suspects that in negotiating this difficult terrain, like other Catholic men and women, he relied on a combination of homemade theology and a sympathetic confessor. This finding of sufficient space to allow the unorthodox, both straight and gay, room to breathe depended on the presence inside the church of a minority of priests who combined charity with a concern for souls and realism regarding the varieties of human nature. Above all it required that both parties refrain from pushing things to their logical limits and that the seeker for absolution give some kind of acknowledgement, however nominal, of the grand architecture of Church doctrine.

Although he did not know it, Hurst belonged to the last generation of gay Catholics to be allowed this luxury. The grim Norwegian proved to be a visitor from the future, as the anomalous wriggle room BDH enjoyed no longer proved possible once the Catholic natural law-based understanding of sexuality was challenged not at the periphery but at the core. One doubts whether Hurst, for all his inventiveness, could have managed to stay inside the contemporary church. Nonetheless his extravagantly baroque sensibility represents a strain which can be traced in church history over the centuries.

At the very least, the pushing of such individuals to the edge of, if not outside, the church represents the loss of a traditional resource and of a distinctive kind of creativity.

As is clear from many accounts of the first and second world wars, mass armies, which are conscription-based and replicate within themselves the varieties and divisions of the societies upon which they draw, find a place for homosexuals. It is only in peacetime volunteer armies, when nothing serious is at stake, that the luxury of homophobia may flourish. In the case of the Catholic church, when it was the church of an entire community, it found a place, however nuanced and uncomfortable, for its homosexual members. The more recent exclusions of baptised gay Catholics from the life of the church, other than on terms which would entail a denial of their essential natures, is surely another sad but unmistakable sign of that institution's retreat from the centre of society. As the densely historical analysis of Alan Bray's recent *The Friend* suggests, the quarrel between the church and homosexual people may not only be unnecessary but also a repudiation of traditions of great antiquity within the Western and Orthodox Catholic traditions. Against this background, in his reconciliation of sexual deviancy and religious observance, BDH emerges as a more traditional figure than he may have realised.

At bottom Brian Hurst conceived of Ireland as a form of verbal magic and a means of transforming the world through the licence of storytelling. Its role was as a leaven to British ponderousness for, "without the Celts and the Jews, the island's culture would be heavy, unseasoned stodge". He responded to a story attributed to Gorky, who had seen an Orthodox priest collapse by the side of the road, take off his boots and address them "There you are, you've been hurting me the whole morning, causing me great pain, but can you go a step without me?" with the comment "That could be an Irish story. Russian and Irish stories are virtually interchangeable. But it could never be an English story." BDH should have known, for he was himself an accomplished anecdotalist. At first Christopher Robbins seems to have been a little disquieted by his subject's meanderings before realising:

> It was not that Brian went off at a tangent, or tended to digress, or was unable to keep to the subject when at work – tangential rambling and digression was how he worked. What resulted was an unceasing cascade

of stories. Tall stories, war stories, funny stories, sad stories, Irish stories, gay stories … stories accumulated over a long and original lifetime. I knew even then that together they pictured a vanished and more elegant world, but saw them at the time as little more than well-spun yarns. Now I realise their true worth. Brian told stories as a way to process life, to parcel up the pain, order the chaos and confusion, and endow meaning to the pointless. Experience was held on to and made valuable by transmutation into anecdote, preferably amusing. Brian put at least as much effort into the story of his life as he did his life's work of film.

Brian Hurst died in 1986 at the age of ninety-one. Years later his biographer took some of his ashes from the graveyard in Dundonald near Belfast and brought them in a champagne glass to Dublin to scatter on Howth Head. In so doing he was following in his subject's footsteps, as years previously BDH had travelled to Howth, equipped with champagne and roses, to scatter the ashes of his sister Patricia. This strange journey provided the occasion for a final display of Hurst's attentiveness to the music of Ireland.

The epiphany began on the evening of Christopher Robbins's arrival in Dublin when, having wandered around the city thinking of his old friend, he dropped into a pub. While waiting for his Guinness to settle he happened to remark to a fellow drinker that he was off to Howth in the morning to scatter a friend's ashes. His companion, a skinny fellow with high rosy cheeks, formless suit and a shirt with a dazzling pattern of tiny blue arrows, responded: "When a frond was a friend inneed to carry, as earwigs do their dead, their soil to earthball where indeeth we shall calm decline, our legacy unknown." Robbins had fallen into the company of a compulsive reciter of *Finnegans Wake*, who needed little encouragement to perform. As he listened, Robbins recalled a conversation with BDH of thirty years previously. This had begun when he provocatively suggested that *Finnegans Wake* "is a load of bollocks". Noting Hurst's displeasure he backtracked slightly, arguing: "The book doesn't make any sense. You can't read it. It is a formless loop of puns and wordplay – language without rules, words spewed out for their sound." This was greeted by a long silence, followed by Hurst's dissent from this "brute assessment of *Finnegans Wake* – a difficult but sublime work". BDH then took a deep breath, adding:

'You are wrong. Ignorantly, unimaginatively, Anglo-Saxonly wrong! *Finnegans Wake* is music. It is song and laughter. It is enormously witty and madly clever. It is a great Irish writer's ecstatic expression of joy in the use of language. It is an endless dream of Ireland and all her history. A book for angels.'

Robbins was not convinced but, assuming it must be "an Irish thing, some sort of Gaelic code", let the matter drop. Now many years later, guided by Brian's ghost to this particular pub, as he listened to the unstoppable riverrun of words of a half-tight man in a cheap suit, for the first time he heard the poetry of "this high falutin' Gaelic literary rap". This was not the worst of closures. Brian Hurst was lucky in his biographer, who has saved a most unusual life from time's oblivion and written a very funny book about a man who was both amusing and strangely wise.

Queen of Lillyput

Queen of the Wits: *A Life of Laetitia Pilkington* by Norma Clarke
Faber and Faber | 384 pp | ISBN: 978-0571224289

CAN YOU imagine a very extraordinary cross between Moll Flanders
and Lady Ritchie, between a rolling and rollicking woman of the town
and a lady of breeding and refinement? Laetitia Pilkington (1712–1759)
was something of the sort – shady, shifty, adventurous, and yet, like
Thackeray's daughter, like Miss Mitford, like Madame de Sévigné and
Jane Austen and Maria Edgeworth, so imbued with the old traditions
of her sex that she wrote, as ladies talk, to give pleasure. Throughout her
Memoirs, we can never forget that it is her wish to entertain, her unhappy
fate to sob. Dabbing her eyes and controlling her anguish, she begs us
to forgive an odious breach of manners which only the suffering of a
lifetime, the intolerable persecutions of Mr. P—n, the malignant, she
must say the h—h, spite of Lady C—t can excuse. For who should know
better than the Earl of Killmallock's great-granddaughter that it is the
part of a lady to hide her sufferings? Thus Laetitia is in the great tradition
of English women of letters. It is her duty to entertain; it is her instinct
to conceal ... Her language is a trifle coarse, perhaps. But who taught her
English? The great Doctor Swift.

Thus Virginia Woolf in *The Common Reader* (1925), in her chapter on Lives
of the Obscure. Laetitia Pilkington's *Memoirs* had been out of print since

1776, having been first published in 1748–54, but were reprinted in 1928 in an English Library edition, edited by J Isaacs, with an introduction by Iris Barry. A new annotated edition, edited by AC Elias Jnr, was published in 1997, and the first biography of Laetitia Pilkington, by Norma Clarke, has now appeared. Woolf's rescue mission has taken a long time to bear fruit, but we are now fully provided with scholarly information about a highly intriguing woman who flourished and suffered in Dublin and London in the early eighteenth century.

Woolf had her dates wrong: Pilkington was probably born in Cork in 1709, and definitely died in Dublin in 1750. She came into an Ireland in a state of solidifying Protestant power in the aftermath of the Williamite wars and the Treaty of Limerick, of increasingly repressive anti-Catholic legislation (which also affected Dissenters), of incremental land dispossession for the Catholic gentry and corresponding aggrandisement of the Protestant Ascendancy, and of the beginnings of the unique cultural project of Ireland's eighteenth century, starting with Berkeley and Swift and ending with Burke and Sheridan, and including Gandon, Johnson, Burgh and Lovett Pearce. The political culture was one of resentful deference to England, from whence flowed most appointments and patronage. (Swift pretended to believe that very good men were chosen in England to be Irish bishops, but were invariably set upon by bandits before they arrived, who then took their places in the episcopal palaces.)

The War of the Spanish Succession was dragging interminably on, not to conclude until 1713. Queen Anne was on the throne, to be succeeded by her Hanoverian cousin, George I, in 1714, bringing the Whigs back into power. George I spoke no English and preferred to stay in Hanover, thus leaving power in the hands of the government. The modern system of prime-ministerial government dates from this time, as developed by Sir Robert Walpole, prime minister from 1721 to 1742. Two Jacobite invasions took place in the first half of the century, one in 1715, the second in 1745. Both ended in ignominious defeat. Jethro Tull invented the seed drill in 1701, the Act of Union between England and Scotland was passed in 1707, the South Sea Bubble burst in 1720 and John Wesley started preaching in 1739. It was a period of relative peace, stability and prosperity, of the rapid development of popular newspapers and pamphlets, and of frequent agricultural crises.

Laetitia's father, John Van Lewen, was the son of a Dutch physician who had settled in Ireland, and her mother descended, according to herself, from the Earl of Kilmallock. Her father was a "man-midwife", a very rare specimen in those days, who became popular with pregnant Ascendancy women, and prospered to the extent of being able to move house constantly to the most fashionable areas of Dublin, ending up in Molesworth Street. Laetitia was an only child for six years; she recounts bad treatment from her mother – "she strictly followed Solomon's advice, in never sparing the rod" – but gentleness and encouragement from her father, who gave her access to his library and provided her with a literary education. She claims to have been able to read Pope at the age of five, "charmed and ravished by the sweets of poetry".

In her teens, she met Matthew Pilkington, a clergyman with no money but with an interest in poetry. Matthew ingratiated himself with her family, and despite his poverty married Laetitia in 1725, when she was sixteen. His lack of worldly goods is represented by his possessions on marriage – a harpsichord, a cat and an owl. The next few years were pleasant and interesting: Matthew and Laetitia became friendly with Dr Patrick Delany, who was the centre of a literary set which included women like the poets Mary Barber and Constantia Grierson, and who was friendly with the biggest celebrity in Ireland at the time, Jonathan Swift, dean of St Patrick's Cathedral. Laetitia and Matthew were both writing poetry at this stage and were very keen to meet Swift. Laetitia accomplished this with a blatantly flattering poem for the dean's birthday, comparing him to Cato and Plutarch.

Swift referred to the Pilkingtons, who were both small in stature, as "a little young poetical parson, who has a littler young poetical wife", or "mighty Thomas Thumb and Her Serene Highness of Lillyput". He was genuinely kind to the young couple, helping Matthew with his career as a clergyman and including them in his peculiar dinner parties at the deanery, which always involved contretemps with the servants over the quality of the food or their alleged purloining of beer. He treated Laetitia almost like an intelligent doll, to be played tricks on, pinched, smacked, forced to take her shoes off, quizzed on her knowledge of literature, and expected to listen to him for hours on end. She willingly put up with all of this, rather like a groupie with a rock star, as she was keenly aware of the value of her connection with him in a world where connections led to patronage and wealth. At this point in her life, her literary aspirations did not include her memoirs, but her account of her relationship with Swift later became a major selling point for them.

In 1732, Swift's patronage procured for Matthew the chaplaincy to the Lord Mayor of London, John Barber, and he decided to go despite Laetitia's protests that a year's absence from her and their three children (mentioned almost in passing) would be too hard for her to bear. When she asked to go with him, he responded that he "did not want such an encumbrance as a wife, that he did not intend to pass there for a married man, and that, in short, he could not taste any pleasure where [she] was". The marriage was obviously in trouble, some of it caused by Matthew's jealousy of Laetitia's literary gifts, which had led to a number of people stating that she wrote better than he did. Laetitia finally got to London three months before Matthew's chaplaincy expired, to find him having an affair with an actress and attempting to pimp his wife to the portrait painter James Worsdale, a transaction which she claims to have resisted.

Returning to Dublin alone (Matthew ended up temporarily in jail in London for trafficking some of Swift's treasonable poetry), Laetitia found herself the object of censure "both traduced for going to London, and for returning from it". And things got worse: Matthew, on his return to Dublin (at his father-in-law's expense), soon began an affair with a wealthy widow, and thus had a motive for divorcing Laetitia; Laetitia's father managed to stab himself accidentally with a scalpel and died soon afterwards, leaving her with no male protection; Laetitia took up with Robert Adair, a young surgeon, when Matthew moved in with his widow, and thus facilitated Matthew's darker purpose. The story of the discovery of Laetitia with Adair in her bedroom at midnight, reading a book – by Matthew and no less than twelve members of the night watch – is one of the dramatic high points of the *Memoirs*.

Matthew, delighted to have finally achieved a cast-iron reason for divorce, called for a bottle of wine to drink the health of Laetitia and Adair, and declared that he would marry them as soon as the divorce was finalised. He then threw them out, Laetitia with nothing but the clothes she was wearing, and nowhere to go but Adair's lodgings. She was pregnant, destitute and disgraced. Her family would not help her, Swift referred to her as "the most profligate whore in either kingdom", and as an unprotected woman she was pursued by rakes and madams, to the point of having to barricade herself in her room at night.

She lost her children. After two years of a truly horrible existence, she decided, in 1739, to go to London and begin again, using an alias but also capitalising on her dramatic story and parlaying her conversational and literary skills into some kind of a living.

Her time in London was eased considerably by her friendship with Colley Cibber, poet laureate, one of the most famous actors of the period, and the author of an autobiography which had sold extremely well. It was Cibber who first planted the idea of writing a memoir in Laetitia's head. She set herself up in lodgings opposite White's club, where the aristocracy gathered regularly, and proceeded to gather subscriptions for her yet-to-be-published book of poetry. She also worked as a jobbing writer, producing poems, prologues and petitions to commission. She established herself as a well-known writer and conversationalist, but her life would always be precarious, without a husband and dependent on uncertain sources of income. Norma Clarke takes her at her word that she never gave sexual favours in return for money, but it is highly unlikely that this was the case. She comes close to admitting to such behaviour on a number of occasions, and her determination to survive very probably demanded a bit of genteel prostitution.

She remained in London until 1747 and had mixed experiences. When she had exhausted her aristocratic connections she quickly found herself in debt, and was imprisoned in the Marshalsea debtors' prison for two weeks. On her release, she managed to set herself up in a shop in St James's, selling books and prints and continuing her work as a commissioned writer. This enterprise ended when the shop was robbed and all her clothes were stolen; her landlord seized what stock remained in lieu of rent. Her maid then ran off with her linen. She wanted to go back to Dublin, but couldn't raise the fare. Just as things seemed to be at their worst, her daughter Betty, whom she hadn't seen since she was a small child, turned up at her lodgings, nineteen, pregnant and unmarried. The reaction of her "saintly methodist landlady" was to evict them both, just before Christmas. They had no choice but to stay in doss-houses, constantly fearful that Betty would give birth in squalid and dangerous surroundings.

They were saved by Colley Cibber, who managed to raise some money from friends, enabling them to get basic lodgings; Betty's child was born in February 1746. Jack, Laetitia's son, also arrived at this time, destitute, charming and needy. She got him work at Drury Lane theatre and spent some of her scarce resources on fitting him out with decent clothes. Jack ended up in the British army, and nearly died as a result of a fever caught while enlisted, but recovered and was responsible for the posthumous publication of Laetitia's final volume of memoirs, as well as for his own autobiography, a useful corroboration of some of Laetitia's assertions.

Laetitia was very happy to be reunited with her children and did everything she could for them, in spite of her own near-destitution at the time. Betty's baby was put out to nurse, and Betty went into domestic service. Both children recounted stories of abuse and neglect at the hands of their father, which further confirmed Laetitia's low opinion of him. James Worsdale came back into her life, and for a period they shared lodgings together. She describes their living arrangements in the *Memoirs*:

> We had four Play-bills for a tablecloth, Knives, Forks, or Plates, we had none ... The Butter, when we had any, was deposited in the cool and fragrant recess of an old shoe, a Coffee pot of mine served for as many uses as ever Scrub had, for sometimes it boil'd Coffee sometimes Tea, it brought small Beer, and I am more than half afraid it has been applied to less noble Uses. (Scrub is the servant in Farquhar's *The Beaux' Stratagem*.)

By 1747 she had had enough of London, and decided to return to Dublin with Jack and try to shame Matthew into doing something for his son. She engaged in a final round of begging letters, getting some vicious responses from previous "friends", and largely due to Patrick Delaney, who was in London at the time, got the fare together. After a long journey at the cheapest rate, they landed at Ringsend, made their way to the city, and got lodgings in Aungier Street. She then laid siege to Matthew, who had abandoned his widow and taken up with the younger Nancy Sandes, whom he wished to marry. Laetitia's inconvenient presence was a major obstacle to this ambition. Despite threats of legal action she failed to extract from Matthew the money he had agreed to in their divorce settlement.

Swift had died in 1745, having left his entire fortune to establish St Patrick's Hospital, his "home for fools and mad". Laetitia knew that her account of her relationship with him would be interesting to many people; she also knew that the implied threat of appearing in the *Memoirs* in a bad light would be enough to persuade many people to subscribe to them in the hope of being treated favourably. She arranged with a printer to open subscriptions, and resumed work on the two volumes she intended to publish, with Jack as her amanuensis. She found a patron in the twenty-three-year-old Sir Robert King, Lord Kingsborough, who accepted her offer to dedicate the *Memoirs* to him and was to give her a great deal of money before their acrimonious parting a year later.

Laetitia had only three years to live after her return to Dublin, but she turned them to good account, promoting and publishing her *Memoirs*, making life difficult for Matthew, helping Jack with his career in the theatre, renewing some old acquaintances and generally amusing herself. After some difficulty getting appropriate lodgings, due to a friend of Matthew's reviling her to prospective landlords, she found a house in Golden Lane, near St Patrick's Cathedral. The first volume of the *Memoirs*, published in early 1748, had proved immensely popular and had created an appetite for the second. Money, for the first time in many years, was plentiful.

Volume II appeared in late 1748, to much interest, acclaim and refutation. During this time she met John Wesley, and had a long conversation with him on "every subject that could convince me he was a man of taste and true breeding". Wesley gave her two guineas and asked her not to mention their meeting in her memoirs. She agreed, and kept her word; we only know of the encounter because she described it in a letter to Lord Kingsborough.

In the summer of 1749, Laetitia's health began to fail; she had always had stomach troubles – she may have suffered from ulcers, or perhaps she had cancer. She continued to work on Volume III of her memoirs, but was losing weight and getting weaker. She and Jack moved to Beresford Street, where she increasingly stayed in bed. Jack's autobiography has a touching account of a final outing to Chapelizod, where she was able to eat duck and peas and drink some white wine. She died two days later. Matthew paid for her funeral, at St Ann's in Dawson Street, and married Nancy Sandes a month later.

Laetitia Pilkington is interesting for a number of reasons: her story is dramatic; her connections were famous; her capacity to survive vicissitudes was remarkable; her ability to turn hardship to good account was admirable. As a female writer in an expressly patriarchal society, she made the very best of her situation. As a woman without male protection, when such vulnerability usually led to seclusion, she defied the customs of her time to live a public, independent life, earning her own living, albeit often by begging. She understood, at the end of her life, that her knowledge of society, allied with her scathing style, provided her with a powerful and lucrative weapon which she could exploit to her advantage; the pity is that she did not act sooner.

The *Memoirs* are a lively mish-mash of gossip, reported conversation, quotes from Milton, Shakespeare and Swift, all of her own poetry, which had never appeared before in one collection, imprecations against her enemies, and particularly the Established Church, eulogies of her friends, and copies of letters sent and received (including an hilarious one from Matthew's widow, to whom she cheekily wrote asking for a subscription to the *Memoirs*: "It is not in your power to defamatonous my Corrector in your wild Memboirs").

Laetitia is one of the original unreliable narrators: her recall of conversations beggars belief, she has many axes to grind, and the paying off of old scores features far too prominently for the health of the narrative. Nonetheless, considerable veracity is attested to by her benign portrait of Matthew as a young husband; she does not paint him as a villain from the start. It is also probable that her recall of her conversations with Swift is pretty accurate: she was young and impressionable, with a very good memory, and he was distinctly memorable. Her account of their meetings still has a kind of freshness and fun that makes it invaluable in any assessment of that most interesting man.

The *Memoirs* are also often very funny. Laetitia had plenty of wit, and knew how to spice it up with malice. Here she is on a number of subjects which exercised her: on Mrs Warren, Matthew's widow: "Old enough she was to be my mother, and big enough to make four of me"; a vengeful poem against a man who tormented her in Mallow, on what a friend did with his impenetrable philosophical writings: "These Sybil leaves, oh spite and shame! / In pieces torn he takes / And wipes a part not fit to name / And plunged them in a jakes"; on clergymen: "Those who want to look further into the deceits of priesthood may trace it even up to the Nile, from whence superstition and the crocodile first sprung, both alike destructive to mankind"; on the Bishop of Salisbury, who refused her alms: " ... an old man with a most unprelatical countenance – for it was full of bubuckles and knobs and flames of fire".

She had no real interest in her surroundings: the account of her circumstances with Worsdale is untypical. Her main interests were in relationships, conversation and literature. She rarely tells us what street she is living in, or what clothes she is wearing, or what food she is eating. She is oblivious to the widespread horrors of poverty in two of the most unequal cities in Europe, except when her own luck is down. To be fair, she understands that life is utterly precarious for many people, but can only look after herself and her immediate family. She is almost equally oblivious to the unfolding city of Dublin, in the process of being completely transformed by the Wide Streets Commissioners into a spacious, architecturally beautiful construct, from a provincial capital into the second city of the United Kingdom. Our sense of period from the *Memoirs* comes from her language and ideas rather than a rich evocation of her physical circumstances.

The early eighteenth century was a period of improvement for women, fuelled by the expansion of the Irish woollen and linen trades and maintained by the widespread use of single women and widows in the burgeoning service industry, as domestic servants, milliners, seamstresses, and similar occupations. Women, for the first time, could achieve financial independence and married women could become contributors of cash to their household economies. Laetitia, still, was unusual in her success as a divorced woman in a world of serious disapproval of such people. Dr Delany and his wife would not publicly acknowledge her after her divorce, although Delany did send her money through intermediaries. The *Memoirs* give us a picture of someone often struggling against great odds to survive with her self-respect intact.

Norma Clarke, in this well-researched and well-written biography, points out that Laetitia had, perforce, to deal with libertines, and that libertines were profoundly contemptuous of women. Even good male friends, like Cibber, could refer to her in carelessly dismissive terms, and she had to swallow this kind of treatment in order to stay alive. The last volume of the *Memoirs* is coarser and more vituperative than the first two; it is likely that as her strength and vitality failed, her bitterness at the palpable injustice of her life increased.

Clarke was lucky to have such an engaging primary source for her biography. Laetitia's voice comes down to us, curious, funny, plucky and well-informed, with great story-telling skill and a dash of pleasant malice. It is to be hoped that this biography will send readers back to the *Memoirs*, to experience this unique woman's voice for themselves.

JOHN HORGAN | 2012

A Scourge
for the Wicked

Muckraker: The Scandalous Life and Times of W.T. Stead,
Britain's First Investigative Journalist by W Sydney Robinson
Robson Press | 281 pp | ISBN: 978-1849542944

THERE ARE few recognisably pivotal points in the history of journalism, but WT Stead's editorship of the *Pall Mall Gazette* is surely one of them. There's hardly a serious journalist who hasn't heard of him, or who would not be aware, in a hazy sort way, of how he scandalised British society almost one hundred and fifty years ago by buying a young girl in order to expose the evil of child prostitution in Victorian England.

And yet, as so often happens in journalism itself, the attention given even to important occurrences and persons is short-lived, as celebrities rise and fall with metronomic regularity. It is almost a century since the publication of the original two-volume biography of Stead by Frederic Whyte, which Robinson describes as useful if "excessively laudatory". Although there has been other relevant work in the interim, particularly JW Robertson Scott's memoirs, which provided Robinson with important insights, Scott's books comprise his memories of numerous editors, and there has really been a Stead-shaped gap ever since.

Robinson has now filled this gap with energy, flair and a fair-mindedness which must, at times, have been difficult to maintain in the face of his subject's bewildering eccentricity, intermittent megalomania, occasional flights of fancy, and a moral compass that did not always point to true north.

It is tempting to suggest that these characteristics may also be found, to some extent, in other editors of note, but that is another day's work and, even if it were true, Stead exhibited them all to such a degree that it is inconceivable that any journalist resembling him today would ever be entrusted by any pin-striped board of directors with the stewardship of a national newspaper. Not the least paradoxical aspect of Stead's character is that when he was asked in 1901 who he considered to be the greatest journalist then living, he named the Irishman EJ Dillon, who was temperamentally almost the diametric opposite of the flamboyant editor of the *Gazette* and was, in Stead's words of praise, "a little man who hides his light under a bushel and shuns the public gaze as the plague".

There are, of course, different theories about how and why journalism changed in the late nineteenth century, in the era that came to be called that of the "new journalism". It is unarguable that newspapers at this point became less staid, less the stenographers to power, and that they found that entertainment and celebrity generated at least as much, and increasingly more, profit than the mere supply of information. Some of the congratulations that flowed into the *Irish Independent* following its first appearance with a new name and a new set of journalistic techniques in 1905 hailed it as a "tabloid". By this, of course, they meant to salute its abandonment of the traditional slavish adherence to interminable accounts of political speeches in favour of leaner accounts of the events of the day, more highly flavoured for public consumption.

Recent scholarship suggests that this new "celebrity journalism" was leavened, in the United States at least, by the need to appeal to the politics of poor immigrants and the working class, and that this segued into the development of radical political campaigning that helped to create and develop mass readership. Robinson's book adds an important dimension to this analysis. He charts the way in which Stead's papers and others came to realise that editors hectoring or lobbying politicians was, in the long run, less effective in influencing political events than using and dramatising issues and topics to build a mass circulation among readers whose opinions and priorities, educated and on occasion inflamed by this journalism, the politicians could not safely ignore. Stead's predecessor as editor of the *Gazette*, John Morley, was of the old school, and believed that every article in the paper should be written by a "qualified expert". Stead, in contrast, believed passionately that it should be the job of journalists to stand "between those who know everything and those who know nothing, and it is his duty to interpret the knowledge of the few for the understanding of the many".

The event at the core of Stead's reputation – the abduction of a young girl to demonstrate how easy it was to purchase a virgin for sex – certainly had the positive effect that Stead had hoped and campaigned for, that is the raising of the age of consent for girls. But Robinson's forensic account of what actually happened in the course of this escapade quite chills the blood. Numerous laws were broken. There were two attempts – the first one, in a brothel, unsuccessful – to examine the child internally, under the influence of chloroform, to demonstrate that she was a virgin. Stead pointedly ignored any evidence that might have tended to challenge his assumption that her parents had no interest in, or feeling for, their daughter. After the second phase of the operation, which involved spiriting her away to France, he to all intents and purposes washed his hands of her, displaying little or no interest in her subsequent welfare. It is hard to come to any conclusion other than that the three-month prison sentence which he afterwards received for his involvement in these events would have been higher but for his role as a crusading editor, and higher still if the moral sensitivities of the era had been more developed in relation to the rights of children generally.

Stead broke the law, he of course argued, in a good cause, and the concept of the "public interest" as a justification for invasions of privacy and even for law-breaking has a strong currency up to our own day. The decision of the High Court to protect the RTÉ investigative report into the Leas Cross nursing home scandal is a case in point, involving as it did the use of hidden cameras by a journalist who misrepresented himself in order to secure employment at the care home concerned. But the verdict on whether Stead could have achieved the same objective by different means, or by means which could have avoided the acute distress – terror even – visited on the thirteen-year-old Eliza Armstrong has to remain open.

It is difficult at this remove to take accurately the moral and ethical temperature of 1885, uninformed as that era was by any developed code of journalistic behaviour or even by any strong sense of human rights, and Robinson provides some useful evidence that it was as difficult to assess then as now. Taking the high moral ground – and appropriate insurance against subsequent retribution – Stead had the vocal and practical prior support of Bramwell Booth, chief of staff of the Salvation Army. He also went so far as to write to three prominent churchmen (the Archbishop of Canterbury, the Anglican Bishop of London, and the Roman Catholic Archbishop of Westminster) to tell them in advance of his intentions. The Archbishop of Canterbury was the only one of these three divines to advise against it, on the altogether reasonable grounds that it was too severe a remedy for the crimes that were allegedly being perpetrated. One might have expected Cardinal Manning of Westminster to be somewhat troubled by the implicit argument that the end justified the means, but Manning not only implied approval by his silence, but remained on close terms with Stead for many years afterwards.

The moral panic created by Stead's articles was double-edged, not that this troubled their author overmuch. The accelerated passage through parliament of what became known, not unfairly, as "Stead's Act", was not rapid enough to prevent the addition to the legislation, by amendment, of a provision criminalising "gross indecency" by a male "with another male person". This provision was not repealed until some eight decades later in Britain, and later than that again in Ireland.

This is probably a minor part of the debit side of Stead's journalistic ledger, given that he had no direct responsibility for it. His megalomania – I may have been kind to him earlier in describing it as "intermittent" – is more problematic. He was heavily involved in influence-peddling at some stages of his career, sometimes for admirable objectives, sometimes in pursuit of a personal agenda that made up in intensity what it lacked in consistency. From a very early age he was imbued with a passionate belief in the divine right, if not of kings, then certainly of editors. Although his predecessor, Morley, was, as depicted in this book, undoubtedly something of a fogey, it is difficult not to sympathise with him, at least to a degree, in his objections to what he described as Stead's attachment to "government by journalism".

Stead once told his clergyman father that he wanted God to give him a "big whip" so that he could "go round the world and whip the wicked out of it". On the eve of taking up his first editorial appointment on the *Darlington Echo* he confided to his diary:

To be an editor! ... to think, write & speak for thousands ... It is the position of a viceroy ... But ... God calls ... and now points ... to the only true throne in England, the Editor's chair, and offers me the real sceptre ... am I not God's chosen ... to be his soldier against wrong?

It is probably fair to say that any modern editor found harbouring such sentiments would be promptly dealt with by the men in white coats. In his subsequent pursuit of these and other – if we are to believe him – heaven-inspired political objectives, Stead had an on-off relationship with Gladstone and Balfour; acted almost as an unofficial public relations manager to Edward, Prince of Wales, and to Cecil Rhodes; engineered the destruction of the innocent Sir Charles Dilke on the basis of a personal animus; and even did his best to support Parnell until a misunderstanding led him to believe – inaccurately and unfairly – that the Irish leader had lied to him about his relationship with Katherine O'Shea. Not all his campaigns were invested with realism or foresight. He succeeded in having General Gordon sent to Khartoum, with results of which everyone has been aware ever since. On Parnell, he assured Archbishop Walsh of Dublin that the whole scandal would quickly blow over. On another occasion, he visited Rome, apparently persuaded that he could convince Pope Leo XIII of the necessity for the emancipation of women.

His own attitude to women was interesting to say the least, and dutifully – if unwisely – often confided to his diary. Before his terminal misunderstanding with Parnell, he regarded the Irishman's relationship with Mrs O'Shea (the significance of which had escaped him) as little more blameworthy than having one glass of post-prandial brandy too many. He pursued and apparently captured, at various stages, the affections of a number of intelligent and spirited women, including a glamorous Russian. There is still disagreement about whether these relationships moved from the emotional to the carnal, with the probable exception of that involving his Russian *femme fatale*, and the evidence is inconclusive enough to support either hypothesis. Among those who remained immune to his charms was Constance Markiewicz. His relationship with his own wife was characterised by a somewhat stern and evidently not uncritical loyalty on her part, and an intermittent uxoriousness on his, leavened not only by the relationships already mentioned but by his habit of surrounding himself, in some of his editorial roles, by attractive, and on occasion clearly smitten female interns.

Some of his ideas have worn better than others. He was in favour of a united states of Europe. He was energetically dismissive of the crime correspondents of his era, criticising them, at the time of the Ripper murders, for bringing out special editions "dripping with gore ... almost as 'creepy' and revolting as the gashed and mangled corpses" of the murderer's victims. His concern for the British underclass at the end of the nineteenth century was unalloyed and fiercely committed. If he was wrong-headed, as he frequently was, it was rarely because he saw commercial advantage in whatever position he was adopting, and his passionate desire to reform the world was interleaved with a patent desire, born no doubt from his own Puritan ancestry, to also reform himself. He was equally successful – or unsuccessful, depending on whether you believe the bottle to be half-empty or half-full – in both these endeavours.

Perhaps the fact that he is nowadays remembered more for the success of his campaign against child prostitution than for the peculiar strategy and tactics he adopted to achieve that objective is, at the end of the day, a reasonable and fair response to the life of a complex, driven and skilful wordsmith to whom all modern journalists are at least partially in debt and who, at the end of the day, was as unknowable as all humans are in the deepest personal sense. Robinson has done a fine biographical job, which can be read with pleasure and profit, even if he might with advantage have taken the risk of ahistoricism head on and essayed a more rounded and detailed assessment of his subject in his concluding chapter.

And what of Stead's inheritors? Investigative journalism as such has always been a hit and miss affair. Douglas Gageby of *The Irish Times* believed – despite his support for journalists like Michael Viney – that it was not really the appropriate territory for a daily newspaper, which had so many other, equally vital, functions to fulfil, and it is certainly true that investigative journalism is only one of journalism's many essential tasks, a number of them routine, even humdrum. The weeklies, Gageby thought, were the place for the more exotic growths.

The reason is not far to seek. Investigative journalism is extraordinarily expensive. It takes weeks, and sometimes months, of a reporter's time, and at the end of it all the hypothesis/story may fall flat on its face, or an editor may simply run out of money. The pioneering work of journalists like Joe McAnthony and his brave editor, Conor O'Brien, at the *Sunday Independent* pointed the finger of suspicion first at the highly dubious international activities of the Irish Sweeps organisation in 1973, and at Ray Burke as long ago as – wait for it – 1974. McAnthony's reward was to have his modest wage differential abolished as part of a general wage round in the Independent stable. When he asked O'Brien whether it could be restored, the latter advised him, with considerable and genuine regret, that if he was seriously interested in enhancing his career in journalism he might be better off trying somewhere else. RTÉ then aborted a six-month contract with him, paying him but refusing him entry to the station to make programmes. At this point he went to Canada, where his talents were eagerly snapped up by the Canadian Broadcasting Corporation, for which he made a number of award-winning investigative documentaries.

The trajectory of contemporary Irish journalism provides evidence to support this curate's egg scenario. Publications like *Magill* and *Hibernia* have blazed a trail, accompanied intermittently by the weekly newspapers, but daily newspapers have had little enough to show. Even their current interest in the salaries and expenses of public servants and politicians, together with leaks from tribunals, while useful and sometimes valuable additions to public discourse at a time of economic crisis, are largely based on data-mining, on the Freedom of Information Act or on the private or political agendas of conveniently anonymous sources as much as on investigative journalism in its truest sense. Luckily this is not universal: the urge to dig and to expose is still present: one story from an Irish newspaper has made it successfully into Unesco's *Global Investigative Journalism Casebook*. Little wonder that the comparatively better-funded RTÉ has been the medium which has, in recent times, consistently broken most of the new ground, even though the quality has been uneven. The ground-breaking work of the early *Seven Days* was impressive in places: later, Michael Heney's potentially explosive documentary on the Irish Sweeps scandal was deep-sixed for years, despite its accuracy, and Mary Raftery's ground-breaking documentaries on clerical child abuse had to overcome many obstacles before they were screened. More recently, RTÉ's targets have been occasionally arbitrary, and some of its attempts in that genre have misfired, not least the spectacular Father Reynolds own goal.

Investigative journalism in the United States appears at first sight to be healthy: a whole new generation of non-profit organisations – some sixty in total – has sprung up. Usually operating in tandem with traditional media outlets, they are hugely supported financially by trusts. Only one of them – Politico – makes a profit. The others are supported (Propublica to the tune of $10 million annually) by the charitable organisations for which the USA is justly famous, or even by crowd-funding, in which individual journalists or teams of journalists pitch ideas over the web for funding in small individual amounts by the population as a whole. But how deep are the pockets of these organisations and individuals, and how long will the goodwill last?

The Irish public, swamped by information but too often deprived of meaning and analysis, may be unaware of how fragile are the links of the chain that support the investigative endeavour. At the end of the day, expensive and risky investigative journalism may well seem, to cost-strapped editors and managements, to be an option that can be dispensed with, and perhaps not as profitable as hiring people who can produce controversial opinions for money. In a media world where the competition for public attention is fiercer than ever, ego can all too easily trump effort. And in the welter of discussion about the deadly serious economic threats which all forms of journalism are facing at the moment, there is little realisation of the magnitude of the loss that would occur if investigative journalism – the really tough kind, the kind that identifies the areas where real political and economic and social power reside and explores them skilfully and fearlessly – is allowed to wither on the vine. As the American critic Eric Alterman has pointed out, it has been left to a fiction writer to explore this modern dilemma in real time – to portray the dilemma facing any editor who has to attempt to balance the monetary cost of a story against its societal value.

In this context, Robinson's book is a kind of parable, focusing as it does on the erratic but ultimately fascinating life of a man whose work, hit and miss alike, exemplified the core value of all journalism, and especially of its investigative strand: that it is writing and broadcasting with a public purpose, a public responsibility, and a public role.

Sharp Mind,
Sharp Tongue

Hugh Trevor-Roper: The Biography by Adam Sisman

Phoenix | 624 pp | ISBN: 978-0753828618

HUGH TREVOR-ROPER had an enviable professional career. As a young historian, whose research on the England of Archbishop Laud had been interrupted by the outbreak of the Second World War, he found himself working with the Secret Intelligence Service, in areas involving penetration and deception of German intelligence. As a result, when the war came to an end, he was exceptionally well-placed, in terms of both connections and skills, to investigate the mystery surrounding Hitler's fate.

It was urgent that this should be clarified. Although the government quarter in Berlin, including Hitler's bunker, had fallen in April 1945 to Soviet troops, the Stalin regime, which certainly knew the truth but preferred mystification, professed to believe that the dictator was still alive. In a short but intensive period of investigation Trevor-Roper located and interviewed a number of those who had been present with Hitler at the end, tracked down a copy of his political testament (a predictably barren document), reconstructed the sequence of events during the final weeks, and managed to capture the hysterical edge, a peculiar combination of banality and desperation, of life inside the bunker. He also established beyond any doubt that Hitler had taken his own life. The work that resulted, *The Last*

Days of Hitler (1947), was a masterpiece of forensic history whose insights – for example that Hitler presided over a court rather than a government – are still compelling.

In the postwar period Trevor-Roper established himself as a leading authority on seventeenth century England, his method being to use disagreements with fellow historians as a means of clarifying fundamental issues. He emerged in disputes with opponents such as RH Tawney and Lawrence Stone, regarding the economic causes of the English Civil War, as a dangerously well-informed and at times merciless controversialist. He also had other registers, most notably on display in his essay on Arnold Toynbee's *A Study of History*, where he employed a combination of empiricism and knockabout comedy to puncture what he saw as vatic nonsense dressed up as history. (The piece was never republished, perhaps because it was so rude.)

For Trevor-Roper the "storm over the gentry", as his exchanges with Tawney and Stone came to be known, widened out into a broader enquiry into the transformations to which seventeenth century Europe was subject. Although unusual among English historians of his generation in his interest in the work of the French *Annales* school, with its emphasis on the deep material and sociological factors which constituted the background to the historical scene and which constrained its actors, the focus of his interests turned increasingly from economics to ideas. Trevor-Roper, who had nothing but scorn for metaphysics – particularly in its Christian inflection – was fascinated by ideas in their historical context, by their ability to influence choices and actions and to generate change. His theme, as he put it in a letter of 1958, was "events and the intellectual impact of events, their cumulative pressure on the human mind".

Trevor-Roper was far from neutral in his feelings regarding the historical process. He was no friend of royal absolutism, and rejoiced in the changes whereby the religious perspectives of early modern times gave way to more secular modes of understanding. As a young man he wrote: "More and more, as I read history, I believe in the Whig historians. There is no getting away from the fact: they are right." A lifetime later he repeated what was essentially the same claim, asserting in *The New York Review of Books*: "In political philosophy I am a Whig: I believe with Montesquieu and Hume, in the equal validity of different social forms, and, with Burke and de Tocqueville, in the organic strength and corrective balance of a complex society nourished by living traditions." Although claiming to be a pluralist, there can be little doubt that he regarded English history, with the Glorious Revolution at its heart, and the institutions and distribution of power to which that history gave rise, as a particularly felicitous embodiment of his ideal. Towards the partner nation, which linked its fortunes with England in the Anglo-Scottish Union of 1707, his feelings were mixed. While deeply admiring the Scottish Enlightenment, he was scornful of the nation's attachment to local particularities and delighted in exasperating the sensibilities of his Scottish readers.

Trevor-Roper viewed Ireland largely in terms of its impact on the balance of power in England and seems to have regarded the seventeenth century New English presence on the island as a colonial enterprise imposed upon the "native papists". Although his Irish references are few, they are of a sort which are likely to set teeth on edge. In a characteristic moment, in an essay on James Ussher, he spoke of the archbishop's need to assert Protestant ideas aggressively in the face of "the Catholic gentry, who still dominated society and sat in parliament, and the sinister unintelligible babble of the priest-led Celtic peasantry". Such phrasing was not an accident or an occasional infelicity but clearly deliberate. This approach, if excessively high-spirited, was capable of discerning unexpected connections. When he visited Prague for the first time, it reminded him "more of Dublin than of Rome, the great palaces and buildings of a foreign aristocracy gradually crowded out by the shoddy hutches of a peasantry come to town".

Trevor-Roper was a man of limited sympathies. These did not extend to such figures as "an Apulian peasant" grovelling "abjectly before a bottle of tinseled pig-bones in a tawdry southern church". Although it is difficult to imagine any member of the *Annales* group writing of the mental world of the Mediterranean peasantry in comparable terms, Trevor-Roper would no doubt have replied that the contents of that world were not only false but of little intrinsic interest. While such prejudices might seem to be disabling in a historian, in fact his Whiggery, allied to an intense curiosity and wide-ranging erudition, acted as a source of energy and generator of insights. His perspectives were predominantly elite, his masters being the great high-cultural historians from Gibbon to Burckhardt, with whose works he maintained a constant intellectual dialogue. His great theme, which he approached again and again from varying perspectives, might be described as the line of thought which led from Erasmus and Grotius, across the bloodstained seventeenth century, to Hume, Montesquieu and the *philosophes*. Trevor-Roper differed from such Victorian celebrators of the triumph of rationalism as Lecky and Bury in his sense of the complexity of that line, of the subterranean routes it took, and the arcane symbolism – drawing upon such unfamiliar sources as Hermetic magic and Renaissance alchemy – in which it sometimes expressed itself. He also differed from them in his sense that what mattered were ideas in their social and historical context, how they were used by absolutist princes and Counter-Reformation popes, by Anglican divines and Calvinist preachers, and how they interacted with other forces to influence men's actions.

Trevor-Roper mapped this seventeenth century world in a series of deeply impressive essays on such topics as "Religion, the Reformation and Social Change", "The General Crisis of the Seventeenth Century", "The Great Tew Circle" and "The Religious Origins of the Enlightenment". As his biographer Adam Sisman notes, in approaching this theatre of conflicting commitments and interests, Trevor-Roper's approach was "remorselessly secular", with the underlying assumption being that "differences of doctrine are merely masks for political differences". While this was so, we should perhaps not ask from the essays what their author could not give. They are, in their own terms, dazzling performances, which still retain their ability to excite because of their subtlety, range and the convincing ease with which connections are made. By redrawing a particular landscape they raise new issues, change emphases and alter the way one thinks about the seventeenth century. The conventional expectation of Trevor-Roper's generation was, however, that a historian was something more than an essayist and should produce at least one major work, which would be a definitive contribution to scholarship. Destiny seemed to point him towards the English puritan revolution, whose history he appeared uniquely well-qualified to write. This was begun, endlessly promised to his publisher with delivery endlessly postponed, and in the end, although a substantial portion was written, the work was never completed.

Trevor-Roper's fundamental problem was one of form. He deeply admired Gerald Brenan's *The Spanish Labyrinth*, the work of a strong-minded independent scholar, which had been produced outside the university system and which provided one of the earliest and most authoritative accounts of the origins of the Spanish civil war. (In a letter of 1954 he commented that he knew nothing of the author, adding: "I suppose, from his name, he is Irish – though his mind isn't.") He particularly admired Brenan's ability to combine a narrative of the sequence of events which led to the outbreak of the war with a deep structural analysis of disequilibriums in Spanish society, which he traced back to the seventeenth century. Trevor-Roper aspired to bring a similar breadth to his history of the English puritan revolution, but found the linking of narrative and structural analysis difficult to manage. As he explained in a letter of 1958 to the art historian Bernard Berenson, while conventional history was adequate for the routine business of politics or war, it failed in revolutionary periods "because it cannot penetrate to the depths of a society which are then stirred up, or the heart of those intractable problems round which human muddles are woven like some great untidy cocoon". The analytic method had its own limitations for, while only it could reveal the social depths, "such an essentially static method cannot explain the movement which, by agitating the surface, stirs up those depths and brings out the horrible monsters that lurk there". Trevor-Roper found the problem of reconciling these approaches intractable and, while certain that Marxist claims to have done so were groundless, did not succeed in resolving the problem himself. As a result, his history of the puritan revolution remained unfinished.

These difficulties left it open to his colleagues to note his comparatively modest output and to regret, with a certain smugness, that such great promise remained unfulfilled. That assessment has changed in the years since his death as an impressive series of works, which he had completed but never published, has appeared. The most surprising, and probably the most important, of these has been *Europe's Physician: The Various Lives of Theodore de Mayerne*, a work which viewed the cultural and political life of early seventeenth century Europe via the biography of its most famous doctor. There was also *The Invention of Scotland*, in which Trevor-Roper sought to discommode Scottish nationalists by dismantling the myths by whose means, as he believed, they deceived themselves regarding the character of their country. *Letters from Oxford* was perhaps the most accessible of these posthumous publications. This was a collection of letters written by Trevor-Roper over an eleven-year period to the art historian Bernard Berenson. These provided a fascinating perspective on postwar English, and in some degree European, intellectual history, viewed through a well-informed and intelligent, if at times somewhat complacent, pair of eyes. As an unsympathetic obituary later noted, he was "more ironical about others than about himself".

The personal qualities attributed to him at the time of his death had been remarked on early. In 1953 the publisher Hamish Hamilton commented uneasily after a weekend spent in Trevor-Roper's company, "we found ourselves wondering if one so young and gifted ought to spend quite so much time hating people". The lack of human sympathy which marked his personal relations was also evident at an intellectual level. In reviewing an early collection of Trevor-Roper's essays, Harold Nicolson found much to admire but deplored the "absence of even average human compassion". Part of the fascination of Adam Sisman's biography is that it provides us with some pointers to the origins of his subject's coldness and willingness to offend. Hugh Trevor-Roper was the son of a Northumberland country doctor. The family setting in which he grew up was an emotionally bleak place, with a cold, disapproving mother and a disengaged father who had contracted out of parenthood. In Sisman's account it was "a grim household without warmth, affection, encouragement, spontaneity or natural feeling of any kind". The predictable result of such an upbringing was that Hugh became an abstracted child, lost in his own thoughts and unheeding of those around him.

In spite of his distance from others, Trevor-Roper was at times capable of displaying considerable charm. This quality was deployed in two significant friendships, both with wealthy, intellectually distinguished older men. Although differing in their settings, both relationships displayed similar patterns. The first was with the expatriate American man of letters Logan Pearsall Smith, then famous as a stylist and for producing aphorisms such as "Some people say life is the thing, but I prefer reading." The second was with Berenson. While both of these relationships were socially consequential, in that they admitted the younger man to interesting and in many ways desirable circles – in Berenson's case as a regular visitor to his beautiful villa outside Florence – at their heart was a shared passion for knowledge. The earlier friendship, with Pearsall Smith, was of particular importance in shaping Trevor-Roper's intellectual style.

Although he had a series of relationships with younger men, Pearsall Smith was particularly drawn to Trevor-Roper and at one stage intended making him his heir. In an intriguing vignette, Sisman reports how Trevor-Roper left the older man's eightieth birthday party early, when he grew irritated at his host's unending homosexual teasing. Although skilled at keeping the prurient and coquettish Pearsall Smith at a safe distance, he evidently valued him immensely as a mentor. Pearsall Smith's philosophy, he later wrote with considerable admiration, was "that humanity is ridiculous, but that there is a pleasure in observing its antics even amid our own gesticulations, and that it is redeemed from utter meaninglessness by its ideals, though many of these are very odd; and that style is an ideal too …" It seems likely that Trevor-Roper, an inexperienced and self-absorbed young man of intense yet frozen emotions, found in Pearsall Smith a usable model for the intellectual life. What was involved was an aspiration to an amused, undeceived, and well-informed contemplation of the human comedy, to pleasure in what the world presented, without commitment and in full knowledge of its limitations. Judgments will differ, but it seems to me that there was something unearned about the alacrity with which Trevor-Roper embraced the Pearsall Smith model, that it was a strategy for holding life at a distance rather than understanding it, and could be seen as a stance towards experience rather than a response to it. As his biography and letters reveal, at its worst this could tumble over into a form of Bloomsbury knowingness.

Trevor-Roper's life was marked by those honours and rewards which England loads upon its intellectual grandees. He was successively regius professor of modern history at Oxford and master of Peterhouse College Cambridge, while in 1979 he received a life peerage as Lord Dacre of Glanton. Trevor-Roper was undoubtedly an establishment man, who felt there was an immense propriety about the rituals and procedures of English life. The photographs of him in his Oxford setting and as "Independent National Director" of Times Newspapers, which illustrate Adam Sisman's biography, exude a sense of ease with the roles he has been asked to play. Although he evidently enjoyed this institutional grandeur, it could be argued that in the end the price it exacted was excessive.

The best remembered of Trevor-Roper's misfortunes was when, as a figure of standing within Rupert Murdoch's empire, he allowed himself to authenticate the forged "Hitler Diaries" on the basis of a hurried and insufficient examination. This was a disaster waiting to happen. He had already got into the habit, common among right-wing intellectuals exasperated by the feeble-mindedness and predictability of the left, of producing fluent and convincing journalism on topics such as Greece, China and Cuba – about which he knew comparatively little. In the decades since he researched *The Last Days of Hitler* he had lost touch with German studies and there must be a suspicion that the skills he once had in this area had become somewhat rusty. Even more catastrophically, in attempting to assess the "diaries" he was working to a journalist's rather than a historian's timetable and was dealing with a man for whom rules of evidence were a matter of indifference, if not contempt. When, late in the day, Trevor-Roper realised that he could no longer stand over the authenticity of the "diaries" and must reverse his opinion, Murdoch famously responded "Fuck Dacre. Publish", showing in this as in other matters his ability to turn everything he touched into dross. It is strange that Trevor-Roper found his reputation at the mercy of this man, as he had already taken the measure of his destructive nihilism. Murdoch, he believed, was animated by a hatred of England as it was. He wished to "moronise and americanise the population" and "to destroy our institutions, to rot them with a daily corrosive acid". It has been plausibly suggested that the reason for his remaining on as an independent director of the Times organisation following Murdoch's assumption of ownership was out of loyalty to the newspaper as a major national institution. This proved to be a misjudgment.

In common with his Times directorship, Trevor-Roper's mastership of Peterhouse, the position with which his academic career ended, proved to be a barren experience. Although unsatisfying, it was not without its ironies. In one view, prior to Peterhouse, Trevor-Roper had passed a lifetime in Voltairean clowning, attempting to bait Catholic contemporaries whose views of the world were as patriotic and rational as his own, and to recast individuals such as Father Martin D'Arcy, a scholarly and pious if somewhat worldly figure, who was one of the most prominent Catholics in Oxford, as if he were one of the Jesuit advisers of King James II.

In Peterhouse this shadow-play ended, as he found himself, a Whig among Tories, in a college whose tone was robustly conservative (critics would have called it reactionary). In this setting he had to deal with colleagues such as the historians Maurice Cowling and Edward Norman, who were devout and intellectually committed Anglicans. Trevor-Roper was unimpressed by the Peterhouse tradition of history which they represented, describing one of its most illustrious figures, Herbert Butterfield, as "a very undistinguished historian". His Peterhouse experience was a predictably miserable one, characterised by pettiness and ill feeling on the part of his colleagues and unending administrative wrangles. In a final irony, shortly after he had accepted the mastership, Trevor-Roper was offered a senior position at the European University in Florence. If he had been in a position to accept, it is hard to believe that the final chapter of his career would not have been more creative than its melancholy finale in Cambridge.

Adam Sisman's biography provides a wide-ranging, acute and convincing account of an extremely interesting man. It allows us to get some sense of how his limitations sat side by side with his superb gifts and how the deployment of both were part of a single process.

FERGUS O'FERRALL | 2015

Scholar and Gentleman

Charles O'Conor of Ballinagare, 1710–91: Life and Works
Luke Gibbons and Kieran O'Conor (eds)

Four Courts Press | 296 pp | ISBN: 978-1846821110

CHARLES O'CONOR of Ballinagare is a seminal, but until now a somewhat neglected figure. His key role in founding the modern study of Ireland's language, culture and history has been appreciated only by a relatively small band of scholars.

Each essay in this long-awaited book – which originated in a conference held in May 2006 – brings new perspectives and insights in appreciating O'Conor's multi-faceted career. Charles O'Conor, in all his endeavours, had, as Luke Gibbons and Kieran O'Conor point out, "to negotiate public life under the double exclusions of the Penal Laws and colonial rule". Yet he came to play a central role "in realigning the politics of lineage and descent with the emergent civic order of representative politics and parliamentary democracy – even if the question of representation for Catholics went against the grain of Protestant rule in Ireland". Luke Gibbons, in his essay on O'Conor and "the print culture and the counter-public culture" notes that "Charles O'Conor's disappearance from Irish history, particularly those versions that culminate in the triumph of the nation, has much to do with the perception that he went over to the other side, or at best, in Joep Leerssen's words, 'had a foot in both camps'." However it is precisely the fact that he was a vital bridge between the

Gaelic world, the Enlightenment and the Anglo-Irish Protestant Ascendancy that gives him his seminal role.

O'Conor was the most authoritative voice of native, Gaelic-rooted Ireland and one of the most important cultural mediators between native and Ascendancy Ireland. The crucially important interface between native Ireland and the Protestant elite was the field of learning and literature. In addition O'Conor sought to utilise the tenets of liberal Protestantism – and indeed to write in the voice of a liberal Protestant – to advance the early struggle for Roman Catholic civil, political and economic rights and freedoms. In this he appealed to the Enlightenment patriotism of some in Protestant circles who supported aspects of the Catholic struggle. O'Conor, in hindsight, may well be judged the key seminal figure in the emergence of nineteenth century Irish Catholic historical and political consciousness: others built upon his foundations in the more confrontational era dominated by Daniel O'Connell.

Who then was Charles O'Conor of Ballinagare and how did he exercise such an important role? He was born in January 1710 in Kilmacranny, Co Sligo, where his family was living in straitened circumstances having lost its lands following the defeat of the Jacobites in the 1690s. His father, Denis O'Conor, came of a cadet branch of the O'Conor family whose head is the O'Conor Don – the former kings of Connacht and high kings of Ireland. His mother was Mary O'Rourke, daughter of Col Tiernan O'Rourke of the O'Rourke family of Bréifne. The O'Rourkes too had lost all in the Williamite victory.

Therefore we may situate Charles O'Conor in a network of defeated, and in many cases exiled, Jacobite Catholic families: his father-in-law, for example, Col O'Rourke, died at the battle of Luzzara in 1702 while in the French service. He had a number of relatives serving the French or Jacobite cause and his uncle, Dr Thaddeus O'Rourke, bishop of Killala, a Franciscan with a continental education, lived with the O'Conors and played a key role in educating the young Charles.

In the early 1720s, after many years of legal wrangling, the O'Conors recovered a part of their lands. This involved a legal agreement with their Protestant neighbours the Frenches. Yet even as late as 1777 there was an expensive and stressful threat when an impoverished brother converted to Protestantism and, under the Penal Laws, sought thereby the estate. It is important to recollect that Catholics could not assert or defend their ownership rights in property or indeed maintain civil, cultural or religious institutions of any kind for most of the life of O'Conor of Ballinagare. In practice the O'Conors recovered about eight hundred acres and a gracious house was built at Ballinagare in 1727, partly from the masonry taken from a late medieval O'Conor tower house. Previously, in the 1680s, the O'Conor estate had been over 3,700 acres. Jeremy Williams and Kieran O'Conor have a fascinating chapter in this book analysing the physical remains of the house which yields valuable insights into the minds and lives of the O'Conors at the height of the Penal Laws. Ballinagare Castle – more accurately house – was built in a modern style but it was designed to look smaller than it was when viewed from the front as the family presumably did not want to overly advertise its position as a Catholic, Irish-speaking landlord in a Protestant state.

Nevertheless, as O'Conor and Williams illustrate, the house itself

> with its mix of old and new, provides a metaphor for Charles O'Conor's life and, indeed, the lives of all the O'Conors of Ballinagare, in that they were deeply rooted by blood and ancestry in the landscape and aristocratic culture of north Roscommon since early medieval times and yet were closely connected with contemporary Enlightenment values and in close contact with relatives and friends serving with the Irish Brigade on the Continent. Paris, St. Germain-en-Laye and Vienna may have been distant in physical terms but they were never very far from Ballinagare.

This pleasant house and estate provided the economic basis for Charles O'Conor's education and later for his scholarly life and advocacy of the Catholic cause. As Catholic schools were proscribed by law he attended local hedge schools and received a classical education there and at home. From his early youth he kept diaries in Irish which offer perhaps the best-documented example of hedge-school education that we have. Diarmuid Ó Catháin's excellent chapter in this book refers to the influence of Bishop O'Rourke as he helped the young Charles in his study of Latin, English, Irish and the psalms. Books that belonged to the bishop are still to be found in the library of Clonalis House, Castlerea, Co Roscommon, where so much of Charles O'Conor's literary heritage is stored. Remarkably, we are told that O'Conor's library has not been fully catalogued – surely a priority task for eighteenth century scholarship. O'Conor benefited from the lore of representatives of the hereditary learned families, such as the O'Duignans, thereby absorbing knowledge from the last of generations of gifted scribes and historians. He was well-equipped therefore to deal with the Irish manuscript tradition. The famous Turlogh O'Carolan (1670–1738) was a frequent visitor, as he was to Gaelic families such as the O'Ferralls of Mornine in Longford. Clonalis House still preserves a harp said to have belonged to O'Carolan.

O'Conor was sent to Dublin in about 1727 to continue his education. He was taught mathematics, science and French by Fr Walter Skelton (1664–1737). He associated with a very vigorous circle around Tadgh Ó Neachtain (c 1671–c 1751) and his father Seán (d 1729) from Drum, Co Roscommon. In Dublin the young student expanded his range of contacts, copied and exchanged Irish manuscripts, and benefited from the literary milieu; his contacts included Dr John Fergus, the Irish scholar and bibliophile, and Aodh Buí Mac Cruitín (Hugh MacCurtin), author and poet. His student days laid the basis for O'Conor's later career, which oscillated between Dublin and Roscommon.

In 1731 Charles married Catherine, daughter of John Fagan, a merchant of Boyle, a marriage which brought some capital into the O'Conor family. Charles and Catherine had two sons (Denis and Charles) and a daughter (Bridget). His wife died prematurely in 1741. Charles and his family lived at an out-farm at Ballynaba until the death of Charles's father in 1750, when he inherited the estate. In 1760, however, he handed it over to his elder son, Denis, and built a smaller Georgian house, which he called his Hermitage (illustrated in the book). He lived at the Hermitage until his death in 1791, the arrangement enabling him to focus on his scholarly pursuits and advocacy of civil rights for Catholics.

O'Conor became a voracious reader, constantly seeking out and acquiring books and manuscripts. Diarmuid Ó Catháin states that virtually every important Irish manuscript in Ireland passed through his hands and he acquired a unique collection of at least fifty-nine manuscripts. He attached primary importance to saving Gaelic manuscripts from destruction as the vital records of the old Gaelic order and was interested primarily in what might be termed the "elite" legacy of the manuscript tradition rather than oral or more popular lore. As interest in Irish scholarship grew he became the person to consult and had a wide correspondence, as is evident in *Letters of Charles O'Conor of Belanagare: A Catholic Voice in Eighteenth-Century Ireland*.

O'Conor's life was devoted to two major concerns – his scholarly interests and his discreet political activity aimed at achieving civil rights for Catholics. He spent part of every year in Dublin when he was not at Ballinagare or the Hermitage and kept up a remarkable range of personal contacts in Catholic and Protestant circles. He became a close friend of Archbishop John Carpenter (1729–86) of Dublin, with whom he shared many intellectual interests. His introduction of Carpenter, by then archbishop of Dublin, to leading Protestant establishment antiquarians in 1773 was described by him as a "revolution in our moral and civil affairs", illustrating the enormous gulf that required to be bridged between Catholics and Protestants in the fields of learning and scholarship.

Among the riches in this study are a number of essays on O'Conor's vital role as the preeminent Irish language scholar of the eighteenth century. Mícheál Mac Craith recounts how O'Conor controversially tackled James Macpherson's famous Ossian publications: as Mac Craith observes, Macpherson was, to say the least, "a creative adaptor"; O'Conor, in a new edition (which is almost better seen as a new work) of his *Dissertations* in 1766 (first published in 1753), refuted Macpherson on historical, topographical and chronological grounds. Today perhaps it is hard to fathom the enormous popular impact of Macpherson's work but O'Conor was best qualified to counteract negative portrayals of the Irish people by invoking a golden age of Gaelic civilisation prior to colonisation.

Nollaig Ó Muraíle emphasises the importance of O'Conor's crucial work on Irish language manuscripts in the absence of any significant impact of the printing press on the Irish language until well into the nineteenth century and the age of John O'Donovan. He provides a valuable account of O'Conor and his company of scribes (and of O'Conor's own scribal activity), poets and particular collectors of manuscripts such as Dr John Fergus. Lesa Ní Mhunghaile further enriches our appreciation of O'Conor's momentous contribution to Irish language scholarship, outlining the networks he employed from the 1720s until his death in 1791. Maura O'Gara-O'Riordan explicates in detail O'Conor's complex involvement with a manuscript copy of the *Annals of the Four Masters* which he acquired in 1734 and which is now in the Royal Irish Academy.

Charles O'Conor was realistic about the Stuarts' failure after the defeat of the Boyne and he saw that the only practical way forward for Catholics lay in achieving constitutional change through reasoned argument and professions of loyalty to the Hanoverian monarchs. The long saga of the struggle for Catholic Emancipation began in 1756 when, together with Dr John Curry of Dublin and Thomas Wyse of Waterford, O'Conor founded the Catholic Association – the first organised attempt to obtain legal acknowledgement of Catholic civil and property rights. It took over seventy years for emancipation to be achieved, when Daniel O'Connell, helped by another Thomas Wyse, and indeed supported by Charles O'Conor's grandson Owen O'Conor, gave birth to Irish democracy in the 1820s, a struggle I have described in *Catholic Emancipation: Daniel O'Connell and the Birth of Irish Democracy 1820–1830*. O'Conor was a key progenitor of our constitutional democratic tradition, and of the liberal Catholic tradition, which O'Connell supremely represents. Like O'Connell, he was determined to situate Ireland within the European Enlightenment. As Gibbons and O'Conor note, Charles O'Conor wished to place the Irish past within the domain of philosophical history and the Irish present into "a tolerant and culturally diverse republic of letters". He had, for example, the first English translation of Montesquieu's 1751 *De l'esprit des loix* (*The Spirit of Laws*) at his disposal; he annotated his copy in Irish. In the 1750s he wrote a number of notable pamphlets, such as *The Case of the Roman Catholics* (1755), highlighting the grievous disabilities under which his co-religionists suffered.

John Wrynn shows O'Conor rescuing the Irish past from antiquarianism and seeking to place it rather in the domain of philosophical (or developmental) history as he saw that this was central to the inclusion of Ireland in "the moral histories of human progress hitherto confined to Judeo-Christian antiquity and the glories of classical Greece and Rome". He thus combated a long line of colonial detractors from Giraldus Cambrensis in the twelfth century to Spenser, Davies, Ware and Temple in the early modern period, and to near contemporaries such as Sir Richard Cox – these had sought to deprive the Irish past of any claims to civilisation in order to justify conquest and domination. He also took David Hume to task for his anti-Irish prejudices in his historical work in the *Gentleman's Magazine* in 1763. Ian McBride in his impressive history of eighteenth century Ireland, *Eighteenth-Century Ireland: The Isle of Slaves*, wryly notes the effects:

The discreet lobbying of O'Conor and Curry, aided by Edmund Burke in London, eventually persuaded Hume to moderate his tone in the 1770 edition of his works, with the rather anticlimactic result that 'barbarous savages' was changed to 'enraged rebels' and 'insulting butchers' softened to 'insulting foes'.

O'Conor's struggle to root the concept of liberty – the key lodestar of the Whig political tradition – in Gaelic Ireland and ancient Irish laws was indeed an uphill task, not only among the pervasively ignorant but even more so among the so-called "enlightened" of his times. In his *Dissertations on the antient history of Ireland* (1753) he had maintained that the ancient Irish constitution "was founded originally on democratic principles ... the government which prevailed in Ireland, was a mixed monarchy, wherein the kings were elected out of a certain royal family for their virtue and achievements". His pamphlets and work on Irish history were key tools in what today we would call "consciousness-raising" in both Catholic and Protestant circles. O'Conor's pamphleteering activities brought him in contact with the famous Dublin printer George Faulkner, who was sympathetic to Catholic claims. It seems that it was through Faulkner and his circle that from the 1760s O'Conor became friendly with Protestant scholars who were growing more interested in Irish culture and antiquities.

Two important figures in this context were Dr Thomas Leland (1722–85) and Francis Stoughton Sullivan (1719–66) of Trinity College Dublin. Through Leland, O'Conor obtained access to the library of Trinity College and to the Irish manuscripts Leland was acquiring for it. This networking took shape in a number of antiquarian societies which eventually coalesced in the Royal Irish Academy, of which, in 1785, O'Conor was a founding member. The authoritative work on this period is *Golden Ages and Barbarous Nations: Antiquarian Debate and Cultural Politics in Ireland c.1750–1800* by Clare O'Halloran, which has a valuable chapter on the role played by O'Conor in the creation of a community of scholars which argues that the political context for such scholarly endeavours "was characterised by a recent and abrasive policy of land confiscation and settlement and by the still ongoing process of Anglicisation, whereby the indigenous language, Irish, was being steadily replaced by English as the medium of social and economic progress". Genealogies were feared by Protestants as they might establish who the original owners of their lands had been, further undermining any sense of their own legitimacy as landlords. One can only imagine how they might have perceived Charles O'Conor, a descendant of the royal O'Conors of Connacht – the last family to hold the high kingship of Ireland.

Indeed there was in O'Conor's work a submerged subversive and anti-colonial mentality. Clare O'Halloran notes that the late Oliver MacDonagh observed that "history [is] but a dialogue between present apprehensions and knowledge of what has gone before", and she concludes that the 1780s and 1790s were "perhaps the most difficult period in which to attempt the formation of a community of antiquaries in Ireland". It is all the more remarkable that O'Conor made a "bridge" which in the long term facilitated the ending of the apartheid.

In an insightful chapter, Luke Gibbons draws attention to one of the most original aspects of O'Conor's work – "his concern to square the 'backward look' of antiquarianism and romantic nostalgia – the staples of emergent cultural nationalism – with the distinctively modern discourses of agrarian improvement and economic progress". Ireland's economic underdevelopment was due to colonial neglect and mismanagement and did not arise because the Irish were a primitive or indolent race. For O'Conor, Catholic thinking could embrace Enlightenment schemes of land reclamation, drainage, inland waterways, mining and so forth as well as drawing upon Irish pedigrees of territory, law, language and political legitimacy. O'Conor, notes Gibbons, "was thoroughly committed to modernization but he differed from his ascendancy counterparts in envisaging it as benefiting the country as a whole, Protestant and Catholic, Anglo-Irish and native Irish".

Olga Tsapina explores, in a brilliant chapter, how for a variety of reasons the Catholic Enlightenment – a complex international phenomenon that spanned the Continent and the British Isles – has long been overlooked in Ireland, while Hilary Larkin, examining O'Conor and the *philosophes*, observes that this is a reason why he "has never entered into the mainstream Irish historical canon". It is heartening, however, that Ian McBride's excellent work on the eighteenth century, referred to above, strongly emphasises the Irish Enlightenment and, in particular, O'Conor's central role. The Enlightenment, however, has not yet been incorporated into the necessary revision of more popular traditionalist nationalist history in Ireland. Until the work of the late Oliver MacDonagh and other scholars, this neglect of the Irish participation in "enlightened" thought also affected Daniel O'Connell's reputation as the major carrier of Enlightenment values which gave rise to his liberal Catholicism and his focus on universal liberty.

Now that the Irish people are rapidly moving away from a narrow, sectarian nationalism, both O'Conor and O'Connell have much to teach us about alternative ways of conceiving our nation and providing for the diverse anthropology of those who live on the island. Larkin provides a most insightful account of O'Conor's reading of Montesquieu, his critiquing of Voltaire and his hostility to Hume. She concludes that O'Conor "remains definitely and self-consciously an Enlightenment figure – hailing the present age in Europe as one of civil liberty and emancipation from prejudices, and looking to a future that would break the deadlock of a sectarian past. He optimistically welcomed the 'free spirit of inquiry' that would enable politicians and historians to challenge the status quo and solve society's problems in a rational way."

It is important to note the depth of anti-Catholicism in much Enlightenment thought, particularly in France – repression of the Irish majority did not become a chic *cause célèbre* of the day, as Larkin observes. She recounts how Daniel O'Conor, brother of Charles, met Claude Adrien Helvétius, the French *philosophe*, in 1763:

> Conversation soon turned to the Penal Laws and Helvétius showed himself far from sympathetic to the Catholic cause, unreasonably asking why they did not solve the matter by becoming Protestants. O'Conor patiently replied that they were attached to their religion and besides could not be admitted into the Protestant polity without swearing away the main articles of their faith. Helvétius scoffingly asked: 'where the Devil would be the great harm in that, surely you are not so idle as to have any regard to these fooleries? Is your brother a Protestant?' On Daniel replying in the negative, Helvétius asked was Charles bigoted as to his religion. 'Sir, he is too enlightened to be a bigot' the Irishman returned simply. This apparently had no effect on the philosopher who advised the O'Conors to all become Protestant and thus protect themselves against the worst of the laws.

From Charles O'Conor's letters and works – as well as from his life – we obtain a vivid picture, in the late Alan Harrison's words, "of a learned, humane, tolerant, urbane Irishman who employed his talents in what he perceived to be the best interests of his country. His was a patriotism that has been obscured by subsequent events of Irish history and by the establishment of a confrontational rather than a conciliatory approach to Ireland's problems." O'Conor was indeed, as Ó Catháin has observed, an astute, complex, subtle, resourceful and deep man. Much remains to be done in relation to his life and career: his role in the struggle for Catholic civil rights, for example, requires a full and detailed examination. His diaries and his library need scholarly attention, especially as the comprehensive Old Irish family archive at Clonalis House is so unique. In the longer term we need a full-scale literary and political biography. In the meantime, Gibbons and O'Conor's collection of essays is a book to feast upon and one which deserves wide attention.

ENDA O'DOHERTY | 2015

The Romantic Englishman

George Orwell: English Rebel, by Robert Colls

Oxford University Press | 330 pp | ISBN: 978-0199680801

IN EARLY 1936 the publisher Victor Gollancz commissioned George Orwell to conduct an investigation into the plight of the unemployed in England's industrial North, a project that led to the book *The Road to Wigan Pier*. Unemployment and hardship in Lancashire and Yorkshire were, on the face of it, not subjects that Orwell could have been expected to know that much about. True, he had written vividly about tramps and tramping, "spikes", charity wards and common lodging houses, but he had little experience of England outside London and the home counties and few friends or acquaintances who were working class or came from a non-privileged background. His own sentimental education had been forged in the sleek landscapes of the Thames valley or, later, genteel Southwold on the Suffolk coast – the England inhabited by those he was to term "the lower-upper-middle-class", the people who kept the country running and who, though they owned no land, still felt they were "landowners in the sight of God".

If he did not have much relevant experience, what Orwell could offer his publisher were energy and passion, and a small but growing reputation as a young man with something to say. He also needed the money. Years later he told a friend that he would never have undertaken the trip north had it not been for the size of the advance Gollancz offered: £500, a rather large sum at the time for a writer still in his early thirties. As a man with not much taste for the high life, he reckoned he could survive for two years on that, and afford to get married.

On January 31st he set out by train for Coventry, staying the night there in a bed and breakfast establishment: "very lousy, 3/6 ... Smell as in common lodging houses. Half-witted servant girl with huge body, tiny head and rolls of fat at back of neck curiously recalling ham-fat." From Coventry, on through Birmingham and the Black Country, he was mostly to walk, the better to see his surroundings ("Wolverhampton seems frightful place. Everywhere vistas of mean little houses ...") On February 5th he arrived at the home of his contact in Manchester, the trade unionist Frank Meade. He was now more or less at his destination and immediately began to observe his surroundings, and arrive at conclusions:

> The M.[eade]s have been very decent to me. Both are working-class people, speak with Lancashire accents and have worn the clogs in their childhood, but the atmosphere in a place like this is entirely middle-class ... I am struck again by the fact that as soon as a working man gets an official post in the Trade Union or goes into Labour politics, he becomes middle-class whether he will or no i.e. by fighting against the bourgeoisie he becomes a bourgeois.

From Manchester, he was sent on to Wigan, where he met the socialist electrician Joe Kennan ("a very short, stout, powerful man with an extraordinarily gentle, hospitable manner") and the unemployed miner Paddy Grady ("intelligent and well-informed"). Kennan found him lodgings in the town but he was soon forced to move again as his landlady became ill and had to go to hospital. His new digs, over a tripe shop, was not an improvement: "Social atmosphere much as [at previous lodgings] but appreciably dirtier and very smelly." By February 21st he had had enough:

> The squalor of this house is beginning to get on my nerves ... The most revolting feature is Mrs F. being always in bed on the kitchen sofa [she was an invalid]. She has a terrible habit of tearing off strips of newspaper, wiping her mouth with them and then throwing them onto the floor. Unemptied chamber pot under the table at breakfast this morning ... I

hear horrible stories, too, about the cellars where the tripe is kept and which are said to swarm with black beetles. Apparently they only get in fresh supplies of tripe at long intervals. Mrs F. dates events by this. 'Let me see, then, I've had in three lots of froze (frozen tripe) since then,' etc. I judge they get in a consignment of 'froze' about once in a fortnight.

Orwell was not, however, in Lancashire (and later Yorkshire) just to comment on the accents, manners and physical appearance of the working class, the strange things they ate and the smell of their houses. He also took notes on pay and conditions in the mines; on the various kinds of working class houses and the rents that were charged for them; on the different grades of social assistance payment and how people who had become unemployed or who were injured at work might manage (or not) on such a diminished income; on diet (and why poor people don't want the "dull wholesome food" others might think good for them); and on the lives of women, their intensive domestic labour and pride in their homes – when they had half-decent ones.

After twelve days in Wigan he went down a mine (the first of three such visits). Writing about the experience later, he has one clear point he wishes to make about the coal industry and its workers: that it, and they – in the England of the time – are the bedrock of all other industrial activity, of all capitalist profit and hence the main source of the "dividends" on which many of the wealthier members of society depend for their civilised lives and which they could not live without: "In the metabolism of the Western world the coal-miner is second in importance only to the man who ploughs the soil. He is a sort of grimy caryatid on whose shoulders everything that is not grimy is supported."

Orwell's account of his visit to Crippen's mine in Bryn, near Wigan, a superb piece of journalistic writing, forms the second chapter of *The Road to Wigan Pier* and has also been anthologised separately as "Down the Mine". The chapter focuses alternately on the miners who dig the coal and those who unthinkingly consume it, the latter portrayed primarily as the comfortable, even the decadent classes – as if coal was not burned too in redbrick terraced houses in working class towns. Here are the fillers, who shovel the freshly mined rocks onto a conveyor belt from a kneeling position, splendid, heroic creatures in spite of the cruelly demanding labour they are engaged in:

They really do look like iron – hammered iron statues – under the smooth coat of coal dust which clings to them from head to foot. It is only when you see miners down the mine and naked that you realize what splendid men they are. Most of them are small … but nearly all of them have the most noble bodies; wide shoulders tapering to slender, supple waists, and small pronounced buttocks and sinewy thighs, with not an ounce of waste flesh anywhere.

And here are the uncaring rich, who warm themselves in their drawing rooms and studies on the products of the miners' labours, oblivious to the grinding effort that has gone into filling their grates:

> … it is brought home to you, at least while you are watching, that it is only because miners sweat their guts out that superior persons can remain superior. You and I and the editor of the *Times Litt. Supp.*, and the Nancy poets [Spender, Auden, Day Lewis etc, a favourite Orwell smear] and the Archbishop of Canterbury and Comrade X, author of *Marxism for Infants* – all of us *really* owe the comparative decency of our lives to poor drudges underground, blackened to the eyes, with their throats full of coal dust, driving their shovels forward with arms and belly muscles of steel.

Orwell brought to Wigan his intelligence, connections brokered by his political (chiefly Independent Labour Party) friends in London, some convictions about socialism gleaned from his reading, no doubt some knowledge of local conditions based on specific research, and certain attitudes to exploitation, power and the possibility of political change which we might surmise were as much informed by his experience of the oppressive regime of colonial Burma as by parliamentary politics in 1930s Britain (in which he took little enough interest). What he did not bring with him was any particular understanding of the British working class, of their history, traditions, aspirations or modes of organisation. Robert Colls writes:

> That they shared a certain organizational talent he accepts, but there is no sense of leadership or thought or even point of view in his account [in *The Road to Wigan Pier*]. For a man on the brink of breaking his ties with 'bourgeois intellectuals', it is strange that Orwell does not know any labour history, seems to regards socialism as some sort of fad … shows

no knowledge of the Socialist Sunday Schools and Leagues of Youth ... [or has] no interest whatsoever in the more gregarious aspects of life in the industrial town – the chapel oratorios and concert parties, or the rambling and cycling clubs, or the boxing booths, banjo bands, and brass bands, the weekly hops, the free-and-easies, the charabanc outings, and Lancashire's famous Wakes ... Lancashire was the home of football, but there is no football in Orwell. Yorkshire was a stronghold of the Workingmen's Club and Institute Union, but when he attends their delegate meeting in Barnsley he does not approve of the free beer and sandwiches ... The friendly societies took the subscriptions of half of all working-class men in 1914, but Orwell says not a word on how they had managed to organize such a vast undertaking, nor indeed on how, along with all the other mutual societies, sick clubs, and boxes, they had secured their place in law to allow them to do so. There is no fun, no ambition, no zest, no obscenity, and precious little sociability in Orwell's north. A night out in Blackpool would have done him (and English literature) the world of good. Where are the comedians? Where is George Formby, Wigan's favourite son? Where are the factory lasses? Where's our Gracie? He says that all trade-union and Labour party officials are middle-class, automatically so, and shows almost no time for those bulwarks of working-class defence – the Miners' Federation, the cooperative societies and guilds, the trades councils, the Labour party, and the multi-layered and infinitely resourceful female communities of the street. He notes the poverty, but where is the thrift? He notes the grind, but where's the Ritz Super [cinema] ... ?

Victor Gollancz, who might be said to have been "close to the thinking of the Communist Party of Great Britain", was not entirely pleased by the book which Orwell submitted to him in December 1936 and for which he had paid so large an advance. Not a great deal of exception could be taken to the first part, which was a fairly straightforward account of conditions in the North. Indeed Gollancz at first proposed – though the suggestion was not accepted – that this should be published on its own as a Left Book Club edition. Into the second part, however, Orwell had stuffed his analysis and his always plentiful opinions, many of them strongly expressed and often focusing on the kind of people who formed a large part of the readership of the Left Book Club. Here are the urban, middle class intellectual socialists:

> the more-water-in-your-beer reformers of whom Shaw is the prototype, and the astute young social-literary climbers who are Communists now, as they will be Fascists five years hence, because it is all the go, and all that dreary tribe of highminded women and sandal-wearers and bearded fruit-juice drinkers who come flocking towards the smell of "progress" like bluebottles to a dead cat.

Famously, there is the attraction of socialist doctrine for "cranks":

> One sometimes gets the impression that the mere words 'Socialism' and 'Communism' draw towards them with magnetic force every fruit-juice drinker, nudist, sandal-wearer, sex-maniac, Quaker, 'Nature Cure' quack, pacifist, and feminist in England.

And finally, rising to an apparent pitch of impotent frustration:

> If only the sandals and pistachio-coloured shirts could be put in a pile and burnt, and every vegetarian, teetotaller and creeping Jesus sent home to Welwyn Garden City to do his yoga exercises quietly.

Perhaps more than a little of this is tongue in cheek. One conclusion, however, can be tentatively drawn before moving on: at this stage of his life and intellectual development, Orwell preferred to portray socialism as chiefly a middle class fad and, while he was quite ready to idealise the working class "other" if it came to him in the right shape, he showed virtually no interest in working class politics or social organisation as they actually existed.

On returning from Wigan, Orwell and his new wife, Eileen, moved out of London to rent, for 7s/6d a week, a disused cottage in remote Wallington in Hertfordshire which had formerly hosted a village shop. Energetically, he tackled the overgrown garden, sowed vegetables, built a henhouse, bought chickens and geese and introduced into the family the goat Muriel (who was to resurface as a character in *Animal Farm*) and a black poodle called Marx. He also reopened the shop, selling small grocery items, and sweets to local children. By 1936, however, political events in Europe were occupying more of his attention and late that year he decided to go to Spain to fight fascism.

With a letter of introduction from friends in the ILP, Orwell travelled, via Paris, to Barcelona. The party's man on the spot, John McNair, directed him to the local barracks of the militia of the Partido Obrero de Unificación Marxista (POUM), where he signed up as "Eric Blair, grocer". It was here, at the Lenin Barracks, that Orwell experienced another socialist epiphany when he noticed, standing by a table, an Italian militiaman, "a tough-looking youth of twenty five or six, with reddish yellow hair and powerful shoulders".

> Something in his face deeply moved me. It was the face of a man who would commit murder and throw away his life for a friend ...
>
> As we went out he stepped across the room and gripped my hand very hard. Queer, the affection you can feel for a stranger! It was as though his spirit and mine had momentarily succeeded in bridging the gulf of language and tradition ... I hoped he liked me as well as I liked him. But I knew that to retain my first impression of him I must not see him again.

Orwell was dispatched to the Aragon front, where he saw action twice, in what seemed to be pointless skirmishes between two equally miserable and underequipped squads of combatants. His rifle was an 1890 Mauser; he also noted that "we had no tin hats, no bayonets, hardly any revolvers or pistols, and not more than one bomb between five or ten men ... no range-finders, no telescopes, no periscopes, no field-glasses except a few privately owned pairs, no flares or Very lights, no armourers' tools, hardly any cleaning materials".

After a brief period of leave in early May, spent in Barcelona, where Eileen had joined him, Orwell returned to the front at Huesca, where he was made lieutenant of an ILP platoon. It was here that he was shot, an experience he described with typical Orwellian detachment and precision.

> The whole experience of being hit by a bullet is very interesting and I think it is worth describing in detail ...
>
> I had never heard of a man or an animal getting a bullet through the middle of the neck and surviving it. The blood was dribbling out of the corner of my mouth. 'The artery's gone,' I thought. I wondered how long you last when your carotid artery is cut; not many minutes, presumably. Everything was very blurry. There must have been about two minutes during which I assumed I was killed. And that too was interesting ...

He was evacuated to Tarragona and eventually Barcelona, where he recovered quite quickly from his wound (the high-velocity bullet, fired from relatively close at hand, had gone clean through his throat; had it been a millimetre to the left it would have killed him). In Barcelona the political atmosphere had soured considerably, the government having declared the POUM illegal; now its units were being disbanded and its members arrested. The degree of hostility that existed between the communist element in the anti-Franco coalition and the anarchist and Trotskyist elements was scarcely surprising (the communists called the POUM Trotskyist, though strictly speaking they had been banished from that faction). As early as December 1936 (and thus somewhat before the events), *Pravda* had ominously announced that "In Catalonia the elimination of Trotskyites and Anarcho-Syndicalists has begun. It will be carried out with the same energy as it was in the Soviet Union." The dispute in Spain between these two currents – let us say "orthodox" and "left-wing" communism – revolved around strategy. The POUM and the anarchists believed that the war could be won only by continuing and deepening the revolution: in practice this meant that any power, or position or property the masses had seized they must remain in control of. The orthodox communists – for the moment at least – backed the position of moderate socialists and democrats in the government that the essential purpose of the war was to save the Republic, and that if there was to be any hope of achieving that it must be prosecuted with efficiency, an efficiency which ran counter to far-leftist and anarchist modes of organisation, or disorganisation.

Orwell, having seen the paltry nature of the military effort that the POUM had mounted on his section of the Aragon front, was at first quite amenable to this "realist" position (indeed he fervently wished to join the International Brigades at Madrid, where the "real" struggle was taking place). However, as the civil war within the civil war developed he became more angry at the lies the communists, and their allies in the left-wing and liberal press at home in Britain, were telling about his comrades, who were now being represented as "Trotsky-Fascists" and fifth-columnists: the distance between having a wrong strategy, and thus perhaps hindering a unified war effort, and being "objectively fascist", or quite simply fascist, could be a short – and often fatal – one in Stalinist communism.

If Orwell, after a good deal of hesitation, came down in favour of the POUM analysis, this was, Colls argues, "not so much because he believed the line but because [he] believed the men who believed the line". The communist smearing of the POUM, he wrote,

> implied that scores of thousands of working-class people, including eight or ten thousand soldiers who were freezing in the front-line trenches ... were simply traitors ... It is not a nice thing to see a Spanish boy of fifteen carried down the line on a stretcher, with a dazed white face looking out from the blankets, and to think of the sleek persons in London and Paris who are writing pamphlets to prove that this boy is a Fascist in disguise.

This is strong writing, and the themes and tone are of course familiar, with the contrast between the shivering soldiers on the front line and the sleek persons (intellectuals, no doubt with merrily burning coal fires) who are writing lies about them from their comfortable metropolitan studies. Colls, however, contends that in relation to the Spanish war Orwell, and the extreme leftists, simply had it wrong. It was quite legitimate at this point in the struggle, he argues, for the central government to wish to put an end to the murderous excesses of militia justice and "people's tribunals", with "private revolutionary patrols, crossings, checkpoints, holding centres, safe houses"; indeed such an assertion of control was crucial to the constitutional credibility of the government. As for the military situation, the Soviet Union was the only significant power that was helping the Republic: it had been their tanks, not the militias, which had stopped Franco outside Madrid in November 1936 and the Republic's few victories, at Jarama and Guadalajara in early 1937, could not have been won without Soviet armour. Colls's position on this, it should be stressed, is not a pro-communist but a pro-government one. Many historians of the war would back this analysis. Most tellingly, however, there is Orwell's own retrospective judgment, from the essay "Looking Back on the Spanish War", published in 1943:

> The Trotskyist thesis that the war could have been won if the revolution had not been sabotaged was probably false. To nationalize factories, demolish churches, and issue revolutionary manifestoes would not have made the armies more efficient. The Fascists won because they were the stronger; they had modern arms and the others hadn't. No political strategy could offset that.

In spite of this later revision, the political attitudes that the Spanish conflict had awoken in Orwell were to remain strong for several years.

In one of his many tirades against "cranks" Orwell relates that he was, while living at Wallington, travelling through the nearby town of Letchworth when his bus stopped and two "dreadful-looking" old men got on.

> They were both about sixty, both very short, pink, and chubby, and both hatless. One of them was obscenely bald, the other had long grey hair bobbed in the Lloyd George style. They were dressed in pistachio-coloured shirts and khaki shorts into which their huge bottoms were crammed so tightly that you could study every dimple. Their appearance created a mild stir of horror on top of the bus. The man next to me, a commercial traveller I should say, glanced at me, at them, and back again at me, and murmured 'Socialists', as who should say, 'Red Indians'.

The appearance of these two grotesques in Letchworth at this time can have had only one explanation: they were there to attend the summer school of the Independent Labour Party, a ginger group just to the left of the official Labour Party. In spite of his apparent aversion to cranks, Orwell attended the school himself in the following year and in 1938 he joined the ILP, writing in its journal, *New Leader*, that the time had come when "one has got to be actively a Socialist, not merely sympathetic to Socialism". It was not, he stressed, that he "had lost all faith in the Labour Party" (the first sign that he had ever had any, his biographer Bernard Crick remarks). But he was relying on the ILP in particular to resist "the temptation to fling every principle overboard in order to prepare for an Imperialist war". In a long article in *The Adelphi* in December 1938 he strongly criticised Labour for being half-hearted in its resistance to what he saw as the inexorable drift towards war with Germany, urging it, instead of colluding in British rearmament, to make stronger appeals to the German working class to resist Hitler. If the war were to be fought, he believed, it would be little more than an ignominious scrabble for markets between Britain and France on the one hand and Germany and Italy on the other. The only blessing would be that, given the power of aerial bombing, it would certainly be over very quickly. But declaration of war and attempted conscription and mobilisation would also give to the working classes of each of the belligerent countries the chance to stage a revolution.

Something quite marvellous happened in summer 1939, and as is so often the case it was announced in a dream. In an essay entitled "My Country Right or Left", published in 1940, Orwell wrote that though the fact that war was on the way had, since at least 1936, been obvious to anyone except an idiot, the prospect of conflict had, for a long time, been horrific to him: indeed he had even made speeches and written pamphlets against it. However, on the night before the Russo-German pact was announced (August 23rd, 1939), he dreamed that the war had started (it in fact started, for Britain and France, on September 3rd). In spite of his previous position, this "realisation" brought him relief, and he knew that he would support the war and, if he could, fight in it. He had been educated, and well-educated, in upper middle class patriotism, and now that England was in a jam he would have no option but to heed the call. Patriotism, however, he insisted, was a quite different thing from political conservatism, and his enlistment in his country's service was, he felt sure, going to be accompanied by unexpected, and quite dramatic, developments:

> Only revolution can save England, that has been obvious for years, but now the revolution has started, and it may proceed quite quickly if only we can keep Hitler out. Within two years, maybe a year, if only we can hang on, we shall see changes that will surprise the idiots who have no foresight. I dare say the London gutters will have to run with blood. All right, let them, if it is necessary. But when the red militias are billeted in the Ritz I shall still feel that the England that I was taught to love so long ago and for such different reasons is somehow persisting.

A combination of poor health (tuberculosis) and political unreliability was to keep Orwell out of the armed forces, but he did, in June 1940, manage to join the Local Defence Volunteers, later to become the Home Guard, a formation to which he attributed great revolutionary potential, seeing it, in Bernard Crick's words, "through blood-red spectacles as a potential people's militia". Those born in later decades may be more familiar with the body through the adventures of Captain Mainwaring and Sergeant Wilson's valiant platoon at Walmington-on-Sea.

Once the war got going Orwell had no difficulty in identifying wholeheartedly with it. In a letter of January 1940 he wrote that "[t]he intellectuals who are at present pointing out that democracy and fascism are the same thing depress me horribly", forgetting that he had spent much of the previous four years pointing out the same thing ("Fascism and Bourgeois 'democracy' are Tweedledum and Tweedledee" for example). Still, the prosecution of the war and the prospect of revolution remained intimately linked in his mind. In late 1942 he was telling the New York readers of *Partisan Review* that "old-style capitalism can't win the war … now, as two years ago, one can predict the future in the form of an 'either – or': either we introduce Socialism or we lose the war". Not that his predictions always worked out: in May 1942 (again for *Partisan Review*) he was writing that "I wouldn't give Churchill many more months of power". Orwell may not have been quite a Trotskyist (indeed he was to adjust quite happily, after 1945, to supporting the left-wing social democrats of the Labour Party's *Tribune* group) but he had enough of the revolutionary socialist spirit for a number of years after Spain to regard the ultimate upheaval as being always just around the corner: explanations would then be required as to why it didn't happen, when the real question was why it ever *should* happen, particularly in a country with as pacific a political culture as Britain. Eventually however, the penny seemed to drop: in January 1943 he wrote, again for his American audience, that

> the growing suspicion that we may all have underrated the strength of capitalism, and that the Right may, after all, be able to win the war off its own bat without resorting to any radical change, is very depressing to anyone who thinks. Cynicism about 'after the war' is widespread, and the 'we're all in it together' feeling of 1940 has faded away.

Yet even in this sudden lurch towards pessimism he was to be somewhat off the mark, as the Labour landslide in the general election of July 1945 would show. Many British people did apparently feel, after all they had been through, that they were "in it together" and they had no wish to go back to the Tory normality of the 1930s, with millions unemployed. The Labour Party, having won 393 seats to the Conservatives' 197, was to be in government for the rest of Orwell's lifetime.

The centrepiece of Robert Colls's fine study of Orwell, which is sympathetic yet sceptical in tone, crammed with persuasive insights, bracing in its judgments and written in a pleasingly informal and occasionally idiosyncratic style, is his chapter on Orwell's Englishness ("England the Whale"). Colls sees Orwell's change of attitude towards his country, which he dates to the very early years of the war, as a psychological watershed, a belated coming to terms for the sometimes haunted author with his background, education and even "the British nation-state ... an old and not entirely dishonourable form of political life". How one feels about this may depend to a degree on how one feels about Britain (or even England). Robert Colls is a professor of cultural history and the author of a well-received study, *Identity of England*, and one may assume that he is not unduly embarrassed by the celebration of his native land. Orwell himself, however, recognised that what he saw as the natural gentleness and deep-seated hostility to dictatorship or even the military mindset characteristic of his compatriots was achieved at the cost of a certain hypocrisy: either they were unaware of what their empire was up to or they simply chose to ignore it. Be that as it may, in a series of sparkling essays written during this period, "this most deracinated of intellectuals" (India – Henley – prep school – Eton – Burma –Southwold – Paris – London – Wallington – Spain – London – Jura), who seemed to be always trying to get away, focused on what it was to be English, in the extended meditation *The Lion and the Unicorn* and in perceptive and beautifully written individual essays on Dickens, Kipling, boys' comics, "dirty" postcards, the English murder and PG Wodehouse.

Orwell has often been credited with having elevated political writing to an art (the phrase appears with great regularity in book blurbs). The judgment, which is in essence a sound one, is usually made with more of an eye on the essays, reviews and occasional journalism than on the major fictions of the final decade, *Animal Farm* and *Nineteen Eighty-Four*, in which Orwell honed his vision of totalitarianism in general and Soviet communism in particular. In weighing this assessment, however, it might be useful to separate out its terms, "political" and "writing", for while it is undeniable that Orwell's writing is of the highest order (and often more so in his essays than his novels) the quality of his political judgment – with the exception of his deep central insight into the nature of Stalinist communism – remains questionable. Indeed if he had taken to betting on the basis of his political forecasts he would have been bankrupt several times over.

If Orwell was, as his friend Cyril Connolly wrote, "a man ... whose personality shines out in everything he wrote", we must ask if this was, in the essays, frequently a rather manufactured personality, made up of an outsize helping of what is usually called common sense – robust and often hectoring – filtered through an apparently unshakable self-assurance: Orwell's assertions are never simply the case – they are things *everyone* knows, things *obviously* true, *indisputably* true, *self-evidently* true, clear to anyone except *a complete idiot*. And this is so even when they seem arbitrary, ridiculous or simply plucked from the air. Here, for example, is Orwell on England:

> Few Europeans can endure living in England, and even Americans often feel more at home in Europe.
> [The English] have no aesthetic feelings whatever.
> The English electoral system ... is an all but open fraud.
> In England, all the boasting and flag-wagging, the 'Rule Britannia' stuff, is done by small minorities.

And rather puzzlingly:

> In no country inhabited by white men is it easier to shove people off the pavement.

Stefan Collini, in a chapter in his book *Absent Minds*, has extensively documented Orwell's "intellectual's anti-intellectualism", his rather concocted plain man's irritation at pretension, the "come-off-it" commonsensical mode that was to become a popular journalistic device, evolving eventually into what Collini has called the "'no bullshit' bullshit" style of Orwell's disciple Christopher Hitchens and others. Indeed there is little doubt that the typical Orwellian form of polemic was a conscious construction, since almost all who knew him agreed that personally he was a rather shy and gentle man. In 1938 he wrote to the poet Stephen Spender, whom he had often pilloried as a member of the "pansy left":

> You ask how it is that I attacked you not having met you, & on the other hand changed my mind after meeting you ... Even if when I met you I had not happened to like you, I should still have been bound to change my attitude, because when you meet anyone in the flesh you

realize immediately that he is a human being & not a sort of caricature embodying certain ideas. It is partly for this reason that I don't mix much in literary circles, because I know from experience that once I have met & spoken to anyone I shall never again be able to show any intellectual brutality towards him, even when I feel that I ought to ...

Over the decades Stalinists and other Marxist-Leninists have attempted to blacken Orwell's reputation, but with remarkably little success. But was he, as they tend to suggest, in his final decade on an inexorable journey to the political right? Would he, if he had survived into old age, have ended up cheerleading for Thatcher? The question is, of course, unanswerable. But was he already in his lifetime becoming a renegade? Much has been made of his supplying, in 1949, the names of people he suspected of being communist fellow travellers to his friend Celia Paget, who worked for the Information Research Department, a branch of the Foreign Office whose brief was to write anti-communist propaganda for use in continental Europe in the immediate postwar era. But here Orwell's action seems quite harmless: no one was being fingered, no one seemed likely to disappear; the advice he gave Paget was simply not to employ people for work they might be neither sympathetic to nor trustworthy in. And what exactly is wrong with not wishing to abet communists in dissolving liberal democracy and civil freedoms?

In the essay "Why I Write" (1946), Orwell maintained that "Every line of serious work that I have written since 1936 has been written, directly or indirectly, against totalitarianism and for democratic socialism, as I understand it." There is little reason to doubt this statement or to think that Orwell might have been moving away from it in his last few years, when the Attlee government was in fact achieving more for democratic socialism than at any time in English history before or since. Orwell's socialism may have been ill-defined and contradictory, but it was deeply felt. It certainly derived to some degree from guilt about his own fairly comfortable upbringing, his education and the role he had played as an enforcer for British imperialism in the Burmese police. It was also based on a clear romanticisation of the "ordinary Englishman" (Colls speaks shrewdly of his *narodnik* tendencies) and a settled view that the misery of the working class in hard times was intimately linked with the comforts of Orwell's own class: the miner was the "grimy caryatid on whose shoulders everything that is not grimy is supported": a huge obstacle to any significant move to the right on Orwell's part must surely have been his considerable distaste for extreme wealth.

Certainly his oddities often infected his political judgment and made him a particularly unreliable guide to what the future might hold. At the same time they seem to have been the fuel that drove his magnificent prose writings, which, in a perhaps very English way, can be wildly eccentric, hilarious, perverse or brilliant. We could do worse than conclude with one of the best summings up of the Orwellian virtues, and of the accompanying flaws of "personality", which in his writing often function aesthetically as virtues. It is from VS Pritchett:

> Mr George Orwell has many of the traits of the best English pamphleteers: courage, an individual mind, vehement opinions, an instinct for stirring up trouble, the arts of appealing to that imaginary creature the sensible man and of combining original observations with sweeping generalization, of seeing enemies everywhere and despising all of them. And like the two outstanding figures of our tradition of pamphleteering, Cobbett and Defoe, both of whom had his subversive, non-conforming brand of patriotism, he writes a lucid conversational style which wakes one up suddenly, like cold water dashed in the face. The sting of it is sometimes refreshing; sometimes it makes one very angry. For Mr Orwell likes his friends no better than his enemies and in the name of common sense is capable of exaggerating with the simplicity and innocence of a savage. His virtue is that he says things that need to be said; his vice that some of these things needed saying with a great deal more consideration. But, damn thoughtfulness! Pamphleteers have to hit the bull's-eye every time, or, failing that, someone else's eye. Mr Orwell's standards of accuracy and judiciousness are in the tradition and may be compared with those of Shaw, the greatest pamphleteer of our time. I will give one key example from *The Lion and the Unicorn* and be done with it: 'It is a strange fact, but it is unquestionably true, that almost any English intellectual would feel more ashamed of standing to attention during "God Save the King", than of stealing from a poor box.'

Pritchett, who knew his Orwell, concluded: "'Unquestionably' is the word I like in that sentence."

The Irish
Literary
Tradition

DENIS DONOGHUE *reflects on the relations of three major figures of twentieth century poetry, WB Yeats, TS Eliot and Ezra Pound, three "presences" who he finds mostly misunderstood each other, not by being deaf but by being hard of hearing to rhythms other than their own.*

John McGahern, writes RACHEL ANDREWS, *seethed with disgust for the political system and the sectarian theocracy in which he was born but still laments the loss of the spiritual solace offered him by religion in his youth, "the sense of our origins beyond the bounds of sense, an awareness of mystery and wonderment, grace and sacrament".*

JOSEPH M HASSETT, *himself a trial lawyer, studies the obscenity trials that faced Joyce's* Ulysses *in the United States and the sometimes dubious strategies adopted by the defence.*

The second volume of Samuel Beckett's letters covers the war years and the huge success of Waiting for Godot. *The writer's sympathy and generosity are a keynote of the volume, writes* BENJAMIN KEATINGE, *and Beckett's own complaints, "a lugubrious background grouse-against-the-world", are tempered by his willingness to alleviate the burdens of his friends.*

JAMES WARD *is impressed by a new biography of Jonathan Swift, an eighteenth century figure who is still our contemporary, having "perfected the art of crafting phrases snappy enough to become slogans but which, on closer inspection, yield disturbing and contradictory meanings".*

Three Presences

ON APRIL 2nd, 1916, one of Yeats's plays for dancers, *At the Hawk's Well*, received its first performance in Lady Emerald Cunard's drawing room in Cavendish Square, London before an invited audience. Michio Ito danced the Guardian of the Well. The guests included Ezra Pound and TS Eliot. For all I know, this may have been the only afternoon on which Yeats, Eliot and Pound were together in the same room. Many years later, Samuel Beckett wrote a play, like *At the Hawk's Well* about waiting; waiting for someone who is supposed to arrive but doesn't, a variant of waiting for a transforming flow of water which is never received because the Guardian of the Well distracts those who are longing for it. In *Happy Days* Winnie utters the first line of *At the Hawk's Well*, "I call to the eye of the mind", one of many literary allusions that she recalls – or rather that Beckett recalls on her behalf. I draw a loose connection between these occasions to suggest a literary context for the relations I propose to describe: Yeats and Eliot, Yeats and Pound.

We know when Eliot converted to the Anglican Communion – he made his formal profession on June 9th, 1927 – but we don't know precisely when he converted to Yeats: that took much longer. The first time he wrote about Yeats was in the *Athenaeum*, the issue for July 4th, 1919, a memorably severe review of *The Cutting of an Agate*. Eliot apparently found Yeats's entire sensibility weird. As much in his prose as in his verse, he said, Yeats "is not 'of this world'

– this world, of course, being our visible planet with whatever our theology or myth may conceive as below or above it". Eliot assumes that he is central, and by comparison Yeats is exotically peripheral. The difference between Yeats's world and ours, Eliot continues in consternation, "is so complete as to seem almost a physiological variety, different nerves and senses". It was not – or not merely – a matter of Yeats's interest in ghosts, mediums, leprechauns and sprites. "When an Englishman explores the mysteries of the Cabala," Eliot writes, "one knows one's opinion of him, but Mr. Yeats on any subject is a cause of bewilderment and distress."

> The sprites are not unacceptable; but Mr. Yeats's daily world, the world which admits these monsters without astonishment, which views them more familiarly than Commercial Road views a Lascar – this is the unknown and unknowable. Mr. Yeats's mind is a mind in some way independent of experience; and anything that occurs in that mind is of equal importance. It is a mind in which perception of fact, and feeling and thinking are all a little different from ours.

Eliot does not define whom he has in mind by "ours", or justify bringing forth their values as a decisive criterion. He does not explain how "experience" can be appealed to as a system supposedly held in common. He claims that Yeats's sensibility cannot be assessed by any available standard:

> In Mr. Yeats's verse, in particular, the qualities can by no means be defined as mere attenuations and faintnesses. When it is compared with the work of any English bard of apparently equivalent thinness, the result is that the English work in question is thin; you can point to something that it ought to be and is not; but of Yeats you cannot say finally that he lacks feeling. He does not pretend to more feeling than he has, perhaps he has a great deal; it is not feeling that standards can measure as passionate or insipid.

Eliot's problem with Yeats is that he cannot see either his thought or his feeling as having issued from any common source:

> He seems, in his disembodied way, to happen on thoughts, thoughts of 'wisdom,' and if we are not convinced, it is because we do not see by what right he comes by them.

Perhaps, Eliot allows, Yeats got these wise thoughts from his dreaming; but, even if this is so, "Mr. Yeats's dream is identical with Mr. Yeats's reality", a qualification or continuation of himself.

Eliot quotes, in evidence, four short passages from *The Cutting of an Agate*, including one – inaccurately quoted indeed – in which Yeats says that the poet must "be content to find his pleasure in all that is for ever passing away that it may come again, in the beauty of woman, in the fragile flowers of spring, in momentary heroic passion, in whatever is most fleeting, most impassioned, as it were, for its own perfection, most eager to return in its glory". "It is a style of Pater," Eliot justly says, but then he indulges himself in a little racial prejudice, saying "it is a style of Pater, with a trick of the eye and a hanging of the nether lip that come from across the Irish Channel, all the more seductive". Yeats, he says, "sometimes appears, as a philosopher of aesthetics, incoherent":

But all of his observations are quite consistent with his personality, with his remoteness. His remoteness is not an escape from the world, for he is innocent of any world to escape from; his procedure is blameless, but he does not start where we do.

At this point in his review, Eliot moves toward thinking that to make sense of Yeats you have first to remember that he is an Irishman. To be an Irishman, he thinks, is to be deprived of certain attributes of sensibility, notably of wit, a quality he defined in his essay on Andrew Marvell as featuring "a tough reasonableness beneath the slight lyric grace":

You cannot find it in Shelley or Keats or Wordsworth; you cannot find more than an echo of it in Landor; still less in Tennyson or Browning; and among contemporaries Mr. Yeats is an Irishman and Mr. Hardy is a modern Englishman – that is to say, Mr. Hardy is without it and Mr. Yeats is outside of the tradition altogether.

What "the tradition" is, Eliot on this occasion does not say: presumably he means a structure of values which Irish men and women lacked, even though Irish culture could point to the various forms of intelligence exemplified by Swift, Yeats, Wilde, Joyce and Shaw. Yeats's mind, Eliot says further in the review is, in fact, extreme in egoism, and, as often with egoism, remains a little crude; crude, indeed, as from its remoteness one would expect. There is something of this crudity, and much of this egoism, about what is called Irish Literature: the egoism which obstructs from facing, and the crudity which remains through not having had to face direct contacts. We know also of an evasion, or rather an evacuation of reality by the very civilized; but people civilized to that extent are seldom artists, and Mr. Yeats is always an artist. His crudity and egoism are present in other writers who are Irish; justified by exploitation to the point of greatness, in the later work of Mr. James Joyce.

Joyce, too, seems to be understandable only if you take him to be an Irishman, with the attributes and defects which go with that condition:

> Mr. Joyce's mind is subtle, erudite, even massive; but it is not like Stendhal's, an instrument continually tempering and purifying emotion; it operates within the medium, the superb current of his feeling. The basis is pure feeling, and if the feeling of Mr. Yeats were equally powerful, it would also justify his thought. Very powerful feeling is crude; the fault of Mr. Yeats's is that it is crude without being powerful. The weakness of his prose is similar to that of his verse. The trouble is not that it is inconsistent, illogical or incoherent, but that the objects upon which it is directed are not fixed; as in his portraits of Synge and several other Irishmen, we do not seem to get the men themselves before us, but feelings of Mr. Yeats projected. It must always be granted that in verse at least Mr. Yeats's feeling is not simply crudeness and egoism, but that it has a positive, individual and permanent quality.

It may have been this quality, common to Yeats and Joyce, which enabled Eliot to think that Yeats had anticipated Joyce in the most far-reaching invention in modern literature. Reviewing *Ulysses* in 1923, Eliot wrote:

> It is here that Mr. Joyce's parallel use of the *Odyssey* has a great importance. It has the importance of a scientific discovery ... In using the myth, in manipulating a continuous parallel between contemporaneity and antiquity, Mr. Joyce is pursuing a method which others must pursue after him ... It is simply a way of controlling, of ordering, of giving a

shape and a significance to the immense panorama of futility and anarchy which is contemporary history. It is a method already adumbrated by Mr. Yeats, and of the need for which I believe Mr. Yeats to have been the first contemporary to be conscious ... Instead of narrative method, we may now use the mythical method. It is, I seriously believe, a step toward making the modern world possible for art ...

Eliot doesn't say where Yeats adumbrated the mythical method. I assume it entailed redeeming a mere fact from its penury by presenting it in the light of a higher or a larger perspective. If so, I think Yeats did this notably in such poems as "A Woman Homer Sung" and "No Second Troy".

It is surprising, then, in view of this achievement, that Eliot continued for several years to comment derisively on Yeats's dealings with occult images and motifs; though these were also the years in which he recognised the power of Yeats's later poems. In *The Use of Poetry and the Use of Criticism* he wrote:

No one can read Mr. Yeats's *Autobiographies* and his earlier poetry without feeling that the author was trying to get as a poet something like the exaltation to be obtained, I believe, from hashisch or nitrous oxide. He was very much fascinated by self-induced trance states, calculated symbolism, mediums, theosophy, crystal-gazing, folklore and hobgoblins. Golden apples, archers, black pigs and such paraphernalia abounded. Often the verse has an hypnotic charm: but you cannot take heaven by magic, especially if you are, like Mr. Yeats, a very sane person. Then, by a great triumph of development, Mr. Yeats began to write and is still writing some of the most beautiful poetry in the language, some of the clearest, simplest, most direct.

In *After Strange Gods* – the Page-Barbour lectures that Eliot delivered at the University of Virginia in 1933 – he referred to Pound as "probably the most important living poet in our language" and to Yeats as "the other important poet of our time", while subjecting both poets to rebuke. His complaint against Yeats, which he adopted largely from IA Richards's *Science and Poetry* only to make the criticism even more pointed than Richards made it, was that Yeats's "supernatural world" was "the wrong supernatural world":

It was not a world of spiritual significance, not a world of real Good and Evil, of holiness or sin, but a highly sophisticated lower mythology summoned, like a physician, to supply the fading pulse of poetry with some transient stimulant so that the dying patient may utter his last words. In its extreme self-consciousness it approaches the mythology of D. H. Lawrence on its more decadent side. We admire Mr. Yeats for having outgrown it; for having packed away his bibelots and resigned himself to live in an apartment furnished in the barest simplicity. A few faded beauties remain: Babylon, Nineveh, Helen of Troy, and such souvenirs of youth: but the austerity of Mr. Yeats's later verse on the whole, should compel the admiration of the least sympathetic.

Not that Eliot had entirely done with rebuke:

Though the tone is often of regret, sometimes of resignation:

> Things said or done long years ago,
> Or things I did not do or say
> But thought that I might say or do,
> Weigh me down, and not a day
> But something is recalled,
> My conscience or my vanity appalled.

and though Mr. Yeats is still perhaps a little too much the weather-worn Triton among the streams, he has arrived at greatness against the greatest odds; if he has not arrived at a central and universal philosophy he has at least discarded, for the most part, the trifling and eccentric, the provincial in time and place.

Eliot seems to have in mind, without saying so much, that Yeats is inferior to Dante in the matter of a central and universal philosophy.

It soon appears that Eliot's conversion to Yeats – or rather to the later Yeats – was made sometime between late 1933 and 1935. By 1935 he had come to appreciate Yeats's significance; first in relation to the Abbey Theatre, which "kept poetry in the theatre" and "maintained literary standards which had long since disappeared from the English stage"; and then for the poetry itself, of which Eliot said that "Mr. Yeats has been and is the greatest poet of his time". "I can think of no poet, not even among the very greatest, who has shown a longer period of development than Yeats." Development "to this extent is not merely genius, it is character; and it sets a standard which his juniors should seek to emulate, without hoping to equal". I think Eliot had Shakespeare in view when he appealed to a long period of development as evidence of genius and character.

When Yeats died in 1939 and Eliot accepted the invitation to deliver the first annual Yeats lecture to the Friends of the Irish Academy, at the Abbey Theatre in 1940, he retained the theme of a poet's development and remarked how Yeats "had to wait for a later maturity to find expression of early experience". Reading the poems again in the light of a complete development, Eliot found the turning point in the 1914 volume *Responsibilities*, with its "violent and terrible epistle" and these great lines:

> Pardon that for a barren passion's sake,
> Although I have come close on forty-nine,
> I have no child, I have nothing but a book,
> Nothing but that to prove your blood and mine.

So he regarded Yeats, poet and dramatist, as "pre-eminently the poet of middle age", by which he appears to have meant that in the play *Purgatory* and in such poems as "In Memory of Eva Gore-Booth and Con Markiewicz" and "Coole Park 1929" "one feels that the most lively and desirable emotions of youth have been preserved to receive their full and due expression in retrospect ... For the interesting feelings of age are not just different feelings; they are feelings into which the feelings of youth are integrated."

I have quoted enough to show that Eliot changed his critical assessment of Yeats, probably in 1934, and that his sense, up to that point, of Yeats's achievement was irregular and erratic. The impersonal animosity of the review of *The Cutting of an Agate* – for it amounts to that – can be explained, but only in part, by Eliot's need to put a considerable distance between himself and Yeats, each of whom could be regarded as a Symbolist, however differently they shared in French Symbolism as Arthur Symons expounded it in *The Symbolist Movement in Literature*.

It is my understanding that Symons led Yeats through the early chapters, with Mallarmé as the main figure, and that Eliot made his own way quickly through the several chapters until he reached Laforgue, the poet he found most useful in his attempt to discover his own voice. Still, Eliot's animosity is hard to explain. The poems in *Responsibilities* and the play *At the Hawk's Well* were available to him for several years before he committed the asperities in his review of *The Cutting of an Agate*. In *The Use of Poetry and the Use of Criticism* he scolded Richards for not quite appreciating Yeats's later work, though he himself was slow to appreciate it. Richards could only plead that he had written *Science and Poetry* before *The Tower* came out in 1928. The presence of Yeats, Swift, and Mallarmé in the "familiar compound ghost" of "Little Gidding" is Eliot's final tribute to three great predecessors; if we add Dante and Shakespeare, we nearly make up the whole account.

Yeats and Eliot were not familiars; they met occasionally and agreeably, but they were not companions. Yeats and Pound make a different relation: they were friends and remained friends, especially after the three winters they spent in Stone Cottage, Coleman's Hatch, Sussex. The friendship continued over the years and found fulfilment in a shared Rapallo. One of the many differences between Eliot and Pound, in their relations to Yeats, was that Pound did not change his opinion. From the first years in London, he sought out the writers he regarded as important, but he did not haggle over their attributes. When he had decided on their quality, he rarely changed his opinion. On December 10th, 1912, three years after meeting Yeats, he wrote a letter to *Poetry*, Harriet Monroe's new magazine:

The state of things here in London is, as I see it, as follows:

I find Mr. Yeats the only poet worthy of serious study. Mr. Yeats' work is already a recognized classic and is part of the required reading in the Sorbonne. There is no need of proclaiming him to the American public ... I would rather talk about poetry with Ford Madox Hueffer [not yet Ford Madox Ford] than with any man in London. Mr. Hueffer's beliefs about the art may be best explained by saying that they are in diametric opposition to those of Mr. Yeats.

Mr. Yeats has been subjective; believes in the glamour and associations which hang near words. 'Works of art beget works of art.' He has much in common with the French symbolists. Mr. Hueffer believes in an exact rendering of things. He would strip words of all 'association' for the sake of getting a precise meaning. He professes to prefer prose to verse. You would find his origins in Gautier or in Flaubert. He is objective. This school tends to lapse into description. The other tends to lapse into sentiment.

Mr. Yeats' method is, to my way of thinking, very dangerous, for although he is the greatest of living poets who use English, and though he has sung some of the moods of life immortally, his art has not broadened much in scope during the past decade. His gifts to English art are mostly negative; i.e., he has stripped English poetry of many of its faults. His 'followers' have come to nothing. Neither Synge, Lady Gregory nor Colum can be called his followers, though he had much to do with bringing them forth, yet nearly every man who writes English verse seriously is in some way indebted to him.

It is clear that Pound was on Hueffer's side. Poetry should be at least as well-written as prose, especially the prose of Stendhal and Flaubert. The unit of perception is the visual image. Beware of glamour and associations. If mind is "the regenerative part of nature", you should not rely on impressions that merely happen to reach your retina. If you do, you will find one impression displacing another: your work will not develop.

In his memoir of Gaudier-Brzeska, Pound stated the same preference without naming names:

> There are two opposed ways of thinking of a man: firstly, you may think of him as that toward which perception moves, as the toy of circumstance, as the plastic substance receiving impressions; secondly, you may think of him as directing a certain fluid force against circumstance, as conceiving instead of merely reflecting and observing. One does not claim that one way is better than the other, one notes a diversity of the temperament. The two camps always exist.

But Pound evidently thought that one way – the way of conceiving instead of merely reflecting –was better than the first: it was the basis of his aesthetic. "Imagisme is not Symbolism."

Over a few years, Pound came to think that whatever Yeats did in the way of Symbolism, Eliot did it better; and whatever Hueffer did in the way of Realism, Joyce did it better, at least in *Dubliners*, *A Portrait of the Artist as a Young Man*, and the realistic chapters of *Ulysses*. Pound's review of *Responsibilities* in May 1914 may be thought to point to a change of style on Yeats's part, but it doesn't; not quite. There is a new note, as Pound remarks, in such poems as "No Second Troy" and "The Magi", but Yeats is still a Symbolist; although his work has become "gaunter, seeking greater hardness of detail". It is "no longer romantically Celtic". Pound seems to say that Yeats, still incorrigibly Symbolist, has recognised the force of contingent detail: the change, the new note, is evident in some of the poems in *The Green Helmet and Other Poems* (1910) and *Responsibilities* (1914). But Yeats has not changed his fundamental allegiance to Symbolism. He has not joined Pound, Gaudier-Brzeska, Wyndham Lewis, H.D., Hueffer and Joyce in the service of what we now call Objectivism. Even in later years, when Pound wrote of his early days with Yeats, he recalled him as a convinced Symbolist.

Some time in 1911, Yeats and Pound happened to be in Paris together, but perhaps not on the day on which Pound emerged from the Metro at La Concorde and saw beautiful faces all around him. He wrote a poem of thirty lines, but he destroyed it because he judged it work of second intensity. Six months later he wrote a poem of half that length and destroyed it too. A year later, with the Japanese hokku in mind, he wrote a poem of three lines including the title:

> In a Station of the Metro
> The apparition of these faces in the crowd;
> Petals on a wet, black bough.

Later he said of it:

> I dare say it is meaningless unless one has drifted into a certain vein of thought. In a poem of this sort one is trying to record the precise instant when a thing outward and objective transforms itself, or darts into a thing inward and subjective.

The poem, as Hugh Kenner said of it, "is energy, is effort. It does not appease itself by reproducing what is seen, but by setting some other seen thing into relation." It is an instance of "juxtaposition without copula", to use a phrase we associate with Marshall McLuhan. That is why it points toward Objectivism, an option taken up by Pound and several poets of similar disposition, including William Carlos Williams, Marianne Moore, Louis Zukofsky, Basil Bunting and George Oppen. Objectivism steps aside in favour of the thing seen, to begin with, even though the sense of that thing must eventually become, as Pound says, "inward and subjective". On the same visit to Paris, as Pound recalled it in Canto 83, he saw Yeats as

> Uncle William dawdling around Notre Dame
> in search of whatever
> paused to admire the symbol
> with Notre Dame standing inside it
> Whereas in St Etienne
> Or why not Dei Miracoli:
> mermaids, that carving ...

Most of the work in that passage is done by "Whereas". Yeats is merely receiving impressions. Notre Dame is not seen by an act of conceiving, a flow of energy directed upon it. Yeats's mind is "in search of whatever", of nothing in particular. Whereas Pietro Lombardo's carved mermaids on Santa Maria dei Miracoli in Venice are there only to be seen: the mind of the one who looks at them is concentrated on their detail, it does not wait for a symbolic halo to surround them. It is the difference between modelling and carving, in Adrian Stokes's terms. The passage I've quoted from Canto 83 gave credence to a common view of Yeats – Donald Davie expressed it well in his first book on Pound – as a poet who never looked hard at anything; that he divined the emblem more ardently than the swan that produced it: "Another emblem there!" In Symbolism, you could nearly keep your eyes closed and attend only to the echo of word and word, so little are objects in space allowed to enforce their claim on you. Paul Valéry said of the poets who succeeded the French Symbolists that "they opened again, upon the accidents of being, eyes we had closed in order to make ourselves more akin to its substance". When Pound noted that Yeats was susceptible to the associations that hang near words, he pointed to the Symbolist's interest in effects purely linguistic, not derived from nature or verifiable by appeal to that value: they are linguistic through and through. In his earliest years as a poet, Pound was himself susceptible to those effects, but he worked free of them and turned for guidance to the poet

Gautier and his insistence upon the detail of apprehension. Pound became a Luminist even before he called his allegiances Imagism or Vorticism.

Pound's references to Yeats are genial nonetheless. He never forgot the friendship that developed between them in their winters at Stone Cottage, where Yeats had him read scholarly works about witches and demonology as well as Doughty's *The Dawn in Britain*. Late in Canto 98 Pound scolds Yeats, Eliot, and Wyndham Lewis for having "no ground beneath 'em", by contrast with Orage, who apparently had the desired ground. Orage, like Pound, knew that the ground of a society is the system of economics which governs it – a system clarified to Pound's satisfaction by CH Douglas. Sometimes, as in Canto 80, Pound made a little fun of Senator Yeats, but in the same Canto he agreed with "old William" that "the crumbling of a fine house / profits no one / (Celtic or otherwise)" and in Canto 77 he recalled with no sign of dissent "uncle William" murmuring "Sligo in Heaven" when "the mist finally settled down on Tigullio", a tribute repeated in Canto 114.

Yeats's most sustained comments on Eliot's poetry are in his introduction to *The Oxford Book of Modern Verse* (1936) and a BBC talk on "Modern Poetry" which he gave in the same year. On both occasions he referred to Eliot as a satirist, indeed as a mere satirist. In the *Oxford Book* he represented him through the four "Preludes", "The Hippopotamus", "Whispers of Immortality", and "Sweeney among the Nightingales". Eliot, he said,

> has produced his great effect upon his generation because he has described men and women that get out of bed or into it from mere habit; in describing this life that has lost heart his own art seems grey, cold, dry. He is an Alexander Pope, working without apparent imagination, producing his effects by a rejection of all rhythms and metaphors used by the more popular romantics rather than by the discovery of his own, this rejection giving his work an unexaggerated plainness that has the effect of novelty.

Maintaining the reference to Pope, Yeats said that Eliot "has the rhythmical flatness of *The Essay on Man* – despite Miss Sitwell's advocacy I see Pope as Blake and Keats saw him – later, in *The Waste Land*, amid much that is moving in symbol and imagery there is much monotony of accent" – to illustrate which, Yeats quoted these lines:

> When lovely woman stoops to folly and
> Paces about her room again, alone,
> She smoothes her hair with automatic hand,
> And puts a record on the gramophone.

"I was affected, as I am by these lines," Yeats recalled, "when I saw for the first time a painting by Manet." "I longed," he said, "for the vivid colour and light of Rousseau and Courbet, I could not endure the grey middle-tint – and even to-day Manet gives me an incomplete pleasure; he had left the procession." And as if the word "procession" reminded Yeats of another one, he continued: "Nor can I put the Eliot of these poems among those that descend from Shakespeare and the translators of the Bible":

> I think of him as satirist rather than poet. Once only does that early work speak in the great manner:

> > The host with someone indistinct
> > Converses at the door apart,
> > The nightingales are singing near
> > The Convent of the Sacred Heart,
> > And sang within the bloody wood
> > When Agamemnon cried aloud,
> > And let their liquid siftings fall
> > To stain the stiff dishonoured shroud.

There, Yeats seems to say, Eliot rose to the grand occasion of Agamemnon, as Yeats himself did in "Leda and the Swan".

But Yeats comes close to being insolent when he refers to Eliot's religion as lacking "all strong emotion" by comparison with the religion of John Gray, Francis Thompson, and Lionel Johnson: "a New England Protestant by descent, there is little self-surrender in his personal relation to God and the soul". *Murder in the Cathedral*, Yeats says, is "a powerful stage play because the actor, the monkish habit, certain repeated words, symbolize what we know, not what the author knows". But Yeats has one complaint about the play:

> Nowhere has the author explained how Becket and the King differ in aim;
> Becket's people have been robbed and persecuted in his absence; like the

King he demands strong government. Speaking through Becket's mouth Eliot confronts a world growing always more terrible with a religion like that of some great statesman, a pity not less poignant because it tempers the prayer book with the results of mathematical philosophy.

And Yeats quotes Becket's speech beginning: "Peace. And let them be, in their exaltation."

In the BBC talk on modern poetry, after describing Eliot as "the most revolutionary man in poetry during my lifetime, though his revolution was stylistic alone", Yeats associated him with writers to whom "what we call the solid earth was manufactured by the human mind from unknown raw material":

> They do not think this because of Kant and Berkeley, who are an old story, but because of something that has got into the air since a famous French mathematician wrote "Space is a creation of our ancestors." Eliot's historical and scholarly mind seems to have added this further thought, probably from Nicholas of Cusa: reality is expressed in a series of contradictions, or is this unknowable something that supports the centre of the see-saw.

To illustrate this, Yeats quoted from "Burnt Norton" the passage that begins: "At the still point of the turning world".

Yeats's feeling for Pound's poetry was much warmer than his feeling for Eliot's, but the more he thought of it the more he talked himself into vehemence and exasperation. He represented Pound in the *Oxford Book* by "The River-Merchant's Wife: A Letter", a passage from "Homage to Sextus Propertius", and Canto XVII. But he begged off saying anything about the Cantos as a whole. As in the revised *Vision*, with twenty-seven Cantos available to him, he could make nothing of them:

> I have often found there brightly printed kings, queens, knaves, but have never discovered why all the suits could not be dealt out in some quite different order.

In the introduction to the *Oxford Book* he said that "like other readers I discover at present merely exquisite or grotesque fragments", but he was content to suspend judgment till the poem was complete – a fulfilment he did not live to see. Meanwhile he was irritated by Pound's "unbridged transitions, unexplained ejaculations, that make his meaning unintelligible". "Ezra Pound," Yeats said, "has made flux his theme; plot, characterization, logical discourse, seem to him abstractions unsuitable to a man of his generation." "He hopes," Yeats said, "to give the impression that all is living, that there are no edges, no convexities, nothing to check the flow; but can such a poem have a mathematical structure?" Pound told Yeats that the Cantos would eventually number one hundred, but not that the structure of the poem would be mathematical. Yeats saw flux everywhere in the cantos, but he did not see – what Kenner saw – that "Pound's work, say from Lustra to the last Cantos, is the longest working-out in any art of premises like those of cubism".

Indeed, one wonders how much of Pound's poetry Yeats kept up with and liked. It appears that whenever he thought of the poetry, he let one poem stand for the rest, and quoted it – "The Return" – without comment both in the introduction to the *Oxford Book* and the revised *Vision*. The poem gratified Yeats, we can infer, because of its theme, the return of the pagan gods. Pater wrote two stories – "Apollo in Picardy" and "Denys L'Auxerrois" – in which a god of the old dispensation survives and comes into the modern world still as a force of nature, to destroy or be destroyed. Pound's poem, which Yeats evidently liked even though he never understood *vers libre*, conducts the reader's mind though syntactic changes, variations of rhythm and phrase, and changes of grammatical tense which represent the gods as they were and as they, waveringly, are:

> See, they return; ah, see the tentative
> Movements, and the slow feet,
> The trouble in the pace and the uncertain
> Wavering!
> See, they return, one, and by one,
> With fear, as half-awakened;
> As if the snow should hesitate
> And murmur in the wind,
> and half turn back;

These were the "Wing'd-with-Awe,"
Inviolable.
Gods of the winged shoe!
With them the silver hounds,
Sniffing the trace of air!
Haie! Haie!
These were the swift to harry;
These the keen-scented;
These were the souls of blood.
Slow on the leash,
pallid the leash-men!

One of the most admirable qualities of the men of 1922 – to call them that for short – was their readiness to accept strong criticism from their friends without letting it damage the friendship. Eliot acknowledged, in effect, that he had no interest in Pound's poetry for what it said but every interest in the ways it discovered of saying it. Pound had nothing good to say about Eliot's later poetry. In *Time and Western Man* Wyndham Lewis attacked a quality of modern style, with Joyce as a chief exemplar. Pound tried to show Yeats the error of his diction, but his failure made no difference to their friendship. He admired Joyce's realism but regarded *Finnegans Wake* as an elaborate mistake. Yeats referred to Pound as a man "whose art is the opposite of mine, whose criticism commends what I most condemn, a man with whom I should quarrel more than with anyone else if we were not united by affection". He had intended to put Pound into the first version of *A Vision* as an exemplar of Phase 23 of his lunar cycle, but thought better of it. The only reference to Pound that remained in the first version was in a remarkable paragraph of apocalyptic criticism:

> I discover already the first phase – Phase 23 – of the last quarter in certain friends of mine, and in writers, poets and sculptors admired by these friends, who have a form of strong love and hate hitherto unknown in the arts.

Yeats is thinking of Wyndham Lewis and Brancusi and of other artists who are "masters of a geometrical pattern or rhythm which seems to impose itself wholly from beyond the mind", the artist "standing outside himself":

I find at this 23rd Phase which is it is said the first where there is hatred of the abstract, where the intellect turns upon itself, Mr Ezra Pound, Mr Eliot, Mr Joyce, Signor Pirandello, who either eliminate from metaphor the poet's phantasy and substitute a strangeness discovered by historical research or who break up the logical processes of thought by flooding them with associated ideas or words that seem to drift into the mind by chance; or who set side by side as in [Pirandello's] *Henry IV*, "The Waste Land," *Ulysses*, the physical primary – a lunatic among his keepers, a man fishing behind a gas works, the vulgarity of a single Dublin day prolonged through 700 pages –and the spiritual primary, delirium, the Fisher King, Ulysses' wandering. It is as though myth and fact, united until the exhaustion of the Renaissance, have now fallen so far apart that man understands for the first time the rigidity of fact, and calls up, by that very recognition, myth – the Mask – which now but gropes its way out of the mind's dark but will shortly pursue and terrify.

Pound is not characterised there by his works. Richard Ellmann has elucidated the pursuit and terror by saying: "Yeats implies that in these writers myth, instead of merging with fact in a symbolic whole, has collided with it to produce a frenzied miscellany." "This is a prelude," Ellmann says, "to the manifestation of myth in some fearful, dehumanized form." It is as if these writers forgot the lesson of Eliot's review of *Ulysses* and of Yeats's adumbration of a particular production of meaning and value. Myth has become ideology, a rough beast we cannot hope to understand or control.

I have called these three writers "presences", mainly in deference to Yeats's use of that word as the title of one poem and a crucial invocation in another. The poem "Presences" impels one to say that a presence is someone who doesn't need to be named; a figure, an archetype, in this poem harlot, child, or queen. In "Among School Children" Yeats invokes, as if this poem were an ode – which it partly is:

O Presences
That passion, piety or affection knows,
And that all heavenly glory symbolize ...

The word "Presences" is capitalised, as if to honour the entities addressed, before exercising the harsher honour of doing justice to them at the end of the stanza as "self-born mockers of man's enterprise". I interpret the presences as perfections projected by human desire – passion, piety or affection – and therefore fit to symbolise heavenly glory: what else could do so? They are bound to be "self-born mockers of man's enterprise", since that enterprise is necessarily imperfect by comparison with those perfections. So I follow Helen Vendler at a distance when she says that "the presences are not Divinities to be addressed in vertical aspiration; they are self-born and deceiving solaces, created by our longing for perfection in the things we love". They are not, I think, solaces. "Created by our longing for perfection in the things we love", they mock our imperfections, subject only to the consideration that the imperfections are categorical; they are in the nature of the human case. Wallace Stevens writes that "the imperfect is our paradise", which is to say that it is as much of paradise as we can know, unless we believe in a greater paradise and find it fulfilled at length in another mode of being. The *OED* allows us to think of a presence also as an absence, "a divine, spiritual, or incorporeal being or influence felt or conceived as present": it points us toward the "sovran Presence" in *Paradise Lost* and, in Wordsworth's "Tintern Abbey": "I have felt / A presence that disturbs me with the joy / Of elevated thoughts." So it is not fanciful to think of our three poets as presences, not divinities indeed but objects of our devotion, so far as we love the literature they embody, imperfect as that, too, is. If we have to think of them as self-born mockers of man's enterprise, we do so only in the fateful end and after we have spent most of our lives addressing them in vertical aspiration. If these poets mock man's enterprise in the end, they practise such mockery by misunderstanding one another, by being not deaf but hard of hearing to rhythms other than their own.

The above essay is based on a lecture delivered to the Yeats International Summer School in Sligo in July 2009.

RACHEL ANDREWS | 2010

Minding the Language

Love of the World: *Essays* by John McGahern

Faber | 350 pp | ISBN: 978-0571245116

GUSTAVE FLAUBERT once wrote that to write well is everything. John McGahern quotes this sentence, and many others, from Flaubert – one of his writerly heroes – in the course of an essay on *Dubliners* published in this collection of his non-fiction work which, appearing three years after his death, provides a new aspect to a voice familiar until now through fiction and autobiography.

In the essay, McGahern's chief concern is to consider the quality of Joyce's prose, which the author himself described as being "a style of scrupulous meanness" and to which McGahern ascribes an "authority and plain sense" that clearly reflects how he believes fiction – indeed all writing – should be approached. For McGahern, Flaubert's dictum is an imperative: that is why he quotes him so liberally throughout. In order to be able to write well, he believes, one needs to find "a unique expression, endlessly reworked and enriched, until it is pared down to an individual style, to the point where the man behind the work is his work and eventually becomes one with it". *Dubliners* is a great work of art, he concludes, because, in the book "the method is that people, events, and places invariably find their true expression ... Everything is important in *Dubliners* because it is there and everything there is held in equal importance."

There is serious attention paid to the art and craft of writing in *Love of the World*, reflecting McGahern's priorities as a writer. He did not write quickly – taking twelve years between his greatest literary success, *Amongst Women* (1990), and his next publication, *That They May Face the Rising Sun* (2002) – and he constantly rewrote his work, even after it had been published: he regularly reworked his short stories and revised *The Leavetaking* (1974) ten years after its first appearance. He was also a ruthless editor, paring *Amongst Women* down to two hundred pages from its original twelve hundred, in the process creating spare, exact prose in which no word or phrase is redundant.

The workings of his craft are evidenced in "Five Drafts", the first piece in the collection, in which he writes and rewrites a paragraph on sexuality, love and the church, but his thoughts on that which is inherently important within good prose reappear time and again throughout the collection. In "The Solitary Reader", he recalls his early writing years: "Words had been a physical presence for me for a long time before, each word with its own weight, colour, shape, relationship, extending out into a world without end. Change any word in a single sentence and immediately all the other words demand to be rearranged. By writing and rewriting sentences, by moving their words endlessly around, I found that scenes or pictures and echoes and shapes began to emerge that reflected obscurely a world that had found its first expression and recognition through reading." The short stories of the Canadian Alistair MacLeod he finds to be written in a "language of precision and deep eloquence"; referring to the concluding story in one of MacLeod's collections, he writes that "everything is right and sure-footed as the story reaches its delicate and inevitable ending". In his discussion of *Dubliners*, he criticises George Moore as a writer of "self-expression: he constantly substitutes candour for truth". *Dubliners*, on the other hand, has no self-expression: "its truth is in every phrase".

Nor is good prose necessarily something that is found only in fiction: in an essay commemorating *Irish Times* journalist Dick Walsh, McGahern notes that "the style he forged is highly individual. Mixing the language of the street and field and public house with clear English, it is immediately engaging." He also admires Walsh's dedication to uncovering sloppy language in pieces that drew attention to the way in which governments and other organisations attempted to divert the public's attention from reality. "He saw

Orwell's reference to the effect of Stalinism on western thinking as equally applicable to the 1990s," writes McGahern, "and he detailed how 'slovenliness of language makes it easier for us to have foolish thoughts'."

For McGahern, there is no difference between how a writer writes and that which he chooses to write about. Aside from Flaubert, he also quotes Henry James, who wrote that "art and morality are two perfectly different things, and that the former has no more to do with the latter than it has with astronomy or embryology. The only duty of the novel was to be well written; that merit included every other of which it was capable." At the end of "A Literature without Qualities", he writes that while serious work can be written out of a conflict such as the Northern Ireland Troubles, it can only be so in so far as "it attracts a writer of talent, and given no more or less importance than a comparable talent['s] interest in a woman combing her hair or adjusting or ... someone tending their garden or getting ready to meet their beloved". Finally he concludes that: "All good writing is local and is made universal through clear thinking and deep feeling, finding the right expression and in so doing reflects all the particular form is capable of reflecting, including the social and the political."

All this, of course, is merely an illustration of how and why McGahern wrote. Colm Tóibín once said in an interview that "John McGahern taught me that it's OK to write repeatedly about the same things". Those things involved a tracing and retracing of the story of his own life, incorporating into his fictions the places and memories of that life, along with the rhythms of a daily existence. He wrote most fully the story of his childhood in *Amongst Women*, his tale of Irish family life in which the dictatorial Michael Moran operates as a tyrant within the family home but is a frustrated, impotent character in the outside world, but the same themes of violence, abuse and the power of the church are also in evidence from the beginning of his writing career: in his first published novel, *The Barracks* (1962), through to *The Dark* (1965), *The Leavetaking* and *The Pornographer* (1979). At the end of his life, he left aside the mask of fiction to write *Memoir* and tell his own story directly – the heartbreak of losing his beloved mother at a young age, the cruelty of a tyrannical father, his early years as a teacher and writer, during which *The Dark* was banned and he was dismissed from his job because of the book and his marriage, in a registry office, to a Finnish divorcee – but what is striking about this work is how closely it mirrors, in theme, in style, in description, the preoccupations of the world of his imagination: he was constantly retreading the same ground.

His essays make clear that this was a conscious decision, and it is this clarity of thought that allows his work to avoid parochialism or narrowness of focus. In a short essay, "The Local and the Universal", delivered as a lecture at Listowel Writers' Week in 2004, he says: "Everything interesting begins with one person in one place, though the places can become many, and many persons in the form of influences will have gone into the making of that single woman or man ... The universal is the local, but with the walls taken away. Out of the particular we come on what is general, which is our great comfort, since we call it truth, and that truth had to be continually renewed."

He sought this "truth" from other writers: reviewing the work of Alistair MacLeod, whose short stories centre on people and a way of life in Cape Breton, Nova Scotia, he writes:

> The work has a largeness, of feeling, of intellect, of vision, a great openness and generosity, even an old-fashioned courtliness ... The small world on Cape Breton opens out to the vast spaces and distances of Canada ... Unwittingly, or through that high art that conceals itself, we have been introduced into a complete representation of existence, and the stories take on the truth of the Gaelic songs their people sing.

And it was at the heart of his own work. For example, in writing that MacLeod's "careful work never appears to stray outside what quickens it, and his uniqueness is present in every weighted sentence and the smallest of gestures", McGahern could be referring to his own fictions.

Nowhere is this more in evidence than in the novel *That They May Face the Rising Sun*, which is, on the face of it, a gentle account of quiet rural life, McGahern's depiction of the place and people that surrounded him in the sparsely populated area of Co Leitrim where he lived and worked. But although the countryside is depicted with meticulous, loving accuracy, as it is in *Memoir*, in some of his short stories and in the essay "County Leitrim: the sky above us", the book is no rose-tinted retreat from the reality of life. The rhythms of the novel may be slow, careful and unashamedly rural, but its considerations are universal. A conversation, for example, between Joe

Ruttledge, who has come back from England with his wife, Kate, to the place of his childhood, and a local character, Patrick Ryan, in which Ryan discusses the people of the rich houses he has worked for in the past, reflects the limitations of a country mentality, where everybody knows everybody and their business, but also something much more fundamental about the human condition.

> When he turned to speak of the rich houses he had worked for, his voice changed: it was full of identification and half-possession, like the unformed longing of a boy. 'Most of the people in this part of the country will never rise off their arses in the ditches. You have to have something behind you to be able to rise.' Rise to what? came to Ruttledge's lips, but he didn't speak it. 'I suppose they'll move around in the light for a while like the rest of us and disappear,' he said. 'They wouldn't like to hear that either, lad,' Patrick Ryan replied trenchantly. 'All the fuckers half-believe they are going to be the Big Exception and live forever.'

The tone is contemplative, subtle, but not evasive, and it is the same tone that suffuses his essay on Co Leitrim, published originally as a foreword to a book of photographs. In the piece, McGahern celebrates the rural landscape in the same manner as he has done in his fiction and autobiography, writing of "the low drumlins around the countless lakes" where "the soil is hardly an inch deep" and of the "irregular hedgerows of whitethorn, ash, green oak, holly, wild cherry, sloe and sycamore" that "divide the drumlins into rushy fields". Echoes of the beginning of *Memoir* abound when he writes: "Along the lake edges and river banks there are private lawns speckled with fish bones and blue crayfish shells, where the otter feeds and trains her young. The foxglove is here, and the orchid, with thousands of other wildflowers."

But, like all his work, the piece goes further than the merely elegiac. He describes stopping at the British army checkpoint on the way to Enniskillen, a town he and his wife visited regularly, and the description is as detailed and accurate as his considerations of the countryside.

> There are ramps and screens and barriers and a tall camouflaged lookout tower. A line of cars waits behind a red light. A quick change to green signals each single car forward. In the middle of this maze armed soldiers call out the motor vehicle number and driver's identification to a hidden

computer. Only when they are cleared will the cars be waved through. Suspect vehicles are searched. The soldiers are young and courteous and look very professional.

Only once were formalities broken at that checkpoint, when an officer asked if the couple could bring him two loaves of wholewheat bread upon their return from Enniskillen. Later, the soldiers were edgy until the situation was explained to them. 'Oh that nutcase,' a soldier said, just as the officer himself appeared, pulling money from inside his combat jacket. 'Thank you very much indeed. We were completely out of wholewheat bread.' When the money was refused – 'with the compliments of the country' – he looked at a loss for a moment, before coming to attention and honouring us with one of the sharpest salutes I have ever seen, out there beneath the mountains, in the middle of the wilderness. I wish the whole commerce of Northern Ireland could be as simple as that human request.

McGahern was at times criticised for not being political in his writings. Indeed he was avowedly not so: in a tribute written after his death, Colm Tóibín discussed how, at a literary conference where writers were urged to display political commitment, McGahern firmly dissented. "It is a writer's job to look after his sentences," he said, "nothing else." He remained exacting in this focus: he refused to get involved in any protest about the banning of *The Dark* because, in the words of Chekhov, "The minute the writer takes up a pen he accuses himself of unanswerable egotism and all he can do with any decency after that is to bow." In "The Solitary Reader", he recounts an incident at the Booker Prize dinner in 1990, the year *Amongst Women* was shortlisted. As Kenneth Baker, then chairman of the Conservative Party, paused to tell McGahern how much he had enjoyed his work, the writer and critic AN Wilson called out: "Do you realize, Mr Baker, that the novel glorifies the IRA?" McGahern knows better: "*Amongst Women* glorifies nothing but life itself, and fairly humble life ... All the violence is internalized within a family, is not public or political; but is not, therefore, a lesser evil."

What he did not do was avert his eyes. The subtle comment made about the North in the Leitrim essay becomes a kind of refrain, both in that essay, where he writes that a feud between two local farmers stretching so far back in time that both have forgotten the cause is "not dissimilar to what is taking place on a larger scale in Northern Ireland", and in others. In the essay "Life as it is and Life as it Ought to be", in which he remembers the Protestant farmer Willie Booth, he writes that when he is asked about the North, he says that it wasn't part of his experience, and that one can only speak of what one knows. What he does know is that to him it is "now stranger than France or Britain or the United States ... Behind all the surface good manners, I feel much of it is deeply hidden, even aggressively so. All that one hears at first hand or notices seems to emphasize that sense of difference."

He is less oblique, even coldly furious, in his discussions of his own society. The essays "It's a Long Way from Mohill to Here" and "Shame in a Polling Booth" seethe with disgust for the contemporary political system and are as relevant today as when they were written. Time and again he refers to the sectarian theocracy into which he was born, which demanded subservience and discouraged individual speech and thought. But even as he unflinchingly details the results of that suppression: compulsory retirement upon marriage for women, the breaking of pelvic bones during difficult births in hospitals, the bitterness of the emigrants on the building sites in Britain, he avoids easy certainties. In the essay "Whatever you Say, Say Nothing", he reminds us that many ordinary people living in that climate "went about their sensible pagan lives as they had done for centuries, seeing all this as just another veneer they had to pretend to wear like all the others they had worn since the time of the Druids," and notes that "many who entered the Church at the time were victims themselves". It is these opinions, held but not worn like a mantle, that underlie his non-political fictions – Joe Ruttledge speaks out against violence towards the end of *That They May Face the Rising Sun* – making them much more than a lament for an old way of life.

What he does lament, most particularly in the essay "The Church and its Spire", is the loss of the spiritual solace offered him by the religion of his youth, writing that: "I have nothing but gratitude for the spiritual remnants of that upbringing, the sense of our origins beyond the bounds of sense, an awareness of mystery and wonderment, grace and sacrament, and the absolute equality of all women and men underneath the sun of heaven. That is all that now remains. Belief as such has long gone." In that same essay, he writes that after independence church and state became inseparable, with "unhealthy consequences for both", but that the "spiritual need will not go away". "If it is no longer able to express itself through the Church," he writes, "it will take some other form." For McGahern himself, that form was clearly the art of writing.

John McGahern was first and foremost a fiction writer – as Declan Kiberd writes in his elegant and informed introduction, he hoarded his best energies for his stories and novels – and this collection is at its best when the essays give insight to the voice behind those writings. Some of the work included here is too short or incidental, and a less unwieldy, more focused book might have served writer and reader better. When it is good, however, the book serves as a glimpse into the workings of a thoughtful and dignified mind, who has left us, once again, and as he surely would have wished, with the well-written word.

The Trials of *Ulysses*

LITERATURE AND law meet each other head on when a book is alleged to be obscene. The law's enforcers assert that the very presence of the book harms society, and seek to ban it. This clash was described in apocalyptic terms by Jane Heap as she faced criminal charges in 1920 for publishing an episode of *Ulysses* in *The Little Review*, a magazine she co-edited with her lover, Margaret Anderson, the founder of that pioneering publication. Heap wrote that "art is and always has been the supreme Order" and thus is the only human activity "that has an eternal quality". Standing on this premise, she expressed her view of the trial in a harrumph: "What legal genius to bring law against Order." Anderson saw the issue the same way. She believed that a work of art could not be obscene. The only pertinent question to be asked about *Ulysses*, she wrote, was whether it was a work of art.

Anderson and Heap's views would be substantially vindicated thirteen years later by a judicial decision that cleared *Ulysses* of obscenity charges in the United States, a watershed event that accorded literary criticism a prominent role in obscenity cases. Indeed the role of literary criticism in obscenity trials became so central that the 1960 English trial which exonerated *Lady Chatterley's Lover* was described as "probably the most thorough and expensive seminar on Lawrence's work ever given".

But Anderson and Heap themselves were convicted of a crime in 1921 for publishing an episode of a work that was later declared the greatest English-language novel of the twentieth century. The struggle between law and literature never ends. It is as old as Plato, who banished poets from his Republic because he distrusted their seductive appeal to the emotions. It is as recent as the next politician who, like American presidential contender Rick Santorum, promises more vigorous enforcement of obscenity laws. Given the neverending nature of this struggle between law and literature, it is worth examining how obscenity cases are won or lost, and the two trials of *Ulysses* are good case studies because different approaches brought very different results.

The case against Anderson and Heap began when John Sumner, secretary of the New York Society for the Suppression of Vice, swore out a warrant complaining of the distribution of the July–August 1920 number of *The Little Review*, which contained the last section of the Nausicaa episode of *Ulysses*. As Pound put it to Joyce, "'Nausikaa' has been pinched by the PO-lice". Anderson and Heap were charged with violating a broadly worded New York statute that criminalised the distribution of "any obscene, lewd, lascivious, filthy, indecent, or disgusting" material.

Ten passages, consisting of about two single-spaced typewritten pages, were the basis for the charges. Focusing on Bloom ejaculating as he watches Gerty MacDowell leaning backwards on Sandymount Strand, they included these Bloomian musings:

> Near her monthlies, I expect, makes them feel ticklish ... but then why
> don't all women menstruate at the same time with the same moon?
> Wonder if it is bad to go with them then.
> Mr. Bloom with careful hand recomposed his shirt.
> Lord, I am wet.
> For this relief much thanks.
> Short snooze now if I had. And she can do the other.

Then-prevailing judicial decisions, following an 1868 Queen's Bench decision, *Queen v Hicklin*, defined a work as obscene if it tended to excite sexual desire. Lawyers called upon to defend the book might choose between a variety of possible approaches.

First, there is the seemingly obvious argument that exciting sexual desire – an enterprise necessary to preserving the species – ought not be declared out of bounds for literature. Anderson and Heap put this position somewhat differently. For them, literature, by definition, could not be obscene. A second approach, at the level of the minor premise, is the argument that, in fact, the book does not excite sexual desire. This appeals to the advocate as the path of least resistance because it operates within the contours of existing legal precedent.

Midway between these approaches is the tenebrous field where the arguments of lawyers often attempt to reshape the law. Among the prominent features of the legal landscape at the time *Ulysses* was serialised and published were two subsidiary rules stated in Hicklin. The first was that the obscenity of a work is to be measured by its effect – not on the law's typical reagent, "the reasonable man" – but on the most susceptible potential reader – "those whose minds are open to such immoral influences". The second troubling Hicklin rule was that any obscenity in a book violated the statute, no matter how beautifully written the book might be as a whole. As one New York court put it:

> Charm of language, subtlety of thought, faultless style, even distinction of authorship, may all have their lure for the literary critic, yet these qualities may all be present and the book be unfit for dissemination to the reading public.

This view has ancient roots. It was the very beauty of Homer and Sophocles that convinced Plato of the danger of their language and imagery. Under this approach, the better the writing the more dangerous the obscenity.

The task of the advocate for Anderson and Heap was to find the ideas, verbal formulae and persuasive force to change these Hicklin rules so that Joyce's literary achievement would weigh more heavily than the shock effect of Bloom's wet shirt or Gerty's monthlies. New York lawyer John Quinn, who had provided the funds that enabled Ezra Pound to bring *Ulysses* to *The Little Review*, was an almost automatic choice to defend Anderson and Heap. But he was unsuited to the task for a number of reasons, most of them unknown to his clients. The first was his paternalistic belief that unwitting recipients of magazines through the postal system should be protected from *Ulysses*.

Quinn's October 16th, 1920 letter to Pound reflects his view that "There are things in *Ulysses* published in number after number of the *Little Review* that never should have appeared in a magazine asking privileges of the mails. In a book, yes. In a magazine, emphatically no."

Secondly, Quinn believed that the only way Joyce could profit from *Ulysses* was by sale of a limited edition in book form, and that serialisation would lead to a criminal conviction that would scare publishers away from the book. Finally, the most serious obstacles to Quinn's success were a terrible misogyny compounded by prejudice against Anderson and Heap's lesbianism. His disgusting letter to Pound rants against the "female urinal" from which *The Little Review* was published and accuses his clients of having the "perverted courage of the bugger and Lesbian". A deeply disturbed part of his mind associated the periodic publication of the magazine with the menstrual cycle. His letter fulminates about his clients' "menstrual defecations", "the monthly mensurations", as he put it, by which Anderson and Heap have "urinally and menstrually violate[d] the law". His follow-up letter continues the same terrible trope. Borrowing a word from one of the Bloomian musings being attacked by Sumner, Quinn refers to issues of *The Little Review* as "monthlies". Quinn was a man of great abilities and a ready patron, but his mind suffered from painful limitations as an advocate for liberated and liberating women like Molly Bloom, Gerty MacDowell, Margaret Anderson and Jane Heap.

Quinn's limitations were unfortunate because, despite the generally forbidding terrain created by the Hicklin precedent, there was room for manoeuvre. Judge Learned Hand, in a 1913 opinion in a case in which Quinn represented the defendant, had characterised Hicklin as reflective of "mid-Victorian morals" and questioned "whether in the end men will regard that as obscene which is honestly relevant to the adequate expression of innocent ideas, and whether they will not believe that truth and beauty are too precious to society at large to be mutilated in the interests of those most likely to pervert them to base uses".

Judge Hand's opinion was an open invitation to the advocate for an author like Joyce to establish that the law ought not bar portrayal of the serious and beautiful way in which reality reveals itself in the sexually tinged imagination. Moreover, that very case was articulated for Quinn in a long letter written by a brilliant man of letters trained as a barrister in Dublin, eighty-one-year-old John Butler Yeats, father of poet William Butler Yeats and an 1862 graduate of Trinity College Dublin.

Yeats realised that "it is really a grave issue ... whether the books of Joyce and such as he are to go free or not". He recognised in Joyce "an intense feeling for what is actual and true" and saw that "the whole movement against Joyce and his terrible veracity, naked and unashamed, has its origin in the desire of people to live comfortably, and, that they may live comfortably, to live superficially".

Yeats's keen eye focused on the statutory term "filthy", the etymological root of obscene. "That such a man" as Joyce "should write filth is incredible," Yeats declared. Citing two other graduates of Trinity College, he argued that Joyce's "intense feeling for what is actual and true" stands midway between worship of "the beautiful", as exemplified by Wilde, and fixation on "the ugly", as exemplified by Swift. With avuncular familiarity, Yeats remarked that Wilde "said to my son that intellect could refine anything ... Beauty was the God of his heaven, and ugliness its devil."

In contrast to him stood Dean Swift, who "died in mental misery; broken down by what? – his passion for the ugly, by that constant contemplation of the hideous". What Yeats called these "two types of men of great imagination and genius, and both Irishmen" defined the boundaries. Midway between them stood Dante, who, as Yeats said, "never shrank from the hideous and the obscene" and who taught Joyce "that terrible hardness, that hardness of which Wilde had so little and Swift too much".

Yeats's powerful ideas fared worse than the seed that fell upon rock. Quinn perverted them terribly in his argument to city magistrate JE Corrigan at a preliminary hearing on the charges against Anderson and Heap. Converting Yeats's aesthetic argument into a moral one, he argued that it is beauty that corrupts, but filth that deters, and contrasted "the strong hard filth of a man like Joyce with the devotion to art of a soft flabby man like Wilde". This is bad criticism and worse advocacy. The idea of confessing filth, but pleading hardness in avoidance was not an inspired one.

Quinn's other argument was another perversion of Yeats. The latter had argued that "Joyce brings with him what will protect him from the silly ... for Joyce is very difficult reading". Quinn reduced this subtle observation to the absurd "syllogism" that the reader would either understand the "Nausicaa" episode or not. "If he understood what it meant," Quinn argued, "then it couldn't corrupt him, for it would either amuse or bore him. If he didn't understand what it meant, then it could [not] corrupt him." Magistrate Corrigan had no trouble penetrating this thinking. The passage "where the man went off in his pants", Corrigan ruled, was unmistakable in meaning and "smutty, filthy within the meaning of the statute". So much for the syllogism.

Quinn's account of the ensuing trial before three city court judges – contained in letters to Joyce and Shane Leslie – shows how far he departed from Heap's absolutism and Anderson's desire for a defence based upon her belief that *Ulysses* was the "the prose masterpiece of my generation". Branding the judges as "stupid" because they were unlikely to be interested in reading *The Little Review*, Quinn boasted to Joyce that he had appealed to their ignorance, confessing that he had made "what many people in court called a brilliant argument", which he described as "the only tack that could be taken with the three stupid judges". This bit of brilliance was the assertion "that no one could understand what the thing was about" and thus it could not corrupt anyone. Before Joyce had time to digest this revelation, Quinn was regaling him with the "good point" he made that the anger manifested in the prosecutor's argument was "my best exhibit" because it showed that "what *Ulysses* does" is to make people angry, but "it doesn't drive them to the arms of some siren".

Confusing the effect of being the prosecutor in an obscenity trial of *Ulysses* with the effect of reading the book, Quinn deprived the occasion of the seriousness it demanded. "The judges were rocking with laughter," he wrote to Joyce, "and again I thought I had them." The joke, however, was on Joyce, Anderson and Heap. Anderson and Heap were fined fifty dollars each, and it was stipulated that no further instalments of *Ulysses* would be published. Quinn welcomed the ban on serialisation, and was convinced that an appeal would fail and thereby harm Joyce's ability to market the book as a whole. Thus he had decided in advance of trial that there would be no appeal from the assumed conviction. He informed Anderson a few days before the trial that he would not make a record of "witnesses, experts and critics, and passages of comparative literature" for an appeal as he would have done had he "thought there was a fighting chance in the matter". Although Quinn sufficiently altered his view at the last minute to concede that expert testimony might be admissible to mitigate punishment, the thrust of the expert testimony he offered was directed only to the point that *Ulysses* would not corrupt readers, but did not demonstrate its quality as literature. No appeal was taken. Quinn never forced the judicial system to confront the core issue – the quality of *Ulysses* as literature. Within about a year of the time an appeal would have been decided, New York's highest court decided in the Halsey case that the book in an obscenity case must be considered as a whole, and that expert opinion is admissible as to an author's reputation and a book's merit. Joyce's work had been found obscene without Quinn's having sought an appellate ruling on these important issues. Reflecting on Quinn's performance as counsel, Joyce commented to his patron Harriet Shaw Weaver that the offence was less grotesque than the defence.

One of the most dispiriting aspects of Quinn's defence was the way it trivialised Joyce's book, and books generally. The gist of his argument was that the book could cause no harm because it really had no effect. That fatuous untruth has never been exposed more simply than in the retelling of the story of Paolo and Francesca by Joyce's master, Dante. In Book V of the *Inferno*, Francesca tells how, as she and her tutor read the story of Lancelot,

> several times that reading urged our eyes to meet, and took the color from our faces; but one moment alone it was that overcame us. When we read how the longed-for smile was kissed by so great a lover, this one, who never shall be parted from me, kissed my mouth all trembling. [Referring to the go-between who urged Guinevere to kiss Lancelot, Francesca continues:] A Galleotto was the book and he who wrote it; that day we read no farther in it.

Appropriating a line from Dante's *La Vita Nuova*, Francesca identifies the force that seized the lovers as *"Amor, ch'al cor gentil ratto s'apprende"* – Love, which is quickly kindled in a gentle heart. Neither Dante nor Joyce was willing to pretend that the erotic imagination lacks power, or that literature is incapable of conveying it.

It was more than a dozen years before a court would grapple with the essence of *Ulysses*. In 1932, Random House founder Bennett Cerf, with the sage advice of attorney Morris Ernst, set out to clear the path for the book to reach the wider audience it deserved. To be sure, they had the benefit of the fact that the novel as a whole had been published in Paris and had received some (if far from overwhelming) critical approbation. On the other hand, they had to deal with the concluding Molly Bloom monologue, which Joyce characterised as "probably more obscene than any preceding episode". Importantly, they brought a willingness to insist upon the veracity and value of Joyce's work.

The brief presented on behalf of Random House pictured Joyce as a distinguished man of letters, quoting encomiums from the likes of John Middleton Murry, Rebecca West, Arnold Bennett and Ernest Boyd. Moreover, Ernst delivered copies of critical commentary by Stuart Gilbert and Paul Jordan Smith to the trial judge, John Woolsey, who already had a copy of Herbert Gorman's biography of Joyce. Ernst's summation on Joyce's stature as a man of letters echoed Yeats, who had argued: "That such a man as Joyce should write filth is incredible." Ernst said almost the same thing: "It is monstrous to suppose that a man of the stature of Joyce would or could produce a work of obscenity." Authors of critical works will be interested to know that Woolsey's decision noted that his reading of *Ulysses* was accompanied by perusal of "a number of other books which have now become its satellite".

It remained necessary to come to grips with the text. Confronted with a charge that *Ulysses* is obscene, the mind of the advocate seems incapable of resisting the argument that it is too obscure to excite. Ernst put it this way:

> [*Ulysses*] is far too tedious and labyrinthine and bewildering for the untutored and the impressionable who might conceivably be affected by it. Such people would not get beyond the first dozen pages.

Referring to a case that had relied on the difficulty of James Branch Cabell's *Jurgen* in finding it not to be obscene, Ernst argued that "beside [*Ulysses*], *Jurgen* is a child's primer. It is not only the language that is baffling; the construction is almost unbelievably involved." As an example of the difficulty of the language, Ernst cited some words selected at random from the book, including whelks, cataletic, houyhnhnm, crubeen, parallax, cygnets, entelechy, yogibogeybox, apocrypha, tympanum, demisemiquaver, videlicet, cruiskeen, oxter, topiary, and epicene. Moreover, he argued, "incomprehensible paragraphs" recur again and again. Those who have struggled to parse the section of "Proteus" beginning "Ineluctable modality of the visible" will be pleased to find it cited prominently among the incomprehensible.

One can empathise with the advocate's desire to elude the question of obscenity with the red herring of obscurity. But sooner or later, a rigorous assessment of whether *Ulysses* was barred by the statutory ban on obscene works must come to grips with the fact that the essence of *Ulysses* – its warp and woof – is Joyce's conviction that sexual desire lies at the heart of things. Ernst sought to whistle his way past this core issue, arguing that "though the element of sex is present, it is relegated to a position of relative unimportance". To their credit, the judges faced with the task of applying the statute to the book were not so facile. The current of erotic imagination that animates *Ulysses* could not be swept under the rug.

The judicial wrestling with this lively question resulted in an unusual instance of resolving a legal question in terms of literary technique. Without explicitly using the term "stream of consciousness", Judge Woolsey opined that Joyce was experimenting in a new literary genre in which he attempted

> to show how the screen of consciousness with its ever-shifting kaleidoscopic impressions carries, as it were on a plastic palimpsest, not only what is in the focus of each man's observation of the actual things about him, but also in a penumbral zone residua of past impressions, some recent and some drawn up by association from the domain of the subconscious. He shows how each of these impressions affects the life and behavior of the character which he is describing.

The important point here is that the characters are not consciously indulging themselves in erotic imaginings. Rather, the primal energy of Eros is forcing itself on the characters. Accordingly, if there is a strong sexual undercurrent in *Ulysses*, it is not the fault of either Joyce or the reader:

> If Joyce did not attempt to be honest in developing the technique which he has adopted in *Ulysses* the result would be psychologically misleading and thus unfaithful to his chosen technique. Such an attitude would be artistically inexcusable.

Woolsey's analysis brought him exactly to where John Butler Yeats was in his 1920 letter to Quinn. Yeats had written that the reason for the outcry against Joyce was his terrible veracity. Woolsey made the same point:

It is because Joyce has been loyal to his technique [Woolsey wrote] and has not funked its necessary implications, but has honestly attempted to tell fully what his characters think about, that he has been the subject of so many attacks and that his purpose has been so often misunderstood and misrepresented.

Law and literature blend seamlessly here because it is Joyce's mastery as a writer that convinces Woolsey that it would be wrong for the law to silence him. Woolsey was responding to a feature of Joyce's writing pinpointed by the great University College Dublin professor Augustine Martin, who wrote that Joyce's literary achievement was the invention of "a range of technical and linguistic resources" of the necessary "power and range" to break "the sound barrier of ... social reticence, the wall – at least the facade – between the public and private self that Victoria's reign had so consolidated, and which the Catholic Church in Ireland had so reinforced". Joyce's piercing of the sound barrier between public and private showed Woolsey the way to break the hold of the Victorian Hicklin case on the law of obscenity.

We know that the prosecution urged Woolsey's special attention to Molly Bloom's soliloquy. Importantly, Ernst's emphasis on the quality of *Ulysses* as literature provided Molly with a platform from which she commanded serious attention. In the argument Molly crafted from her bed in Eccles Street, Woolsey could not help but find the rationale for putting off pretence and recognising the role of the erotic imagination: "What else were we given all those desires for I'd like to know?" is a question sharply posed by Molly that demanded an answer from a judge being asked to ban a book that draws attention to the fact of those desires. Those desires and their manifestations "didn't make me blush," argued Molly: "why should it either? It's only nature."

Woolsey's implicit acceptance of Molly's argument enabled him to swallow the admittedly "strong draught" of *Ulysses*. It remained to reconcile his conclusion with the law of obscenity, which still adhered to the twin views of the old Hicklin case that the measure of obscenity was the impact of isolated passages on the susceptible. A controlling federal case, *United States v Bennett*, so held. A better critic than legal scholar, Woolsey simply plunged ahead with the *ipse dixit* that the proper test was a reading of the book in its entirety in terms of how it would affect "a person with average sex instincts

– what the French would call '*l'homme moyen sensuel*' – who plays, in this branch of legal inquiry, the same role of hypothetical reagent as does the 'reasonable man' in the law of torts".

Sitting as the trier of fact, Woolsey thus had the unenviable task of offering himself as the barometer of whether *Ulysses* excited lustful thoughts. But even the valiant judge paled at this prospect. Instead, in an extraordinary departure from the notion that the advocates have a full opportunity to present their cases to the decision-maker – Woolsey reported what was, in effect, the combined decision of himself and two friends. His carefully hedged report avoided the question whether and to what extent any of the three had been stimulated to lustful thoughts in the course of duty. Instead, the report was that "in its entirety" the "net effect" of *Ulysses* was not "to excite sexual impulses or lustful thoughts".

Woolsey's opinion was vulnerable to an argument that, whatever the "net effect" of *Ulysses*, it contained specific passages that were obscene, and that the book thus ran afoul of the statute under the traditional Hicklin rule, as adopted in Bennett. The new United States Attorney, Martin Conboy, made exactly that argument in appealing Woolsey's decision to the Court of Appeals.

Conboy had no trouble convincing Judge Martin Manton, whose dissenting opinion rhetorically inquired: "Who can doubt the obscenity of this book after a reading of the pages referred to, which are too indecent to add as a footnote to this opinion?" Unfortunately for Conboy and the prosecution, the two other members of the three-judge panel were Learned Hand, who had questioned the soundness of the Hicklin rule twenty years previously in Kennerley, and his cousin Augustus Hand, two wonderfully educated judges of robust intellect and trenchant pen. Learned Hand's private pre-conference memorandum to his fellow judges, now available in the Harvard Law School library, gives us an unvarnished insight into his thinking. The core of his view was that some passages of the novel were undeniably obscene, but "the offending passages are clearly necessary to the epic of the soul as Joyce conceived it, and the parts which might be occasion for lubricity in the reader are to my way of thinking not sufficient to condemn a very notable contribution to literature". Seeking to write an opinion that would not be mined for quotable phrases, the two Hands recognised that Learned should not be the author.

Writing for the two-judge majority, Augustus Hand quickly showed his appreciation for Woolsey's reliance on Joyce's technique. Hand identified Joyce "as a pioneer" of the "'stream of consciousness' method of presenting fiction" which "attempts to depict the thoughts and lay bare the souls of a number of people ... with a literalism that leaves nothing unsaid". Then, in one of those touches that makes judging an art, Hand, with an eye on precedents that permitted a greater range of candour in scientific works, framed "the question before us" as "whether such a book of artistic merit and scientific insight should be regarded as 'obscene' within section 305(a) of the Tariff Act". Molly would have been proud to see her insight labelled scientific.

With characteristic candour, Hand conceded "that numerous long passages in *Ulysses* contain matter that is obscene under any fair definition of the word cannot be gainsayed; yet they are relevant to the purpose of depicting the thoughts of the characters and are introduced to give meaning to the whole, rather than to promote lust or portray filth for its own sake".

Again meeting the prosecution head on, Hand observed that "it is argued that *United States v Bennett* ... stands in the way of what has been said, and it certainly does". Exercising his power as an appellate judge, Hand simply interred Bennett as departed dogma. Citing his opinion in *United States v Dennett* that works of physiology, medicine, science and sex instruction are not within the statute, though to some extent and among some persons they may tend to promote lustful thoughts, Hand concluded that "we think the same immunity should apply to literature as to science, where the presentation, when viewed objectively, is sincere, and the erotic matter is not introduced to promote lust and does not furnish the dominant note of the publication".

By focusing on the quality of Joyce's novel as literature, and creating a presumptive dichotomy between literature and obscenity, the *Ulysses* decision fundamentally altered the law of obscenity. At the same stroke, the decision created a significant role for literary criticism in obscenity trials by holding that, in determining whether obscenity is the dominant note of the publication, the trier of fact is to be guided by the "relevancy of the objectionable parts to the theme" and "the established reputation of the work in the estimation of approved critics". In affirming Woolsey's decision that *Ulysses* was not obscene, the court relied on the fact that "*Ulysses* is rated as a book of considerable power by persons whose views are entitled to weight".

Conboy urged his superiors in the Department of Justice to seek discretionary review by the Supreme Court, but they declined. The voyage of *Ulysses* through the courts thus came to an end. Several conclusions can be drawn.

First: a successful voyage was by no means assured. Witness the initial failure, and the dissent of Judge Manton, whose views were probably more representative of the general run of the judiciary than those of the more liberal-thinking Hands.

Second: nonetheless, as evidenced by the acquittal of the seller of Théophile Gautier's *Mademoiselle de Maupin* in 1918, the verdict in favour of *Jurgen* in 1922, and the Halsey departure from Hicklin the same year, the building blocks for a successful defence were available at the time of the 1921 trial of Anderson and Heap. What was needed was an unbiased lawyer committed to literature's right to be heard.

Third: the lawyers tended to be cautious, arguing the case somewhere short of the level of the major premise. Although Ezra Pound had urged Quinn that obscenity statutes were "unconstitutional from a Jeffersonian point of view", it would not be until 1957 that the United States Supreme Court would hold in the Roth case that the principle of free speech animating the First Amendment to the United States Constitution protects a book that excites sexual desire so long as the book is not "utterly without redeeming social importance", a position approaching, if not wholly adopting, Anderson and Heap's view that literature could not be obscene. In defence of the general caution of the lawyers, it is worth remembering that the initial reaction of many established writers was also cautious, to the point of hostility. DH Lawrence thought *Ulysses* the dirtiest, most obscene thing ever written. Virginia Woolf found it "underbred", the work of a "self-taught working man" or of a "queasy undergraduate scratching his pimples". To her credit, before herself adopting the idea of describing Mrs Dalloway's stream of consciousness on a single day in June, she conceded that Joyce's novel had "genius, I think, though full of stunts". Edmund Gosse thought Joyce "a literary charlatan of the extremest order" and *Ulysses* "infamous in taste, in style, in everything". Katherine Mansfield couldn't "get over the feeling of wet linoleum and unemptied pails and far worse horrors in the house of his mind". Shaw thought *Ulysses* "a revolting record of a disgusting phase of civilisation", albeit "a truthful one". Even those who praised the work, like Eliot, tended to ignore its strong erotic current in favour of technical or structural themes. WB Yeats was a partial exception. He wrote to Quinn that the first chapters in *The Little Review* "surpassed in intensity any novelist of our time", but later confessed that a partial reading of the rest left him hating it when he dipped in and out but impressed to the extent – admittedly limited – that he read it in the right order, in which case he found in it "our Irish cruelty and also our kind of strength". In general, the early writer-readers were no more anxious than lawyers and judges to confront *Ulysses* head on.

Fourth: even so, lawyer Quinn suffered defects greater than caution. He lacked the personal conviction to force the courts to confront the right of *Ulysses* to be heard. Moreover, his unpardonable bias against Anderson and Heap and his antipathy to their enterprise disqualified him for the fundamentally important task of protecting their right to publish. Joyce's biographers, Ellmann and Bowker, John Butler Yeats's biographer, William Murphy, and Quinn's own biographer, BL Reid, have deferred to Quinn's judgment that the case against Anderson and Heap was unwinnable. But Quinn thought the same thing about the case against *Jurgen* in 1920 and he turned out to be wrong when his successor as counsel proved victorious two years later. Without hindsight or speculation, it is possible to say that the arguments that Quinn did advance were poor ones, and unworthy of *Ulysses* and Joyce.

Fifth: tellingly, Quinn knew that there were better arguments than the ones he advanced. In a letter to Shane Leslie the year after the adverse *Ulysses* decision he articulated the argument that would ultimately carry the day in Judge Woolsey's decision more than a decade later. Quinn's letter anticipates Woolsey – and echoes John Butler Yeats – in saying that "there is no humbug in *Ulysses*, no pretense about morality ... There are the facts and the dialogues, simple, unadorned, unashamed, without sentiment and without sentimentality. An orgy of thought and speech and action fused into a work of art by the inspiration of a man of genius." Quinn probably said something similar in a memorandum he submitted to the Solicitor of the United States Post Office in June 1919, arguing against post office suppression of an earlier issue of *The Little Review* containing an earlier episode of *Ulysses*. The National Archives' copy of Quinn's memorandum was destroyed and no copy has been located, but we know that Anderson, who disapproved of

Quinn's handling of the trial, thought his memorandum to the Solicitor a "magnificent defense". Ezra Pound thought it "the best apologia for [Joyce] that has been written" and Eliot found it admirable and was prepared to publish it in *The Egoist*. Quinn declined to permit publication. He claimed that it was written too hastily and that he lacked time to revise it. The fact is that he shrank from using the defence that would ultimately succeed, and declined to be associated with that defence in public. His prejudice against Anderson and Heap, and his reluctance to be publicly identified as a champion of what, in a letter to Pound, he called "sex literature", were a disservice to both law and literature. Fortunately, other lawyers, judges and critics did justice to *Ulysses* and Joyce.

Sixth: the federal decisions in the *Ulysses* case contributed significantly to a maturing of the American law of obscenity, and, after the book had been published in England, the Obscene Publications Act of 1959 incorporated the essence of the *Ulysses* decision into English law. The argument that carried the day in *Ulysses* was the compelling one that regard for truth itself requires that Joyce's terrible veracity be heard. That argument had its roots in the fictional reverie of Molly Bloom. Plato was right: fictions subvert orthodoxies.

The above essay originated with a lecture delivered in 2012. The underlying issues are treated more fully in Hassett's book The Ulysses *Trials: Beauty and Truth Meet the Law, published by The Lilliput Press in June 2016.*

Much the Same

The Letters of Samuel Beckett 1941–1956 by Samuel Beckett; George Craig,
Martha Dow Fehsenfeld, Dan Gunn and Lois More Overbeck (eds)
Cambridge University Press | 886 pp | ISBN: 978-0521867948

THE SECOND volume of Beckett's correspondence, covering the years
1941–1956, which saw his emergence as a writer of stature, comes to us courtesy
of Cambridge University Press complete with four pages of praise from the
reviews of Volume 1. Variously described as "an elating cultural moment" (*New
York Times* Sunday Book Review), "a heroic achievement by the editors" (*The
Irish Times*) and a "cornucopia" (*The Times*), most commentators welcomed
the scrupulous editorial framework which editors George Craig, Martha
Dow Fehsenfeld, Dan Gunn and Lois More Overbeck have given each letter.
Minute annotations are provided, together with careful translation to English
of those letters written in French or German. Nothing is left to chance and
light is thrown on the recondite allusiveness in which Beckett often cloaked
his 1930s correspondence.

The punctilious attention to detail continues in Volume 2, but there
are some differences. Instead of including 60 per cent of the extant
correspondence as in Volume 1, the editors find space for only 40 per cent.
This is partly due to the additional space needed for George Craig's excellent
translations from Beckett's French since this is famously Beckett's medium
during the "siege in the room" which this volume charts. Beckett's chief
correspondent is no longer Thomas MacGreevy but the art critic Georges

Duthuit (1891–1973), with whom he composed "Three Dialogues" and whom he used as a sparring partner for his radical ideas on visual and verbal representation in art and literature.

The tone of the correspondence also differs, with Beckett's concern for others, his sympathy and generosity (as for example towards the widowed Mania Péron and her two sons, Michel and Alexis) being a keynote of the volume, his own complaints, a lugubrious background grouse-against-the-world, tempered by his evident willingness to alleviate the burdens of his friends. And, of course, midway through this volume, his own life fortunes are dramatically transformed with the first production of *En attendant Godot* at the Théâtre de Babylone, Paris on January 5th, 1953. These are the years when Beckett was "damned to fame". They also include the trauma of the Occupation, from which almost no correspondence survives; the first letter reproduced here is a card dated February 17th, 1945 addressed to Beckett's family in Ireland and sent care of the Irish Legation in Paris. There are the privations of the aftermath of war, during which Beckett and his partner, Suzanne Deschevaux-Dumesnil, lived in particular penury at their small apartment at 6 rue des Favorites in the 15th arrondissement, but where Beckett enjoyed an intensive period of creativity, composing, of course: *Molloy*, *Malone meurt*, *L'Innommable*, *En attendant Godot* as well as the *nouvelles* (*La Fin*, *Le Calmant*, *L'Expulsé* and *Premier Amour*) and *Mercier et Camier*, *Eleuthéria* and *Textes pour Rien*, all in French.

On the biographical plane, three other important events punctuate this volume: the death of Beckett's mother in August 1950, the death of his elder brother Frank in September 1954 and his increasing tendency to withdraw from Paris and seek refuge in the village of Ussy-sur-Marne where, in 1953, his cottage was completed. Thus these letters are increasingly sent from Ussy rather than rue des Favorites, with Beckett variously declaring himself: "not very well", "feeble", "uncomfortable", "in a bad way", "green and rotten", "spineless" or "dismal" according to his mood. Indeed what Beckett later called "the fearful symptoms" (*Ohio Impromptu*) are evoked more than once in his letters from Ussy. Concluding a letter to Mania Péron on August 28th, 1951, Beckett writes: "Right, off to bed. So as not to sleep. To listen to the darkness, the silence, the solitude and the dead", while an earlier letter to Georges Duthuit (July 20th, 1951) refers to "the images that insomnia brings

– no, I prefer nightmares". Beckett the haunted insomniac, familiar from Volume 1, dwells in this volume too and just as Beckett enumerated his physical and mental symptoms to MacGreevy in Volume 1, here he reiterates his "unrelieved wretchedness" to his closest correspondents.

Now that we have reached the halfway point in this monumental four-volume selection of the letters (out of 15,000 in total), it may be worth reflecting on what has and will be accomplished in this undertaking. It is probably fair to say that the trajectory of Beckett's life is too well-known and the extant letters too widely quoted in James Knowlson's authoritative biography for new revelations to be forthcoming. Indeed, in some ways, Knowlson was granted a freer hand than the editors of this volume since he quotes from letters written between 1945 and 1956 which do not appear here. The false distinction drawn up by Beckett's executors between what has relevance to his work and what is extraneous and personal has handicapped the Beckett letters project from the outset. Thus, much of his "business" correspondence with Jérôme Lindon and other publishers, translators and directors is reproduced, some of it revealing, much of it dispensable. Meanwhile, some beautifully revealing letters, freely available courtesy of Knowlson, are omitted, such as much of Beckett's correspondence with his American lover, Pamela Mitchell. For example, the following excerpt from a letter dated August 6th, 1954 is partially quoted as a footnote, but the full letter from which the quotation comes is not reproduced:

> Soon the leaves will be turning, it'll be winter before I'm home. And then? It'll have to be very easy whatever it is. I can't face any more difficulties, and I can't bear the thought of giving any more pain, make what sense you can of that, it's all old age and weakness, why will you not believe me?

To say that this is "not relevant" to Beckett's work, in its humane, tender and stoic tone and content is not consistent with any realistic view of the relationship between life and work. Similarly, Beckett's vigil over his brother's deathbed, which is related candidly to Mitchell in this period (summer 1954) and clearly conveyed in Knowlson's biography, is only patchily conveyed here. Indeed the link which Knowlson persuasively makes, thanks to the letters to Mitchell he quotes, between the death of Beckett's brother and the genesis of *Endgame* is not so evident in this selection because of the editorial policy.

Therefore, what we have is a truncated volume of letters with many crucial omissions, omissions which are perhaps more regrettable than in Volume 1, where important cuts were also made.

If Philip Hensher, writing in *The Guardian* (December 9th, 2011) is able to claim that "whatever their relative status as writers, Beckett's published letters so far have a tenth the interest and value of Evelyn Waugh's", it is partly because of this misguided editorial policy and also because the "business" side of Beckett's life, which so many of these letters are drawn from, has little of the personal candour and compassion which he reveals elsewhere, notwithstanding his richly diverse dealings with Lindon and others. It is true that his letters to Georges Duthuit, in particular, are both personal and pertinent to the work. But what is one to make of the following, written in July 1951 to Duthuit, which mixes gardening chores, philosophy, biology, nature and personal grief in an entirely tangled and unsystematic way:

> Behind the wheelbarrow, painted by Suzanne in red, I do not think of Pascal, ever since the article by the biologist Rostand in the *Table Ronde*. Never seen so many butterflies in such worm-state, this little central cylinder, the only flesh, is the worm. First flights of the young swallows, the parents who feed them on the wing. Yesterday, about 2p.m., a year ago my mother was dying, not even capable of forgetting that, or of thinking of it too late.

Such is the nature of letter-writing: it is an unsystematic art which blends, necessarily, the personal and the quotidian with the literary and the philosophical. Trying to draw a dividing line between these across a lifetime of correspondence is not possible. Although the editors claim that their "selection has been more straightforward" than with Volume 1, owing to "an abundance of work-related letters" and that "there remain only a very few letters which the editors would have included but which were not approved" by the Estate, this begins to look somewhat questionable once Knowlson's coverage of the same period is compared with this selection.

However regrettable these lacunae may be, there still remains much to be grateful for in this second volume. The letters to Duthuit match those to MacGreevy in Volume 1 as a kind of intellectual fencing match in which art is the occasion to express the impossibility or futility of expression. The epistemological uncertainty of Beckett's prose and the philosophical paradoxes of "Three Dialogues" are articulated more fully here as, for example, Beckett to Duthuit in August 1948:

> I shall never know clearly enough how far space and time are unutterable, and me caught up somewhere in there … One may as well dare to be plain and say that not knowing is not only not knowing what one is, but also where one is, and what change to wait for, and how to get out of wherever one is, and how to know, when it seems as if something is moving, which apparently was not moving before, what it is that is moving, that was not moving before, and so on.

In this, and similar passages, one hears the thoughts of Molloy as he speculates on the "extreme complexity" of the astral movements he witnesses at Lousse's house. Instead of advancing a little further along what Beckett in "Three Dialogues" calls "a certain order on the plane of the feasible", Beckett postulates another axis of being, perception and creation which turns away from conventional expression "weary of its puny exploits" to express a kind of radical will-lessness or abulia even in the act of writing or painting. The phraseology of "Three Dialogues" is echoed in Beckett's letters to Duthuit and one can easily see how Beckett "wrote up" the Dialogues for publication in *transition* in December 1949:

> Not to have to express oneself, nor get involved with whatever kind of maximum, in one's numberless, valueless, achievementless world; that is a game worth trying all the same, a necessity worth trying, and one which will never work, if that works.

Beckett's love of the paradox and the self-cancelling doubt which is the signature of his mature prose is fully articulated to Duthuit and we can understand, reading these letters, why, when he finally found a publisher (Éditions de Minuit) prepared to publish his three novels (*Molloy*, *Malone meurt* and *L'Innommable*), it was for the last of the three which he waited impatiently to appear.

Perhaps the most important of these letters to Duthuit has already appeared in print, notably in the 2006 book *Beckett After Beckett* (ed SE

Gontarski and A Uhlmann, University of Florida Press). Dated March 9th, 1949, it is one of the key letters in the collection where Beckett spells out how he finds, in Bram van Velde's painting, "the absence of relations of whatever kind". Just as in his 1931 monograph on Proust, or in his comments to MacGreevy on Jack B Yeats or Cézanne, Beckett is most revealing about himself when the "occasion" for expression is something or someone other than himself. As he writes to Duthuit:

> And I shall tend irresistibly to pull Bram's case over towards my own, since that is the condition of being in it and talking about it ... We have waited a long time for an artist who is brave enough, is at ease enough with the great tornadoes of intuition, to grasp that the break with the outside world entails the break with the inside world, that there are no replacement relations for naïve relations, that what are called outside and inside are one and the same.

We see here perhaps a mature formulation of "the breakdown of the object" and "rupture of the lines of communication" already postulated in Beckett's 1934 review of "Recent Irish Poetry". Such a rupture is, as Beckett gleefully suggests in "Three Dialogues", barely sustainable, putting the subject in "an unenviable situation, familiar to psychiatrists". As Beckett's post-Trilogy prose suggests, there is no easy way to "go on" in this predicament.

There is, we may suggest, a certain heroism in this position which also constitutes the paradoxical dynamic of Beckett's prose. The "onwardness" found there inhabits a plane of indigence which Beckett has written himself into, "illogically", beyond the "plane of the feasible". If anyone doubts the sincerity of what *Disjecta* calls Beckett's "Words About Painters", we find the following letter of December 1951 written to Bram van Velde and his partner, Marthe Arnaud-Kuntz:

> Above all, let Bram not get the idea that I'm moving away from him. The very reverse. The farther I sink down, the more I feel right beside him, feel how much, in spite of the differences, our ventures come together, in the unthought and the harrowing. And if there had to be for me a soul-mate, I make bold to say that it would be his soul and no other ... Bram is my great familiar. In work and in the impossibility of working.

As one reads these letters, one is struck as much by certain continuities in Beckett's career as by the very obvious discontinuities. There are indeed important turning points: Beckett's resignation from Trinity in 1931, his abandonment of Ireland in 1937, his wartime experiences in the Resistance and the flagrant success of *En attendant Godot* in 1953. Equally, Beckett's writings show an uneven and unpredictable line of development. There is a gulf between *More Pricks Than Kicks* (1934) and the more achieved prose of *Murphy* (1938) and similarly between these and the wartime novel *Watt* and the Trilogy and post-Trilogy prose. Having said this, it is apparent that philosophical positions laid out, often in obscure publications, in the 1930s, hold good for the mature writer. By the same token, Beckett was a loyal and tenacious friend and correspondent, so that when he re-emerges after the war, he picks up with his old network of associates and friends – George Reavey, the van Veldes, Con Leventhal, Ethna McCarthy, as well as with George Belmont/Pelorson, whose wartime record contrasted with that of Beckett – in a way which demonstrates Beckett's well-known generosity of spirit, sometimes absent in Volume 1 of the *Letters*. At the same time, this volume shows Beckett developing a new network of friends – publishers like Jérôme Lindon and Barney Rosset, actors like Roger Blin, translators like Richard Seaver and Elmar Tophoven – whom he trusted to interpret, publish and promote his work. The period 1945–1956 charts this re-emergence (with 1945 being the real starting date of the book), which is also a period of prodigious professional growth and artistic achievement.

Nonetheless, as letter after letter testifies, for Beckett "the essential doesn't change" and a deeply ingrained pessimism, tempered by sympathy and loyalty, pervades these pages, as one would perhaps expect it to.

So much for Beckett the man. But do these letters reveal new things about Beckett the writer during this, the most fertile period of his career? Undoubtedly the exchanges with Duthuit will provide scholars with illuminating background to Beckett's major novels in French. By contrast, he speaks with less intellectual freedom to other correspondents. In line with his admonition in *Watt*, "no symbols where none intended", Beckett cautioned more than one theatre director against reading too much into his plays. Thus writing to German director Carlheinz Caspari in July 1953, he states:

If my play contains expressionist elements, it is without my knowledge … Nor is it, for me, a symbolist play, I cannot stress that too much. First and foremost, it is a question of something that happens, almost a routine, and it is this dailiness and this materiality, in my view, that need to be brought out. That at any moment Symbols, Ideas, Forms might show up, this is for me secondary.

From the outset of *Godot*'s popularity, therefore, Beckett discouraged actors and directors from asking the inevitable questions: Who is Godot? Who are Pozzo and Lucky? What are these four characters doing on stage? Beckett's consistent response was to deny all privileged insight and to claim that if he knew the answers to these questions, he would have answered them in the play. Towards the end of Volume 2, we see the beginnings of his revealing correspondence with his American director Alan Schneider, already accessible from Maurice Harmon's edition *No Author Better Served*, published in 1998.

Beckett's famous reticence and his reluctance to grant interviews was not always consistent, so that, on occasion, he would drop hints or provide skeletal background information about himself to curious individuals. Hence, amid many uninspiring letters concerning contracts, proofs, translations and productions, we find a few unexpected gems. Among these one could include some notes on *Godot* written in January 1952 to one Michel Polac of Radiodiffusion Française for broadcast with a radio excerpt of that play in which Beckett claims, somewhat disingenuously: "I have no ideas about the theatre. I know nothing about it. I do not go to it." Beckett was also happy to correct the misapprehensions of a German translator, Hans Naumann, in a letter of February 17th, 1954:

Since 1945 I have written only in French. Why this change? It was not deliberate. It was in order to change, to see, nothing more complicated than that, in appearance at least … You may put me in the dismal category of those who, if they had to act in full awareness of what they were doing, would never act. Which does not preclude there being urgent reasons, for this change.

Such morsels as this remind us of Beckett's cryptic ways of helping, or at least not hindering, those who contacted him about his work, especially if they were introduced via Jérôme Lindon or another trusted friend. We can take note, for example, of Beckett's cheerful assistance to Niall Montgomery, an old Dublin acquaintance, in a letter dated December 2nd, 1953, for an article he was writing about Beckett's work. Equally, we find Beckett dispensing liberal advice to his translators and complaining that his "queer French" will not "go" into English. Indeed, such were the demands on Beckett after the initial success of *Godot* in 1953 that we frequently find him overwhelmed by the "wastes" of (self-)translation which his scrupulous nature led him to undertake. Beckett's sense of obligation extended, not just to the people around him, but to the works themselves and his interventions in theatre productions and in the translations of his work stemmed from an evident protectiveness he felt about what he had created.

For the interested reader or Sunday afternoon Beckettian, Knowlson's biography remains the fullest source of information about Beckett's life during this period. *The Letters of Samuel Beckett 1941–1956* helpfully sets out many important and revealing letters, expertly translated and annotated. Nonetheless, one must regret the unspoken missed opportunity this volume represents in terms of reproducing a complete range of Beckett's correspondence for these years. However, even if the editors "fail again" or even "fail better" with Volumes 3 and 4, they will still have accomplished a Herculean labour for which all of us will be grateful.

This Life a Long Disease

Jonathan Swift: *His Life and His World* by Leo Damrosch

Yale University Press | 512 pp | ISBN: 978-0300164992

LEO DAMROSCH'S new biography of Jonathan Swift closes by detailing some of the many indignities suffered by its subject after death. As he lay in state in St Patrick's Cathedral, souvenir hunters plucked locks from what remained of his hair, leaving his already bald head utterly stripped. The image is apt for a satirist who went about the task of laying bare the reputations and personal habits of others with relish. It recalls perhaps the remark made in *A Tale of A Tub* about seeing a woman flayed alive: "you will hardly believe how much it altered her person for the worse". Here, as often in Swift's writing, humiliating violence grates against the banality of polite sentiment and rhetorical amplification makes the second look more inexcusable than the first. Readers are left to puzzle for themselves whether the appropriate response might be compassion, callous amusement or some strange blend of the two.

Such a mixture was perhaps more common in Swift's time, which unlike our own, did not place a premium on heart-wringing sincerity. Context is important and Damrosch's new biography provides this amply. His focus, as his subtitle says, is not just on Swift's life but also his world. This dual perspective helps avoid a pathologising mode, something which is very easy to slip into when writing about Swift: if some features of the life look unusually mordant or morbid by our standards, they were not out of place in that world. *A Modest Proposal*'s baby-eating humour still has the capacity to shock but in the week of its publication one Dublin shop made a window display of a mummified corpse to attract passers-by, likening the skin's texture to a freshly-baked cake of puff pastry.

On a similarly gruesome note, Damrosch informs us that the original of the *Tale*'s flayed woman may have been the desiccated corpse of a convict displayed under glass in the library of Trinity College during the time Swift studied there. When its face was eaten by rats, a new one was duly peeled from another more recently executed body and mounted on the faceless cadaver. We tend to think of grotesque fascination with bodily degradation and its public display as peculiarly Swiftian, but perhaps he just used the materials that came to hand around him. He seems to have been an early adopter of the mantras of modern creative writing – "write what you know" and "show, don't tell" – and they led him to some interesting places.

Even allowing that life in the eighteenth century could be brutal and strange, and death itself no guarantee of peaceful repose, contemporaries occasionally found Swift a bit odd. His first biographer, Lord Orrery, was often left cold by what he called his "peculiarity of humour". His generally disapproving *Remarks on the Life and Writings of Dr Jonathan Swift* (1751), published with what looked then like indecent haste six years after its subject's death, provoked spirited responses from Swift's cousin, confusingly named Deane Swift, and his friend Patrick Delany. They argued that Orrery had fundamentally misrepresented a subject whose instinct was to conceal his better nature for fear of being thought vain. Swift biography ever since has vacillated between sympathy and outright disgust. Damrosch is more forgiving than a lot of his predecessors, many of whom found it difficult to get past the objectionable side of Swift's personality. There is a long tradition, which Damrosch does not follow, of viewing the life and the works as variations on an unholy trinity of misanthropy, misogyny and madness. Atheism, asexuality and impotence have been thrown into the mix by such distinguished authors as Sir Walter Scott and George Orwell.

Admittedly Swift did not do much to help himself, announcing "I hate and detest that animal called man" or taking as his own La Rochefoucauld's maxim that "in the adversity of our best friends we find something that does not displease us". But for most such remarks there is usually a mitigating context which goes some way to relieve the shock of initial impact. His avowal of misanthropy is part of a satiric tradition also found in the poetry of John Wilmot, Earl of Rochester. Like Swift, Rochester was probably great fun to be around at times. Swift qualified his own denunciation by adding that despite hating mankind "I heartily love John, Peter, Thomas, and so forth." He adopted the maxim from La Rouchefoucauld as an epigraph to a poem, "Verses on the Death of Dr Swift", which meditates self-mockingly on his own posthumous reputation. News of his decease is just about significant enough to occasion a passing remark during a card game where the news is received "in doleful dumps / 'The Dean is dead: (and what is trumps?)'"

But even in this poem there is a fine line between self-deprecation and backhanded self-regard, as expressed though Swift's self-conscious use of the titles "Dean" and "Doctor". Swift bought his doctorate, and even though he used the title at every opportunity (more than a hundred and seventy times in his poems, at Damrosch's count) he always thought he was cut out to be more than a dean. The post was an administrative one, involving the day-to-day running of St Patrick's as a working church. A dean does the work that a bishop is too important to do, and Swift had tried hard to become a bishop. He failed through a combination of misjudgement, bad luck and unwillingness to oblige on the part of those who owed him favours. Swift tended to dwell on his failures and was not shy about blaming people he felt had let him down. It is difficult to know whether he had a talent for self-sabotage or whether he was hindered along the way by unhelpful patrons and ungrateful friends, as he liked to maintain. Either way, becoming universally known by the title "Dean Swift" or just "the Dean" was a permanent reminder of ambition thwarted and talent unrewarded. In maturity, as Damrosch notes, Swift became "a collector of grudges". It would be difficult to observe otherwise.

Although candid about Swift's faults, overall this is a generous and sympathetic account of one who had by the standards of his class relatively few advantages in life, and who, aside from his literary gift, did not make the greatest use of those that came his way. Born in Dublin to a mother who had recently arrived from England to seek the charity of distant relatives, he was a posthumous child and possibly an illegitimate one. It is impossible to speak with certainty about this, because there is virtually no reliable information about Swift's early life. Along with his relations with women, it forms a puzzle at the centre of any biography.

Swift himself, as ever, is not much help. He left a brief autobiography and some other scattered remarks on his childhood, which tend to take the form of mythmaking exaggerations or rueful prognostications of future disappointment. On the question of Swift's parentage and later *amours*, Damrosch returns to long-established but often disregarded theories, including those of Denis Johnston and Sibyl le Brocquy, who sought out fascinating and tragic intrigues beneath the Dean's scrupulous propriety. Previous generations of Swift scholars tended to have little time for these, but Damrosch argues for the plausibility of two conjectures in particular: that Swift's father might have been Sir John Temple rather than the late Jonathan Swift senior, and that this had serious repercussions for his relationship with Esther Johnson, aka Stella.

If the theories are to be believed, Stella and Swift were set on a fatal path when the twenty-one-year-old Jonathan went to England to work as secretary to Sir William Temple, a retired diplomat and son of Sir John, master of the rolls in the Dublin court of chancery. Based on possible interactions between Sir John and Swift's mother Abigail, Johnston speculated that the former might have been Swift's real father. There is, as Damrosch concedes, no evidence for this but it does make for a great story, more suited to a scandal memoir than the life of a middle-ranking Church of Ireland cleric. When Swift arrived at Moor Park, Sir William Temple's Surrey estate, there was certainly no acknowledgement that he and Temple might have been half-brothers. If the secret was known, it did not beget affection. Swift was probably treated more like a member of Temple's domestic staff than an equal. A letter of recommendation Temple wrote for him to Sir Robert Southwell, which Damrosch quotes at length, does little to suggest that Temple held him in high regard. He seems effectively to have been asking Southwell to take Swift off his hands, writing with "the offer of a servant", whom Temple had been "obliged … thus far to take care of".

The description of Swift as a servant was not automatically belittling – letters were routinely signed off with "your humble servant" – but Swift's de facto status within Temple's household may help explain why he was so interested in, and sociable with, domestic servants throughout his life.

"Directions to Servants" is one of his funniest mock-treatises. Through all of his travels Gulliver is only really at home in the country of the Houyhnhnms under the tutelage of one of the "under servants" in a household of super-intelligent horses. He is supposed to have used his own servants as a test audience for the *Travels*, reading passages aloud to them and redrafting until they felt he had got it right. A monument to his favourite, Alexander "Saunders" McGee still stands in St Patrick's Cathedral, erected by "his grateful master", Swift. It was to have been inscribed "friend and master" until Swift was persuaded against it.

In the Temple household there was one who occupied an inverse position to Swift's, a servant treated more like one of the company. This was Esther Johnson, better known by Swift's pet name for her, Stella. While speculations about Swift's parentage are wild but compelling, Damrosch thinks that critics have been on surer ground when they deduce that Johnson must have been Sir William Temple's "natural" daughter. Temple bequeathed property to her with a total value of a thousand pounds and probably took other steps to ensure that she was provided for throughout her life. These don't seem like the actions of a master to a servant, however grateful. What is certain is that Swift's bond with Stella, often reduced to prurient whispers, nudges and winks, was as close as it was fractious. Eavesdropping on it through the assortment of prose and verse in which it has come down to us is utterly compelling.

The poems he wrote to Stella, to which she sometimes replied in verse, are teasingly affectionate, with the occasional flareup of temper. Replete with an invented language and mysterious deletions, the series of letters he wrote to her from London, usually known by the editorial title *Journal to Stella*, is a document of strange and beguiling creativity and intimacy. It would be worth reading even if Swift had never got round to *Gulliver's Travels*. The account of Stella's life and character written by Swift in the hours after her death is a candid and moving performance by one not known for his ability to play it straight. It is nonetheless a performance and indeed there is something theatrical, if not melodramatic about many of Swift's utterances. It is not so surprising that Johnston and le Brocquy followed WB Yeats in writing plays about him. Although Swift doesn't seem to have had much interest in theatre beyond a friendship with William Congreve, a lot of his work reads as if meant to be performed. *A Modest Proposal*, like *A Tale of A Tub* and even *Gulliver's Travels*, is an extended monologue which depends on dramatic irony for its effect. There are also chamber pieces such as "Polite Conversation" and "A Dialogue in Hibernian Style" which were based on talk overheard and transcribed by Swift.

Damrosch puzzles as to why Swift called La Rouchefoucauld his favourite author – one answer is that like Swift, he excelled at writing maxims. Claiming a French aristocrat as a model might have appealed to Swift's sense of himself as born to better things, but a more everyday source for such utterances would have been the villains and anti-heroes of the Restoration stage. The terse, epigrammatic quality which makes Swift's style so quotable today seems sometimes to have more in common with this kind of theatrical language than with the prose of his contemporaries. This isn't always a good thing. Although Damrosch follows Orwell in praising the famously plain and transparent style, Swift sometimes pursued concision to the point of brutality. A long exposure to his writing can sometimes send one in search of an antidote, such as the long, languorous sentences of Sir Thomas Browne.

There is no mistaking the dynamism of Swift's dramatic style, however, and it is not surprising that his biographers have set out his life as a correspondingly theatrical stew of conflict, secrecy and revelation. The denouement to the tragedy is supposed to have come in 1716 when Swift and Stella were married in secret by the Bishop of Clogher, only to find that they were blood relations, star-crossed by the consanguinity of their respective "real" fathers, Sirs John and William Temple. Again, evidence for this is scant, but it provides an explosive climax to the middle act of Swift's life and allows us to see pathos as well as misanthropy in the increasingly embittered and estranged writing of the 1720s and 30s, from *Gulliver's Travels* through *A Modest Proposal* to *The Lady's Dressing Room*.

Allowing for caveats about veracity, Damrosch's telling of the secret marriage tale is one of the centrepieces of the biography, along with an extended focus on the other woman in Swift's life. Esther Van Homrigh, the daughter of a Dutch merchant, was named Vanessa by prefixing the "Van" of her surname to a shortened form of her first name. Although Swift performed the same surgery on himself, mangling the Latin Decanus (Dean) to Cadenus for the intriguing and unusually long poem "Cadenus and Vanessa", it is hard sometimes not to see a controlling impulse behind all this name-changing. Combined with a penchant for conceiving imaginary worlds populated by fabulous creatures and governed by unhinged grotesques, his imaginative fecundity had an edge to it which recalls no one so much as Lewis Carroll.

Whatever she thought of her new name, which along with the phrase "sweetness and light" is a Swiftian coinage that has passed into general use, Vanessa's tale is shorter and even sadder than that of Stella. Swift was deep into some kind of long-term relationship with Johnson when Van Homrigh came along to flatter his fortysomething vanity. Much ink has been spilled over their famous use in correspondence of the word "coffee" as possible code for sex. Swift concluded one letter with "Adieu till we meet over a pot of coffee, or an orange and sugar, in the Sluttery, which I have so often found to be the most agreeable chamber in the world." It is certainly a suggestive set of phrases, but some critics have argued that although Swift's language and intentions may have been carnal Vanessa's weren't. Damrosch disagrees: he states unequivocally that "Vanessa loved him passionately and longed to be loved in return". Whatever transpired in the sluttery, there was a final, dreadful, falling out before Vanessa died, probably of tuberculosis, in 1723. Along with Jane Waring, an early marriage prospect whom Swift renamed Varina, and Lady Acheson (regaled or harassed late in life as "Skinnibonia"), Stella and Vanessa headed a list united by characteristics that Swift clearly found desirable: all were highly intelligent, most were very thin, and half of them were called Esther.

Damrosch's portraits of Stella and Vanessa are notably strong and rounded. He is reluctant to caricature either as victim or muse and is equally wary of the accusations of misogyny that continue to dog Swift. He relishes a tale of Stella's fatal wounding of a household intruder and successfully defends Vanessa against charges laid by several previous biographers of being needy and desperate. On Vanessa and on the possibility of Stella's parentage he brings in supporting evidence that previous biographers have tended to overlook or dismiss, and is not afraid to criticise them for having done so. Damrosch is not on the whole overly reverential towards those who have gone before him in writing Swift's life. These include the formidable *Jonathan Swift: The Man, His Works and The Age* by Damrosch's onetime colleague Irvin Ehrenpreis.

Long regarded as definitive, this three-volume work stretched to over two thousand pages and took from 1962 to 1983 to complete. Ehrenpreis insisted that Swift was deeply scarred by a strict, almost Calvinist, religious sensibility, and that he was always in search of replacements for his absent father. Damrosch dispenses early on with these orthodoxies, pointing out that there is much less evidence to support such interpretations than for many of the incidents and anecdotes rejected by Ehrenpreis as apocryphal "Swiftiana". While Ehrenpreis's triple-decker still commands respect for its thoroughness and scale, the same cannot be said by Damrosch for David Nokes, author of the most widely read academic biography after Ehrenpreis. Although his book still has the best title of any Swift biography (*Jonathan Swift: A Hypocrite Reversed*), Nokes is frequently castigated for misreading Swift – literally in the case of a letter which Damrosch says he ascribed to the wrong addressee.

It's probably not accidental that *A Hypocrite Reversed* is the least sympathetic of modern Swift biographies. Damrosch has more time for those writers on Swift who display infectious enthusiasm for their subject. As well as the previously mentioned Johnston and Le Brocquy, he praises Victoria Glendinning, whose 1998 *Jonathan Swift* is a readable and entertaining work not primarily aimed at academics. Like Glendinning, Damrosch enjoys putting glamour and mystery back into a life that in the hands of other biographers had come to resemble (in the words of Swift's friend Alexander Pope) a "long disease". Lives, whether long or short, in the eighteenth century abounded in pain and discomfort, and Damrosch refuses to see physical suffering as inevitably symbolic of psychic malaise. Even writing was hard work. Swift wrote by the dim, smoky and undoubtedly stinking light of a bulrush soaked in bacon fat because he could not afford candles for the cathedral deanery. It is humbling to think of the sheer number of words he produced in such conditions while also holding down a full-time job. Swift's work was also affected by at least one serious debility, which has been diagnosed retrospectively as Ménière's syndrome. Now recognised as a disorder of the inner ear, it causes deafness and vertigo, affecting sufferers' balance so that they are prone to falls and exhausted by the sheer effort of trying to stand upright. It is sad to read that Swift thought his illness had been caused by eating fruit. Even though he loved to eat and cultivate fruit, achieving the considerable feat of growing nectarines outdoors in Dublin, he tried to avoid plums, peaches, and the like throughout adulthood, so he thought, for the good of his health.

Medical intervention made things worse. Swift's friend the physician John Arbuthnot tried to help out by providing remedies which sound disgusting and which, like most eighteenth century medicine, had no beneficial effect and caused active harm – luckily for Swift this was confined to the pills' stated purpose, the induction of vomiting. Damrosch's unstinting and unsentimental discussion of such details comes in the form of mini-essays on relevant topics, which make good on the "world" promise of the title and add breadth to the chronological progression of individual chapters. He is a particularly good explicator of the politics of the time, which do not easily admit of concise summaries; his tone, though not intrusive, is worldly, with flashes of deadpan humour conveyed in the short punchy sentences he uses to round off a paragraph. These include the droll observation that "it rains a lot in Ireland" (possibly an autobiographical reflection on sodden overseas research trips) and the assertion he makes in discussing the allegorical significance of Gulliver's preferred fire-fighting technique in Lilliput: "urine is still urine". He also favours linguistic *aperçus*, reminding us that "conscious" could mean "conscience-stricken" and that a journal was originally the record of a single day. The combination of pleasure in detail with a measured and clear take on the big issues produces a reliable one-volume reference biography for scholars which is also entertaining enough to provide good reading for anyone with an interest in Swift or his times.

One of the claims Damrosch makes near the beginning of his book to explain the need for a new biography is that "Swift matters". This is, I think, justifiable. "Burn everything that comes from England except their people and their coal" used to be his most famous (and most misquoted) soundbite but in recent years changed priorities and transformed relationships have pushed another of his statements to the fore, one in which Swift calls for a law to be passed that would make it mandatory to "hang up half a dozen bankers every year". Swift matters not just because he said some things which, taken out of context, can be readily assimilated to modern populist sentiment. He perfected the art of crafting phrases snappy enough to become slogans but which, on closer inspection, yield disturbing and contradictory meanings.

He also (naturally) had an epigrammatic statement for this reading process, likening satire to "a sort of glass" in which beholders are likely to discern everyone's face but their own.

Not all his reflections will appeal. In a time of austerity he preached in a sermon that Ireland's working poor, "the natives" as he called them, were "from their infancy so given up to idleness and sloth, that they often choose to beg or steal, rather than support themselves with their own labour". Where compassion was due, he presented people as passive objects of suffering, "wretches" who deserved little beyond pity. In the end he became such an object himself. Having been declared of unsound mind in 1741 he was exhibited by unscrupulous carers, presumably for a fee, to anyone who cared to come and gawk. Had any of them, one wonders, read the passage where a caged Gulliver is hawked around the country fairs of Brobdingnag? Samuel Johnson wrote in a poem that Swift died "a driveller and a show", and went on in his *Lives of the Most Eminent English Poets* to add to an already flourishing body of negative, unsympathetic biography. Damrosch's balanced, informative book provides thoughtful relief from that tradition.

Poetry

The depth of Seamus Heaney's engagement with the matter of his childhood, writes BARRA Ó SEAGHDHA, goes far beyond nostalgia: we are dealing with a kind of imaginative loyalty that underpins a whole life, with the poet insisting on working and reworking the material given him by birth and inheritance.

DEIRDRE SERJEANTSON finds Clive James's solution to the problem of translating Dante's rhyme into English a highly successful one, accomplished with remarkable sensitivity and immaculate scholarship.

EILÉAN NÍ CHUILLEANÁIN writes that although critics often focus on Paul Muldoon's talent for weirdness and his technical games, the weirdness, like Flann O'Brien's version of Mad Sweeney, perhaps corresponds to the weird predicament of humanity.

Reviewing Philip Coleman's study of John Berryman, CALISTA McRAE recalls that after graduation the poet headed to Cambridge. In a later poem, he portrays himself exclaiming "Yeats, Yeats, I'm coming! It's me!" – in what McRae writes must be "one of the most ebulliently silly apostrophes in twentieth century poetry".

Dublin, writes GERARD SMYTH, has been central to the poetic imagination of Thomas Kinsella. No other writer since Joyce has so fervently mapped the city, and few writers have known it so intimately.

The Harvest In

Stepping Stones: *Interviews with Seamus Heaney* by Dennis O'Driscoll

Faber and Faber | 560 pp | ISBN: 978-0571242528

WITH THE thousands of reviews, articles, interviews and full-scale studies that Seamus Heaney's work has already attracted, it is hardly necessary here either to introduce Heaney or to use *Stepping Stones* as a mere stepping stone back to the familiar squabbles over his poetic territory – whether the land is overgrazed or overgreen, whether he should have moved out of the area entirely, whether a diploma in experimental farming techniques might not have been advisable at some stage, whether he is drawing attention away from other worthy neighbours, whether he has reinforced the traditional confinement of women's work to home and farmyard, whether he is merely walking the fields out of habit ...

Most newspaper reviews of the book contented themselves with describing the nature of the enterprise: Dennis O'Driscoll's proposing the idea of a volume of interviews; Heaney's agreeing but asking that matters should be conducted in writing; Heaney's responding to a selection of the many possible questions forwarded by O'Driscoll; and the careful crafting of answers that this allowed. Most reviews were positive, though a few emphasised that the book was for the devotee rather than the casual reader. Some offered a juicy plum or two (a subtle jab to the ribs here; a sketch of a literary legend there) as if to assure us that the pie had been fully inspected.

Some commented wonderingly on the fact that, in a period obsessed with the lives of the famous, Heaney had managed to avoid becoming the victim of a biographer. This is indeed a remarkable feat; it may at least partly be put down to the fact that he has inspired a degree of loyalty among friends that would be the despair of any scandal-sniffing biographer, compounded by the fact that there seems to be so little scandal to sniff out in the first place.

There is an implicit valuation of his wife's judgment in the way Heaney speaks of the process of making and keeping friends but, beyond some emblematic moments, Marie and the children figure almost exclusively insofar as they intersect with the writing life. As O'Driscoll says, Heaney has every right to keep the details of his personal or family life to himself; this stance is also consistent with the autobiographical, but ultimately non-confessional, impulse in his poetry.

A short-lived, rather arty Irish magazine of the 1980s once carried an interview with the Russian poet Joseph Brodsky. As question followed question, the reader could observe with a kind of awe the poet's gathering realisation that the interviewer knew absolutely nothing about him or his work. This is not the kind of thing that Dennis O'Driscoll is going to be accused of. We may assume that, at the outset, he already knew man and work intimately, but the sheer mass and detail of the questions and promptings suggest an additional thoroughness of research. Thus, if we are not entirely surprised at some of what O'Driscoll knows – wasn't there a phone call from Czesław Miłosz during that party? – we have to doff our caps when he casually drops this kind of thing: but you were skilful enough to play for the Castledawson minors, and you even received a trial for the Derry county team. O'Driscoll would not, we suspect, be a regular visitor to Semple Stadium in his home town of Thurles. Though his name figures prominently on the cover of *Stepping Stones*, as it deserves to, his performance as interviewer is, on the whole, an admirably self-effacing one.

There is no appendix listing all the unanswered questions, so if there are matters where we sensation-seeking readers might have liked a little more detail, we can only guess whether O'Driscoll was uninterested or diplomatic, or whether his curiosity might have been rebuffed. Only very rarely, as in the case of Ted Hughes, does a sequence of questions suggest an opinion different from Heaney's.

If a volume of *Selected Heaney Interviews* ever appears, it will almost unavoidably include much repetition in both questions and answers. The steady journey through the career that this volume provides overlaps of course with previous articles and interviews – how many times has Heaney recounted the way in which he heard that he had received the Nobel Prize? – but it is usefully self-contained and internally consistent. Any committed lover of Heaney's poetry will want to stand at the poet's shoulder as he casts an eye back over fifty years of work, and even dippers into the stream will be rewarded by a striking formula here, a vivid pen picture there, not to mention corrections to the record, wordplay and assorted Heaneyisms. And if *Stepping Stones* does take us from book to book, it retains a conversational quality by hopping back and forth in time and nipping up side paths as it goes along – as well as in the light, unlaboured tone of much of what Heaney says.

Heaney has the widest readership of any poet writing in English today. If he had written a relatively conventional autobiography, he would have been guaranteed even more readers than *Stepping Stones* will have. The opening chapter sends out a clear message that this is not going to be merely a relaxed stroll down memory lane, that it is a book for those who are willing to pay attention. It does indeed go down the lanes of south Derry but in a way that appeals rather too much to both the quantity surveyor and the devotee in us. There is a reason for this, but the effect is almost disconcerting at first, as this selection of questions might suggest:

> *What kind of traffic is on the road in the forties? Was there a family car? Did your mother cycle sometimes? What about the travelling shop? Was there barter of any sort – trading of eggs, for example? When I reach the farmyard, what outbuildings do I see? What's inside them? What's in the yard?*

And Heaney obliges with the appropriate detail:

> Well, as you come down the lane, you're looking into the first farm building, the one we called simply 'the shed'. It stood at the gable end of the house, a wooden-framed, zinc-roofed job, open at one end, the other walls made from flattened-out tar barrels. Old tar barrels, for some reason, were in plentiful supply. They'd had the bottoms knocked out

of them and were unriveted and unrolled so as to make a tin panel that could be nailed up on a wooden frame. Inside the shed there might be some bags of grain or potatoes or fertilizer or a farrowing crate. It had a clay floor. A smell of old meal. Implements in the corners. Swallows' nests up on the rafters.

And besides the shed?

Walk on with the gable of the house on your left and the shed on your right and you're into the back yard. One side of that is defined by the dwelling house and opposite, on the other side, say fifteen yards away, you have the byre and – later on – a pig house. The byre was an old structure, a cow house, no windows; cow stalls on your left when you went in, with room for four cows; stalls again on your right, although these weren't used for cattle in my time, more for storage of fodder. Beast smells and manure smells. A 'groop' as it was called, a sunk trench in the concrete floor running to a back outlet, to drain the piss and catch the cow dung.

And so on. (This opening section might have been revisited to bring it more into line with the later chapters – and perhaps also to keep more casual readers on board.) Flats in Belfast, rooms in Harvard, a cottage in Wicklow – these and other places will be evoked later, but not in such detail. Heaney's writing places – the room in the cottage in Glanmore or the one at the top of the house in Sandymount – are refuges, or rather nests in which memory can hatch images of the original space. This book certainly confirms what needed little confirming: that Heaney has never stopped feeding off the matter of his childhood. What the book also does, by virtue of taking us on a journey from the poet's childhood to his three score years and ten, is to lead us to reflect on the extraordinariness of this in some ways ordinary life. From one point of view, it is only the survival of the poetry that matters, but in an age in which many poets feel obliged, or pressurised, to justify both the act of writing itself and the values embodied in particular poems, Heaney's is a case worth lingering over. Ultimately what emerges from *Stepping Stones* (despite its relaxed tone) is a life held together by a set of interconnected literary and human values.

Given the extraordinary attention Heaney pays to the detail of Mossbawn, his childhood home, it would not be going too far to refer to it as a sacred place of his imagination – and in Heaney's case, as is well known, the poetic imagination is intimately bound up with memory. Not only did going to boarding school reduce his active connection with life at Mossbawn at an early stage, but the family's move to an inherited farmhouse some miles away a few years later, soon after the shocking death of the poet's young brother, reinforced the separation, and of course he would go on to live in various homes in Ireland and abroad. But it seems that, whether he is in Belfast, Dublin, Wicklow or Harvard, Heaney has to feel the thread of connection with rural Derry.

The depth and length of his engagement with the matter of childhood suggests that what is involved goes far beyond nostalgia: we are dealing with the kind of imaginative loyalty that underpins a whole life. Regardless of where he is living at the time or what creative phase he is in, Heaney persists in working and reworking the material given him by birth and inheritance. We might recall the lines from "The Badgers" in *Field Work*:

> How perilous is it to choose
> not to love the life we're shown?

We are dealing not just with a poet's loyalty to his own imaginative world, but with human loyalty too: it is as though Heaney could not bear to live with himself if his life-journey away from home involved any posture of superiority or condescension. He is a man of learning, a man of words, who refuses to contemplate any position that would disrespect the near-speechlessness of his father. ("The Stone Verdict" in *The Haw Lantern*, a kind of elegy, is a strikingly conceived exploration of this aspect of the father/son relationship.) It is noteworthy too that, in a section of the book looking at Catholic/Protestant relations and political attitudes among neighbours, there is a forceful snap to Heaney's response to this question regarding his mother:

> *How did your mother's 'whatever you say, say nothing' attitude in sectarian Ulster square with some of the characteristics you ascribed to her earlier – her alertness to 'sectarian strains' and her readiness to be 'provoked by the hidden operations of the system'?*

I suppose this should go on the record once and for all. My mother's attitude was not at all expressed by the phrase 'whatever you say, say nothing' – nor, I should say, was mine. Her use of it and my use of it put it very much in inverted commas. The phrase was a knowing acknowledgement of the power structure, a Catholic nod in answer to the Protestant wink that got the jobs and the houses. It was ironical rather than instructional. It was fundamentally an expression of anger rather than of acquiescence.

While Heaney can be seen as defending himself against misreadings of one of his most famous lines and poems, he is also clearly intent on rescuing his mother from any imputation of servility.

The social discomfort involved in homecoming is acknowledged in a passage in "Casualty", from *Field Work*, written in memory of a neighbour who died in an explosion:

Incomprehensible
To him, my other life.
Sometimes, on his high stool,
Too busy with his knife
At a tobacco plug
And not meeting my eye,
In the pause after a slug
He mentioned poetry.
We would be on our own
And, always politic
And shy of condescension,
I would manage by some trick
To switch the talk to eels
Or lore of the horse and cart
Or the Provisionals.

An anecdote in *Stepping Stones* shows Heaney's continuing awareness of the gap that might open up between the poet and his neighbours – in the gentler context of Co Wicklow in this case. Heaney has described the enforced simplicity of life at Glanmore Cottage, with its lack of running water. Asked about being socially isolated as a newcomer to Wicklow, Heaney has just mentioned the parties in Garech Browne's house in Luggala, attended by artists, musicians, film-makers … But he returns to the unspectacular daily life which was more the norm:

> We were lucky, all the same, in our neighbours: the Johnsons on one side, who had a dairy herd, and the Chapmans on the other, who did more arable farming. I remember soon after we landed, coming up the road from the village and being faced with about ten or twelve cattle galloping down the hill towards me, with Mrs Johnson well back behind them. I realized they had broken out and had to be turned, so I spread my arms and let a shout out of me the same as I would have done at home on our own land, and the beasts halted. I got them turned and, from that moment, I think I was regarded as OK.

He may mix with the great and famous on occasion but being OK with the neighbours and retaining skills picked up in childhood still matter. In this sense, as in others, Heaney will not betray his origins. Generations of British people from rural or working class homes have been cut off from their family and neighbours, and emotionally mutilated in many cases, we may surmise, by the need to adopt an accent as social camouflage or a defence against snobbery at university. This is the sacrifice that social or political success demanded. If it is occasionally possible in Ireland to meet, for example, a pastiche Trinity accent amid the broader and more honest vowels of a Co Limerick family, there is in general less pressure to put on a voice. Heaney has worked on his reading voice, but only in terms of clarity and delivery. The sense of being comfortable with the voice that registers his origins is part of what makes him such a successful reader – with subdued musicality and neither the histrionics nor the relentless jokiness that make many poetry readings so agonising. This is one area among many where Heaney is happy to express his gratitude or indebtedness to Ted Hughes:

> The one who helped me in that regard was Ted Hughes. Ted held fast to the pitch of his first voice, stayed generally faithful to his first accent … He managed to sound out his inwardness without crossing the line

towards ingratiation. When he spoke his poems, it was as if he was
retrieving them rather than reciting them. Hearing him made me want
to do likewise.

This sense of unproblematic voice, which goes from the speaking voice of
the man who reads to (though here some qualification must be in order)
the implicit authorial voice, may be something that certain schools of
criticism would see as inherently problematic; for Heaney and his listeners,
it is more a mode of validation and perhaps also of respect. It is possible to
dismiss this position as conservative, but can critics really insist that poets
write according to a set philosophical agenda? And can the ways in which
language and identity are to be doubted be prescribed dogmatically? How
radical, in any case, is the radical dissolution of all positions (except tenured
positions in Critical Theory departments)? In poetry, and probably in music
or philosophy too, it is the fullness of engagement, the fullness with which a
world is brought into being or tested, that matters – after which, readers and
critics can have their say.

As a writer, Heaney's voice has been troubled by doubt or has wobbled
towards uncertainty at various points, but there is an underlying faith in
the possibility of giving untroubled voice. The wobbles, we might say, are
eventually assimilated to the texture of the voice or are overcome; the poet's
voice changes with the years – and Heaney will, within limits, try out new
voices – but, typically, a continuity is maintained. His failure to dissolve or
fragment his voice in correct modernist-into-postmodernist style lies behind
some of the exasperation which is directed at him.

Muldoon's intellectual narcissism and power-play are much more
forgivable because the poems gesture towards the dissolution of the ego into
a multiple play of identities and voices; the monotone under the fizzle, the
amusicality with which this is accomplished – the sophisticated drone into
which John Ashbery has long settled also comes to mind – is little commented
on by those who are less interested in a line that moves through time and space
than in raw material for exegesis, in the exemplification of a theory or in the
solving of a puzzle. (Musicality here is not to be confused with the pastoral
or with the living remains of nineteenth century convention: by analogy, we
are talking as much of Boulez or Ligeti as of Vaughan Williams or Sibelius.)

When Heaney's "Parnassian" or self-imitating poems have fallen away, the poems that remain standing will continue to demonstrate a variety of music and a degree of variation within the voice. It is the luxury of readers to enjoy what is to be enjoyed in Heaney but to value other approaches and writers at the same time. It is not that Heaney's poetic mode and procedures are right in any general way; it is that they seem to be right for him. In poetic technique, as in other areas of life and writing, he does not take his inheritance as a bag of tricks to be casually shouldered.

To think about the span of life encompassed in *Stepping Stones* is to realise just how easy it would be for someone like Heaney to consider the past another country. It was open to him – through some happy intertwining of ability, personality, application and luck – to move, step by step, away from his childhood world. Already, for someone of his background to go to boarding school was to be marked out as different. To go to university was a further step away. Then there was third-level teaching, a steadily expanding reputation as a poet, international fame, prestigious positions at Harvard and Oxford, friendships with some of the most eminent writers and intellectuals of his time, a string of honours culminating in the Nobel Prize for Literature ... At this stage, we are far indeed from the boy perched in a tree overlooking a road in South Derry, the boy fascinated by frog-spawn or collecting blackberries. It would be easy to think of that childhood world as the accidental beginning of a self-shaped and highly successful career. Instead, Heaney chooses to return endlessly to his beginnings.

Was it right to list luck alongside ability, personality and application in the paragraph above? Or is it a combination of the triad of ability, personality and application that makes some of what happens to Heaney appear like luck? Whatever the truth of the matter may be, it seems that people have always been happy to give to Heaney. A primary school teacher offered to give him lessons in Latin outside of school hours, thus helping him on his way to boarding school and university. It was hinted, while he was at Queen's, that the path to postgraduate study at Oxford might be made smooth for him. (It was Heaney himself who failed to follow through on the matter, for various reasons.) Not only did he have a book published ahead of some slightly senior contemporaries but he was taken up by Faber as a relative unknown at a time when the Faber poetry list was the one that mattered.

It was Heaney's luck that the young Helen Vendler, soon to become an influential voice in the American literary critical world, was entranced by his work in the early 1970s and was to become a major interpreter and advocate, as well as a friend. Towards the end of the same decade, Elizabeth Bishop having reached retirement age, Heaney was offered some teaching at Harvard at just the right moment for him. And so it goes – friendly hands helping him towards the top, with few if any bodies left in the bushes along the way (though envious mutterings may be heard here and there).

Some of what Heaney has had to deal with – the scrutinising of every line for what it says about the state of the nation, the world, the relations between men and women; the distance between the home ground of his imagination and the world in which he operates as a writer – may be the price of success. There is a limit to the sympathy that will be felt for carriers of that burden, but it cannot be denied that Heaney has carried it with more grace than most. Should we simply say that he has managed the journey and the burden well? The language of management – with its hint of manipulation or calculation – does not quite do justice to what is involved.

A particular memory world, a particular intelligence, a particular talent: these are the givens, as it were. However, it is the handling of the materials and the handling of the life over decades that mark Heaney out. Here it becomes impossible not to speak in terms of vocation, a concept that can be related to such terms as discipline, patience, conscience, respect and perhaps husbandry – and then to alertness, intuition, the weather eye. Heaney was given a particular piece of the world to tend. It has never been in his nature, it would seem, to make wild, unprepared moves. Caring for his patch of land is a matter of attention and repetition. At the same time, if you keep your nose to the ground at all times, if you don't keep an eye out for possibilities or for changes in the weather, if you don't notice the field that might be acquired from the ageing farmer next door, then the farm may slowly run down. Heaney seems to gather experience and then let intuition, or what comes his way, guide him at a certain point – and though success of various kinds (publication, position, prizes) came early to him, he has never been in a rush; instead, he has seemed to ease his way forward. *Stepping Stones* reminds us that, for Heaney, the poet is not simply a producer of individual poems but a person with a special responsibility: the poet's intuitive, emotional and intellectual equipment must be kept in good order if the long-term internal conversation from poem to poem is to be sustained. Even if the terminology changes somewhat over time – and Heaney is here distinguishing between craft (a certain formal excellence) and technique – something of this is already to be found in "Feeling into Words", a well-known, relatively early essay:

> Technique, as I would define it, involves not only a poet's way with words, his management of metre, rhythm and verbal texture; it involves also a definition of his stance towards life, a definition of his own reality. It involves the discovery of ways to go out of his normal bounds and raid the inarticulate: a dynamic alertness that mediates between the origins of feeling in memory and experience and the formal ploys that express these in a formal work of art. Technique entails the watermarking of your essential patterns of perception, voice and thought into the touch and texture of your lines; it is that whole creative effort of the mind's and body's resources to bring the meaning of experience within the jurisdiction of form.

There is the groundwork, the maintaining of the equipment, but also alertness for the moment when discovery beckons. Certain values are inherent in the vocation of poetry when conceived in this fashion, values that will also shape the life of the poet. A quarter of a century later, Heaney is saying something similar, this time in relation to Eliot:

> What one learns ultimately from Eliot is that the activity of poetry is solitary, and if one is to rejoice in it, one has to construct something upon which to rejoice.

From the beginning, there is a celebratory, praise-giving side to Heaney's gift, a pleasure in the detail of the world that is intimately bound up with pleasure in the detail of language, in verbal forms adequate to the world. He has been associated almost to the point of caricature with language evocative of sod, clay, bog, wetness ... but his range runs to the perfectly pitched memory of sunlit domesticity in "Mossbawn, Sunlight" and on to the airy world of "Squarings".

In keeping with the notion of vocation, Heaney seems quickly to have developed a feeling for material that could trigger sustained exploration and revisiting. There are repeated references to this throughout *Stepping Stones*, the title itself of course evoking ongoing movement rather than fixed achievement.

> And once I opened those channels, I got the surge, definitely …
>
> There was a terrific sense of having arrived somewhere, and at the same time a definite anxiety. Would you get off the ground again – and on course – and then get landed again safely …
>
> From the moment I wrote it, I felt promise in 'Bogland'. Without having any clear notion of where it would lead or even whether I would go back to the subject, I realized that new co-ordinates had been established …
>
> It seemed the right poem to close with since it didn't seem to stop after the last line. I don't know how to explain the dam-burst …
>
> It was a visitation, an onset, and as such, powerfully confirming …
>
> The pattern was always the simple one of setting out, encountering tests and getting through to a new degree of independence …
>
> I was sitting in this most beautiful reading room with the rain coming down on the glass dome. Suddenly I wrote a few lines and it became a twelve-line, four three-lines, thing. It felt given, strange and unexpected; I didn't quite know where it came from, but I knew immediately it was there to stay. It seemed as solid as an iron bar … The form operated for me as a generator of poetry.

It is hard to imagine any poet managing a lifetime of pure celebration. Lust and rage were energisers of Yeats's imagination, generators of his poetry. In Heaney's case, guilt and doubt – or perhaps the working through of various seams of guilt and doubt – seem to have become primary generators, though he will always emerge for air from time to time. So much has been written about the particular forms of guilt involved – particularly in relation to political and personal choices made in the 1970s – that there seems little point in scrutinising that particular ground here. It is true that Heaney took it on himself to question his own gift in its relationship, or adequacy, to the political traumas and violence of the period. The poet felt his personal dilemmas and voice "amplified within a larger historical acoustic", to steal a phrase from his essay on MacDiarmid, but also potentially diminished by it.

Though there is quite a lot of incidental detail on the politics of the North (a subject that is probably not Dennis O'Driscoll's forte) in *Stepping Stones*, Heaney tends to underplay the intensity of his own engagement (however slantwise) with the matter – preferring at this point to look back to the writing of the poems themselves:

> What I felt at the beginning of the Troubles was what any poet would have felt in the circumstances, a certain undefined accountability. Implicated in the politics, yes, but without any real appetite for the political role.

Heaney's reading of his own position is very nuanced, as might be expected. In *Stepping Stones*, he is interesting on the sectarian realities he encountered in the fifties and sixties. He is quite frank about the mixed emotions and pressures he felt as a member of the Northern minority, of the Irish majority (if we may put it thus), and as a writer with friends among and dealings with the British establishment, literary and other, during and after the hunger strike crisis. (For a very different interpretation of one episode recounted here, Danny Morrison's website can be consulted.) The subtle way in which Heaney was sounded out about the possibility of becoming poet laureate is interesting both as, let's admit it, pure gossip and as an insight into the workings of British power. Though a few of his phrases have been picked up by politicians, it is no disrespect to him to say that, in analytical terms, he does not take us much beyond standard nationalist positions. (His brief summing up of the unreality of the Peace People's position is absolutely spot on, however.) At the same time, there is quite an evolution from 1960s poems such as "Requiem for the Croppies" and "Docker" to the later poems on the Troubles.

The national and sexual politics of *North*, in particular, has thrown up some fine criticism but a few points may be made here. First, the noise around the poems means that the voice of the poems themselves, or the poems as experienced, is easily forgotten. Second, as already suggested, there is no particular reason to look to Heaney for political insight as such. Third, where the Troubles are concerned, the Heaney that matters is neither the willing or unwilling lender of phrases to politicians nor the permanent exhibit in the museum of incorrect choices, but, as Vendler emphasises, the poet working from image to image and from poem to poem, trying (and sometimes failing) to do justice to the challenges thrown at him by the violence that is rending his (extended) home ground. Fourth, after the much criticised sexual politics of *North*, Heaney went on to write the outstanding love poems that appeared in *Field Work*.

If, as suggested earlier, Heaney has taken doubts and guilts into the heart of his writing process, it may be that he took on too much of a load in the late seventies. Thirty years later, *Field Work* still retains a curiously unsettled quality: alongside the starry but guilt-invaded lyricism of "Oysters", the hushed tenderness of "Homecomings", the deft plaiting and replaiting of "The Harvest Bow", the surprising crop of mature love poems, the estranged formality of "A Dream of Jealousy", the almost palpable surge of history through the funeral scene in "Casualty", there are eruptions of overwrought language and imagery as well as failures of touch (as in the end of "The Strand at Lough Beg", the focus of indirect self-accusation later). There was no knowing where Heaney was going. The book that followed, *Station Island*, is still hugely important to him. The title poem, an internal dialogue cast as a dialogue of the poet with literary and personal ghost-voices, both accusing and enabling, enacts a ritual casting-off of oppressive burdens. A key event in the poet's personal narrative, the poem in itself may prove less central to readers of Heaney as time goes on. Some freedom of voice is immediately achieved in the Sweeney Redivivus section that follows the poem proper, a freedom built on in *The Haw Lantern*, though with something stiff and willed about it at times.

Some have speculated, and Heaney himself does not disagree, that the loss of both parents in the 1980s brought grief, of course, a revisiting of personal and family history that is seen in many poems, but also the psychic freedom of being his own man rather than a dutiful son. If Heaney was always at heart a celebrator, a venerator, a singer, it is the final, untroubled release of the praise-singer in himself that sings off the page in the eleventh chapter of *Stepping Stones*, devoted to *Seeing Things*, and especially to "Squarings".

> I felt free as a kid skimming stones, and in fact the relationship between individual poems in the different sections has something of the splish-splash, one-after-anotherness of stones skittering and frittering across water ... Many of the lines just wafted themselves up out of a kind of poetic divine right ... I learned what inspiration feels like but not how to

summon it. Which is to say that I learned how waiting is part of the work
... I got into the habit of swooping on anything that stimulated memory
or association ... It felt given, strange and unexpected ...

Even lifted out of context, these extracts convey Heaney's excitement at
even the memory of that run of poems, the moment when he came into
his reward. As already suggested, Heaney's vocational conception of poetry
meant that he had to trust that his disciplined tending of the ground over
years would lead to harvest. It is implicit in his whole handling of his own
gifts, as in the way he assesses other writers, that, if the writing self is kept
open and tuned throughout a life, the poems will come through and renew
themselves accordingly. In the elation over the coming of "Squarings", there
may also be gratitude, or relief, that his core beliefs – a bet on the future, as
with any life-choice – have been validated. Heaney had never counted on a
romantic pattern of brief flares and long splutterings. Though in the coda
to *Stepping Stones* he wonders if he should not have sometimes disregarded
"Miłosz's injunction and my own censor and let bad spirits rather than good
spirits choose me, as he says, 'for their instrument'".

Heaney gives the impression of largely accepting himself, the life he was
given, the life he has led and the work he has done:

*In a television interview, to mark your fiftieth birthday, you spoke of three
phases in a writer's life – the starting out, the taking stock (at around thirty),
and the new freedom of later life. Does this still seem valid to you as an
analysis – or has your perspective changed, now that you are approaching
seventy? Is there a fourth phase?*

If there is, I haven't got to it yet. But I can imagine it – a phase of solitary
wandering at the edge of the mighty waters. What I said in that interview
I have repeated often since, but in a somewhat different way. I believe
the three phases turn out to be cyclic, that there are renewed surges of
endeavour in your life and art, and that, in every case, the movement
involves a pattern of getting started, keeping going and getting started
again. Some books are a matter of keeping going; some – if you're lucky
– get you started again. *Seeing Things* was a new start. There, for once, the
old saw came true: life began, or began again, at fifty.

It is from within this overall pattern that Heaney speaks in *Stepping Stones*, but of course we are not talking about a manual of untroubled poetic serenity and, as both the conversation with O'Driscoll and a reading of the later poems make clear, anger and self-questioning have by no means been eliminated. Nor, lest the impression be given that *Stepping Stones* rises entirely above the literary fray, does Heaney grant absolution without penance to those who have annoyed, angered or slighted him down the years. He is, after all, a poet of memory. If Michael and Edna Longley resented the fact that Heaney was more highly rated within Philip Hobsbaum's famous Group, "they had a status drawn from their own examining board, so to speak, one that consisted of themselves and Derek Mahon and, at that time, Eavan Boland". Heaney suggests that there was "no begrudging of achievement per se. The awkwardness or resentment set in when one was promoted over the other by publication or praise or later by the award of a prize."

There is reference to an episode recounted by Michael Longley when, with drink taken, Heaney was told, rather vehemently, that Mahon was the better poet. Heaney is no prize-fighter, but he can throw a nice punch while gliding out of reach:

> Michael told Jody Allen Randolph that 'we competed with each other more ferociously than perhaps we now remember', but I don't think I considered myself 'in competition' with anybody. Admittedly I may have been the cause of it in others, which only means, come to think of it, I was raising the standard without even trying.

It is clear, too, that Heaney has not enjoyed the relentless critical attention he has received from Edna Longley. His attitude to James Simmons's criticism is even clearer:

> What bothered me in the end was the disjunction between his snotteriness in print and his pleasant ways when we'd meet, but it all arose from big temperamental and cultural differences. And deep down my irk was eased by the realization that Jimmy was just getting back at me. Without my ever having to tell him, he knew I didn't rate his poetry very highly.

Because it is a summing up, Heaney is more unbuttoned in *Stepping Stones* than we are used to. Seán Ó Riada was a very important and energising cultural figure in the 1960s, but there has been a tendency in some quarters to mythologise his achievement as well as his personality. Heaney, who elegised him in *Field Work*, catches both the energy and the theatricality.

Did you get on well with Ó Riada?

Well, yes, but I have to say his posturing irked me. Swirling the snifter of brandy and brandishing the cigar. Setting himself up as commissar, interrogating rather than conversing. I remember walking into the Club Bar that week [late 1968] and being asked rather grandly – in front of Kinsella and Montague – 'And where do you stand on the North?' I should have said that, unlike the company I was in, I'd stood on it for thirty years, but I just let it go. I admired him even if I didn't get close.

Heaney's Ó Riada does not cancel Kinsella's beautiful prose tribute to a friendship in *Fifteen Dead*, but it has its own truth.

Silence has been the poet's main critical tool where some of his contemporaries are concerned. There is also an implicit self-evaluation in the company he keeps in his essays, and in the great writers he summons up, or is visited by, in his poems. (Kinsella is one of the few living Irish writers to be written about at length; their temperaments may be different, but Heaney would respond to Kinsella's unwavering concentration on the building, unbuilding and rebuilding of his own imaginative world.) On the whole, and this is an aspect of the thrift that was mentioned earlier, Heaney has concentrated his energies on working his own ground. Ultimately, it is up to us readers, and the readers of the future, to decide how much of his work we value and how he stands in relation to his predecessors and contemporaries. In addition to criticism by silence, Heaney also displays critical thrift – an excess of it, perhaps, for those of us who might like to witness more meeting of worlds – when he simply turns away (not always in dismissive fashion) from forms of writing not relevant to him:

Whatever the Beats and the Liverpool Poets were doing, it didn't put me through the eye of my own needle the way 'The Bull Moses' or 'The Windhover' did. I had a feeling of being dispersed rather than concentrated.

Asked about sound poetry, he replies, not surprisingly: "No, I have nothing to declare in that area." About Charles Olson, Robert Duncan, William Carlos Williams and company, he has more to say, as here:

> I just couldn't slip the halter of the verse line and the stanza. I came to happy enough terms with Carlos Williams, whose ear is actually very delicate, but I couldn't spread out and let go projectively.

He is prompted to return to the subject later:

> Charles Olson and Robert Duncan were serious, completely dedicated poets, with an elevated concept of their role, but when I think of them the image that comes to mind is of two life-size figures waving and creating this larger than life shadow play. There was too much gesture for my taste and too little gist.

We might wonder what Heaney has made or would make of Charles Wright's stunningly compacted lyrics in "Skins", "Tattoos" or the volume *China Trace*, but the question is not raised. Another comment, arising from discussion of his translation of *Beowulf*, sums up Heaney's attitude to American writing: "The experience was physical and the result different from the generally frictionless idiom of transatlantic poetry."

Such comments, when set alongside others distancing himself from "open-weave" poetry and various positive references to poetry as felt in the body (there is even a reference to muscle-tone) point to the consistency of Heaney's world: even if he later "takes off", he starts from an object, a gist, a body, a grid, an enclosed rather than an open field, a form that can take pressure. His first urge as a writer was to touch, to dig, to excavate. Later he might look skyward and let gusts of strangeness and exaltation blow through his imagination, but he is a poet of attachment, even at his freest. For an artist to claim unlimited freedom would imply an art disconnected from human and natural life, from limits, from endings, from death.

In the later sections of *Stepping Stones*, there are many illuminating comments on translation, on age and writing, and on the writers Heaney admires. Ted Hughes and Czesław Miłosz are his two unshakable reference points, in life as in poetry, returned to again and again. He is never afraid that expressing admiration for the qualities of others might lead to some diminution in his own position or authority. The poet's credo can be found in his many essays, by implication and in partial statement in his poems, but here it is presented anew in a conversational style that can shift easily to the epigrammatic and the reflective. A reviewer should not be a pig digging up every truffle in the wood; readers will sniff them out for themselves. Heaney holds the line steadily, falling neither into false modesty nor into arrogance. It would be difficult not to emerge from *Stepping Stones* without increased respect or liking for the man and understanding of the poet.

O'Driscoll raises the matter of the many conferences, launches, conferrings and other public events in which Heaney participates. "Ongoing civic service, I suppose," Heaney responds. The grace and patience with which he handles such demands on his time and energy point to another aspect of the poetic vocation as he conceives it. Life has been good to him in many ways; poetry has enriched his existence both privately and in the social and intellectual worlds it has opened up to him. In return, though under no obligation to roll up his shirtsleeves and take part in the *meitheal*, he performs his neighbourly duty as few in his position would.

To anyone who is considering inviting Heaney to perform such duties again, a reading of the later sections of the book, and of the coda, is recommended. Perhaps the poet should be left master of his own time. He has made an excellent recovery from the stroke he suffered some years ago. He speaks touchingly – humorously too – of this, of the sheer joy of existence in its best moments and of the potential nearness of death. Whether a further late harvest of poems is due or not, Heaney deserves to enjoy these years as he sees fit. He sees no reason not to keep going. And we have the poems, the essays and now *Stepping Stones* to be going on with.

The poet and critic Dennis O'Driscoll died in December 2012. Seamus Heaney died in August 2013.

DEIRDRE SERJEANTSON | 2013

A Single Volume Bound by Love

The Divine Comedy by Dante Alighieri, translated by Clive James

Picador | 560 pp | ISBN: 978-1447242192

IN 1509, Pope Julius II commissioned Raphael to paint the frescos which decorate the Stanza della Segnatura in the Vatican. The result was the series of conversation pieces we know today, involving the great men (and a very few great women) of Western civilisation arranged according to their own particular species of genius: the philosophers of the School of Athens; the poets clustered around Apollo on Mount Parnassus; the theologians at a heavenly altar for the Disputation of the Eucharist. In this exalted company, Dante Alighieri is unique in appearing twice. On Parnassus, he can be seen standing at Homer's right hand; but the same aquiline profile and laurel crown is also visible on the adjoining wall, where, in the company of Thomas Aquinas and Gregory the Great, he can be seen playing his part in theological debate.

Raphael's twin portraits are a tribute to the poet's range as it appeared at the beginning of the sixteenth century – canonical writer, honorary saint. But he was shortly to be reinvented. The new Protestant reformers, busily gathering material, noticed that Dante's hell was well populated with popes being punished for their misdeeds. This was a coup for the anti-papal cause. Dante was deemed a Protestant *avant la lettre* and was duly co-opted to appear in polemical texts like the bestselling *Catalogue of Witnesses to the Truth* (1556) in the pages of which he rubbed shoulders with Martin Luther and

Jean Calvin. The Vatican, meanwhile, was not to be deflected from its own opinion. Certain inflammatory passages were recommended for excision from the *Commedia*, but Raphael's vision of the sanctified poet held true. In the Stanza della Segnatura, Dante continued to stand undisturbed among the saints at their centuries-long holy hour.

This potential for radical reinvention has served Dante well. It has certainly kept his translators busy. In the late eighties, Theodore Cauchey calculated that we had forty English translations of the whole *Commedia*, all fourteen thousand lines of it; twenty of the *Inferno*; eleven *Purgatorios*; six *Paradisos*. His numbers are already out of date: there are at least five new accounts of hell, including those by Ciaran Carson (2002) and Sean O'Brien (2006); and the list does not include translations of shorter excerpts or works showing a looser influence. That catalogue would start with Chaucer, and would rapidly spool from the compiler's grasp under the weight of the names: Milton, Browning, Byron, Eliot, Joyce. William Blake spent his last day on earth sketching illustrations for the *Commedia*. Mary Shelley invoked Dante in her political writings as a champion of liberty, and Éamon de Valera may have expected something similar when he set out on December 6th, 1921 to chair a paper comparing the linguistic fortunes of Dante's Tuscan with those of contemporary Irish. He was interrupted with the news that the Anglo-Irish Treaty had been signed in London that morning, but presumably, Dante continued to stand for freedom regardless.

More recently, we have had the video game Dante's Inferno (2010), in which the muscle-bound poet cleans up the underworld; and Dan Brown has just released his *Inferno* (in which a muscle-bound Harvard professor of symbology cleans up the underworld). There is something in Dante to justify almost all of these remakings – not just in his enormous cast of characters, but in his own history. He was politician as well as poet, lover as well as scholar. He was even, like every male citizen of Florence, an occasional soldier. If he did not also find time to set up, in his more accessible works, codes warning of fiendish schemes to control the world's population through the dissemination of incurable viruses, at least someone else was on hand to make good that oversight.

Dan Brown's *Inferno* will jostle in the bookshops with Clive James's new verse translation. In a long tradition of reimagining the *Commedia*, they both play their parts. What is perhaps unexpected is that, of the two, it is James's poem which challenges the pieties of Dantean translation. To be at the centre of a conspiracy theory is virtually a mark of literary distinction (look at Shakespeare's *Sonnets*), but the body of theoretical writing about translating Dante suggests that some of James's changes will appear more dramatic than the mere introduction of a few chase scenes through the Palazzo Vecchio.

The first of these is a question of form. The *Commedia* is written in Dante's signature *terza rima* (aba bcb cdc). He is so powerfully identified with this stanzaic structure that his followers can invoke him simply by arranging their lines in groups of three. Yeats wrote "Cuchulain Comforted" in prose, but recast it in unrhymed tercets, presumably to lend Dante's weight to his vision of Cuchulain in the underworld. True *terza rima*, however, is not easy to pull off in English – the lack of rhyme words makes it difficult to sustain. Mary Sidney employed it some time around 1600 to write her translation of Petrarch's *Triumph of Death*. The metre contorts her lines – she has to fight them into submission, where Petrarch's Italian seems to tumble naturally into rhyme. Translators of Dante have experienced similar struggles. Dorothy L Sayers retained the original form but sacrificed much of Dante's meaning to the exigencies of her metre. Longfellow, on the other hand, kept the tercets, but not the rhyme. Mark Musa, author of the Penguin Classics edition, followed Longfellow's example, producing unrhymed iambic pentameter in stanzas three lines long. Other forms have been tried, but this remains the most popular option: the tercet seems to operate throughout the world of translations as the visible guarantor of communion with Dante.

It is interesting, therefore, that James repudiates the bond. In place of trios, he gives us quatrains and a pattern of loose rhymes: abab, ababa, and other minor variations. Rhyme itself is controversial. Musa's introduction suggests that it is unwarranted: "It cannot be proved that rhyme necessarily makes a verse better: Milton declared rhyme to be a barbaric device, and many modern poets resolutely avoid it." The fact remains, however, that the experience of reading Milton is very different from that of reading Dante. Milton relies on the gravitational pull of his verse paragraphs to carry the reader along, but this effect depends on a magnificent distortion of English: he holds his sentences in suspense, and keeps the eye moving, by withholding his verbs over a page at a time. To duplicate this technique in a translation of Dante would be untrue to the effect of the *Commedia*, which is in turns more intimate, more demotic, and more obscene than anything in Milton. The conversational tone was not hampered by the demands of the rhyme scheme: for Dante, the abundance of rhyme words in Italian made *terza rima* a rhythm which could at least be made to sound unforced. Meanwhile, the interlocking pattern of sounds and echoes compelled the reader onwards through the long poem.

Clive James's quatrains are the highly effective compromise of a poet who has absorbed all of this; who is aware both of the demands of form, and of the limitations of the English language. He uses rhyme like Dante, to give movement and lightness to his five hundred pages of text, and to punctuate his points: each of the cantos, for instance, ends on a rhyming couplet, like the close of act on the Elizabethan stage. At the same time, the demands of the cross-rhymed quatrains are less strenuous than that of *terza rima*, so that his verse has a Byronic flexibility. It can accommodate lyrical hymns to the dawn as well as the detail of doctrinal exposition in heaven. It can also manage the mockery of the damned. Here Virgil, outraged that the demons have wilfully misdirected him through hell, complains to the hypocritical Friar:

> My Leader stood with bent head, mortified.
> 'The one that hooks the sinners over there
> Sold us a bill of goods,' he said, whereat
> The Friar grinned. 'Yes, wasn't that unfair?
> I think I once heard, in Bologna, that
> The Devil sometimes has resort to vice.
> He has been known to say what isn't true.
> I've heard he isn't really very nice.'

Quatrains have the quality of being, by their very nature, more capacious than the traditional tercet. In James's hands, this affords the opportunity to effect another small revolution: he folds the editorial glosses into the body of his text. Editions of Dante tend to come shored up with explanatory notes. There are early-modern copies where the verse is a small island, barely holding its ground against the encroaching waves of commentary. You can dip in for whatever Dante left unexplained: the name of the pope who made "the great refusal" by resigning the papacy (presumably no longer a mortal sin); the time of year signified by the confluence of the stars; probably, in fact, a warning about artificially created viruses designed to wipe out a tenth of the world's population unless there's a Harvard symbologist available to save the day. This sort of commentary tradition adheres to very few works – the Bible, Virgil, Ovid – and translators have generally been content to preserve the ambiguity of the text, leaving the commentators to pin down the meaning in the margins. Sometimes the alternative was dangerous: when William Tyndale was working on English Bible in 1534, he and his proof-reader came to blows over the question of whether introducing explanatory paraphrase into the body of the text represented a blasphemous meddling with scripture. They were right that the whole enterprise was risky: Tyndale was executed eighteen months later.

To judge by the reaction to the absent footnotes in certain reviews of the American edition, James should have approached his decision with no less of a *frisson*. His risk, however, has paid off: the needful information, whether it be the likeliest identifications for anonymous characters, or details for a reference grown obscure, is supplied unobtrusively and accurately. The scholarship which informs his reading of controversial points in the poem is immaculate: a necessary precaution, perhaps, in a book dedicated to his wife, Prue Shaw, one of the most distinguished Dante scholars of her generation. More remarkable is the sensitivity with which he approaches the task. Early on, for example, Dante introduces his guide through hell, the poet Virgil. He does so indirectly. The figure encountered in the dark wood says that he is the poet who sang of "that just son of Anchises". Anchises was the father of Aeneas: the shade is claiming authorship of the *Aeneid*. James adds the more telling name to the mix. In his version, Virgil announces

> I sang about Anchises son, the just
> Aeneas, pious, peerless.

It is one thing to have your reading interrupted while you identify Anchises in the footnotes. It is another to be deprived of the particular readerly pleasure of making connections. Dante was constantly gesturing beyond his text to a vast hinterland of literary tradition. Now, just as for the *Commedia*'s earliest readers, there is satisfaction to be gained in connecting the allusion on the page to others stored in the memory. James is not immune to its appeal. He might furnish the name of Aeneas within the text, but next to it he makes an addition. Aeneas is "pious": the Virgilian epithet which followed that hero through an entire epic. It is as "Pious Aeneas" that he fled Troy, and he continued pious as he seduced and abandoned Dido to her death in Carthage and arrived in Italy to fight Turnus. The interpolation affords us the pleasure of recognising the reference, but it also gestures towards a central theme in the *Commedia*, and offers a moment to contemplate it. Aeneas's ruthless piety is the essence of Roman virtue – loyalty to fatherland – but it is not the piety of Christians: Virgil is eventually left on the threshold of paradise, uncomprehending. James might gloss the hard places, but he isn't going to spoonfeed us.

The properties of form and metre, however controversial, are only the accidents of translation. The crucial distinction, or so it would appear, in recent approaches to the *Commedia* lies in the conception of Dante: man for all seasons, or local bard. TS Eliot was the advocate of the universal Dante, but, he suggested, this quality was partly the result of a fortuitous fact of language as spoken in Florence around 1300:

> Dante's universality was not solely a personal matter. The Italian language, and especially the Italian language in Dante's age, gains much by being the product of universal Latin. There is something much more local about the languages in which Shakespeare and Racine had to express themselves.

It is true that the slippage between Virgil's language and Dante's is very slight. Dante can move from Latin to Italian in the confines of a single sentence. It may have been that quality which laid the portals of the *Commedia* open to Eliot and his immediate predecessors, the *Dantisti* of the classically educated nineteenth century, and allowed them to pluck out characters caught in the web of universal passions: Tennyson's defiant Ulysses, Rossetti's tender Francesca. Their versions, however, remain intrinsically local in spite of themselves. Ulysses's heroism is the fervour of the Victorian explorer, or the Victorian missionary, not the sublime discontent of Dante's sailor. Francesca's sweetness is the product of nineteenth century Romanticism, and not a reflection of the mendacious and bitter beauty met on the winds of hell.

Even the language of the poem is far from the pure Tuscan which Eliot saw as the next best thing to Latin. In fact, the *Commedia* is a polyglot medley. We hear Virgil's classical Latin, but also snatches of the Vulgate. Arnaut Daniel addresses us from purgatory in the Provençal of his own verse. There is a language of hell, often left unattempted by translators who simply reproduce Dante's nonsense sounds "Pape Satàn, pape Satàn aleppe!", but here rendered with aplomb: "The Pope pops Satan, Satan pips the Pope". And there is the opposite of language: Dante and Virgil come to the ninth circle of hell, which is guarded by Nimrod, who built the Tower of Babel and thus oversaw the shattering of a unified human language into mutually incomprehensible fragments. Dante's Nimrod speaks one indecipherable line: "Raphèl maí amèche zabí almi", which James neatly represents with a string of words meaning "word" in incompatible tongues: "Palabra wort kotoba word parole!" Even the Italian in the poem is not homogenous. We are constantly reminded of the other dialects around him – from Sicily, Sardinia, Lombardy – because Dante moves through the poems following familiar accents, snatches of patois, the particular sounds of home.

This sense of place seems to underlie the most significant recent translations of the *Commedia*. We are perhaps more attuned to the local than we used to be. Shakespeare was once the ultimate repository of grand universal types: now we ransack him for perspectives on Captain MacMorris's Irishness. There is something intrinsically untranslatable about the local and specific, which is liberating for the translator: he or she can admit the impossibility of the task and set about finding a set of equivalents. Derek Walcott's Caribbean epic, *Omeros*, is a poem about the aftermath of colonisation in his home, the island of St Lucia. The conceit is borrowed from Homer, but once the narrator descends into the island's underworld, his imagery comes from Dante. The *Inferno*'s Malebolge is the circle of the fraudulent and here Walcott bestows on it a new generation of sinners:

> [the] bubbling lead erupted with speculators
> whose heads gurgled in the lava of the Malebolge
> mumbling deals as they rose. These were the traitors
> who, in elected office, saw the land as views
> for hotels and elevated into waiters
> the sons of others, while their own learnt something else.

Irish writers have tended to see in the walled city of hell an image of Belfast's watchtowers during the Troubles. Ciaran Carson makes this explicit in his introduction, and his *Inferno* is set out among borders and precincts. Heaney's 1979 collection *Field Work* is in conversation with Dante throughout. One of the poems, "The Strand at Lough Beg", an elegy for his cousin lost in sectarian violence, begins with an epigraph from the *Purgatorio*, but the debt to Dante comes into focus in the final poem of the collection, his translation of the Ugolino episode from *Inferno*. The reader encounters Ugolino in the depths of hell, among the murderers. He is frozen in a fierce embrace with Archbishop Ruggiero, upon whose head he gnaws, as he explains through his story. Ugolino tells of being locked in a tower by Ruggiero and left to starve with his sons. They died one by one, and he, blind and starving, ate their bodies. The account is not an honest one: Ugolino leaves out his own betrayals, and his part in the internecine conflict which led to the destruction of his family. The innocence of the victims and the manner in which a generation might be consumed by the quarrels of its fathers comes across in Heaney's spare rendering of Dante's text, but he stamps it as Irish with one interpolated image: Ugolino, gnawing the head of his enemy, is here made "a famine victim at a loaf of bread".

The truth of Dante's rage at corruption and folly is cast into clearer relief by the transplanted details of these translations, and James, in his *Divine Comedy*, shows that he recognises the power of this form of renewal. As with Heaney, the telling choices in his diction are discreet in themselves, but overwhelming in their impact. His vision of hell, for instance, emerges out of the shadow of the concentration camp. When Dante and Virgil pass through the gates to the underworld, they encounter the monster Minos, who sorts the damned into the varying circles of hell and thereby decides their fate. Minos was a classical figure, the judge of the dead in the *Aeneid*. James gives him an edge of more familiar horror:

> Here, deciding who'll be sent
> To which reception, the Selector looms
> Whose name is Minos.

"Reception" is a warning, an incongruously modern word; the capitalisation of the official "Selector" brings the scene into focus. It conjures up the spectre of Josef Mengele, Selektor at Auschwitz, who prowled the queues of new arrivals, choosing them for labour, for medical experiment and for the gas chamber. It reflects fresh significance back on the beginning of the previous canto, where Dante, with the "naked troop" of the dead, passes through the gates to hell and looks up at the mottos carved upon them. They may not claim that "Arbeit macht frei" – if anything, they are more honest, and more sonorous in James's wonderfully monumental rendering, "Forget your hopes. They were what brought you here.", but the images readily overlap. The victims of the concentration camps are not to be identified with the *Inferno*'s justly condemned sinners, but the comprehensive cruelty and barrenness of Dante's hell finds a sound equivalent here. It is an essential counterbalance to the fascination and colour of the stories which emerge from the depths: without the suffering, Dante's point is missed.

James is the right generation to have the image of the prison camp seared into the imagination. He was born in 1939, and his father was a prisoner of war who died on his flight home to Australia in 1945. The collision of these two types of hell in the poet's mind, however, may come from another source. Primo Levi, before the outbreak of war, had been a student of Dante. In 1944, imprisoned in Auschwitz, he turned to him again, reconstructing the *Commedia* from memory as a bulwark against the horrors of the camp. James has written extensively about Levi, and will know the chapter of *If This is a Man* in which Levi guides another prisoner through the *Inferno*. The poem was a refuge, but it was also an apt motif: against the backdrop of the smoke and the gas, Levi and his companion are another pair of pilgrims in hell. Levi bestows his humanity and vulnerability on James's Dante; around him, the devils and the sinners suddenly look worse.

Here, as elsewhere, James undermines the distinction of a local and a universal Dante: as with Heaney and Walcott and Carson, its very specificity draws attention to its broader relevance. For the original reader, Dante must have been neither local nor universal but both simultaneously. It is true that Dante discovered his own neighbours on the roads of hell, which must have thrilled the readers from across the way; but he also encountered a shared tradition which transcended Tuscany – the shade of Myrrha risen from her father's bed, Hecuba barking like a dog with grief, Francis of Assisi wooing poverty like a courtly lover. We can (nudged when needed by the notes) lay claim to that broader heritage – but the local dimension is not out of reach. The denizens of thirteenth century Italy have taken up residence in the townlands of our minds. We are on nodding acquaintance with Ugolino even without knowing Dante, because of introductions from Heaney and Rodin and Fuseli. This means that the experience of reading the poem has changed, even aside from questions of language and verse form. James, characteristically, grasps this. His *Commedia* is caught in the act of evolving. This is Dante in purgatory, describing scenes of ruin:

> And Troy I saw in ashes. Ilion!
> Pride brought your topless towers low …

The topless towers are anachronistic. They belong to Christopher Marlowe, who, some time around 1592, set *Dr Faustus* to woo Helen of Troy, possessor of the "face that launched a thousand ships / And burnt the topless towers of Ilium". Similarly, Virgil takes his final leave of Dante while channelling WE Henley's "Invictus": "Of your soul / I make you captain." The neutrals rush past on the bank of the Acheron, "their pride to have no prejudice". This is not lazy writing. It is an act of creative fidelity to the experience of reading Dante.

The *Commedia* is an encyclopedic text. The sum of human knowledge at the cusp of the Renaissance, whether astronomical, theological or philosophical, is gathered in its pages. All of Dante's literary ancestors were contained in it. He chats with Homer and Lucan, but he also borrows their effects – so, for instance, the thieves who are constantly turning into snakes and back again are borrowed from Ovid's catalogue of transformation, the *Metamorphoses*. To recreate that effect of all-inclusiveness, James performs another type of translation. The Troy of the modern imagination is provided with Marlowe's topless towers, so here, they are wisely allowed in.

If the *Commedia* is a drama about salvation, it is also a poem about reading and writing. Dante constantly draws attention to both the crafts at which he is employed. He takes advice from the great poets in their little conclave in Limbo, and he contemplates the dangers of poetry when Francesca quotes his own verse back to him to justify her fall. Divine spirits form letters to spell out words of praise on the face of heaven, and each new book contains an appeal to its own muse for assistance in finding the right words for the task of describing what was to follow. Virgil reads his thoughts, and figures met along the way invite him to read their stories in the books of their faces. Translation adds a further layer of complexity to these encounters, but it does not necessarily impose a further barrier between the reader and the poem. Because it forces attention on the process of reading and writing – the choices about metrics, the decisions about equivalent turns of phrase – a good translation can also offer the reader a straight path to the heart of Dante's design. James has translated the meaning along with the words, so that his *Divine Comedy* is, for the twenty-first century English speaker, something very close to reading Dante in 1317: not the same thing, which is impossible even in Italian, but a journey which allows the same discoveries to be made along the way. On that long road, Clive James treads before us, a trustworthy and companionable guide.

'... Thank you for what brings
My will and yours together: what I learn
From my teacher, master, leader.' So I said.
On the high, hard road I followed, and he led.

Rousing the Reader

One Thousand Things Worth Knowing by Paul Muldoon

Faber | 128 pp | ISBN: 978-0571316045

PAUL MULDOON is our most Wildean writer in the twenty-first century. In many ways Wildier than Wilde, but the comparison still appears just to me. His verse exhibits wit and skill, informed by a steady, serious gaze. He is an international poet with a reach as far as the transatlantic English into which the world's culture empties itself, but also a grounded one; when the Irish reader encounters in the hologram-maze of his references the word *gliomach*, she wonders how many of her foreign counterparts know they can consult the online Dinneen.

His work of course reflects his life: as transatlantic professor at Princeton, the jet engine ferrying him home, but not allowing him to forget the millions of less fortunate exiles who laboured without a chance of return, commemorated in his earlier poem "The Loaf"; as father in a world of globalised youth, as possessor of a sensibility that enjoys the rootless and changeable mash of contemporary culture without becoming deracinated himself. Enjoyment is bubbling up everywhere, the hilarity of a bookish child loose in a library, of the writer in a university not tethered to a period, of the person free to come and go, who saw classifying him as an "exile" as belittling "the likes of Brodsky or Padilla" in *The Prince of the Quotidian*.

It is located even more in the nature and the possibilities of poetic language. Wilde's dictum "A truth in art is that of which the opposite is also true" is balanced by the opposite and equal truth, that language does bear a relationship to truth, and the poet's job is to find a provisional balance between these two realities. The oppositions are frequently binary, fictions of poetry presenting themselves as both true and false. The invocations, the conjurings and the clues can cluster in a brace of lines that have the blatant form of a statement. In the opening poem of *One Thousand Things Worth Knowing*, "Cuthbert and the Otters", "This style of nasal helmet was developed by the Phrygians // while they were stationed at Castledawson" has a seismological sense both of the actual shifts of history (it was the Celts who overran the Phrygians, in Asia Minor, it seems; conquerors and conquered have changed places – and they change places in the other sense too) and the steadiness of fact (the places haven't changed at all). It is also absurd if deft, the absurdity recalling us with a bump to the world of what we know, or know we can't know.

At other points it's a dizzier ride, as the book's title turns up in a poem written for the National Gallery's exhibition *Lines of Vision*, "Charles Émile Jacque: Poultry Among Trees", where he slithers gracefully from a hen to an LA motorcycle cop; while one can only fall in with his assessment of the fantasy otters who turn up out of the tale of St Cuthbert to join Seamus Heaney's funeral cortege:

> Like the Oracle
> at Delphi, whose three-legged stool
> straddles a fiery trough
> amid the still-fuming heaps of slag,
> they're almost certainly on drugs.

The slagheap, the reference to Cuthbert of Lindisfarne, whose remains were transported to Durham in the tenth century to be safe from Viking raids, are in Heaney's memorial poem because it is also a work commissioned by the Durham Book Festival last year. Grief, jetlag, archaeological erudition and a palimpsest of maps where the post-industrial wasteland of the North of England is superimposed on (or possibly subterraneanly introduced into) the village of Bellaghy, produce a kaleidoscope of perspectives. An occasional poem makes the most of the misfit between the occasion and the continuities of the poet's life.

The great resource of language is the negative, and that rampant fertility in copious ways of saying, variously, "not" is often the fragile wisp that yokes his airy mismatches. In "Pip and Magwitch" a cigar compared to an Egyptian mummy is "dismissive of the chance / it will ever come into its inheritance". "Almost certainly" appears repeatedly in "Cuthbert and the Otters" as a challenge to the reader's disbelief. The negative can also take the form of the well-known effect of grief: "I'm at once full of dread / and in complete denial." Again, an actual historical fact (sixth to seventh century this time) is slammed under our noses: "It's no time since Antrim and Argyll / were under Áedán Mac Gabráin's rule."

In the English-speaking world there is, we know, no agreement as to the importance of history: the joyful Irish infatuation, the British imperial revision, the shallowness of the recorded past in North America, clash and distort themselves here. So history becomes a transparent pool in which facts swim, nobody can know at what depth or in what true dimensions. But they do point to truths, they have weight and bodies and have their impact in the present. In the poet's funeral, the line about Áedán Mac Gabráin is followed by "We come together again in the hope of staving off // our pangs of grief", and further down "I want to step in to play my part", and again "I want that coffin to cut a notch // in my clavicle." That notch is perhaps related to another declivity, in "A Dent", a poem in memory of his friend and teacher Michael Allen:

> The depth of a dent in the flank of your grandfather's cow
> from his having leaned his brow
> against it morning and night
> for twenty years of milking by hand
> gave but little sense of how distant is the land
> on which you had us set our sights.

– "gave but little sense of" – there it is again, the fragile slender link between the incommensurables among whom we live.

The truth of history is not only private. "Barrage Balloon, Buck Alec, Bird Flu and You" is addressed to a friend of Protestant background, the painter Dermot Seymour, genially recalling the days when they would, in the atrocious 1970s in Belfast, in their twenties, "devoutly skive / off for the afternoon to the Washington or the Crown Liquor Saloon", naming too another couple of drinkers, Boston and Lowther, murdered and dumped in a burning car, just around that same era, because their friendship crossed the religious divide. "We treated the wicker fence / that ran between us with such reverence", and if the poem celebrates the Irish beasts Seymour has accommodated in his faithful landscapes, it also includes the toothless lion paraded on the small streets of North Belfast by the notorious Fenian-basher and B-Special "Buck Alec" Robinson.

Paul Muldoon is not, I think, setting out to be just even-handed about the factions in the North when he adds a poem on Rita Duffy's *Watchtower II*. The painting, which is on the book's cover, shows the horrible army watchtower with in the background the green fields of south Ulster, in which some post-Troubles rings have turned to smuggling steroids and green diesel; "green" takes on a new meaning which is suspiciously close to its old meaning:

> By far the biggest hassle
> is trying to get rid of the green sludge
> left over from the process. It infiltrates our clothes. It's impossible to
> budge.

Viewed simultaneously from outside and inside the culture, the incommensurables hang there, held in the poet's gaze. Other poems show his wanderings taking him farther away, and he encounters more remote connections; in "At the Lab", the pollen from a bog in Ireland washes up in North America; in "Some Pitfalls and How to Avoid them",

> native scouts
> will still be able to follow our route across America
> by the traces of mercury
> in our scats.

Two large poems, "Cuba 2" and "Dirty Data", are epic attempts to hold the whole of complex systems suspended and presented. In "Dirty Data" the renaming of Ben Hur as "Ben Hourihane", the juxtaposition of multiple imperialisms, Roman and British and American, the half-heard phrases distorted and decoded, are like motes dancing in a sunbeam seen through half-closed drowsy eyes – one has the impression that between these revolving veils an avenue to a true perception might suddenly reveal itself, but I can't say that I have been alert enough, so far, to spot the moment. As with the water splashing in the Hawk's Well in Yeats's play one might be distracted and miss it, but I will keep watching. "Cuba 2" has a Yeatsian streak, the poet recalling some of his own greatest hits while flabbergasted by the timewarp of the suspended island. I find it more satisfactory in that the poet's own presence and the reality of place provide a resonance that seems lacking in "Dirty Data".

There are other simple and graceful poems in the collection too. "Camille Pissaro: Apple-Picking at Eragny-sur-Epte" starts from the resemblance of the apple-picker with his long basket-rake to the centurion who pierces Christ's side on the cross; a whole evolution of art swarms and settles in the gap. Translations from Old Irish do their bit to ground the book in the scholarly inheritance as well as the disturbed Irish present.

Critics often focus on Muldoon's talent for weirdness and his technical games; the first, like the weirdness of Flann O'Brien's version of Mad Sweeney, seems to me to correspond to the weird predicament of humanity. It is hardly the main business of poetry to be normal, though this poetry turns out to be fit to take on the weight of normal life when called on. If he is allowably skittish in responding to Heaney's funeral (because he is writing about another poet, and indeed one who had given him licence to write in his own way), he can more collectedly focus on the human condition, and its limits and infinities, in the poem for Michael Allen. And while there are hoops and laces of rhymes that signal to each other and hold poems in place, even as the language spills out of their restraints, they appear to me to be somewhat beside the point in the pleasure his poetry gives.

It is language itself, its multiplicity and its straining after meaning, that is illuminated by his work. If the jingling of the rhyming refrain in "The Loaf" irritated me (and other readers I think) to the point of spoiling the experience of reading, that poem's gimlet-eyed focus on history, work and suffering is equally typical of Paul Muldoon over his writing career. These – the formal traps and the clustering relevant excrescences

– are the entanglements he has passed through in his strenuous quest for communication. In this latest book, the fluid metamorphoses of words and themes intimate to the roused reader just how many difficulties, preoccupations, assumptions buried in language itself get in the way of the task. In "Cuba 2" he opines that "the best poems meanwhile give the answers / to questions only they have raised". Circular as it appears, that statement appears to me both elegant and true, and it surely applies to the poems in *One Thousand Things Worth Knowing*.

I Am An Automobile

John Berryman's Public Vision: *Relocating the Scene of Disorder* by Philip Coleman
University College Dublin Press | 260 pp | ISBN: 978-1904558491

IN A LITERAL sense, John Berryman's public image is comprised mostly of his massive beard. First cultivated when the young American poet was trying to look as refined as possible in England in the 1930s, and alternately shaved off and let flourish in subsequent decades, the beard dominates images of Berryman. Saul Bellow described him as "meteor-bearded like John Brown". Robert Lowell wrote an elegy that called him "brush-beard" and said "the Victorians waking looked like you". PJ Kavanagh, remembering Berryman, declared "I feel your dreadful beard, / Even now." Geoffrey Hill commemorated him as a "face-fungused wizard"; David Wheatley wrote Berryman a "Beard Song".

John Berryman was born John Smith, in Oklahoma, in 1914; his early life was upended when, after a failed land speculation, his father shot himself. His mother soon remarried; the eleven-year-old took his stepfather's name. After graduating from Columbia College, Berryman headed to Cambridge: "Yeats, Yeats, I'm coming! It's me!" a later poem has him exclaiming from the ship, in one of the most ebulliently silly apostrophes in twentieth century poetry. His first meeting with Yeats was almost sabotaged by Dylan Thomas, who "very nearly succeeded in getting me drunk earlier in the day".

After the years in Cambridge, Berryman's life became more tumultuous, filled with what he called "whims & emergencies, discoveries, losses". He shifted around the US teaching; he married, had affairs and was divorced (repeatedly); he worked on scholarly projects, tried to get his poetry published and found that many of his friends failed to understand or like it. Some attention came with the mid-fifties poem "Homage to Mistress Bradstreet", but it was not until the first instalment of *The Dream Songs* that Berryman became a celebrity. (The several books that appeared later, near the time of his 1972 suicide, were taken mostly as indications of his decline.)

The Dream Songs baffled, charmed and irritated its first readers. Robert Lowell's early review ended in a rare admission of semi-appreciative bewilderment: "How often one chafes at the relentless indulgence, and cannot tell the what or why of a passage. And yet one must give in." Spoken by an imaginary character named Henry, whose turbulent life often follows Berryman's closely, the sequence describes problems with alcohol, marital fidelity, insomnia, an onslaught of bills, the suicide of a father, an alternating fear of and desire for death. *The Dream Songs* both made and circumscribed Berryman's reputation: it won him recognition and a number of major awards, and it was taken by many readers as a straight transcription of his own thoughts and plights.

In a July 1967 issue of *LIFE* magazine, for example, Berryman is photographed repeatedly, holding forth in a pub in Dublin; the beard is on prominent display. "Whisky and ink, whisky and ink. These are the fluids John Berryman needs," the accompanying profile begins. Soon it tells us that "His consumption of alcohol is prodigious and so is his writing." While doing so it falls into a tradition, already congealing by the late sixties, of focusing somewhat gleefully and unreflectively on Berryman's self-destructive tendencies. (Berryman himself played into his role as *poète maudit*, later echoing the whisky-and-ink cadence in a cartoonishly drunken couplet: "Madness & booze, madness & booze. / Which'll can tell who preceded whose?")

Berryman's fame arrived a few years after ML Rosenthal coined the term "confessional" in a review of Robert Lowell's 1959 volume *Life Studies*. Rosenthal himself later expressed misgivings about the term's use, admitting that "very possibly the conception of a confessional school has by now done a certain amount of damage". The term has furthered readings that reduce poems to unfiltered, exhibitionistic utterances: *Life Studies* as autobiography produced while Lowell was involuntarily confined to one mental hospital, Sylvia Plath's *Ariel* as something similar to the patient histories she transcribed when working as a secretary in the psychiatric division of another.

While such conflations have become less common for other mid-century American poets, they have persisted for Berryman. "Maudlin" is one word frequently used of him; "egotistical" is another. One writer called *The Dream Songs* nothing but alcohol-fuelled emoting, saying that the poems "slide sideways into intellectualizing, pride, boredom, talk, obfuscation, self-pity and resentment". Although such a summing up is harsh and extreme, it has been echoed by a number of established readers. Harold Bloom, for example, has dismissed Berryman as a poet championed by critics who "like their American poets to be suicidal, mentally ill, and a touch unruly". The cover on a recent edition of Berryman's *Selected Poems* (that of Faber's 2007 volume) is of six emptied shot glasses, stacked, tilting, on a table that shades off into dark blue; the glasses continue the representation seen in *LIFE*'s photos of the poet gesticulating at a pub.

In contrast to the images that preponderate in Berryman's myth and photographs, the cover of *John Berryman's Public Vision* presents us with a shaved, thin-faced, extremely ordinary-looking man in his mid-forties. Berryman's gaze is sharp, possibly tired, a little unsettling: it is hard to tell whether he is looking directly into the camera or beyond it.

The less recognisable jacket photo is emblematic of Philip Coleman's project. Coleman has (in the introduction to another book published in 2014) referred to Mark Doty's lines about Berryman's "iconic thick glasses // glinting like the sidewalk / in the cold, iconic thick beard" as presenting not merely a "popular visual image of the poet" but an icon of "the misguided critical assumption that Berryman ... failed to engage with the world around him". Coleman questions the tradition of viewing Berryman as "a poet of solipsistic disengagement and self-absorption", unable to handle his tempestuous personal life, let alone look up long enough to consider American politics. He demonstrates that Berryman thought both passionately and carefully about the modern world, and about poetry's public value.

In contrast to potentially suffocating readings of Berryman as concerned only with his own mind and suffering, Coleman argues that his poetry is far more than id, psychosis, and despair: the "development of Berryman's poetry throughout his career can be charted ... as a 'calling into question' of the nature of human subjectivity" and a "sense of what it meant to be a human being in the twentieth (or 'American') century". *John Berryman's Public Vision* brings out Berryman's intelligence – which has often been ignored in favour of accounts that emphasise a wild, whisky-inspired genius – through a range of works, both the often-quoted and the completely forgotten.

Coleman begins by discussing the weaknesses and reductive tendencies of the confessional label, and lays out how it has, in Berryman's case, encouraged glib fusions of biography and poetry. As Coleman notes, the photo of the emptied glasses on the Faber *Selected* suggests that "the often ugly realities of Berryman's private life ... frame [the] selection in a way that insists the poetry should be read only as a footnote, a perverse postscript to the poet's troubled life and death".

To begin to change our focus from Berryman's personal crises to his public vision, Coleman explores "Formal Elegy", which was written after John F Kennedy's death and which has received little previous discussion (perhaps, in part, because it does not fit the stereotype described above). The poem begins in heartsick ambivalence: Berryman perceives that the assassination stemmed "from matters of principle – that's the worst of all – / & fear & crazed mercy". He sees in the assassin, whom he does not name, a pernicious combination of deranged emotion and rocklike certainty – the certainty that the poet lacks.

Later in the elegy, the poet seems to become a literal vehicle:

> I am an automobile. Into me climb
> many, and go their ways. Onto him climbed
> a-many and went his way.

This elegy is, in part, a meditation on a poet's role in political events. Although his ideas are read by "many" his readers "go their ways", changed or more likely not, after encountering the poem; those carried by Kennedy, however, "went his way". (Berryman's syntactic parallels also recall Yeats's statement that "We make out of the quarrel with others, rhetoric, but of the quarrel with ourselves, poetry.")

"But what did Berryman believe his poetry could 'do'?" Coleman's first chapter asks. He finds an answer in one of the poet's unpublished lecture notes, on Coleridge's idea of a synthesising imagination. According to Coleridge, poetry reconciles "opposite or discordant qualities"; this concept, Coleman suggests, gave Berryman "a way of explaining the kind of radical inclusiveness that he had been attempting in his own poetry from the beginning of his career". The notion of far-reaching inclusiveness, of yoked opposites, has often been used to explain much of what makes his style engaging: its inclusion of quasi-Miltonic syntax and a bizarrely fragmented grammar, of Latinate vocabulary and contemporary slang, of iambic pentameter and Ogden Nash. But Coleman's study extends this idea of radical inclusiveness, showing how Berryman attends not only to his own mind, but to the "scene of disorder" outside it. The mental dramas of *The Dream Songs* are themselves given new vigour by consideration of how they encompass politics and ethics.

The subsequent chapters of *John Berryman's Public Vision* each take up roughly a decade in the poet's work, from the late 1930s to the early 1970s. Coleman proceeds from Berryman's first book, *The Dispossessed*, quoting generously and expressively. In contrast to a tradition of focusing exclusively on *The Dream Songs* (a number of readers have stated that this is the only Berryman worth reading), Coleman takes the entire body of work seriously. It is a delight to read his analysis of the early poetry, and of the several depreciated books from the 1970s.

As the examination of Berryman's lecture notes on Coleridge suggests, Coleman presents new finds from the wealth of archival material held at the University of Minnesota, drawing on letters, manuscripts, unpublished essays and heavily marked-up books. They reveal his breadth of interests and his decades of evolving thought. Throughout his superbly thorough study, Coleman directs our attention to the richness of Berryman's allusions, and thereby to how his wide reading makes its way into his poems. For example, when he examines the late volume *Love & Fame*, which a number of critics have attacked for its bragging (about sexual conquests, or rubbing shoulders with Yeats), he notes that the title recalls Keats's "When I have fears that I may cease to be", which ends:

> then on the shore
> Of the wide world I stand alone, and think
> Till Love and Fame to nothingness do sink.

Coleman charts the four-part book's shift, in which Love and Fame – or "lust and notoriety" in the words of a particularly hostile critic – do vanish into thin air, as the speaker turns to political, religious, and ethical questioning.

In each chapter, Coleman lays out several poems that confront events beyond the personal. By the third section of *Love & Fame*, for example, the speaker can turn to argue on behalf of "The Minnesota 8", an anti-Vietnam War group jailed for trying to destroy draft records. Berryman first published this poem in his local paper in response to a letter that called for their execution; although he once declared that Kierkegaard "wanted a society, to refuse to read 'papers, / and that was not, friends, his worst idea", he did read the paper, assiduously. In one of the more memorable early poems – "World-Telegram", which Coleman also discusses – Berryman evokes the unhierarchical jumble of newspaper headlines, from the sensational ("Man with a tail heads eastward for the Fair") to the blandly distant ("Berlin and Rome are having difficulty") to the twee ("All this on the front page. Inside, penguins").

This book is bracingly wide-ranging, as regards both Berryman's range of works and those works' numerous sources. However, it might have arrived at further insights by occasionally taking a baggier method, one that pursued elements that don't fit in these tightly argued chapters. (Because Coleman is writing against several decades of received ideas, digressions from his primary argument are rare, and sometimes their absence is missed.) One aspect that he raises but only briefly discusses is that Berryman's effort to address the world at large was often a struggle. The first line of *The Dream Songs* – "Huffy Henry hid   the day" – foregrounds retreat and avoidance; and as Berryman says near the end of "World-Telegram":

> If it were possible to take these things
> Quite seriously, I believe they might
> Curry disorder in the strongest brain …

Berryman's accomplishment might be brought out still more fully by taking into account both his outward and inward turns. A book like *Love & Fame*, for example, is in part a study of narcissism; one could press more closely at how the desire to take part in the world interacts with the impulse to talk about oneself. While *Love & Fame*'s progression from complacency to contemplation is undeniable, it is not straightforward; from line to line, this speaker's attitudes toward his earlier exploits jostle against each other, sounding alternately petulant, conscientious, self-congratulatingly modest or corrosively self-mocking. There remains a need to discuss, in detail, his poetry's tonal fluctuations, and its tension between ambivalence and the impulse to speak plainly. (The poem for "The Minnesota 8" is an example of Berryman at his most strident and direct – but as Coleman notes, the poem was removed from the second printing of *Love & Fame*.)

Each of Coleman's forceful chapters, however, directs us to numerous areas in which Berryman's work cannot be regarded as confessional solipsism. He draws attention, for example, to the range of his formal innovation. Even a disregarded work like the Kennedy elegy, with its ten sections that move spikily between free verse and metre, reveals his unforgettable syntax and rhythms: "Scuppered the yachts, the choppers, big cars, jets. / Nobody goes anywhere." After Kennedy's death, the yachts and jets are swept away even before they are listed; the hefty pentameter, in which stressed syllables pile up the way that the expensive, vulgar vehicles do, suddenly gives way to a short, bare, paralysed statement.

Berryman's language, especially his syntactical inversions, is like no other in the twentieth century; we see his grammar straining as early as "The Dispossessed", and by the time of "Homage to Mistress Bradstreet" it is extremely wrenched:

> Out of maize & air
> your body's made, and moves. I summon, see,
> from the centuries it.

Here, as Berryman addresses the seventeenth century poet Anne Bradstreet, his crumpled syntax pushes "centuries" of distance between "I" and the "it" of "your body"; but the sentence does end with Bradstreet evoked. Here the expressiveness of Berryman's syntax is almost didactic – see also how he animates the first sentence at the last possible minute, with "and moves" – but by the time of *The Dream Songs* its strangeness is more varied and slippery. Two stanzas from "Dream Song 49" show Berryman's innovations in concentrate; its grammatically crazy sentences fall into an abcabc rhyme scheme, and quite a bit of good pentameter:

> Old Pussy-cat if he won't eat, he don't
> feel good into his tum', old Pussy-cat.
> He wants to have eaten.
> Tremor, heaves, he sweaterings. He can't.
> A dizzy swims of where is Henry at;
>   somewhere streng verboten.

His language is pervaded by his symptoms. "Tremor", without article or verb, suggests that the speaker suffers from one unending bout of trembling, and "sweaterings" has undergone a more severe change. Sweat seems to have turned into a made-up verb, sweater, which we might define as "to sweat constantly with no end in sight". This new word becomes a participle, sweatering, making it even more endless – and then, in a nonsensical attempt to adhere to grammatical rules, it takes on the -s of a normal third person verb.

> How come he sleeps & sleeps and sleeps, waking like death:
> locate the restorations of which we hear
> as of profound sleep.
> From daylight he got maintrackt, from friends' breath,
> wishes, his hopings. Dreams make crawl with fear
> Henry but not get up.

Henry's plight seems interminable: the intense disjunction of that last sentence leaves him trapped in the middle of the sentence, with no escape.

In the exuberantly self-pitying language above, we find another counter to the idea of the maudlin, self-absorbed poet: the humour. Although Coleman does not discuss this more playful side in detail, it is a crucial aspect of Berryman's perspective, and of his constant, fluctuating ambivalence. The relish of mishap we hear in his prose – for example in the account of meeting Yeats when nearly perilously drunk – is equally prevalent, though more elusive, in the poetry. (Berryman prefaced a 1966 reading of *The Dream Songs* by declaring, "Prepare to weep, ladies and gentlemen. Saul Bellow and I almost kill ourselves laughing about the *Dream Songs* and various chapters in his novels, but other people feel bad. Are you all ready to feel bad?") Much of what makes Berryman appealing derives from how he pushes the serious against the seemingly non-serious, and the personal against the public.

John Berryman's Public Vision ends with a look at Berryman's influence in the world today. Slow to find fame, and relatively quick to undergo a sag in his reputation in the eighties and nineties, Berryman seems to have attracted more interest in the past few years. He has been the subject of a few recent studies, such as Brendan Cooper's *Dark Airs: John Berryman and the Spiritual Politics of Cold War American Poetry* and Samuel Fisher Dodson's *Living at the Intersection of Need and Art* (a study of *The Dream Songs*), as well as a collection of essays that stemmed from a 1993 conference, edited by Coleman and Philip McGowan.

As to Berryman's influence on poetry, Coleman finds it in many places of the English-speaking world – in particular the fascinating legacy in Ireland. This past year also saw the publication of *Berryman's Fate*, which Coleman edited, and which compiles a number of short, Berryman-instigated poems by writers across the US, Ireland, England and Canada. About half take inspiration from the three-sestet *Dream Song* form, such as David Wheatley's "Beard Song": "Chinny-chin-chin, I spared you those years, / wrapping you tight in the seaweed tangle / of my first beard." Many others pay homage to Berryman through quotation, pastiche, or remembered anecdote.

Given *Love & Fame*'s records of conquests, and the *Dream Songs* that imagine "a lark with Sappho, / a tumble in the bushes with Miss Moore", it is interesting that a number of the poets who have drawn on Berryman's style are women. Just as Berryman takes up other people's and even other objects' voices – a seventeenth century Puritan woman, a "demented priest", a literal lost sheep, an automobile, a helicopter – Lucie Brock-Broido swirls through personae. (In her first book, *A Hunger*, speakers include a little girl trapped in a well, an insane twin, and the young Edward VI.) Brock-Broido also shares Berryman's tendency toward jarring ampersands and expressively bent syntax. Much as he blends the Romantic and the slangy, she mixes a pre-Raphaelite vocabulary into the contemporary:

And where are you now, my posthumous.
      Have you been bad, unplugging
The blue appliance cord that keeps you juiced into this
      World, particular with myrrh and bile?

Berryman is also re-embodied in Anne Carson's "Twelve-Minute Prometheus", published in the *London Review of Books* in 2008. The poem seems half collage; its echoes of Berryman range from the imperceptible to the pronounced. For example, it quotes repeatedly from "Dream Song 28", which is spoken by the literal lost sheep mentioned above. Berryman's sheep fears that "There may be horribles" and wishes for "the strange one with so few legs" to return: "I'm too alone. I see no end. ... The sun is not hot. / It's not a good position I am in."

At the beginning of Carson's poem, Prometheus speaks nearly those exact lines: "I'm too alone, the sun is hot, it's not a good position to be in." But where Berryman's sheep ends with the aphoristically gloomy "If I had to do the whole thing over again / I wouldn't," Prometheus revises this sentence:

HERMES: But if you could start over –
PROM: I'd do it all again.

Whether one can hear an affirmative, defiant Berryman behind Prometheus's adjustment seems open to interpretation. Coleman's study, however, ends with a poem that shows us similar determination, spoken by "a poet-king ... who persists with his performance in spite of all the world can throw at him." It is from Berryman's posthumous *Delusions, Etc.*, and entitled "King David Dances":

Aware to the dry throat of the wide hell in the world,
O trampling empires, and mine one of them,
and mine one gross desire against His sight,
slaughter devising there,
some good behind, ambiguous ahead,
...
with the ponder both of priesthood & of State
heavy upon me, yea,
all the black same I dance my blue head off!

Coleman's focus on Berryman's public vision – "the ponder both of priesthood & of State" – also speaks to Berryman's almost indiscriminately voracious intellect and his curiosity about "Earth so gorgeous & different from the boring Moon," as *Love & Fame* put it. (That truculent jab at the "boring Moon" is a good instance of how Berryman escapes the saccharine through a sudden change of tones, or sheer non sequitur.) One is reminded that Berryman is also the poet who began a 1962 reading by announcing, "Uh, it's pleasant to be here, and it's pleasant to be – too, never mind just here."

GERARD SMYTH | 2015

Solitary Prowler

Confronting Shadows: An Introduction to the Poetry of Thomas Kinsella by David Lynch

New Island | 306 pp | ISBN: 978-1848402874

IN HIS poem "A Technical Supplement" Thomas Kinsella states:

> But for pleasure there is nothing to equal
> sitting down to a serious read.

Kinsella's poetry, his outlook on life, have always been of the most serious kind; and so too is this superb exploration of his work by David Lynch – as indeed it should be in the instance of a poet whose uncompromising dedication to his art has been exemplary, always refusing to make his work presentable to trends, and often against the current, as Lynch reminds us.

Lynch contends that this stance has been to Kinsella's cost and presents him as a writer with a declining readership who seems to stand in isolation. It is a point he hammers home perhaps just a bit too much: Kinsella is "a writer regarded as central and at the same time marginal", one whose "central influence in Irish poetry" has waned. That this has happened – though I believe not quite to the extent that Lynch asserts – says more about the audience for poetry and their wants than it does about Kinsella and his work.

Setting out the purpose of his study, Lynch declares that he is not an academic or a poet, or any kind of specialist in critical writing, but that his book emanates from a reading of the poet. That reading is indeed a close and penetrating one that takes in Kinsella's broad range of concerns: family origin, history and its consequences, politics, love, marriage, the natural world, the abuse of political and bureaucratic power, the act of artistic creation and the larger issues such as Hiroshima ("Old Harry") and the false promise of the Kennedy era ("The Good Fight"), as well as the "established personal places" of this Dubliner's Dublin where so many of his poems are set and of course the exploration of self that is the most abiding theme throughout his work.

In delving into the Kinsella cauldron, Lynch's intensity of focus is a match for the poet's own intensity. He sifts his way through the material of the poems and the poet's imaginative and schematic processes to present the reader with a vivid understanding of how, from early to late poems, a single fabric has been formed. Lynch's insightful commentary weaves its way from poem to poem with careful cross-reference between various poems, periods and shifts in the Kinsella *oeuvre*. What Lynch clearly establishes is the unified authority overarching all of the work; the sense of a poetic mission from start to finish. He is especially engaging in his thinking on the role of the loner – Lee Harvey Oswald, Marcus Aurelius – in Kinsella's cast of characters.

Kinsella emerged as one of the generation who faced the post-Yeatsian challenge of finding new means of expression – making it new. His reaction against the legacy of Yeats did not keep him from a close engagement with matters of national and cultural identity; his excoriations of the failures and disappointments of the new republic and the betrayal of the ideals of its revolutionary founders made him a voice of indictment (Lynch identifies one poem as a "stuffed charge sheet against the southern state"). The author sets this aspect of his work against the background of Kinsella's early career as a public servant in the Department of Finance – a vantage point that allowed close observation of the forces of power at work in the new Ireland of the 1960s and where he began his "critique of the commercialised Ireland from within its ideological base".

The poet James Liddy once neatly summed up certain defining qualities: "If Kinsella appears in some ways as not a compulsively readable poet he is an introspective challenger of depth, an anxious recorder of interior space, an inhabitant of native Catholic tensions laced with the appropriate fears". To which you could add that the temper of his imagination is a severe one.

I have devoted
my life, my entire career,
to the avoidance of affectation,
the way of entertainment.

At the core of all his poetry is the ordeal and struggle that confronts the human spirit: a poet of "stoic introspection" who likes to settle for the facts. In his interrogation of that theme, Lynch begins in the Kinsella household of the poet's childhood and positions the magnificent elegy for his father, "The Messenger", as a key poem out of his memory of a "Dublin urban experience", citing it as an "excellent place for a reader to commence their engagement [with Kinsella]".

Lynch puts forward and justifies the argument that this poem draws together Kinsella's "most significant themes and consistent forms" and is "a delicate dance between the personal and historical". The poet's introduction to the daily ordeal, the beginning of what he once called "the continuing encounter with reality" took place in his father's shadow. John Paul Kinsella, to whose memory "The Messenger" is dedicated, was a Guinness worker and left-wing activist involved in the first attempts to form a union at the brewery. The father's trials – including conflict with the Guinness establishment on matters of principle – as well as other "hammerblows" that life delivered would appear to be pivotal in the character-forming of the poet, who as a child witnessed his father "on an election lorry ... shouting about the Blueshirts" and making a protest exit from Mass in a local church. Biographical and personal material, and the home ground of his younger years, have provided the poet with much of his most memorable and powerful work.

Lynch sees the transition that took place in mid-twentieth century Ireland, from a predominantly rural society to one with a burgeoning urban labour force, as an important backdrop to the moulding of Kinsella the poet and places his origins and experiences growing up in a working class environment as central to the development of his poetic identity. His social background has been the instigator of many of his thematic preoccupations.

The shift from country to town is particularly personified in the character of Dick King, the childhood neighbour to whom Kinsella pays homage in his poem of the same name. It is a crucial early Kinsella poem, and one that alerted me to local resonance in his work. King, a man of the Gaelic-speaking west and one of those victims of the decline of the rural economy, is transported to the city where his "second soul / was born in the clangour of the iron sheds"; the grind of his new proletarian life in Dublin may, as Lynch points out, be "grimly painted" in the poem but it is magnificently dramatised in the way that Kinsella brings together two distinctly different and originally separate poems into a composite work, demonstrating the poet's intuitive gifts. (In another Kinsella study, Andrew Fitzsimons's *The Sea of Disappointment*, invaluable for its unearthing of source notes and unpublished poems, there is a reference to an earlier draft of the King poem that suggests the neighbourly bond between King and the poet's father.)

Lynch pays particular attention to the period of his poetic style that "dismayed" the critics: the more opaque and deeper and darker introspective poems of idiosyncratic detail that began with *New Poems 1973*. These poems – allusive, allegorical, of high voltage – were a turning point; the poet enters a different aesthetic zone, the ground of his most testing confrontations.

In a discourse on the writings of the psychologist Carl Jung as an important influence, Lynch brilliantly examines the poet's "intense personal assessment" in these poems and subsequent Peppercanister volumes, such as *Songs of the Psyche* and *Fat Master*, with their symbolic vitality. While Kinsella departed from his earlier formal idioms, his meticulous approach to the making of a poem remained; the quest for exactitude became more rigorous.

These poems certainly did not appease the perception that he can be a "difficult poet". Lynch points out that Kinsella himself is cognisant of his relationship with his readers, that "mingling of lives" that occurs in the reading moment, that he refers to in "A Technical Supplement". He was never a poet to ingratiate himself, but one who demands "the maximum from the audience". As Eamon Grennan has asserted, "Reading Kinsella, among other of its virtues and values, is a sort of discipline." The disciplined poet, it would seem, requires disciplined readers.

As well as being his walking terrain, Dublin has been central to his imagination, as he noted when presented with his Freedom of the City:

"Dublin gave many important things their first shape and content for me." From early to later work he has contemplated and reconstructed the city. No other writer since Joyce has so fervently mapped Dublin in the way Kinsella has, and few writers have known it as intimately. In his poems of perambulation he possesses the same qualities as those ascribed to the Parisian *flâneur* poet Jacques Reda, an "equipoise between internal and external awareness".

His journeys are not just through a particular physical landscape – down Baggot Street or back to Phoenix Street or into the city centre and towards the GPO or the Pen Shop – but deep into the human psyche: the onward path always leading inwards. These are "metaphysical journeys", as Lynch tells us, with the poet "reading the ground". Whether it is the solitary stroll of "A Country Walk", in which the poet enters the "gombeen jungle" of an Ireland turning its back on patriotic ideals or the epic suburban trek of Joycean moments with its inevitable arrival at "the Sea of Disappointment" in "Nightwalker", these journeys, says Lynch, have had "an enabling impact" on the poet's imagination and "act as a consolation of sorts for Kinsella ... that brings a semblance of structure and meaning to life". Both poems are seen by Lynch as embodying Kinsella's rejection of "the priorities of the orthodox capitalist dream" of the new Republic. The poet has continued that solitary prowl through "personal and political history" in later work such as "St Catherine's Clock" and "The Pen Shop".

"Nightwalker" is not the only poem in which the poet's indignation erupts. In "Night Conference, Wood Quay" (another of his indictments, this time against destructive development sanctioned by Dublin's city fathers) his stern and scornful gaze is directed at the "white-cuffed marauders". That scorn is aimed not only at a political elite: the literary and journalistic coteries of the day are not exempted; he takes no hostages in "Open Court", a literary bar scene evoked with a Clarkesque satiric edge: "the overcrowded sty", where

> three poets sprawl,
> silent, minor, by the wall.

In the overcrowded hall of poetry, Kinsella holds a singular position and this study, scrupulous in its attention to the individual poems and guided by the author's passion for his subject, will deepen an understanding of that position. My own suspicion is that the "dethroned god" (as David Wheatley has described Kinsella) is being reinstated. The poems will certainly endure, with studies such as *Confronting Shadows* amplifying their presence in the canon.

Ireland:
Culture and
Society

It is possible, writes DAVID BLAKE KNOX, *to acknowledge that neutrality was the best option open to the Irish government during World War II but still question some of its legacy to succeeding generations. A group of Irish merchant seamen were interned in a German slave labour camp during the war but they are not officially remembered by the state as they did not serve on Irish-registered vessels.*

Two aspects of the Ascendancy converge in the image of the Big House, TERRY EAGLETON *argues. While middle class houses are just places to live in, the gentry house is an evolving organism, full of treasured knick-knacks and wrinkled old retainers.*

Not all Catholics suffered from famine and emigration in the nineteenth century, writes MAURICE EARLS. *Elite Catholics managed to retain significant wealth and to benefit from an educational structure adapted to their various needs, which helped them to survive and thrive in a world shaped by British interests and culture.*

If the independent Irish state was forged by a generation which felt itself in many cases to be both Gaelic and Catholic, the fortunes of these two elements were soon to be seen as clearly diverging, writes NIALL Ó CIOSÁIN. *Catholic social power reached its zenith in the decades after independence, but the language continued its slow decline in spite of the state's avowed project of conservation and revival.*

It is a kind of quiet support for the downtrodden and their folk culture that makes Daniel Macdonald unique in Irish art of his generation, writes CATHERINE MARSHALL, *and art historian Niamh O'Sullivan is to be congratulated for bringing him forward as the major figure he is.*

After an unconscionably long wait, there are now not one but two English-language versions of Máirtín Ó Cadhain's masterpiece Cré na Cille. *They each adopt contrasting approaches to what is involved in translation, and each is a superb example of its own approach, writes* PHILIP O'LEARY.

Missing

IN HIS review of *Documents on Irish Foreign Policy, Vol VII, 1941–1945*, in the Summer 2011 issue of the *drb*, Pádraig Murphy rightly identifies World War II as "the greatest test of the effective assertion of sovereignty that the then relatively new [Irish] state had faced". These documents chart the way in which the policy of Irish neutrality evolved as the global war progressed. They reflect certain divisions within Irish society – as well as providing fascinating insights into the thinking inside the Irish government, and our civil service, during those five critical years.

The documents also offer valuable and unique perspectives from outside this country. Ireland was, after all, one of the relatively few states to keep its diplomats in place across Europe for the entire duration of the war. In this context, the dispatches from Germany are of particular interest. There is much to admire in the skill, determination and flexibility with which Irish politicians, civil servants and diplomats pursued the policy of neutrality – sometimes, in very difficult circumstances – and, as Murphy notes, "all this makes for very gripping reading".

However, I would argue that it is possible to acknowledge that neutrality was the best option open to the Irish government during World War II but still question some of its legacy to succeeding generations. Irish diplomats were not the only Irish citizens to find themselves behind German lines, so to speak, during the war. There are other viewpoints and other experiences that are still missing from what has become the dominant narrative of that period. I would suggest that such omissions still affect us, and will continue to do so until they have been properly acknowledged as an integral part of Ireland's history in the war years.

Like many Southern Irishmen, my father crossed the border into Northern Ireland shortly after war was declared in 1939 and enlisted in an Irish regiment of the British army. He ended up in Burma, arriving in Rangoon just two days before the decision to evacuate and burn that city was taken. He became part of the longest forced retreat in British military history, but was also part of the counter-offensive, when defeat was turned into victory. He returned to Ireland in 1946: to a country that had little direct experience of the global war.

When he died three years ago, he left a mass of papers. Sorting through them, I came across some faded press cuttings. One of these, from *The Irish Times*, was dated May 17th, 1945. It described the homecoming of a small group of Irish merchant seamen who had just been liberated from a Nazi concentration camp, where they had been part of a slave labour force. My father had mentioned that his cousin, William, had died in Bremen in 1945. I had assumed that William was an Allied soldier who had been killed during the invasion of Germany – like one of my uncles. Now I discovered that he had served in the merchant navy, and that the circumstances of his death were much darker than I had imagined.

From another cutting – this one from the *Times* of London – I learned that William's ship was on its way from South Africa to India in August 1940 when it was intercepted off the coast of Madagascar by a German raider. The raider, which was "probably a disguised merchant vessel", took the crew prisoner and sank their ship. The prisoners were eventually brought to Bordeaux in occupied France; from there, most of them were sent on to be interned in Germany. However, the Irish seamen were segregated, and, in the spring of 1941, they were taken with other Irish prisoners to be interrogated by German military intelligence.

The surviving seamen told *The Irish Times* how the Abwehr (German military intelligence) tried to persuade them that they had a common enemy in Britain. At this stage of the war it was still believed that Ireland could be of strategic importance if Germany were to invade England. The Irish seamen were asked to become part of the Nazi war effort. All of them declined the invitation and, towards the end of 1941, they were moved to a concentration camp in Germany. A year or so later, they were moved again: this time, to a merchant navy internment camp.

Throughout their captivity, the Irish seamen consistently refused to sign an agreement to become *freie Arbeiter* – voluntary workers – for the German Reich. In early 1943 they were again segregated, and thirty-two of them – including William – were moved by the Gestapo to Bremen Farge. This was one of eighty-seven satellite labour camps attached to the large concentration camp at Neuengamme in northern Germany.

According to the survivors, they were beaten by SS guards when they arrived at Farge. They were told that, since they were civilians, they were not protected by the Geneva Convention, or the International Red Cross. Their new accommodation was a disused fuel tank buried beneath several metres of solid concrete. The seamen learned that they had been brought to Farge to work on Project Valentin: the codename for an immense underground bunker, where Reichsminister Albert Speer planned to construct submarines on an assembly line, in pre-fabricated sections – like the US "Liberty Ships". Speer's ambition was to build a new U-boat every fifty-six hours.

The thirty-two Irishmen joined more than ten thousand other slave labourers – mainly Russians and Poles – who were working on Project Valentin. This operated on a twenty-four-hour-shift system, with each shift lasting for at least twelve hours. There was one half-hour meal break for soup and black bread: the bare minimum required to keep prisoners alive. According to the survivors, the Irish seamen were assigned to some of the hardest work. Usually, this involved lifting, carrying and emptying heavy bags of cement. The prisoners would inevitably inhale some of the dust during the day, and hack it up in wet balls during the night.

Before they left for Farge, the merchant seamen had written a number of letters to the Irish *chargé d'affaires* in Berlin, William Warnock, explaining their predicament and seeking his assistance. At that time Warnock held pronounced anti-British views. In a breach of diplomatic protocol, he had publicly applauded Hitler's triumphant Reichstag speech of July 1940. In a dispatch sent to Dublin in the same year he predicted confidently that the Luftwaffe's blitz of London would soon have a "shattering effect on the morale of the self-centred and self-satisfied British".

Warnock had earlier advised against seeking the release of James Joyce's Jewish friend Paul Léon from Auschwitz. He had been asked by Dublin to intervene "in case there is danger that Léon be shot". Warnock claimed that the real danger was that such intervention might affect Ireland's "good relations" with Nazi Germany. Dublin deferred to his judgment, and Léon was executed in April 1942. In 1940, Léon had rescued many of Joyce's original manuscripts when their author fled the Nazi occupation of Paris – including the only known drafts of the "Ithaca", "Scylla and Charybdis" and "Penelope" episodes of *Ulysses*. Léon died in Auschwitz, but – sixty years later – the Irish government paid €11 million to acquire those same manuscripts from his family. It is not known if Warnock ever received the Irish seamen's letters: what is quite clear, however, is that he did nothing to help them.

As the tide of war began to turn against Germany, Dr Edward Hempel, the German minister in Dublin, complained that the Irish government's attitude had also changed, becoming "unhelpful and evasive". In this context, it seems that Warnock's apparent sympathy for Hitler's regime came to be viewed as potentially damaging to Irish interests. In late 1943 he was joined by Con Cremin, whose view of Nazism appears to have been a good deal more critical. Cremin sent reports back to Dublin of the Nazis' genocidal treatment of Europe's Jews, and even tried (unsuccessfully) to rescue some of them. In August 1944 he visited the Irish merchant seamen in Bremen Farge. According to the survivors, he told them he was determined that they would be repatriated to Ireland.

Cremin argued that, as non-combatants from a neutral state, they should not be treated as prisoners of war – let alone slave workers. By the end of 1944, his campaign for their release appeared to have succeeded. The Irishmen were loaded onto a train and sent to the port of Flensburg, from where they were to be dispatched to Sweden – and, thence, home on board a Swedish merchant ship. However, Allied bombing prevented them from reaching Flensburg and they were returned to the camp at Bremen Farge.

The camp was run jointly by the SS and the Gestapo and according to the Irish survivors its Kommandant was an unrestrained sadist. In the last weeks of the camp's existence, he went on a homicidal rampage, shooting many prisoners, strangling and suffocating others. On April 10th, 1945, Bremen Farge was abandoned by the SS and most of the prisoners were forced to march to another camp, further from the Allied advance. Farge was finally liberated by British troops in the first week of May – but liberation came too late for William. He had survived nearly five years of captivity, but died on March 2nd soon after a surgical procedure performed without sterilised instruments or any form of anaesthetic in one of the camp huts. He is buried in Rheinberg war cemetery, along with three of the four other Irishmen who died in the camp at Farge.

In 1947, thirteen of the Farge guards were tried for war crimes. The military court heard harrowing evidence of back-breaking work, prisoners shot or beaten to death and pitifully inadequate rations. Despite that, the German government denied legal liability for many years, insisting that the Irish seamen had been paid for their labour. In fact, all such payments were made directly to the SS, in alleged recompense for the prisoners' food and board. It was not until 1999 that a proper scheme for compensation was established, and not until 2004 – fifty-nine years after their liberation – that the few Irish survivors who were still alive received any money.

Not all Irishmen in Germany during the war were treated as badly as the merchant seamen. While they were held in Farge, the novelist Francis Stuart was employed as a lecturer in English literature at Berlin University. This was, of course, the kind of academic post from which all Jews had been excluded since 1938 by the Nuremberg racial laws. Stuart had come to Nazi Germany in 1940 as an emissary of the IRA. Soon after he arrived in Berlin, William Warnock helped him to organise a party to celebrate St Patrick's Day. By 1943, he was making weekly propaganda programmes for Irland-Redaktion – a radio service aimed at Irish listeners. In his broadcasts, Stuart spoke with open admiration of Hitler, whom he compared favourably with Gandhi, and considered to be "a kind of contemporary Samson". He praised the "vision and courage" with which the Führer had defied international "financiers and bankers" – clearly identifiable in this context as Jews – and he expressed his belief that a victory for Germany would lead quickly to the reunification of Ireland.

Stuart came home after the war and resumed his writing career. In the years that followed he became a respected figure in Irish literary circles. In

1982 he was chosen to be one of the first members of Aosdána (the Irish arts academy), and was granted a yearly stipend from our national Arts Council. Then, in 1996, he was elected a *saoi* – the highest accolade in the Irish arts world – joining such luminaries as Nobel Prize winner Samuel Beckett, who had been a friend of Paul Léon and who worked with the French Resistance during the war. The President of Ireland, Mary Robinson, presented him with a gold-plated torc – a symbol of the ancient Celtic bards – as a mark of the state's recognition and esteem.

Only one of Aosdána's two hundred members resigned in protest at Stuart's election. That was the Irish-language poet Máire Mhac an tSaoi. One of those who voted in favour of honouring him was the distinguished novelist and critic Colm Tóibín. In 2001 he looked back upon his decision to do so in the *London Review of Books*: "No one in Aosdána, as far as I am aware, had lost family in the War," he wrote, "All of us were part of the legacy of Irish neutrality, and all of us, debating the issue of Francis Stuart, were living in a sort of backwater, protected from the terrible pain and anger suffered by the families of those killed by the Nazis." Tóibín went on to raise a fundamental question: "I believed and still believe that the honour was justified, but I'm not sure I would believe this if I had lost friends or family."

In 1991 a memorial was unveiled to the merchant seamen from Ireland who died during World War Two. It lists the names of more than one hundred and fifty men who were lost at sea as a result of German naval action. It took many years of patient lobbying for their deaths to be acknowledged publicly in this way. However, the granite monument in Dublin's docklands does not bear the name of my father's cousin William, or of any of the other Irish seamen who were used as slave workers in Bremen Farge and who perished in the Nazi terror. The reason given was that they were not serving on Irish-registered merchant ships when they were captured. Three of the five Irishmen who died in Farge were from Dublin, one was from Mayo and another from Wexford. The Germans could identify these merchant seamen as Irish – even though they sailed under Norwegian, Dutch and British flags. It appears that some of their fellow countrymen have not been so sure.

In the *London Review of Books*, Colm Tóibín affirmed his rejection of the naive belief that "writers should be good people". In fact, Tóibín had once seemed at pains to prove that Stuart was not such a bad person. Writing in the *Sunday Independent* around the time that he was elected as a *saoi*, Tóibín stated categorically that Stuart had no connection with "politics, or antisemitism, or fascism, or Nazism". It seemed then that he accepted fully Stuart's own evaluation of himself as "an ostracized writer, writing for other ostracized people". He felt compelled to revise this opinion, however, following the publication of Brendan Barrington's *The Wartime Broadcasts of Francis Stuart* – which clearly established that the bulk of those broadcasts were not only explicitly political in nature, but were also "consistent with the broad thrust of German propaganda".

As it happens, I share Tóibín's belief that writers needn't be good people. However, I don't think this should exempt any state from an obligation to scrutinise the criteria by which it decides which of its citizens it will honour and which it will ignore. When Mary Robinson, as president of Ireland, presented Stuart with his golden torc, she referred to his role in contemporary Irish culture as "awkward". It seems to me that the history of some of the Nazis' Irish victims raises issues that have proved, in reality, to be much more awkward to address.

Stuart was undoubtedly a talented artist – but he was also someone who admired Hitler, who gave expression to antisemitic feelings and who broadcast extreme anti-British sentiments when Britain was at war with Nazi Germany. The Irish seamen who died in Farge may have been less talented than Stuart, but they stubbornly refused to collaborate with Nazism – and their experience remains missing from the official record.

Stuart was, of course, not the only one to resume his career with some success after the war. William Warnock returned to Germany: this time as a full ambassador to the Federal Republic. He ended his career as Ireland's ambassador to Washington – usually considered the top posting in Ireland's diplomatic service. Warnock dismissed any previous sympathy he held for the Nazis as the product of "youthful enthusiasm": Paul Léon might have taken a somewhat different – and, perhaps, a harsher view.

I don't know why my father told me so little about William's ordeal. Perhaps he was too absorbed with memories of the jungle war he had fought in Burma. He may even have felt a little ashamed that his cousin had not died a "proper" soldier's death. As it turned out, the agonising labour that William and thousands of other slave workers were forced to expend on Project

Valentin was all for nothing: Speer's underground factory was still incomplete when the Second World War ended and no commissioned submarine ever left the bunker. It is now used as a commercial warehouse. An imposing sculpture by Fritz Stein stands outside the site: its title is the inversion of a Nazi slogan – "Extermination through Labour".

TERRY EAGLETON | 2013

To the Manor Born

The Crocodile by the Door: the Story of a House, a Farm and a Family
by Selina Guinness
Penguin Ireland | 256 pp | ISBN: 978-1844881574

THE ANGLO-IRISH Ascendancy were an odd mixture of the soft-headed and the hard-nosed. If they could be a dreamy, spook-ridden, eccentric bunch, they also had a keen eye for the price of an acre or the cost of a domestic servant. Washed up by history and finally dispossessed by their own state, their more progressive wing could nevertheless see themselves as in the van of modernity, held back by a bunch of benighted papists.

WB Yeats, visionary and man of affairs, is a case in point. If he was fascinated by the way leprechauns spin on their pointed hats (though only in the northeastern counties, as he solemnly notes), he was also a tough-minded organiser and political activist, a canny cultural commissar with (as his father once remarked) the virtues of the analytical mind. He was a man as much at ease in a committee as at a seance. There was a garage with a motor car at the foot of his ancient tower. Seeing themselves as an avant garde meant among other things that the Anglo-Irish produced some magnificent champions of the common people. For the most part, however, the only wearing of the green with which they were acquainted was a matter of wellies. There is more than a touch of green wellies about Selina Guinness's highly accomplished memoir.

These two aspects of the Ascendancy converge in the image of the Big House. Houses for the middle classes are just places to live in, but for the gentry they are evolving organisms, repositories of cherished memories, full of treasured knick-knacks and wrinkled old retainers, as much living subjects as physical sites. Individuals come and go, but the grange or manor house lives on, more like a transnational corporation than a bungalow. If this corporate form of existence sets its face against middle class individualism, it is equally averse to what one might call the Byronic style of aristocracy – the swaggering, anarchic, wild-old-wicked-man syndrome, for which nobility of spirit means not giving a toss for anyone else. Like a slightly dotty but much-loved relative, the house has its own quirky ways, its distinctive aura and personality. One almost expects to encounter it settled on one of its own sofas, granny glasses perched on its nose, knitting and crooning. It is a symbol, not in the neo-Platonic sense of a cryptic intimation of eternity but in the sense of a chunk of the material world traced through with human values and meanings, a spot where spiritual and material realms meet and even the most mundane objects are resonant of more than themselves. The stuffed crocodile by the door of Selina Guinness's title, long used in her family home as a kind of mailbox, is exemplary of this. The body of the house incarnates a communal soul and a shared history, so that the invisible is everywhere woven into the visible, the past palpably alive in the decrepit armchairs and herbaceous borders of the present. Such houses are more sacred texts than bricks and mortar.

Yet they are, of course, bricks and mortar too, and sometimes ruinously expensive to maintain. Big Houses may mean culture and civility, but they are also at the nub of a whole system of property, labour and production. As the Marxists would say in their tiresomely mechanistic fashion, they are base and superstructure together. As such, they engage the hard-headed qualities of the gentry as well as its more highminded impulses. The latter can also serve to draw a decorous veil over the former. If one's tenants are sorely exploited, it is, after all, in the name of an age-old tradition and a spiritual ideal.

The Crocodile By the Door is the tale of how a scion of the lower gentry came into possession of Tibradden, a house and farm in the Dublin mountains which belonged to her family and where she lived for a while as a child; and though the story is deeply in love with the local landscape and thronged with tender reminiscences, it is also remarkably well-versed in questions of land values, inheritance tax, rezoning, title deeds and fee-farm grants. It is true that the author needs to bone up on such stuff in order to restore the house and farm, but she appears to take to it like a duck to water. Guinness may have inherited the pieties and sentiments of her ancestors, but the spirit of enterprise that drove them to render their compatriots legless and rentless still courses in her veins. At one point, she describes a map of the Tibradden estate as "fluttering like a bird in my hand", an image which neatly combines questions of property with natural spontaneity. Elsewhere in the book, she discusses the sale of some farmland with her partner, the Irish postcolonial critic Colin Graham, and notes that they may become seriously rich as a result – at which point the discussion suddenly breaks off as Graham spots a buzzard flapping nearby. Nature mercifully intervenes to suspend a train of thought which, pursued too far, might appear less than creditable.

In the manner of Maria Edgeworth's *Castle Rackrent*, another tale about coming from behind to inherit an estate, Guinness's memoir unwittingly allows the reader to make some rather less positive judgments on its narrative than it would formally invite. In this book, the double aspect of the Ascendancy – dreamy and dishevelled on the one hand, shrewdly realistic on the other – comes through as a contrast between the author's uncle, Charles, the previous owner of the farmhouse she inherits, and herself. The contrast is incomplete, not least because Guinness admires her uncle's values and channels her considerable business sense into a project (the refurbishing of Tibradden) which is meant to restore and perpetuate them. To do so, however, she is forced to sup with the devil, dealing with an array of planners, lawyers, surveyors and the like, whose brash, calculative spirit she dislikes but whose manoeuvres she is nonetheless well able to match. Patricians may find bourgeois values distasteful, but they would not be where they are did they not have as quick an eye for a decent turnover as their social inferiors – a class with whom, historically speaking, they cemented some mutually beneficial alliances. Guinness, who seems rather fond of the Sermon on the Mount, accordingly reminds herself of the need to be pragmatic and "not [to be] left marooned on the high moral ground". It is certainly a terrain with a good deal of elbow room.

The book seems not to be fully aware of its mild air of bad faith in this respect, any more than Edgeworth's Thady Quirk seems to be conscious of how assiduously he is working for the overthrow of the titled buffoons on whom he fawns. One would, for example, wish to know a bit more of mild-mannered Uncle Charles's view of his niece briskly bundling a pile of disused white waistcoats and dickey bows into suitcases, selling them to the wardrobe department of the Abbey Theatre without consulting him, and then placing a cheque for the proceeds in his hand. He was, she comments unrevealingly, "surprised". If Charles is rather too laid back, his niece is a mite too overbearing. Full of kindliness and concern, she is sometimes a touch myopic when it comes to registering the effects of her muscular schemes on others, not least on those financially insecure underlings who would be imprudent to rely on her good-heartedness alone.

When a planning consultant asks the chronically vague Charles whether he intends to continue farming his land, it is Guinness herself who steps in to handle the query: "'Uncle,' I interpose, eyeing the consultant, 'I think we can safely say, can't we, that you intend to go on farming for now?'" Charles responds not by asking her to have the courtesy to allow him to field questions about his future himself, even if his future might closely concern hers, but by meekly agreeing, though he manages to make his reasons for doing so sound entirely altruistic. The farm, he informs the consultant, is run by an elderly couple, and it wouldn't be fair to deprive them of their livelihood. It is just the kind of elevating of the human over the economic which is supposed to distinguish gentlefolk from the mercenary middle classes, even if the Anglo-Irish in general were notably deficient in the spirit of *noblesse oblige*. All the same, urban cynic as one is, one doubts that even a landowner as comically incompetent as Uncle Charles would have considered this the sole or prime reason not to have his family's lands bulldozed by developers. There is a sense in which the narrator, perhaps unconsciously, makes use of her relative's disastrous lack of business acumen to justify her own rather too energetic drive. It is not for nothing that her grandmother was president of the Girl Guides.

The problem is that you might undermine the culture you cherish in the very act of seeking to put it on a sounder material base. What if the utilitarian cast of mind required for running a Big House efficiently is at odds with the spiritual values it stands for? How can Guinness preserve her inheritance without disrupting it by the vigour with which she does so? One chapter of the book takes as its epigraph some lines from Yeats which suggest that the burden of responsibility is destroying his love of Nature. Culture in this kind of society needs Mammon to survive, but can you really serve them both? If you can't, then you need to take a sharper look at the nature of the current property system than this book is prepared to do.

If responsibility is a problem, however, so is its opposite. Uncle Charles's patrician casualness with paperwork endangers his workers' livelihoods. Cue, then, the entry of the robustly reforming landowner Selina Guinness, a fierce woman when installed behind a broom but a soft touch when it comes to appeals to her heart. It is just that by the end of the story she too is finding it notably hard to combine efficiency with compassion. In the end, benevolent landowners are no solution to malign ones. Property and inheritance usually turn out to be in some way tainted, as Irish Gothic is aware. The words "gift" and "poison" have a common etymological root. Property means prosperity, but also anxiety. There is a subliminal vein of fire imagery running through the text. Big Houses have been known to burn down. Fretting about your dilapidated dwelling is almost as much part of Ascendancy tradition as smashing a bottle of port over someone's head. It could also lend the class a spurious air of solidarity with tenants whose brand of poverty was rather less genteel. Faulty wiring may be a headache, but it's preferable to living in a boghole.

The landed estate is a place where Nature is converted into culture, like the crocodile by the door. Cattle are reared for profit and crops planted for the market. The book has an account of learning how to deal with lambing which is worthy of a major novelist. It belongs to the ideology of such places, however, partly to disavow their own unglamorous economic motives by an appeal to Nature as a value in itself. Yeats does not encourage us to think of Coole Park as a business enterprise. Guinness's memoir takes the kind of erudite delight in the natural world which (speaking as one who first encountered a tree at the age of thirty-six) seems to be hard-wired into the brains of the upper classes, and upper class women in particular. To be able to name sixteen different varieties of weed is a sure sign of good breeding. *The Crocodile by the Door* is a superbly written book, but its prose style is never more stunningly impressive than when it is registering natural detail: "Mats of leonine aconites, yellow and frilled, have somehow survived beneath the tall bracken, and budding clumps of wood anemones are interspersed through the box hedges that have grown into leggy trees. A thicket of moss roses stands where the paths used to intersect. Their rotting hips speckle the sphagnum below, beads on a viridian pillow."

All the same, the Almighty did not put Nature on earth simply for us to gawp at. You can eat the stuff as well. An insolent hunter creeps into Tibradden and shoots dead a deer, enraging the author so much that she drives round the area in ferocious pursuit of him. Having failed to track him down, she returns to the house and immediately asks one of the farm workers whether he knows how to bleed a deer. "The buck has been killed for venison," she reflects with her customary practicality, "so why not give it a go?" If the hunter didn't get to eat it, she might as well scoff it herself. So she has the beast instantly strung up from a cedar tree, pausing only to reflect that it should perhaps have been disembowelled first, in the hope that a neighbour who is a licensed deer-stalker might be persuaded to prepare the carcass in return for half the meat. The text betrays not the slightest sense of irony in charting this abrupt shift from fury over the death of an animal to a keenness to carve it up. What Guinness really objects to is not deer-hunting but other people nicking her property.

She is not, to be sure, blind to the ambiguities of her situation, which by and large are the familiar contradictions of that oxymoronic animal the benevolent landowner. She is, for example, forced to ask a helper, a woman for whom she has the warmest affection, to leave her house for a while, and guiltily pictures herself as a stereotypical evicting landlord. Yet while insisting that she has no intention of forcing the woman permanently out of her dwelling, despite having the legal grounds on which to do so, she does not question the moral offensiveness of being in possession of such a right in the first place. Instead, she struggles with admirable decency to help people on her estate over whom she ought to enjoy no such power.

There are similar ambiguities in her attitude to Uncle Charles, a man she loves dearly but the consequences of whose privileged indolence she has to clean up. Perhaps she is more critical of him than the book suggests, or than she will allow herself to feel. She is furious when he refuses to enter the council flat of a former domestic servant. "'Stop it,' I'd wanted to shout. 'Thirty years of cooking for you, and you can't show her the courtesy of visiting her in her own home.'" But, "as usual, I said nothing". The Quirk-like phrase is telling.

Is there more of an aggressive-subaltern subtext to the book than meets the eye? Not only does she say nothing, however; on the very next page she is to be found excusing his apparent snobbery. Perhaps, she muses, he couldn't face the sight of the woman's loneliness. Blood proves thicker than courtesy.

Charles the Wykehamist squire gets on well with Colin the working class Belfast boy. There is an affectionate cameo in the book in which Guinness watches the two of them doing a crossword together. Colin's book *Deconstructing Ireland* lies on the floor beside them, and Charles himself is about as deconstructed as you can get without actually falling apart. (Guinness herself, by contrast, is a devout reconstructionist). Both men are postcolonial in their different ways – Charles a relic of a colonialist class, Colin a postcolonial critic. It is an image of harmony, but also of a continuity between the generations, as the author's uncle and husband seem to meld into mutual sympathy. The two men even share the same initials. That Charles finds Colin's theoretical jargon infuriating seems beside the point. In this cosy domestic setting, it would seem tactless to mention that postcolonialism is meant to be a fundamental critique of much that Tibradden stands for. People are so much more important than politics. Personal relationships count for so much more than rebarbative abstractions.

In the end, it would appear, sentiment and heritage win out over the merchant, the clerk and the hot-faced moneychangers, as Guinness tells the developers eager to lay hands on her property to go to hell "with their deals and negotiations". "Deals", however, isn't quite accurate. The offer that would have made the author eye-wateringly rich has actually been withdrawn, and the one she turns down is far less lucrative. In any case, the collapse of the Celtic Tiger means that the development companies are rapidly going down the pan, so there are unlikely to be many more tempting but morally dubious offers. Guinness, who refers at one point to marking a sheaf of student essays on *King Lear*, is the young woman who remains loyal to the patriarch, but who also, unlike the hapless Cordelia, inherits his estate. It seems a suitable compromise between the soft-hearted and the hard-headed.

One Onion, Many Layers

Catholics of Consequence: Transnational Education, Social Mobility, and the Irish Catholic Elite 1850–1900 by Ciaran O'Neill

Oxford University Press | 272 pp | ISBN: 978-0198707714

SOCIAL CLASS is a widely employed conceptual tool in the writing of history yet it is often ignored, and sometimes met with a shrug of indifference, by historians of Ireland. National and confessional perspectives – important as they are – always seem to push class to one side. But class exists in Ireland; indeed it has a long past, with evidence of its presence often taking spectacular material form.

Not all Catholics suffered from emigration and famine in the nineteenth century. Families with wealth, certain forms of cultural capital, influence and power did not register these experiences. Elite Catholics were successors of the traditional landed cohort which, though buffeted and very significantly reduced, managed to survive the eras of expropriation and penal oppression with not inconsiderable wealth retained. This landed element was joined by the many Catholic families who managed to become wealthy during penal times. In the nineteenth century successful professionals were to expand still further the community of elite Catholics.

In the latter half of that century, when the Irish population was falling and the poor were emigrating in vast numbers, the experience of privileged Catholics was the opposite of that of their co-religionists: elite numbers, it seems, rose significantly. Given this remarkable phenomenon and the fact that this body of elite Catholics survived into the independent state, it is surely worthy of study as a social class. Ciaran O'Neill, in his scholarly analysis of Catholic elite education in the latter half of the nineteenth century, joins a small number who have addressed this challenge.

Catholics of Consequence is an interesting and thoughtful book, remote from the characteristic dullness of school histories. The author brings a reflective intelligence to his work, linking the detail of his subject to broader historical and cultural questions. He mentions in passing, and with a hint of criticism, the tendency of Irish historians to privilege "the nation-state as a conceptual lens". Ironically, in this case the result of stepping away from that focus is actually an enhanced understanding of the social currents that were to comprise the nation-state which took form in the twentieth century.

Elite Catholics, who made up approximately three per cent of the later nineteenth century population, were by no means a homogeneous phenomenon. Some had substantial and long-established landholdings. Others had used capital accumulated in the previous century to buy or buy back land. Others were highly successful professionals whose families had recently graduated from the middle classes. (This is the element which saw significant nineteenth century growth.) Some, like the Murphys and Powers from Cork, were prosperous and long-established merchant families, whereas the commercial prosperity of others was more recent. There were also political differences. Some were quite happy to live under the crown while for others the urge to resist English power persisted.

The modern Catholic elite took its initial form in the wake of the final military defeat suffered at the end of the seventeenth century. Under Protestant hegemony, Catholic behaviour became pragmatic and unassertive. However, as the eighteenth century neared its end and the urge in Westminster to penalise Catholics abated, anti-Catholic penal measures were gradually disbanded, leading to the partial opening of the restricted profession of law, and even of Trinity College itself, to Catholics.

In response to these changes there was a huge release of pent-up Catholic energy, which ultimately manifested itself politically in the O'Connellite movement. The ultimate objective of this new political phenomenon was to position property-owning Catholics at the heart of government and administration in a transformed Ireland, an Ireland characterised by an organic relationship between the social classes and a shared anglophone culture. It was a hugely ambitious programme, which among other things envisioned an Irish industrial revolution. Indeed, its heyday was perhaps the only time when elements of the Catholic elite came close to resembling a modern bourgeoisie.

When the O'Connellite movement collapsed, the vision and ambition of its tentative bourgeoisie declined correspondingly. But the erosion of Protestant dominance in the legal and administrative worlds continued, and this occurred at a time when the modern growth of the professions had begun. So, if there was to be no substantial Irish industrial bourgeoisie drawn from the Catholic elite, there was to be a growing and confident middle class and elite Catholic professional and administrative class.

The cultural politics which evolved and which were embraced to advance this process essentially involved a continuation of the O'Connellite tactic of appealing to centres of power in London over the heads of the existing and defensive possessors of privilege in Ireland. But this time the objectives were the micro advantages of position rather than legislative autonomy, an objective which did not focus attention again for a generation following O'Connell's defeat. And when it did revive, in O'Neill's estimation, the desire for autonomy did not centrally engage this elite.

Choice of school, as many a parent will perhaps grudgingly admit, is the first decision affecting status to be made in relation to a child. In the eighteenth century the children of privileged Catholic families were educated abroad. Like many upper class Catholic youths of his time, O'Connell attended school in France. Indeed, his was the last generation for whom the educational journey to France was *de rigueur*. The relaxation of the penal laws not only enabled O'Connell to study law at Trinity, it also enabled the Jesuits, the Holy Ghost Fathers, the Vincentians and others to establish schools for elite children in Ireland. O'Connell's own sons attended Clongowes. Indeed the Liberator contemplated retiring there when he reached sixty-five.

Catholic elite education was about succeeding in a world shaped by British interests and culture, a culture which was residually anti-Catholic and negative in its perception of the Irish. In this demanding environment privileged Irish Catholics sought parity of opportunity within the empire. Clongowes Wood College was set up in 1814, Castleknock in 1835, and

Blackrock College in 1860. These schools offered an English public school-style education, with cricket, rugby and a powerful internal culture which encouraged students to place the school towards the centre of their identities throughout their lives. The idea was that graduates could pass muster in the company of the English elite, who would therefore not be ill-disposed to granting them appointments.

The project was highly successful. At an old boys' dinner at Clongowes in 1896 the Old Clongownian and chief baron of the exchequer Christopher Palles declared: "we are now upon equality with any other persons in the kingdom ... an equality that we are determined to maintain". (Interestingly, O'Connell himself declined the same appointment in the 1830s, but the elite in his era were more muscular in their politics.)

As the nineteenth century progressed and the Catholic elite penetrated senior administrative positions and the legal world, others, noting the pronounced anglicisation of their manners, denounced them as "West Britons". There was perhaps some justice in the charge but "getting by" and "getting on" in the Anglo-dominated world were issues for all social classes. Nationalist newspapers of the 1914–16 period frequently carried small ads for grind schools which prepared students for lower-level civil service positions in the empire. The fact is that the business of "getting on" involved a voluntary anglicisation across Irish society over a lengthy period. Arguably, this was an unavoidable consequence of the intense colonisation experienced in the country. Certainly the phenomenon of anglicisation was observable over a wide social range; not even the Irish Ireland romantics could avoid it. In the end Irish elite schools simply reflected an intensified and highly conscious version of what was a widespread and long-established phenomenon.

When the anti-Catholic laws were relaxed, most English Catholic schools which had decamped to the continent in earlier centuries resettled in rural England. The Jesuit Stoneyhurst was the leading Catholic school; the Benedictine Ampleforth and Downside were others. In the eighteenth century many Irish elite Catholics would have been educated in those or comparable institutions on the continent. The tradition continued into the nineteenth century, with many old families and some ambitious newcomers sending their children to English Catholic public schools. The education was virtually identical to that offered in schools such as Clongowes, but the

English public schools had greater prestige and appear to have been more attractive to landed Catholics. In the latter half of the nineteenth century twenty per cent of the students at these English schools were Irish.

For some of the old Catholic elite the emergence of the professional newcomers was distasteful. In 1840 a correspondent of Lady Bellew criticised her decision to send her sons to Clongowes, saying they would associate with "boys far below them in station".

Religious orders offering elite education in Ireland wished to ensure that any anglicisation of the Irish Catholic elite did not lead to a general apostasy. As O'Neill emphasises, the real core of these schools was a Catholic education. The cricket and the air of polish were, in comparison, more decorative. It might be added that the Jesuits would presumably have welcomed the prospect of a cohort of committed Catholics operating within the upper echelons of the British state. The hope that Britain might abandon its experiment in reformationism had not altogether disappeared from Catholic strategic thinking. A romantic nationalism which advocated full political separation and a Gaelic-orientated public culture would hardly have appealed to Jesuit universalist principles. If nothing else, the religious aura around advanced nationalism would have been apprehended as a competitive phenomenon. Yet given the way things turned out in the early twentieth century, pragmatism presumably required that elite schools emphasised what connections they had with such politics. Connections to The O'Rahilly and others, including Francis Meagher, who said he loved his time at Clongowes but learned nothing of Ireland there, were presumably emphasised. Indeed, the revivalist tide, it seems, temporarily dented the main programme of manners at the school and for a period "hurling, rebellion and Cuchulainn would briefly (though never entirely) replace cricket, loyalty and Tom Brown in the pages of the school annual".

The Jesuits' mission to propertied Catholics extended beyond the elite to embrace also the merely comfortable. Belvedere College was established in the 1840s to offer education to those somewhat down the social scale from Clongowes – and yet above the Christian Brothers' level. Again the objective was to give the boys sufficient polish to set them apart from those beneath them and to render them employable at a respectable level. The order, it seems, had a very exact understanding of class in Ireland. Stephen Dedalus's father who, perhaps foolishly, went into business instead of the professions, found he could no longer afford his son's fees at Clongowes. Mrs Dedalus's suggestion that the boy be sent to the Brothers was rejected out of hand by the knowing *paterfamilias*, who, declaring for Belvedere, said he did not wish his son to be educated with "Paddy Stink" and "Micky Mud". Simon Dedalus, it would seem, shared an understanding of the niceties of social class with Lady Bellew's correspondent.

As in the English public school system, accent was of central importance to the Irish elite. Local accents, when blended with approved Anglo tones, may have given rise to the famed speech of Montenotte or be responsible for Ross O'Carroll Kelly's tortured vowels. Certainly at the beginning of the twentieth century there was a great deal of fun poked at "Cawstle Catholics", including by some who may have been, unwittingly or otherwise, adjusting their lives to take account of Anglo cultural and economic power.

Interestingly, the importance of accent, like class itself, did not vanish with the disappearance of the British. A mother who wrote to *The Irish Times* in 1983 seeking advice on schools clearly appreciated the social aesthetics of accent:

> I sent my first son to the Christian Brothers and he has got pretty good results all round, but he has a frightful Dublin accent ... Now I have to decide where to send my second son. I would prefer to send him somewhere with a bit more polish ... Among those suggested have been Blackrock, Gonzaga ... I have heard that the Jesuits are tops in education. Is this true?

O'Neill considers the politics of the Catholic elite intermittently throughout his book. He argues that the subjects of his study were socially above the typical Irish Parliamentary Party activist and, by implication, also socially above popular revolutionary types. This area is complex and is not the main focus of the book. It is safe to say that this fascinating subject would repay further attention. In O'Neill's reading the Catholic elite were not much involved in the Home Rule campaigns. Thus he rejects Conor Cruise O'Brien's suggestion that they were a ruling class in waiting, permanently confounded by the success of revolutionary politics.

Yet John Redmond, who led the Home Rule movement, was celebrated and honoured by Clongowes. Redmond, of course, was not averse to a continuing British connection and was not as ardent an advocate of autonomy as some in the Irish Parliamentary Party. Perhaps his politics were compatible with the core Clongownian outlook. He said he learned in Clongowes that the "highest duty of a gentleman was in every circumstance of life to play the game". Support for the British war effort was, in a sense, a logical outcome of this outlook and of the conscious self-anglicisation that occurred throughout the nineteenth century in elite Irish schools; it is interesting that there was a disproportionate number of war dead among those who attended such elite schools. Whether the explanation is the influence of Redmond or the result of anglicisation is not clear.

Perhaps, as is still the case across many social classes, students simply took their politics from the home environment and the diversity that existed within the Catholic elite was reflected in the politics of the students. Indeed it may not be too much to hope that questions of this sort may, in time, give rise to research directed at unravelling the many layers of the onion that is social class in Ireland.

NIALL Ó CIOSÁIN | 2015

Gaelic and Catholic?

An Irish-speaking Island: State, Religion, Community, and the Linguistic Landscape in Ireland, 1770–1870 by Nicholas M Wolf

University of Wisconsin Press | 416 pp | ISBN: 978-0299302740

THE CLOSING of Ireland's embassy to the Vatican in 2011, following unprecedented criticism of the Catholic church by a taoiseach in the Dáil, could be said to confirm the end of a particular hegemony within the culture of independent Ireland. A few years earlier, in 2007, a major survey of language use in the Gaeltacht suggested that Irish could cease to be a community language in any part of the state by 2030, a finding confirmed by the updating of that survey this year.

Two of the central elements in the official discourse of the state will therefore have faded almost beyond recognition within the first century of its existence. They followed different patterns, of course – the Catholic Church reached probably the highest point of its political and social influence in the decades immediately following independence, followed by a sudden collapse in moral authority, recruitment and lay practice from about 1980 onwards. Irish on the other hand has been in slower but continuous decline over the same period, despite the state's avowed project of revival and conservation.

If we look back farther, over three or four centuries, we find that the fortunes of these two cultural elements have also been quite different, though their starting points were very similar. In 1600, before the final destruction of the Gaelic social and political order, the vast majority of the population of Ireland shared two features that marked them out from the culture and practice of the state in which they lived, and the state from them. These were religion and language, Catholicism and Irish. By 1900 the picture was very different. The Catholic church was a far more powerful force than it had been in 1600, with near universal rates of practice among its members, control over a wide range of the institutions of civil society, considerable influence in parliamentary and local politics and substantial wealth. Irish, in stark contrast, had relatively few speakers, next to no presence in politics and public life and was concentrated in peripheral regions and among some of the poorest sections of the population.

In some ways this contrast is surprising when we bear in mind a few of the practicalities as well as the philosophical difficulties of cultural change. Religious conversion would have involved changing from one variety of Christianity to another, and arguably entailed less of a cognitive shift than a change of language did. There were widespread and rapid conversions to different forms of Protestantism throughout Europe during the sixteenth century, and in some areas the population later reconverted to Catholicism. In Ireland, there were those who converted from Catholicism to Protestantism and occasionally back again, whether landowner and lawyer in the eighteenth century or starving poor in the nineteenth. Such rapid transitions are not normally possible in the realm of language, and language shift is almost always slow and final. Moreover, changing a spoken language needs to be a collective process as well as an individual one – it is not possible for an individual to switch languages unless many others do so as well. There are of course very strong collective elements in religious belief and practice, and there was frequent community opposition to conversion. Even so, purely individual conversion is conceivable, and indeed Protestant religions have always emphasised individual conversion. Individual language shift is much less likely.

On the other hand, there are aspects of language shift that make it potentially a smoother process than religious conversion. At a local level, language shift normally takes place over a number of generations, with a monolingual generation followed by some bilingual ones, with these finally being succeeded by a generation that is monolingual in the new language. Changing religions, or at least changing churches, by comparison, is instantaneous. This is because religion is a binary variable whereas language isn't – you can speak more than one language, but you can't legitimately belong to more than one religion. Choices are presented more starkly in a religious conversion, and to that extent it might require more explicit and urgent motivation.

In practical terms, in seventeenth and eighteenth century Ireland, probably the most significant difference between Catholicism and Irish was the existence of external support. There were powerful Catholic countries in Europe, and an international Catholic church, for whom Ireland was of continuous strategic importance. The church supplied clergy through Irish clerical colleges abroad, while Catholic states, and to a lesser extent the papacy, could exert diplomatic pressure on Britain. There was of course no Irish-speaking state that could have been a similar support to linguistic practice.

Recent explanations of language shift in Ireland, however, have tended to focus on the material benefits of switching language, and it could well be argued that these were greater than the benefits of changing religion. This is far from obvious though, particularly in the eighteenth century, under what is generally referred to as the penal code. Catholics, whatever language they spoke, were barred from voting, teaching, having guns or buying land. There were no such legal barriers to Irish speakers as such, and fewer immediate material benefits to changing. In both religion and language, the advantages of switching were greater the higher your social status, and there was a steady drift among the better-off towards Protestantism and English, and less so among the general population.

In 1800 therefore, both Catholicism and Irish were still well-entrenched in the mass of the population of Ireland. Indeed some thought that Irish was more likely to survive at that point than Catholicism. A well-placed observer like Whitley Stokes, professor of medicine in Trinity College, Irish-language publisher and former United Irishman, could write in 1799 that "it is easier to alter the religion of a people than their language". Stokes wrote this by way of advocating the publication and diffusion of the Bible in Irish as a way of overcoming the political alienation that was manifested in the 1798 rebellion. That alienation was also from the Catholic Church, since the clergy and hierarchy had vehemently opposed the radical political movements of the 1790s. A Co Cork priest wrote in 1806 that in the previous three decades, "not only all former influence was lost, but even that confidence in their clergy, without which all their exertions must prove abortive, ceased in a great measure to exist among the people".

A century later the Catholic Church was central and Irish was peripheral. What had happened in between? The religious story has been well explored by historians and sociologists. Internally, the Catholic Church carried out a major reform programme, building churches, introducing new devotions and inculcating greater discipline among both laity and clergy – a process known, for better or worse, as the "devotional revolution" after a famous 1972 article by the American historian Emmet Larkin.

Politically, the clergy took a lead in the electoral politics of the period, from O'Connell's Catholic Association in the 1820s to Parnell's Irish Party. Finally, the Catholic Church became a major partner of the state in the general administration of Ireland. Ireland was governed after 1800 by a London parliament that was far better disposed to Catholics than the pre-Union Dublin assembly had been. Its willingness to engage with a Catholic population was fostered by its conquest of a multi-ethnic, multi-religious empire, including French-speaking Catholics in Canada, and cemented by the French Revolution, which produced an enduring alliance between the papacy and Britain, which were both strongly anti-revolutionary. A national Catholic seminary at Maynooth was established and funded by the London government in 1795 to house clerical refugees from the Irish Catholic colleges shut down by the revolution. It was intended to be "the salvation of Ireland from Jacobinism and anarchy", according to its first president, Thomas Hussey. The Act of Union was therefore followed within a few decades by the co-option of the Catholic Church into the official political process. Catholic clergy were regularly consulted by parliamentary inquiries and the commissioners of the new national education system in 1831 included a Catholic bishop.

The story of the Irish language between 1800 and 1900, by contrast, has been much less studied and understood. In many accounts, it simply drops out of sight. This is partly the result of a type of retrospective teleology. The process of language shift was inevitable and irreversible, the argument goes; it had started by 1800; therefore Irish-language culture was effectively finished by 1800 as well, and can be ignored in the nineteenth century. In these accounts, Irish only re-emerges with the revival movements almost a century later. This is perfectly illustrated by one of the major statements of Irish cultural history in recent decades, *The Field Day Anthology of Irish Writing*, which appeared in 1990. Its three large volumes were scrupulously multilingual, with texts in middle and modern English, old, middle and modern Irish, Latin, and Norman French. If you look for texts in Irish from the nineteenth century, however, you discover something very strange – there is no section in the anthology for such texts. There is a section in Volume 1 on writing in Irish from 1600 to 1800. Two volumes and three thousand pages away, there is another section in Volume 3 on writing in Irish after 1900. The clear implication is that nothing of any significance was written or composed in Irish between 1800 and 1900, and moreover that there is no continuity between pre-1800 Gaelic culture and the culture of the revival.

The Field Day Anthology may be an extreme example of the neglect of the nineteenth century, but it is not unrepresentative. Until now, there has been no single book focusing on the social history of language in nineteenth century Ireland. The late Brian Ó Cuív contributed some magisterial chapters to different volumes of the *Oxford New History of Ireland*, but unless and until they are issued on their own these are easily available only in libraries; there are articles of great authority written by Maureen Wall, Seán Connolly and others; and there are some excellent local studies such as Bríd Ní Mhórain's *Thiar sa Mhainistir*, on the barony of Iveragh, Co Kerry.

A decade ago, in a survey of the scholarship in this area, I pointed to this anomaly and suggested that one necessity was an ethnography of Irish-language communities that would separate the question of Irish-language culture from that of language shift and thereby avoid the invisibility mentioned earlier. Such an account would focus on language use in practice as well as on written production, on bilingualism and the co-existence of two languages, and on the interactions of Irish speakers with two institutions that were becoming ever more prominent in their lives, the state and the Catholic church. A study of the petty sessions, small local courts introduced in the 1820s, of the Poor Law of the 1830s, or of publishing and printing, would show Irish speakers engaging with modernity, and not as irremediably pre-modern and doomed to extinction.

The suggestions made in that survey have been closely followed in Nicholas Wolf's major new book, which is now the most complete and best-documented survey available of Irish-speaking communities in the nineteenth century, despite some reservations that will be made presently. It has chapters on the use of Irish in law courts and elections, in education, in Catholic religious practice, and by the Catholic clergy. We read about Irish speakers taking court cases through interpreters, monolingual Irish speakers voting in parliamentary elections, again through interpreters, the recruitment of Irish-speaking parish clergy and the translation of major devotional works into Irish. These topics are all found in the second part of the book, entitled "Encounters". In the first part, "Identities", Wolf explores the attitudes of Irish speakers themselves to their language, which could be strikingly positive, and also their views of monolingualism and bilingualism. An extended analysis of a corpus of jokes about language from the National Folklore Collection shows bilinguals having fun at the expense of monoglots. These jokes are often taken as deriding the broken English of Irish speakers, but Wolf shows that they also ridiculed English-language monoglots. It was bilingualism that was prized, therefore, rather than English per se.

Wolf draws two related conclusions from the two parts of the book. From the first part, "Identities", it is clear that some Irish speakers prized their language and regarded it as superior to others. A deprecating attitude to Irish has often been invoked as a cause of its abandonment, but Wolf makes the important point that this negative attitude did not prevail until the twentieth century (or perhaps the very end of the nineteenth) and cannot be projected back into earlier periods. It was a result of language shift, in other words, not a cause.

A stronger conclusion emerges from the discussion of "Encounters":

> In the century before 1870, as has been shown here, Ireland was not by any means an anglicized kingdom and, indeed, was quite capable of articulating the forms of modernity – whether religious, political, or economic – in the Irish language.

This is a striking statement and a welcome and necessary corrective to presentations of Irish as purely backward and limited in its uses. It should stimulate a great deal of debate and research among cultural and literary historians, and among a more general readership. It is refreshing in particular as it avoids viewing Irish purely in retrospect, as a language whose decline is preordained. But by the same token it raises the question of that decline with renewed urgency – if Irish was adapting so successfully to the modern world, and if its speakers valued it so highly, why did it decline so rapidly and totally? For a community to change its spoken language *in situ*, rather than as the result of migration out or in, is a radical undertaking, and if market activity, interaction with the state, and religious practice were all possible in Irish, what other motivation was there for changing a community language?

Wolf does not address this issue, and it seems to me that, while his argument is valid and valuable, he overstates his case. This is most evident in the sections on "Encounters", where the strategy of argument is to show that Irish was frequently spoken in situations and places that would normally be regarded as domains of English, such as courthouses, schools, shops and markets. Wolf cites newspaper advertisements for shop assistants specifying that they should be able to speak Irish, plaintiffs taking cases in Irish through interpreters, and teachers using Irish out of necessity where pupils did not understand English.

The difficulties with this argument are both conceptual and empirical. Conceptually, the fact that Irish is permitted and spoken in a particular domain or situation does not mean that the domain is not an English-language sphere. The language of commerce was English, and all banknotes and contracts were in English; those contracts would ultimately be enforced in English, since that was the language of the courts, and interpreters were the proof of that; and Irish was spoken in national schools as a way of teaching English.

Empirically, while all these arguments are very well-documented, Wolf's evidence is usually qualitative rather than quantitative. As a result, the reader is never sure how typical are the cases being quoted. The constabulary, for example, began to be stationed everywhere in the country from the 1820s onwards, and might be thought to be purely English-speaking. Wolf quotes five instances of policemen being able to understand Irish, ranging in date from 1832 to 1887. These are fascinating cases, from which we learn for example that plain-clothes detectives valued Irish as a way of obtaining information, but we have no idea how typical they were. Nor are we told whether policemen who understood Irish were happy to speak it in the course of their work. The following description of a tithe protest in Lettermacaward, Co Donegal, in the 1830s offers a contrasting example of the linguistic practices of the constabulary and their attitude to Irish-language monoglots:

> The chief constable, Mr. Taylor, after reading the Riot Act to a people, not one of whom understood the English language, ordered his men to fire, and wounded several.

There is a similar difficulty in Wolf's discussion of Catholic devotional literature in Irish. He gives a long list of translations of seventeenth and eighteenth century works of devotion, to demonstrate that Irish-speaking Catholics were familiar with newer forms of religion. They were almost all manuscript translations, however, and it is difficult to know how widely circulated they were, and consequently how representative of Irish-language belief and practice. An example would be Pinamonti's 1693 book *Hell Opened to Christians*, famous as the source of the sermon in *A Portrait of the Artist as a Young Man*. According to Wolf, this text "had currency in the Irish-speaking world as well: [the scribe and poet Mícheál] Ó Longáin completed an Irish translation from the English for Murphy [bishop of Cork] in 1818". It's not clear if Murphy shared it with others, but since it seems to be the only copy of this text, probably not. Indeed it's quite possible that only Murphy and Ó Longáin ever saw and read it. This equation of two speakers of Irish, only one of them a native speaker, with an "Irish-speaking world" is not persuasive, and in fact Wolf himself has earlier in the book warned against precisely this type of argument.

A related issue is that Wolf's examples are frequently interpreted in a way that maximises the incidence and prestige of the speaking of Irish, sometimes unjustifiably so. This is evident already in the opening pages, where he maintains that "Irish speakers could be found among all social classes and religious persuasions". As an example of gentry speakers, we have the following:

> James McQuige, a Methodist preacher, recalled in 1818 being jostled on Grafton Street by a gentleman 'of most noble appearance' who excused himself in Irish.

This man might not have been a landowner – for all we know he was a well-dressed beggar with fancy airs. A few lines on, we are told that "Protestant labourers spoke [Irish] habitually" with a reference to an 1868 memoir of missionary work in Ulster by an Anglican clergyman. In fact, what the clergyman wrote was that "no person above the labouring class ever speaks it habitually", not exactly the same thing. Moreover, the clergyman goes on to say that "among the Protestants of Ulster of the lower classes, there is a decided prejudice against the language, which they connect with superstition and barbarism and rebellion, and so wish to see it exterminated", which gives a very different impression from Wolf's short summary.

There is also a more general observation to be made about Wolf's overall argument that Irish "was quite capable of articulating the forms of modernity – whether religious, political, or economic". Modernity here is defined as engagement with supra-local institutions, in particular the state and the Catholic church. It was in the century that Wolf is writing about, 1770–1870, especially the early decades of the nineteenth century, that both institutions began to incorporate and address the mass of the people. The population census and the Ordnance Survey mapping, the police, small local courts, national schools and the Poor Law, the essential mechanisms of the modern state, all date from between 1820 and 1840.

The church, having emerged from its semi-clandestine status in the late eighteenth century, was aiming for universal catechesis and devotional observance in the same period. The two were related, and some historians have seen the establishment of the national schools after 1831 as in effect a state bailout of Catholic schools that the church did not have the means to maintain at a time of growing population and increasing poverty. Both also had in common the fact that perhaps half the population they were trying to reach was Irish-speaking and that they had to adapt to that fact. For their part, Irish speakers were faced with new interventions and had likewise to adapt. This adaptation, however ingenious and resourceful, was in the broader sense reactive.

A more active form of modernity that might also be used as a yardstick would be the creation of a print culture and a public sphere. In English-speaking Ireland from the 1760s onwards, the rapid growth of a newspaper press, periodicals, pamphlets and other printed materials created networks of communication and forums for argument that did a lot to shape modern political organisation and consciousness, from the Volunteers and the United

Irishmen through the Repeal movement to the Land League. This print culture is almost completely absent in Irish. There were very few printed books and no newspapers or periodicals (with the exception of the short-lived *Fior Eirionach*, published in Clonmel in 1862, which was in any case a revivalist magazine aimed at least as much at English-speakers as at Irish). Wolf comments that the reading aloud, with translation, of newspapers was a common practice, and this is so. However, it makes the participation of Irish speakers in the public sphere a more passive affair than that of English-speakers. In this it resembles participation in courts, for example, but with the difference that a more active role was possible in print than in the courts but that this didn't materialise. There could not have been an Irish-language state court. There could have been an Irish-language newspaper, but there wasn't.

The obvious comparison here is with Welsh, which in the nineteenth century had a large print element, with up to ten thousand books being published and dozens of periodicals and newspapers, many of them lasting for decades. The contrast is even more marked when we bear in mind that there were four times as many Irish speakers as Welsh in 1800. Welsh was in far better health than Irish in the later nineteenth century, and in fact the number of speakers had quadrupled over the century. From this perspective, Irish was abandoned because it hadn't embraced modernity while Welsh survived because it had.

Many of the Welsh periodicals were produced by clerics, and this brings us to another marked contrast between Welsh and Irish, and back to the relationship between religion and language. By 1850, most Welsh speakers belonged to nonconformist denominations, Methodist and Baptist in particular. These underlined their separateness from the established Church by emphasising the use of Welsh in both church services and devotional reading. The Catholic church in Ireland didn't use Irish to anything like the same extent, and it formed no part of its cultural politics. One sign of this is that the campaign for disestablishment of the state church in Wales took place to a great extent in Welsh, while that in Ireland was conducted exclusively in English.

Wolf recognises the centrality of religion to the story he is telling. Two chapters discuss the Catholic church and another one the Church of Ireland, altogether nearly half the book. The chapters on Catholicism look at the provision of devotional reading material and at the provision of clergy and church services respectively. Both are based on substantial original research in manuscript catalogues and in church archives. Wolf's approach to the devotional texts is to list, categorise and describe them, and to show that they reflect currents in Catholicism that were new (and therefore "modern") at the time. There is some fascinating material here, but the exercise as a whole is vulnerable to the problem discussed earlier, that of typicality. Just over seven hundred manuscripts survive containing religious texts, and by no means all of these would have contained the new texts in question. Even allowing for the fact that the surviving manuscripts are a fraction of what was produced, and that many of them were read aloud, it still seems tiny relative to the print material circulating in English. Wolf identifies twenty-two new devotional texts being printed in the century 1770–1870, and again this seems a lot until one compares it with the hundreds produced in Welsh, and for a much smaller language community.

The following chapter, on the clergy, tackles what Wolf sees as the standard view among historians that the Catholic church was indifferent, even hostile, to Irish, resulting for example in priests without Irish being sent to Irish-speaking parishes. He lists priests who were known for their preaching abilities in Irish and discusses collections of written sermons, mostly in manuscript. Again questions of typicality and volume arise, with one contemporary observer claiming that there were no more than five manuscript sermon collections in all of Connacht in the 1870s.

There is however some strong quantitative analysis as well. Wolf builds on Brian Ó Cuív's tracking of the linguistic capacities of Maynooth students through the census and does the same for clerical students from the diocese of Cloyne using the diocese's own recruitment records. He finds that the proportion of Irish speakers among the Cloyne students was the same as that of the population of the diocese, so that priests were not more anglicised than their congregations. "In any case," writes Wolf, "the ability of priests to speak Irish became less relevant as time went on, since their congregations were increasingly anglophone ... Even where there was a willingness to preach in Irish, however, two difficulties stood in the way in this period: the availability of Irish-language written material from which to deliver a sermon and the growing number of parishioners proficient in only one language, making it difficult to accommodate both ... To accommodate the old, in this scenario, was to risk losing the young who represented the future of the church."

To put the issue like this, it seems to me, is to regard the clergy as the passive providers of services to the laity rather than as the active local representatives of a national and international organisation, whose decisions and practices would have some cultural influence locally. The same is true of Wolf's treatment of the state – it is presented as a supplier of education, dispute resolution and public order to the entire population and therefore adapting itself to the linguistic practices of that population. This approach is clearest in the short discussion of markets and shops, where buyers and shopkeepers needed Irish to complete commercial transactions. In all these cases, the need for Irish grew less as regions shifted from Irish to English. The problem that then arises is that, since all these activities were reactive, the presentation leaves no room for any force that might drive a language shift, let alone one as sweeping as occurred in nineteenth century Ireland.

In part this is the result of a methodological position proposed by Wolf earlier in the book. From the 1960s until the 1990s or so, the most frequent approach to thinking about language use and language shift historically, in the Irish case and more generally, has been based on the idea that language use was differentiated by function and location, what is known as "diglossia". Some domains, in particular high-prestige and public domains, used a higher prestige language, that is, English, while others, normally low-prestige and private ones, were Irish-speaking. In this scheme of things, language shift is the replacement of the lower language by the higher one in domain after domain until there is so little use for the displaced language that it ceases to be transmitted to the next generation.

Wolf disagrees with this approach, maintaining that "no concept has tended to obscure the understanding of scholars of this period more than the idea that eighteenth and nineteenth century Ireland was characterised by diglossia". The first part of the book therefore constitutes a demonstration that Irish was in fact viewed as a high prestige language by many of its speakers, and the second part shows that Irish was present in many of the domains that are held to be English-language ones. Wolf suggests instead, following recent work in sociolinguistics, that language use is determined by the relationships between speakers, that the language you use depends on who you're talking to, rather than on where you are talking, or what you're talking about.

This can be a fruitful approach, but I'm not sure that it displaces an analysis by domains. In the first place, there is often no substantial difference between the two approaches – you meet particular people only in particular domains (a shopkeeper in a shop, a magistrate in court). Secondly, it is very difficult to document or test the idea for the eighteenth or nineteenth centuries, as opposed to the observational and participant fieldwork of contemporary linguists. Wolf produces some examples, all to the effect that people in Irish-speaking areas spoke Irish among themselves and English to outsiders, but only a few other cases. (And one of these cases doesn't actually bear out the argument. It's a description of a seal hunt in Kerry in 1856 during which, according to Wolf, the boatman spoke English to his passengers but gave orders in Irish to his crew. In fact a few pages later the text records him shouting orders in English to the crew at a crucial point in the expedition.)

Finally, such an approach has difficulty explaining language shift. In this presentation, people switch their principal language when enough of those around them are monolingual in the new language. But those other people must have made the transition first, so that language shift is being invoked to account for itself. Of course it is true, as noted earlier, that language is a social phenomenon, maybe the quintessential social phenomenon, so that language shift around you is a compelling reason to change your own language. But as a broader explanation it is circular.

The passivity of speakers in this model of change is the same as that of the clergy, state agents and others discussed above. But of course the personnel of state and church were all active cultural agents, their decisions about language mattered, and they were not always responding directly to the requirements of the population or the laity. One very clear illustration of this is the reaction of the Catholic church and clergy to the various Protestant missionary organisations that conducted evangelical campaigns in Irish-speaking areas between the 1820s and the 1850s. As well as preaching, these societies encouraged devotional reading in Irish and circulated large numbers of Bibles and religious tracts in Irish. The response of the Catholic church seems to have involved a distrust of printing in Irish, if not of the language itself. According to David Greene, the evangelical campaign succeeded in provoking a reaction against the reading of the Irish bible, or indeed any material in Irish at all, which was to do much harm to the already weakened status of the language.

At a local level this seems to have translated in some cases into hostility, and the Celtic scholar John O'Donovan wrote in 1850: "I know that the Catholic clergy, who are the real anti-Irish party at present, are moving heaven and earth to put out the Irish language."

Even if the reaction to vernacular Protestant evangelisation was not uniformly anti-Irish, it is remarkable that there was no sustained campaign of preaching and publication in Irish in response. Very few popular Catholic tracts were published in Irish, and as Wolf points out, the missionary orders that were mobilised to counter the Protestant crusade, mostly new European orders, did not consider the language issue, at the beginning of their campaigns at least. Remarkably, Archbishop McHale of Tuam, usually regarded as a champion of the use of Irish, sent Rosminian priests, who were Italian and English and therefore without Irish, into Irish-speaking north Connemara in the 1850s to counter the evangelising of the Irish Church Missions there.

The cultural resonance of this response can be gauged by comparison with the other Catholic region that spoke a Celtic language, Brittany. At the same time as the Protestant Crusade was beginning in Ireland, and as part of the same broader evangelical movement, Methodist and Baptist missionaries from Wales began to travel through Brittany, preaching and distributing religious tracts and Bibles in Breton, which is related to Welsh. The reaction of the Catholic church in Brittany, by contrast with Ireland, was to mount a counter-offensive in Breton, circulating and encouraging Catholic tracts, periodicals and other publications in that language.

In Ireland, from a pastoral point of view, at least in the short and medium term, it would have made far more sense to encourage the reading of Catholic books in Irish than to wait for the completion of a language shift (or perhaps even to stimulate that shift). The fact that this first option wasn't chosen on any scale suggests that the Catholic church in Ireland was not particularly inclined to use Irish even before the evangelical campaigns.

Traces of hostility to Irish among the parish clergy, or at least of a reluctance to use it pastorally, can be found in the memoirs of some early Gaelic League activists at the beginning of the twentieth century and in folklore collected in the 1930s. In a different mode, differences between the church and language activists flared up particularly during the dispute that led to the dismissal of Michael O'Hickey, the professor of Irish, from Maynooth in 1909, after O'Hickey had criticised the hierarchy for not supporting the inclusion of Irish as a compulsory subject for matriculation to the new National University of Ireland.

Overall, though, tension between the two elements was submerged in the ideology of the new state that was held to be both Gaelic and Catholic. This ideological fusion was brought about by the revolutionary generation of 1916–22, many of whom had participated in the Gaelic League and were at the same time devout Catholics, and was subsequently institutionalised in the new state. The constitution of 1937 was the classic expression of this fusion, making Irish the "first official language" of the state and recognising the "special position" of the Catholic church.

The tension between Catholicism and Irish remained not far from the surface, however, and was exemplified in a memorable exchange in 1932. In that year the Celtic scholar TF O'Rahilly published *Irish Dialects Past and Present*. A single paragraph in the introduction of this book summarised the relationship between religion and language over the centuries. In 1600 "the ties which bound the Catholic Church in Ireland to the Irish language seemed indissoluble" but in the eighteenth century O'Rahilly found "an extraordinary remissness in the supplying of devotional books in Irish". By the nineteenth century, in contrast to the nonconformist churches in Wales, the Catholic church had "definitely turned its back on the Irish tradition".

This summary provoked a thunderous response in the Jesuit journal *Studies* from "J.R.", probably John Ryan SJ, a lecturer in history in UCD:

> [O'Rahilly] might have said a word of the abject slavery under which the people groaned, and the impossibility of getting a hearing as long as the national case was put in a language which the oppressor ignored. If the leaders of the nation, lay and clerical, used English rather than Irish as their medium of expression, they did so for the reason that in this way

alone did they see any hope of winning back for the people their lost national rights … Would Catholic Emancipation ever have come if the case for it had not been put powerfully by Irishmen in the English tongue?

Irish, for Ryan, was a hindrance to nationalist and Catholic politics, because all forms of engagement with the state ("the oppressor") required the consistent use of English, as did the co-option of the Catholic church into the mechanisms of that state. This negotiation and co-option was made possible by a final difference between Catholicism and the Irish language. The fact that Catholicism was an institution as well as a belief system meant that it was possible for the United Kingdom state before 1921 to deal with Catholics as a totality, and for them to deal with that state through the structures of the church. Catholics as such had leaders and representatives, Irish speakers did not, and as a result the state could co-opt the Catholic church, and by extension Catholics, into official structures and forms of power, or at least come to a compromise with them, but not with Irish speakers.

At independence, there were no radical changes in the structures and practices of government and administration (and, apart from the police and the army, remarkably few changes in personnel). Catholics, both clergy and laity, were strongly present in those structures, especially in education, social welfare and disciplinary institutions, and were therefore able to consolidate their position and construct a Catholic hegemony that lasted for more than half a century. Irish-speaking communities (as opposed to Irish-language revivalists), by contrast, were marginal to the new state and partly as a result continued to decline thereafter. As cultural practices, therefore, the Irish language and Catholicism have followed very different trajectories, both before and after independence, and it might even be said that there was some opposition between them. This was hidden, however, by the official ideology of a state that envisaged a polity that was simultaneously Gaelic and Catholic.

The collapse of the Catholic church in Ireland since the 1980s has meant that its practice, like the use of Irish in Gaeltacht communities, is increasingly confined to the older age groups. As elements of a public discourse, however, Catholicism and Irish have gone in quite different directions in that same period. In the recent same-sex marriage referendum, for example, it was striking that they lined up on opposite sides.

The Catholic Church as an institution was strongly in favour of a No, while there was a very visible Irish-language presence on the Yes side. An organisation, "*Tá Comhionannas*", was formed to campaign for a Yes vote. It canvassed, produced posters for the Connemara Gaeltacht, published articles in Irish and had a social media presence. A video of Stephen Fry giving a short speech in Irish for a Yes vote was also available on YouTube. On the No side, while there were individual Irish speakers who were active in the campaign, there was no organisational presence in Irish and no publicity. As we approach the centenary of independence, this contrast between these two elements of Irish public discourse may well continue to grow.

Picturing the People

In the Lion's Den: Daniel Macdonald, Ireland and Empire by Niamh O'Sullivan

Quinnipiac University Press | 160 pp | ISBN: 978-0990468684

WHEN NIAMH O'SULLIVAN published *Aloysius O'Kelly: Art, Nation, Empire* in 2010 she threw down a gauntlet to all writers of art history in Ireland through the depth of research and analysis she was prepared to bring to her subject. The task required her to delve into the archives of the *Illustrated London News* and other illustrated journals of the second half of the nineteenth century, material which she has been able to put to good use again in her role as curator of Ireland's Great Hunger Museum at the University of Quinnipiac.

At that time her work on the *Illustrated London News* alone would have merited a dedicated book. O'Sullivan, however, had taken on far more than that. In looking at the career and work of Aloysius O'Kelly (c 1853–1936) she was faced with a family background of artists and revolutionaries, members of the Fenian movement, connections to the Land League and a sibling elected as an MP for Roscommon, not to mention the artist's own role as embedded journalist in the wars of the Mahdi against British imperial authority in Egypt and the Sudan in the early 1880s. Most difficult of all for a researcher were O'Kelly's frequent changes of name and identity as he ducked and dodged the scrutiny of the anti-Fenian establishment while continuing to work and exhibit in Ireland, Paris, Brittany, London and New York. It took years just to establish the date and whereabouts of his death because of his various aliases and the picaresque careers of family members, but where others had shied away O'Sullivan battled on, adding a wealth of knowledge and research to the history of Ireland and England and providing a new gloss on orientalist studies. The result, on that occasion, was a magisterial book that moved effortlessly between art history, orientalism, colonial studies and detective work that involved archives in different countries and different languages. No other work of Irish art history before or since has managed to meet that level of scholarly detection and breadth.

Did she know, then, when she turned to her most recent project – *In the Lion's Den: Daniel Macdonald, Ireland and Empire* – that she would have another multi-faceted mystery story on her hands? The facts about Daniel Macdonald as assembled by Walter Strickland, later by Anne Crookshank and the Knight of Glin and most recently by Nesta Butler in Vol 2 of *The Art and Architecture of Ireland*, are straightforward and minimal. The fact that those earlier writers pointed to a name change, from MacDaniel to Macdonald, during the artist's short life must certainly have triggered alarms in her experienced head but O'Sullivan knew that however difficult unravelling the story might prove to be, it had to be done. Macdonald was responsible for one of the most important paintings in the history of Irish art, not just in the nineteenth century but for all time.

The painting in question, *An Irish Peasant Family Discovering the Blight of their Store*, is not Daniel Macdonald's greatest painting, nor is Macdonald the greatest Irish artist of his generation when measured against the criteria usually applied to painting, but this work is unique. Alone it carries the weight of an event that changed the course of Irish history for ever, the greatest natural disaster to hit Europe since the Black Death. Moreover, *Discovering the Blight* is undoubtedly the painting that first drew Niamh O'Sullivan to his work in her role as curator of a museum dedicated to the Famine. Painted and exhibited in 1847, at the worst period of the Great Hunger, there is no other known painting about the blight that contributed to the deaths of over a million people and the virtual destruction of a culture through traumatic loss, emigration, dislocation, loss of mother tongue and the erosion of an age-old native tradition that was painted by an Irish artist while the event was still unfolding. An even more important contributory factor in this catastrophe was Ireland's position as a subjugated country in an enormous global empire. For an artist trying to establish himself in London, that meant that the people to whom he might look as potential purchasers of his work were implicated in the tragedy it depicts.

The inherited view of Daniel Macdonald, or Daniel McDaniel as he was first known, was that he was born into an artisan family in Cork city, and that his father was known as a minor painter, cartoonist and writer, among other things. O'Sullivan found this to be, at best, an economical version of the truth. At worst it might signify an attempt to marginalise an artist who dared to represent the unpalatable. By following the vicissitudes of the family from flight and concealment after the Jacobite failure in Scotland, through death at sea and various family adventures, she discovered that the family were blue-blooded Scottish aristocrats who had a very direct claim to the lordship of the Western Isles of Scotland, a claim that Daniel's father, James McDaniel, later Macdonald, did not manage to pursue as far as O'Sullivan has now done. She further reveals that far from being humble artisans, Macdonald counted among his three siblings another artist, his sister Jane, a brother who was a well-known Wesleyan minister, and another brother, Denis, who rose to become a distinguished doctor, inspector-general of the Royal Navy hospitals and fleets and recipient of a knighthood. Perhaps more importantly for a growing artist, O'Sullivan delved into the hub of intellectual activity that Cork boasted to reveal that Macdonald senior enjoyed close friendships with leading writers, folklorists, antiquarians and wits of the day such as Thomas Crofton Croker, William Maginn, the painter Daniel Maclise, Richard Dowden and others and was a regular contributor to the Cork Literary and Scientific Society and a businessman before becoming an artist himself.

Macdonald raised some of the other uncomfortable aspects of colonisation too in his paintings, notwithstanding the fact that he hoped to make a living as an artist in London and had to graft to find patrons in a social climate that showed little sympathy for the situation in Ireland. Yet for reasons that Niamh O'Sullivan tries heroically to reveal, we cannot be sure of why he remained so independent of the establishment with which other more established and better known expatriates from Cork compromised rather than alienate buyers of their work.

It is fascinating that despite a not inconsiderable trail of documentary evidence about Macdonald, very little was known about him until this publication. That cannot be attributed solely, perhaps not at all, to his name change, which, if anything, was likely to excite curiosity rather than the opposite, nor to his early death, before his thirty-second birthday, although that truncated his career before it had a chance to fully develop. It is, in fact, much more likely to derive from dismissals of his work as naive by earlier writers such as Crookshank and Glin and from the politics of his work. To be seen as both naive and from Cork, in the eyes of certain writers, was a bit like being, in the manner of Oscar Wilde's Ernest, guilty of carelessness. His work received little national coverage in Ireland, and although he was well received in his native city and in London, where within a year of his arrival in 1844 Prince George and Princess Mary of Cambridge sat for portraits by him, the unique contribution that Macdonald made to Irish history and visual culture has never been adequately recognised until now.

Crookshank and Glin were aware of Macdonald's famine painting *An Irish Peasant Family discovering the Blight of their Store*, which they describe as "his most dramatic picture … one of the very few contemporary paintings recording the tragic years of the Great Famine" (*Ireland's Painters*), and later they reference it again, this time declaring that it was "as far as we know, the sole surviving contemporary depiction in oils of the disaster". Unlike Niamh O'Sullivan, they do not attach any particular importance to this fact, or wonder why others had not also painted it. Instead they pass on immediately to talk of other things. A painting of such a subject by a "naive" artist did not find an easy place in their account of Irish art from 1600 to 1940, although they did show some interest in his pre-famine painting of *Eagle's Nest, Killarney* (1841), with its fashionably dressed visitors and his portrait of *General Sir Rowland Smyth in Uniform* (c 1845). It has taken a new generation of art historians to penetrate the shield of exclusivity surrounding the canon of Western art that accorded importance to academically trained artists (which Macdonald was not) and valued a hierarchical approach to history, which Macdonald did not practise.

As O'Sullivan rightly points out, Macdonald is important precisely because he was an outsider to that tradition. It appears that his only training was received from his father, who was self-taught. Neither the son nor the father found it necessary to adopt the mores of classical strait-jacketing to their artistic expression. Yet Daniel Macdonald was skilful enough to represent a range of subjects in a manner that neither doffs a cap to the powermongers nor patronises the ordinary people of the country. His paintings of life around him in Co Cork, whether he is recording the visits of polite society to well-known landmarks, exploring the rich culture of folklore, rural sports and faction fighting, or showing the trauma of poverty and eviction, mix the different classes in Cork society with a degree of subtlety that is not compatible with naivety. It allows him to travel where peers like Daniel Maclise, more successful but more bound by the rules, could not follow.

O'Sullivan describes *An Irish Peasant Family discovering the Blight of their Store* as "harrowing", although it was not seen as such by some of the contemporary reviewers she cites. What is surprising is that it carefully avoids the levels of horror that O'Sullivan herself has deftly analysed in the *Illustrated London News* and other news periodicals, although to those as informed as she is about the million or so deaths already recorded by the time this picture was painted, the horror can be readily intuited. What is clear, of course, is that the so-called "fine art tradition" was so in thrall to the centrality and dignity of the human form, and so bound by its own rules of decorum, that it could not embody the kind of abjection that was required. Goya is the only artist who managed to portray human suffering on this scale and he, unlike Macdonald, did not have a colonial authority to cope with. Artists sympathetic to the Irish situation, like John Hogan and RG Kelly, were all too aware of what befell the careers of those identified with the Irish nationalist or Catholic cause and chose to avoid overt reference to it. Artists of Macdonald's generation and background found themselves obliged to pretend that the Famine wasn't happening or to at best disguise it, as Daniel Maclise did in his monumental painting of the *Marriage of Strongbow and Aoife*. Given that situation, Macdonald's achievement in this painting is remarkable, especially, O'Sullivan reminds us in the first paragraph of the book, as he was only twenty-seven and this was the painting with which he chose to introduce himself to London art lovers. The family it depicts, all three generations of them, are facing certain death, in this, the third year of failure of their crop. O'Sullivan is of the view that one of them – the grandmother – has already died and is represented as a black shrouded figure standing at the very centre of the composition, although she may also represent that folkloric figure "The black stranger walking the roads" who gave her name to Gerard Healy's 1945 play.

There are strange stylistic dips in Macdonald's paintings that are immediately obvious if you compare the difference in integrity in his handling of the central figure in *The Fighter* (1844) with that of the man throwing the bowl in *Bowl Playing* (1842) or with the foppish portrait image of Rowland Smyth (c 1845). If we think of the fighter and the Rowland Smyth images, painted within a year of each other, as representing two classes in Irish society or two aspects of masculinity, it is immediately clear that Macdonald is excited by the fighter. Indeed while a superficial reading of this might allow the viewer to dismiss it as a swashbuckling image of a street fighter, O'Sullivan correctly identifies it as having a "confrontational force" quite untypical in Irish art, and being the antithesis of the drunken Irish brawlers that populate the paintings of Erskine Nicol.

Moving from those important subject pictures to his *Eviction* painting of c 1850 or even to the earlier *Sidhe Ghaoithe* or *Fairy Blast* (1841) it could be argued that Macdonald's natural affinity with the poor surfaces through the dignity he affords them. It is abundantly manifest in his deliberate choice of subjects, and although his depictions equally avoid the sentimentality usually associated with Victorian painting and the racism of Erskine Nicol's popular paintings of Irish peasants, Macdonald's attitude is expressed in the restraint and decorum he affords the family in the unsigned *Eviction* painting of 1850, which O'Sullivan attributes to him. Even when painting a subject of lawlessness – *Tasting the Poitin in Ireland* (1844) – Macdonald avoids the usual bawdiness and persuades the viewer that this is a necessary cash-generating activity that might keep the landlord at bay, but at great risk to the family who engage in it.

It is that kind of quiet support for the downtrodden and their folk culture that makes Macdonald unique in Irish art in his generation. There is no need to claim genius for him and it is hard to see him as a prodigy as O'Sullivan does, despite his early precociousness. His treatment of space and anatomy reveal all too clearly his lack of formal training despite O'Sullivan's efforts to link his work to the classical sculptural casts that he had available to him in Cork. His courage and honesty in his treatment of the Irish poor more than compensate for such minor flaws. O'Sullivan is to be congratulated for bringing him forward as the major figure he is, and not least for the level of knowledge that she brings to each telling detail. Who else in the art world knew that the poitín-maker is wearing one shoe only because his day job as a turf-cutter required this luxury but he couldn't afford its partner? If this work does not attain the breadth of O'Sullivan's Aloysius O'Kelly book it is only because it is an exhibition catalogue and has a different job to do.

PHILIP O'LEARY | 2016

We're No Angels

Graveyard Clay: Cré na Cille by Máirtín Ó Cadhain,

translated by Liam Mac Con Iomaire and Tim Robinson

Yale University Press | 368 pp | ISBN: 978-0300203769

IF THE same rules apply in Dublin's Mount Jerome Cemetery as in the Conamara graveyard of Máirtín Ó Cadhain's *Cré na Cille*, Ó Cadhain should soon be hearing that a second English translation of his classic novel has appeared – a little over a year after the first. There is, of course, nothing unusual about multiple versions of significant works of literature hitting the market at the same time. What is unusual, however, is how long it took for *Cré na Cille* to be made available to the wide audience with an interest in Irish writing but without a knowledge of the Irish language. After all, readers of Danish and Norwegian were able to enjoy Ó Cadhain's novel in their own languages for more than decade at a time when readers of English could not share that experience unless they had access to Joan Trodden Keefe's unpublished translation in her PhD dissertation. The frustration of such readers and scholars can only have been exacerbated by having to listen for nearly seven decades while those with Irish smugly told them what they were missing.

This lack of an easily accessible English version of the novel has created several significant problems. Those unable to read *Cré na Cille* really were missing something, both a great work of literature and an essential statement about the continuing importance of the Irish language and its speakers in the evolution of a modern Irish culture. In its own time and place, *Cré na*

Cille was more than a *sui generis* comic masterpiece; it was also Ó Cadhain's zestfully successful attempt to subvert what was then and still is now an influential but pernicious view of the language and its speakers – the idea that the Gaeltacht was a site of stasis, sclerotic fixation on the past, impending silence and linguistic and cultural demise.

In *Cré na Cille*, Ó Cadhain allowed the proponents of this view the playing field of their choice. If they insisted on seeing the Gaeltacht as moribund, he would go a step further and set his novel in a graveyard, with all its characters dead and buried. If they wanted to lament the encroaching silence as emigration drained the Gaeltacht of its population, in particular its youth, he would repopulate it with characters unheard by those above ground but in their own subterranean realm creating a cacophony of distinctive wrangling voices as fundamentally real and generative as the roiling quantum flux beneath the apparent vacuum of interstellar space. Indeed virtually the whole novel is dialogue in the richest and most rambunctious of Ó Cadhain's native Cois Fhairrge Irish.

Ó Cadhain was also aware that friends of the language could be just as blind and dangerous as its enemies. Many in the language movement from its very beginning – one thinks here of Patrick Pearse for example – wanted to put native speakers of Irish on a lofty ideological pedestal, seeing them as all but otherworldly beings out of place in a fallen Anglophone Ireland. Far from being elevated above their countrymen, Ó Cadhain's characters are quite literally earthy, shoved indiscriminately under ground, not isolated in some prelapsarian Gaelic paradise or reservation for colourful residual aborigines but rather involved with unedifying enthusiasm in all the muck and mire of contemporary Irish life in the 1940s.

From its initial appearance, *Cré na Cille* has had a reputation for being a difficult book, with the extraordinary fecundity and allusive richness of Ó Cadhain's Irish being seen as a problem rather than welcomed as the treasure-house it is and would have been seen as had it been written in English. The damaging misconception that Ó Cadhain's Irish is particularly, even uniquely, difficult, a misconception that has probably put readers off enjoying him in the original, has since been effectively addressed by scholars like Róisín Ní Ghairbhigh. The language in *Cré na Cille* may be challenging, but it is certainly no more so than that in many modernist classics in which the linguistic medium is also a significant element of the thematic message. Less remarked on when the novel appeared was a problem that has only grown with time. As Ó Cadhain himself wrote in 1950: "I myself was wrung out of folklore. It was the only kind of 'learning' most of my neighbours had." ("*As an mbéaloideas a fáisceadh mé féin. Ba é an t-aon chineál 'léinn' é a bhí ag formhór mo chomharsana.*")

Only a small minority of Irish people at the time could have made such a statement, and that minority has all but vanished by now. As a result, if *Cré na Cille* depicted a world that was alien to most of Ó Cadhain's countrymen in 1949, that world might well seem all but incomprehensible to readers today. References to folktales, Gaelic literary texts, traditional songs, superstitions, prophecies, cures, curses, and popular religious and cultural practices are everywhere in *Cré na Cille*. Thus a belief in both the evil eye and the malevolent power of *Leabhar Eoin* (John's book), a text borrowed from a priest that allows the one who has it to spare someone from death by substituting another victim, are central to the novel's admittedly disconnected plot. Nor was Ó Cadhain above creating his own parodic "folklore", thus again subverting traditional pieties and their champions. Interwoven with these allusions to the traditional and pseudo-traditional are references to very real events in Conamara, Ireland, and the wider world – the explosion of a mine that kills several local men during World War II, a national politics still haunted by memories of the Civil War, GAA loyalties, an inchoate awareness of Nazi genocide, and different attitudes to the warring parties in the global conflict.

Obviously then, translators taking on *Cré na Cille* face the considerable challenge of bringing into an appropriate kind of English a rich and colourful Irish shaped by very different experiences and outlooks, while at the same time not losing touch with the assumptions and values of Gaelic culture – all while trying to convey a sense of the anarchic and Rabelaisian comedy at the heart of the original. In *Graveyard Clay*, Liam Mac Con Ionmaire and Tim Robinson prove themselves up to the task. Robinson is, of course, already well-known to readers of English for his superb work as a cartographer of Conamara and the Aran Islands and is the author of a series of books on the Galway Gaeltacht that draw on his long and intimate experience as a resident of the islands. Mac Con Iomaire was actually born in Conamara only thirty years after Ó Cadhain and was thus coming of age at precisely the time and place Ó Cadhain was recreating in his novel.

According to their introductory note, "On Translating *Cré na Cille*", it was Mac Con Iomaire who produced "the basis of our translation", which was then worked through "repeatedly, almost phrase by phrase" by the two of them. Their insiders' familiarity with the language and worldview of their source is evident throughout the translation, both in the fluid ease with which the text reads and the subtle ways in which essential information is unobtrusively conveyed. Moreover, they provide an excellent introductory piece on both Ó Cadhain himself and *Cré na Cille* as well as, when necessary and never intrusively, concise and informative notes to bring readers more fully into the world of the novel.

Unavoidably, given the appearance of *Graveyard Clay* so soon after Alan Titley's *The Dirty Dust*, many will wonder which of the two should be read by someone seeking a satisfying encounter with what had become in its inaccessibility a legendary novel, one probably praised more than it was read. The answer to this question is simple – both. There has been a tendency in modern Irish language literary studies to assume that there is only room for a single definitive work in any particular area – one definitive biography, one definitive critical study, one definitive history, one definitive translation. Thus it is hardly surprising that the arrival of two translations of the same work in such short order would raise the question of which should be seen as standard and which judged a less successful effort. But surely it is hard to imagine anyone arguing that there is room for only one translation of *Moby Dick* or one *Ulysses*, particularly when the different versions are indeed different, inspired by diverse ideas about translation itself. And *The Dirty Dust* and *Graveyard Clay* are indeed quite distinctive takes on *Cré na Cille*.

It is, of course, a truism that the two principal approaches to translation are to reproduce the original as closely, even literally, as possible, and to freely recreate the "spirit" of the original given the very different resources of the target language. Thus we have "faithful" and "free" translations. However simplistic this dichotomous view may be in theory, it works very well with our two translations. Mac Con Iomaire and Robinson's *Graveyard Clay* offers a brilliantly faithful rendering of Ó Cadhain's Irish. Indeed its fidelity to *Cré na Cille* goes well beyond its linguistic accuracy. *Graveyard Clay* uses meticulous reproductions by Cian Ó hÉigeartaigh of Charles Lamb's original cover art and portraits of the novel's main characters as they appeared in the first edition. Titley, on the other hand, takes a much looser approach to the text, an approach made immediately clear by his decision to reject the literal translation of the title used by Mac Con Iomaire and Robinson in favour of *The Dirty Dust*, which he feels conveys "some sense of the rhythm of the original, along with the biblical echoes that dust we are and 'unto dust we shall return'". His is the credo of the free translator: "There is no easy equivalence between languages. It is not the meaning itself which is the problem but the tone, and feel, and echo." Still, while willing to acknowledge that "I have taken some liberties with this translation", he is quick to add "but not many".

The liberties to which he refers and which most obviously distinguish his translation from that of Mac Con Iomaire and Robinson concern linguistic register more than anything else. Specifically, this difference concerns the question of how to render into English the demotic language of the villagers. In fact, both translations take a similar approach, with the deliberately stilted and baroque passages spoken by the "Trump(et) of the Graveyard", using an orotund and intimidating English to separate this oracular and timeless voice from the speech of mere mortals. Irish is a language that is by no means deficient in curses and other terms of abuse and opprobrium, and one could think that Ó Cadhain knew them all and used most of them in *Cré na Cille*. Of course there is nothing surprising here given that most of the dialogue – and the book is virtually all dialogue – consists of arguments, accusations, innuendos and insults involving people who know each other (and each other's peculiarities and shortcomings) with a fierce intimacy after long experience going back generations.

There can be no doubt that Ó Cadhain intended their incessant and scurrilous wrangling over trivialities to be shocking to those with an idealised image of the native speaker. These are the sort of childish zero-sum games for status played by actual people rather than by Gaelic angels. Certainly much of the humour in the novel comes from the over-the-top virulence with which his characters engage in debates of paltry significance above ground and none whatsoever in the grave. Far more often than not, the two translations diverge widely in how such passages are translated, with Mac Con Iomaire and Robinson favouring a literal translation – although often the Irish word is a generic term of abuse whose specific meaning is not entirely obvious or relevant – and Titley opting for a more joltingly crude or modern expression.

A handful of examples will have to suffice here. Where in *Graveyard Clay* we find "your goose is cooked" for Ó Cadhain's "*tá a chaiscín meilte*" (literally "his meal is ground"), *The Dirty Dust* has "you're fucked". "I won't give you a red cent" ("*Ní thiúrfaidh mé comhaireamh na sop dhuit*", literally "I won't count the bundles of straw for you") in *Graveyard Clay* is "I wouldn't give you the steam of my piss" in *The Dirty Dust*. Mac Con Iomaire and Robinson's "Sure, there's no pep in him! He's an impotent old thing." ("*Ar ndó' dheamhan preab ar bith ann! Sean-phlúithid é sin*," literally "Of course there's no kick in him! That one is an impotent old man") is Titley's "There's no jizz in him! He's only a wimp and a wanker."

Various Irish terms and expressions translated as "streak of misery" in *Graveyard Clay* become "scumbag", "nasty bitch", "ugly turkey", "snotty shithead", "slitty slut" and more in *The Dirty Dust*. The frequently used curse "*Go ropa an diabhal thú*" (literally "May the devil stab you") is usually rendered "May the devil pierce you" by Mac Con Iomaire and Robinson, but is "may the devil fuck you" in Titley's version. (The relevant pronouns vary as necessary in this curse.) Indeed even "*ababúna*", the protagonist Caitríona Pháidín's untranslatable favourite expression of outrage, regularly left as is in *Graveyard Clay* and spelled "abuboona" in *The Dirty Dust*, is at one point turned by Titley into "Holy fuckaroni". And there are dozens of such examples.

Some may find this language problematic in the mouths of rural Irish speakers in the 1940s, but in fact there is a good deal of crude sexual talk in the original novel. For example, one hardly needs a corrupted Cork mind to read "*go ropa an diabhal thú*" as Titley does. Moreover, as he makes clear in his "Translator's Introduction", "the most common curses in Irish derived from the Devil himself, and to those who believed in him and his works and pomps, this was far worse than any 'fuck' or 'shit' or their attendant pards". In effect it was easier in Ó Cadhain's day – and still is – to shock readers of Irish than readers of English. An unexpected word or phrase, a neologism, a borrowing from English, all of these can be jolting when encountered in Irish. To have the same effect in English requires raising the stakes with a bit of slang or an ever reliable "fuck". Think, for example, of Paul Muldoon's translations of poems by Nuala Ní Dhomhnaill. Thus Titley's linguistic choices make sense given his aim of capturing the spirit of his original for a jaded modern anglophone audience, of letting twenty-first century readers experience the surprise and excitement (and perhaps dismay) that Ó Cadhain's original readers felt seventy years ago.

On the other hand, it should be stressed that the commitment to linguistic fidelity of Mac Con Iomaire and Robinson by no means leaves their translation either stodgy or prim. Abuse is, after all, abuse, and Ó Cadhain was a master at it. While lacking the obvious pyrotechnics of Titley's approach, their impressively faithful version loses little of Ó Cadhain's Rabelaisian vitality. Indeed at times they actually go (a bit) further than Titley himself, as when they translate "*pictiúr*" as "flick" where Titley has "film", "*raicleach*" as "bitch" where Titley has "harridan", "slut" for Titley's "hag", "*giodáinín de ghearrchaile*" as "young little rump of a woman" for Titley's "little slip of a thing", or "*M'anam muise go raibh tú dhá cláradh*" as "you were screwing her" where Titley has "you were having it off with her".

Ultimately, preference for one or the other of these translations will be a matter of personal taste. Each is a superb example of its chosen approach to translation, and neither is unduly limited by that approach. If *Graveyard Clay* is a masterfully faithful version of its original, it is also a rollicking recreation of a comic classic and a damn good read. If *The Dirty Dust* takes liberties with *Cré na Cille*, it does so for reasons that make good sense and that help give modern readers a more immediate sense of how it was experienced by those who read it in Irish hot off the presses. With regard to these two fine books, more is without a doubt better. Máirtín Ó Cadhain has been nobly served by his translators. Someone should tell him.

Novels and Novelists

SIOBHÁN PARKINSON *surveys the work of Nobel literature laureate Herta Müller, whose* Atemschaukel *is based on a series of interviews with Oskar Pastior, a German-Romanian poet who spent five years in a Soviet prison camp. Müller's melding of the documentary and the lyrical, Parkinson finds, presents personal experience with an extraordinary physical directness.*

KEVIN STEVENS *writes that, though American literary life has no shortage of self-aggrandisers willing to play the publicity game – Hemingway, Mailer, Vidal – the media is most interested by those who play hard to get. Don DeLillo and his postmodern predecessor Thomas Pynchon are recent examples, but the gold standard of American literary isolation is JD Salinger.*

If we were asked to say what was the hallmark of English fiction, writes GEORGE O'BRIEN, *we might answer that it's very concerned with manners. American fiction, Henry James and a few others apart, is different. Focusing on striving, it has produced the novel of bad manners. And the crime novel, in its modern form an American invention, is the last word in bad manners.*

CAROL TAAFFE *examines one writer's reading of another. Colm Tóibín returned to the subject of Henry James on several occasions in the years after the appearance of his novel* The Master. *If that work acted like a subtle echo chamber of James's fiction, reading Tóibín's essays feels a little like stepping behind the wizard's curtain.*

A publisher's reader who had been sent a copy of Vladimir Nabokov's Lolita *felt that he could only recommend "that it be buried under a stone for a thousand years". Nevertheless, it was published, first in Paris and then, in 1958, in New York. Humbert Humbert, who relates the story of his infatuation with the prepubescent Lolita, is, writes* TIM GROENLAND, *"one of the great examples of the unreliable narrator in literature". But while he may be unreliable, not to mention reprehensible and possibly insane, he is the only narrator we've got.*

Two collections of short stories and the novel City of Bohane, *writes* MATTHEW PARKINSON-BENNETT, *established Kevin Barry's reputation as one of the most exciting and bold writers of our time.* Beatlebone, *a work of technical brilliance by a literary talent in virtuoso mode, enhances that reputation.*

The Hunger Angel

Atemschaukel by Herta Müller

Carl Hanser Verlag | 304 pp | ISBN: 978-3446233911

*Ich halte die Balance, die Herzschaufel wird zur Schaukel in meiner Hand,.
wie die Atemschaukel in der Brust.*

I hold the balance; the heart-shovel becomes a swing in my hand,
like the swing of one's breath in one's chest.

THE TITLE of this extraordinarily powerful and moving novel translates
literally as "Breath Swing", but it is cited in English as "Everything I Possess
I Carry with me", which is the first line of the text. Apparently, it is under
this title that the book will appear in English. (The UK/US rights have been
acquired by Granta/Metropolitan, who have published other titles of Müller's.)

Herta Müller was born in Romania in 1953; her family belonged to a
German-speaking minority known as Banat Germans (Banat is a place), and
German is her mother tongue. She was persecuted under Ceausescu for non-
cooperation with the regime and left Romania in 1987 and settled in Berlin,
where she still lives, working as a writer and academic.

Most of Müller's work is concerned with the experience of the German-
speaking Transylvanian Saxon minority in Romania, who were subject to cruel
persecution by the Russians after World War II, ostensibly in retribution for
Nazi war crimes. As the war came to an end, Germans of working age living

in Romania were routinely rounded up, deported to labour camps and used as slave labour for the reconstruction of the USSR after the devastation caused by the war. Herta Müller's own mother, as Müller reveals in the afterword to *Atemschaukel*, spent five years in a Soviet labour camp, an experience about which she remained silent for the rest of her life.

This documentary novel is based on a series of interviews with labour camp survivors, and particularly with a German-Romanian poet, Oskar Pastior, who himself spent five years in a Soviet camp and is clearly the model for Leopold Auberg (Leo), the novel's protagonist narrator, a seventeen-year-old German-Romanian who is transported to a camp in Ukraine and spends five years there as a forced labourer. The original plan was for Herta Müller and Oskar Pastior to write this book together, but Pastior died before it was written so Müller wrote it herself.

Herta Müller first came to the attention of Irish readers when *The Land of Green Plums* (originally published as *Herztier*, literally "Heart Beast") won the Impac award back in the late 1990s, and to my knowledge that remains the only one of her novels that has ever been easily available in English. (It has recently been reissued by Granta.) A handful of her books have been translated, but, as you might expect, they were published by small literary imprints and have not had wide currency.

I say "as you might expect", because that is generally the case with translations: English-speakers are unforgiving of foreign names on book covers; add a term like "Transylvanian Saxons"; indeed, throw in a reference to anywhere east of about Klagenfurt; stick an umlaut on the author's name – and you're sunk. (Clever of old Stieg Larsson and Henning Mankell to have such nice unintimidating names – if you must be a foreigner, it seems, the least you can do is be "pronounceable".)

One counterbalance to English-speaking prejudice just might be the Nobel Prize for Literature. (That lights a special glow in the hearts of Irish readers, of course – not only do we recognise this accolade: we feel we almost own it.) Herta Müller was awarded the Nobel Prize in October, to the surprise, even the dismay, of many. Opinions are divided about her work, but to my mind she is unquestionably a world-class writer, an extraordinarily poetic, passionate and uncompromising voice with something important to say to the human condition.

Müller won the Nobel Prize, but *Atemschaukel* itself did not win this year's Deutscher Buchpreis (German Book Prize, the Booker Prize for Germany so to speak), though it was shortlisted for this popular award. Doubtless the presence on the judging panel of one of the book's harshest critics did not help *Atemschaukel*'s cause. Iris Radisch, writing in *Die Zeit* (published online under the startling headline "Kitsch or World Literature?") criticised it for insincerity:

> There is an unserious, disengaged virtuosity [about *Atemschaukel*] that does not do justice to this serious author and her undoubtedly deeply felt outrage. The era of Gulag literature that takes our breath away has reached its natural conclusion, and it cannot be revived at second-hand with harp music and angel songs.

These last words are a reference to the recurring image in *Atemschaukel* of the "hunger angel" – a personification of hunger that is imagined as a kind of demented guardian angel who haunts each of the inmates of the camp. Müller's ironic use of the term "hunger angel" might, I suppose, conjure up a seraph in celestial robes playing the harp, but it is pretty clear that this one is a heartless beast who represents unrelenting suffering:

> Always the hunger is there.
> Because it is there, it comes when it wants to and how it wants to.
> The causative principle is the handiwork of the hunger-angel.
> When he comes, he comes in force.
> The cement and the hunger-angel ... are in cahoots. Hunger tears the pores apart and crawls in. When it's inside, the cement forms a seal over it, and you are cemented.
> The heart-shovel has a scoop as big as two heads side by side. It is in the shape of a heart and concave, big enough to accommodate five kilos of coal or the whole of the hunger-angel's backside.
> The hunger-angel puts my cheeks on his chin, he sets my breath swinging.
> The breath swing is a delirium, and what a delirium!

This hunger-angel is self-evidently no heavenly harpist. (The quotations above are separate, taken at random from various places in the novel.)

Die Zeit published an article by Michael Naumann in contradiction of Radisch's, under the same heading of "Kitsch or World Literature?" Where

Radisch sees kitsch (though to be accurate, she does not use that actual word – it appears only in the heading), Naumann sees a masterpiece:

> Saying the unsayable about everyday fear in a dictatorship – fear of arrest, torture and murder in peculiar ways – is this author's art. She looks with the eyes of the victim on the political masters of terror, and calls it by its name. She is one of the significant imaginative witnesses of our lamentable times.

A more mundane question is raised in *Der Spiegel*, in an article surveying the novels on the Deutscher Buchpreis shortlist, before the award was made:

> Herta Müller's novel *Atemschaukel*, for all it is concerned with life in a communist prison camp, uses a language that is far too elaborate to appeal to a wide audience.

If Iris Radisch is concerned that the language is too flowery – as an English writer might have put it – too self-consciously poetic, for the subject matter, the *Spiegel* journalist considers it "*allzu elaboriert*" – far too elaborate – not for the subject matter, but for a mass audience, and it is certainly true that this is not a novel that is likely to have wide appeal. It is an immensely rewarding read, but it is undoubtedly challenging.

The *Spiegel* commentator's remarks may be rather banal, but his comment raises a question about what it is that readers expect of novels, a question that Müller herself raises in the first chapter of *Atemschaukel*. This chapter, "On Packing", describes the protagonist's pathetically careful packing of his shabby collection of borrowed and made-over items into a makeshift suitcase for the journey to the camp. Among these items is a handful of books: a copy of *Faust*, one of *Zarathustra*, and two poetry books – a large anthology and a particular collection. "No novels," he remarks, "because novels you read just once, then never again."

Which is not true, of course, or at least it is only true of the general kind of novel, the kind with mass appeal. What an unfortunate word we use to label prose fiction of a certain length! – a word brittle with superficiality and suggestive of the throwaway. The word used in German, as in other European languages, is *Roman*. If "novel" suggests triviality, then *Roman*, with its close relationship to "romance", is not much of an improvement. (Perhaps it is reading too much into this throwaway remark of Leo's to make a connection between the word *Roman* – the word he uses to denote throwaway literature – and the word Romania. But there it is.)

Unlike the kind of novel that Leo has no place for in his luggage, there is very little narrative suspense in *Atemschaukel*. The narrative structure has been reduced to a thin, chronological line that begins with Leo's life before his arrest, follows him on his journey to the camp, remains with him for his five years of forced labour, and then comes with him out of the camp and back into his life afterwards. There are chronological markers along the way, which give the reader something to hold onto: we are told that such and such an incident happened in the first year, or that we are now in the third year, or the fifth. But the movement forward in time that is marked by those occasional temporal indicators is otherwise barely perceptible. It's not that kind of novel.

Nor is it character-driven. Characters other than the protagonist/ narrator, Leopold, emerge from time to time – the kindly Trudi Pelikan, the camp nurse; the treacherous camp foreman Tur Prikulitsch; the simple-minded Planton-Kati; Albert Gion, with whom Leo works the night shift – but they are shadowy figures rather than the rounded, developing characters of conventional fiction, and they people the narrative rather than drive it. The narrator acknowledges this when he says that his strategy for overcoming the agony of his situation, if it is successful, will reduce people to cyphers: "Then there will be no more people living in my head, only objects. Then I will push them around on the sore spot, as one pushes one's feet in a dance."

Even Leo himself is something of an enigma. We are privy to his reminiscences, his ruminations, his grim experiences, and the whole novel is relayed in his voice, in turn lyrical, meditative, hallucinatory and distant, closed, matter-of-fact – but though the reader can sympathise with his sufferings, s/he is not invited to empathise with him personally. There are occasional incidents where Leo's emotional life comes to the surface – in particular the scene where he receives a postcard from home announcing the birth of a baby to his parents, and he is devastated at the thought that they have, as he sees it, replaced him in his absence and thereby made him insignificant – but the reader is generally kept at an emotional distance from the character.

The distance that is maintained between character and reader is not amenable to psychological explanation. It's not really – or not only – that Leo is cool because his emotions are flattened by his situation. Again, it's that this is not that kind of novel. This is not a *Bildungsroman* in the unusual setting of a labour camp. It's a book not about its protagonist but about the labour camp itself and the fear, pain, hunger, exhaustion and cold experienced by its inmates and the emotional, psychological and physical deprivation inflicted on them.

It is of course impossible to know how much of the novel as written by Müller is directly taken from what Pastior told her about his experiences. But knowing that it is based on interviews with someone whose personal experience it presents gives the reader a useful strategy for reading the otherwise perhaps unapproachable prose. The voice of the narrator is strong, like the voice of the interviewee in a television or radio documentary, and it is ruminative, speculative, reflective and reminiscent. Like a documentary, the story is told in a fragmentary way, not so much narrated as allowed to accumulate through a series of short chapters, unfolding through a combination of reminiscence, anecdote and lyrical passages. There is a story here, but it is not all joined up, and there are very few causal relationships between events. Or at least, the causal relationships are quotidian and haphazard, rather than the narratively constructed events of plot:

> The naked truth of the matter is that the lawyer Paul Gast stole his wife's, Heidrun Gast's, soup out of her bowl, until she could no longer get up, and so died, because she couldn't do otherwise; just as he stole the soup because his hunger could not do otherwise either; just as he wore her coat with the Peter Pan collar and the scuffed rabbit-fur lapels and couldn't help the fact that she had died; just as she couldn't help it that she hadn't been able to get up; as indeed our singer Loni Mich, who later wore the coat, couldn't help the fact that a coat had become available through the death of the lawyer's wife; ... just as the winter couldn't help being icy cold, and the coat couldn't help being warm; no more than the days could help being a chain of causes and effects; as the causes and effects couldn't help it either that they were the naked truth, although it was all about a coat. (Semi-colons added.)

The structure is almost anthological; the story accumulates through a series of narrated incidents, but each incident is largely independent of the other incidents in the book. The most accessible chapters are anecdotal. They present short scenes or incidents from camp life: the theft of a hoarded piece of bread; an encounter with a Russian peasant woman who gives Leo some soup and the present of a handkerchief; the story of a woman who, having been passed a message concealed inside a partially scooped-out potato, ignores the message and eats the potato; the cutting of the hair of a corpse before burial, so that it can be used to stuff draught excluders.

It seems odd to say this about a character who narrates a whole novel, and who gives such extensive and detailed descriptions of physical things, but Leo is essentially laconic – by which I mean that he leaves large gaps in the narrative, and when he does tell a story, he tells it in a matter-of-fact, documentary tone, in the voice of a witness, not an interpreter. The result is at the same time powerfully anti-sentimental and deeply moving. Our emotions are evoked but never directed. The horror of one inmate's suicide, for example, by throwing herself into a pit of mortar, is conveyed not through expressions of horror but through a series of unrelenting details about her death, ending with the image of her cap riding up to reveal the scabbed-over louse-bites on her shorn scalp. Her fellow-inmates watch in stricken horror, but in the end, what they most regret about her death is that she was buried in her clothes, "when there are living people who are freezing". No gloss on the event could be more horrifying than that matter-of-fact observation. This apparent coldness is explained by one of the five rubrics into which Leo condenses what he has learnt from his experience: "The labour camp we is singular." Or, as he says elsewhere: "You can become a monster if you don't cry. What keeps me from that, if I am not that already, is not much, at most, the sentence 'I know you will come back.'"

That last sentence, spoken to Leo by his grandmother on the night he is arrested, recurs through the novel as the thing that sustains him through the whole five years.

Language and memory are the only things left to the prisoners. Their very bodies are disappearing from overwork and lack of nourishment – "the less body you have, the more it is used to punish you". But they can reconstruct the details of their former lives, even if they torture themselves in the process:

When the hunger is greatest, we talk about our childhood and about food. The women talk more extensively about food than the men, and the women from the villages most extensively of all. With them, recipes are in at least three acts, like plays. The tension rises as various aspects of the ingredients are discussed ... Telling recipes is a greater art than telling jokes. The punchline has to make an impact, even though it is not funny. Here in the camp, a joke begins with 'You take ...'

Interspersed with the anecdotal, more conventionally narrative chapters are lyrical ones where narrative structure is replaced by an ekphrastic, densely descriptive principle. There are dreamlike sequences, litanies and meditations on objects (a shovel, a piece of cloth), creatures (lice, bed bugs, prairie dogs) and substances (coal, cement, chemicals, cinders) that embody Leo's life of enforced labour. We are presented with detailed accounts of things that are brimming with meaning, but it is up to us to divine what it is that they intend or portend. This author is certainly not going to tell us.

Some years ago, Andrea Köhler wrote of Müller's work: "Writing that is not pivoted on pain is tedious. Here it [pain] is anything but expressed. It is physically there."

Müller's extraordinary melding of the documentary and the lyrical presents experience with convincing physical directness. It is as if, by the sheer intensity of the lyrical gaze, she invents a series of objective correlatives whose unstated evocation of emotion is all the more powerful for being presented rather than represented. And so we get an account of a life lived in intense relationship to things, to physical experience and to a world brutally reduced.

Leo is pleased when he is sent to work at a distance from the camp, partly because the journey itself creates a space of time that he can treasure, because as long as you are travelling, you are not working, but also because of the opportunities it gives him to pick up evidence, however humble, of human habitation – nettles, for example, which his grandmother told him grow only where people have settled. It is not the nettles that interest him, though; he is hungry for evidence of civilisation itself:

I saw the people in their yards. I wanted to see people who did not live in the camp, people who had a home, a yard, a room with a carpet, perhaps even a carpet beater. Anywhere that carpets are beaten, I thought, you can believe in peace. Life is civilised there, there people are left in peace.

This book demands a lot of its reader. You have to read its chapters as you would read poems, slowly, attentively, one at a time, and with a suspension of narrative expectation. And you have to yield to Leo's extraordinarily creative strategy for survival, which depends on a use of language and imagination to transform the brutalised world in which he finds himself:

> Because I could not avoid chemical substances, was indeed in their thrall – they consumed our shoes, our clothes, our hands, our mucous membranes – I decided to reassign meanings to the odours of the factory to my own advantage.
>
> I talked myself into aromatic highways and persuaded myself of something alluring about every path on the premises: naphthalene, shoe polish, furniture wax, chrysanthemums, glycerine soap, camphor, heart of pine, alum, lemon blossom. I managed to become pleasantly addicted, because I did not want to allow these substances to have poisonous power over me ... What was pleasant was that chemical substances could be used, like hunger words and eating words, as swear words, and that these words were substantially necessary to me.

The transformative power that he attributes to language is ultimately what saves Leo from brutalisation. Whether that represents an overelaboration of language or a second-hand romanticisation of horror the reader must judge for him- or herself.

KEVIN STEVENS | 2010

One Hand Clapping

In Search of J.D. Salinger by Ian Hamilton

Faber and Faber | 226 pp | ISBN: 978-0571269273

IN THE Information Age, the surest path to celebrity is the long-term, single-minded effort to avoid it. For writers of serious fiction, who function best while keeping the world at bay yet depend on publicity to develop a readership, the paradox of contemporary fame is particularly perilous. For them, the work is all; yet nothing – except perhaps a fatwa – diverts attention from a book as thoroughly as a successful author's insistence on utter privacy.

Of course most writers pass their careers completely unnoticed by the general population, and many of those who toil anonymously welcome any attention that might help sell a few books. But the inexorable advance of media technology continues to hone fame's double-edged sword, to shorten the shelf-life of the work itself and to ensure that huge swathes of the public become familiar with the images and names of renowned authors they will never read. Those writers who refuse to fan the fire of celebrity are the first to be devoured by its flames.

Nowhere is this more true than in the United States, where the cult of celebrity holds a special place for authors and relentlessly cycles their work and personae through what Don DeLillo calls "the all-incorporating treadmill of consumption and disposal". Though American literary life has had no shortage of self-aggrandisers willing to play the publicity game – Hemingway, Mailer,

Vidal – the media is agitated most by those who play hard to get. DeLillo and his postmodern predecessor Thomas Pynchon are recent examples. But the gold standard of American literary isolation is JD Salinger.

Salinger's death in January this year brought down the curtain, if you can say that, on a half-century of wilful seclusion that defines his literary personality and indelibly colours interpretation of his slender published output. "It is my rather subversive opinion," he wrote in 1961 for the dust jacket of his book *Franny and Zooey*, "that a writer's feelings of anonymity-obscurity are the second most valuable property on loan to him during his working years." That arch "second most" is a classic Salinger diversion. The real question is: valuable how? For the hermetic atmosphere these feelings generate? As a testament to purity of motive? As a method of focusing on what's most important? With Salinger it is difficult to say, because in 1965, after a twenty-five-year career that had produced over thirty stories, three story collections and one of the most popular novels ever written, he opted to transform avoidance of publicity into the ultimate literary silence by refusing to publish another word for the remaining forty-five years of his life.

Which is not to say he wasn't writing. In a rare 1974 interview with *The New York Times*, Salinger said, "There is a marvelous peace in not publishing. Still. Publishing is a terrible invasion of my privacy. I like to write. I love to write. But I write just for myself and my own pleasure." According to Joyce Maynard, who had a year-long relationship with Salinger in 1972, he had finished two new novels to that point. His daughter Margaret, in her 2000 memoir, *Dream Catcher*, described how her father filed his unpublished manuscripts with a red label for those works that could be published after his death "as is", and a blue one for those that required further editing.

It will be interesting to see if Salinger's executors allow any of this work to appear. If the arc of his current *oeuvre* is anything to go by, his progression towards elliptical, self-conscious, self-reflexive narrative, which had reached fever pitch in his final published stories, might well make any new material near unreadable. Though perhaps we'll never know. In the meantime, the obsession with his public persona, shaped, whether he liked it or not, by his seclusion, jogs alongside more purely literary assessments of the influence and quality of his work. Inevitably, the jostling of these twin interests blurs the big picture and can lead to confusion – not least for critics themselves – though it can also offer clues to the meaning of literary fame in the US and the stubborn stand-off between American fiction and the forces of mass culture it feels obliged to oppose.

Ian Hamilton's 1988 study *In Search of J. D. Salinger*, reissued by Faber and Faber in April, holds a distinctive place in the history of this blurred pursuit. A serviceable account of Salinger's extant work and a decent summary of what was known of his biography at the time, Hamilton's book would have been a solid but unremarkable contribution except for its own unique and, well, self-reflexive history. Starting out life as *J.D. Salinger: A Writing Life*, the book was first delivered to Random House in 1985, set in type, and sent in bound-galley form to reviewing publications. Salinger got a copy of the galleys and did not like what he read. "He was displeased with my use of his unpublished letters," Hamilton wrote. Subsequently Salinger contacted Random House, insisting that "unless these quotations were removed forthwith, he would take all necessary legal steps to have the book enjoined".

Culled primarily from collections at Princeton and the University of Texas (and all publicly accessible), the letters were central to Hamilton's biography. After all, little else of Salinger's direct speech was in existence. Instructed by Random House to reduce the amount of direct quotation, Hamilton "hacked and juggled" the Salinger quotes in his book so that not more than ten words remained from any single letter, a percentage, it was thought by the publisher's lawyers, well within the concept of fair use. Salinger remained unhappy. The case came before a New York district court, which ruled in favour of permitting publication but left the door open for immediate appeal. Salinger did appeal and the decision was reversed, the appeals court ruling that, as Salinger had the right to protect the "expressive content" of his letters, the book could not be published with even the briefest excerpts.

Undaunted, Hamilton rewrote and retitled the book, removing the offending quotations and adding a chapter on the lawsuit. The result was a different and better work, given depth and scope by the account of the legal tussle. Hamilton's narrative of the case revealed more of Salinger's character than the letters ever would have. His robust efforts to enjoin the original book offered a perfect example of the lifelong paranoia Hamilton's "search" had consistently explored, and was also an object lesson in the perils of the famous trying to protect their privacy. In one of the keenest ironies of the case,

Time magazine, *The New York Times* and other major American publications, in reporting the suit, did exactly what Hamilton was forbidden to do: they quoted freely from Salinger's letters, ensuring that a far broader readership than Hamilton's book would ever have commanded had access to the very words the writer's lawsuit had suppressed.

Hamilton's troubles were typical of those suffered by authors who have taken on the Salinger myth. Yet, as he noted at the beginning of his search, Salinger has always been an irresistible subject:

> He was, in any real-life sense, invisible, as good as dead, and yet for many he still held an active mythic force. He was famous for not wanting to be famous. He claimed to loathe any sort of public scrutiny and yet he had made it his practice to scatter just a few misleading clues. It seemed to me that his books had one essential element in common: Their author was anxious, some would say overanxious, to be loved. And very nearly from the start, he had been loved – perhaps more whole-heartedly than any other American writer since the war.

This love is prompted by the unique seductive power of Salinger's first book and sole novel, *The Catcher in the Rye*, which has sold sixty-five million copies (and counting) since its publication in 1951. From its famous opening sentence, the voice of its narrator and protagonist, Holden Caulfield, is engaging, sympathetic, and pitch-perfect in its evocation of the blend of innocence and aggression that distinguishes adolescence:

> If you really want to hear about it, the first thing you'll probably want to know is where I was born, and what my lousy childhood was like, and how my parents were occupied and all before they had me, and all that David Copperfield kind of crap, but I don't feel like going into it, if you want to know the truth.

Young readers in particular have a sense that Holden is confiding in them, that in spite of the novel's bestselling history each has discovered Holden's charming cynicism for the first time. The knowing hyperbole, the obsession with authenticity, the distrust of social roles – Holden's attitudes, tightly wrapped around his aching vulnerability, have turned him into a perennial emblem of adolescent fragility and discontent, brought to life by Salinger's unerring stylistic touch, which is thoroughly of its time and place and yet durably resistant to datedness.

Yet rereading the novel at several decades' remove from my own teenaged earnestness, I am struck less by Holden's naiveté than by Salinger's. Knowing what we do of the author's self-imposed isolation, it is hard not to read *The Catcher in the Rye* as, in part, an expression of Salinger's impatience with society and an extension of his own desire for escape. Holden's hatred of phonies, his obsession with childhood innocence and his distrust of change condemn him to what Michael Greenberg calls "a hell of second-guessing" where "every motive is potentially corrupt" and purity "is impossible because it opposes the basic machinery of human nature". Yet Holden sees no escape from this philosophical cul-de-sac apart from fantasy. "How would you like to get the hell out of here?" he asks his old girlfriend, Sally Hayes.

> 'Here's my idea. I know this guy down in Greenwich Village that we can borrow his car for a couple of weeks. He used to go to the same school I did and he still owes me ten bucks. What we could do is, tomorrow morning we could drive up to Massachusetts or Vermont, and all around there, see. It's beautiful as hell up there. It really is.' I was getting excited as hell, the more I thought about it, and I sort of reached over and took old Sally's goddam hand. What a goddam fool I was ... 'We'll stay in these cabin camps and stuff like that till the dough runs out. Then, when the dough runs out, I could get a job somewhere and we could live somewhere with a brook and all, and, later on, we could get married or something. I could chop all our own wood in the winter-time and all. Honest to God, we could have a terrific time!'

Holden interrupts his speech to admit to the reader that he is deluding himself. But his creator? On New Year's Day 1953, eighteen months after the publication of *The Catcher in the Rye* and in the first frightening flush of lifelong fame, Salinger did flee to rural New England, moving into a small cottage in Cornish, New Hampshire that lacked electricity, running water or a furnace, where he did chop his own wood and carry water from a spring. And there he remained for the next fifty-seven years, skirmishing with the media, with potential biographers, with rubber-necking fans, and eventually even with the townspeople themselves.

This retreat to the country coincided with a conversion to Eastern mysticism that had a profound effect on Salinger's life and work. The teachings of the nineteenth century Hindu mystic Sri Ramakrishna provided him with the first of many philosophical frameworks for his increasingly ascetic *Weltanschauung*. Ramakrishna believed in the authenticity of all religions and the need to renounce the material world in order to obtain a vision of God. Hamilton is good on this critical period of Salinger's life, especially in his analysis of how these life changes were prefigured in the fiction:

> The yearning for childlikeness that has run throughout his fiction from the beginning has seemed all the more potently sorrowful because its imagined outcome is a kind of blank: flight, early death, or madness. A skilled missionary might have perceived in all this Salinger's susceptibility to swift conversion ... Up until 1952, the order he aimed to belong to was an order based on talent and on the disciplines of art. From now on, though, he will speak of 'talent' as if it were the same thing as 'enlightenment' and will seek in the curricula of holy men a way of dissolving what has all along been for him an irritating, hard to manage separation between art and life.

One of Hamilton's interviewees who knew Salinger during this time, the author Leila Hadley, remembers him writing down for her the titles of the ten best books on Zen and telling her that "he was against all descriptive writing. He couldn't see the separateness of things ... so why bother to describe them?"

The impact of conversion on Salinger's aesthetic perspective is evident in his second book, *For Esmé with Love and Squalor* (entitled *Nine Stories* in the US), which was published four months after his move to Cornish. The stories in this volume were written over the five years leading up to the book's publication and appear in the order in which they were composed. Though most of the pieces are technically accomplished and dramatically even, by the end of the collection Salinger's focus on enlightenment and oriental mysticism has begun to overshadow the realistic portrayal of character and event. Almost every story in the collection features children or childlike characters who embody innocence and vulnerability, in contrast with the adult world, which is inevitably shallow and false, if not downright corrupt.

The book does include several small masterpieces, including the opening story, "A Perfect Day for Bananafish", which so impressed *The New Yorker*'s editors upon its submission in 1947 that they sought and secured right of first refusal on all Salinger's future work. The piece balances wonderfully oblique dialogue with economic action, macabre humour and a shocking ending. The title story, which draws directly on Salinger's experience as a soldier in World War II, has a warmth and resonance that his later fiction fails to capture, and uses the conceit of childhood purity to full effect. But the final story in the book, "Teddy", about a child genius returning home by ship from England with his father, mother and younger sister, fails to sustain these heights. Most of the narrative relates Teddy's conversations about Eastern religion and philosophy with a young graduate student – conversations that go on for too long and sap the narrative and its surprising ending of significant dramatic power.

For the most part, however, *For Esmé with Love and Squalor* is a solid collection, and its stories, all but two published in *The New Yorker*, confirm Hamilton's judgment that the magazine's high standards and careful editorial stewardship marked a turning point in Salinger's career:

> Without access to the magazine's files, we cannot know what was done to these manuscripts by *The New Yorker* editors. We can guess that quite a lot was done … It can be no accident that the slackness and vulgarities that disfigured even Salinger's best stories of the [previous] decade contrived a sudden disappearance in this year … Salinger, it seems, had at last entered a world in which his own fastidiousness would be honored, and perhaps surpassed, by that of his editorial attendants.

The earlier stories were limp partly because he was simply learning his craft, but also because they were written for the "slicks", high-circulation and high-paying magazines that fed a pre-television American market for commercial short stories in the thirties and forties. Before cracking *The New Yorker*, Salinger had written twenty stories for *Collier's*, *Esquire*, the *Saturday Evening Post* and other glossies. These stories remain uncollected, and attempts over the years to reissue them always met with stiff resistance from the author. "I wrote them a long time ago," Salinger said, "and I never had any intention of publishing them. I wanted them to die a perfectly natural death … I'm not trying to hide the gaucheries of my youth. I just don't think they're worthy of publishing."

For the most part, he's right. Here is a passage from "Young Folks", published in *Story* in 1940:

> 'Well. I gotta beat it. See ya later, you two!'
> 'Take it easy!' Edna called after her. Then, 'Won't you sit down?'
> 'Well, I don't know,' Jameson said. 'I been sitting down all night, kinda.'
> 'I didn't know you were a good friend of Jack Delroy's,' Edna said. 'He's a grand person, don't you think?'
> 'Yeah, he's alright, I guess. I don't know him so good. I never went around with his crowd much.'

The dialogue is cumbersome and dated, as if from a mediocre movie of the time. Compare it with this assured passage from "Uncle Wiggily in Connecticut", published in *The New Yorker* in 1948:

> 'Oh, listen! You know who I saw last week? On the main floor of Lord & Taylor's?'
> 'Mm-hm,' said Eloise, adjusting a pillow under her head. 'Akim Tamiroff.'
> 'Who?' said Mary Jane. 'Who's he?'
> 'Akim Tamiroff. He's in the movies. He always says, 'You make beeg joke – hah?' I love him … There isn't one damn pillow in this house that I can stand. Who'd you see?'
> 'Jackson. She was – '
> 'Which one?'
> 'I don't know. The one that was in our Psych class, that always – '
> 'Both of them were in our Psych class.'

This exchange rings true, capturing the cross purposes of real-life conversation even as it carefully arranges itself in a stylised depiction of empty afternoon chat. Salinger's apprenticeship in the forties had paid off, as *The New Yorker*'s editors realised, and the stories the magazine published vindicate John Updike's judgment that Salinger "really opened my eyes as to how you can weave fiction out of a set of events that seem almost unconnected, or very lightly connected".

Yet this fecund period of five years or so at mid-century (which also included the composition and publication of *The Catcher in the Rye*) was not sustained after the flight to Cornish. "Teddy" presages a slide into self-indulgence that was to characterise Salinger's writing as he grew more and more obsessed with his privacy. The epigraph to *For Esmé with Love and Squalor* is: "We know the sound of two hands clapping. But what is the sound of one hand clapping?" In the early fifties, this Zen koan may well have had a glow of mysticism that has since been lost in the mists of cliché, but it does serve as an apt metaphor for the progress of Salinger's career from this point.

Post-1953, Salinger's public output was a grand total of five stories, all published in *The New Yorker*: "Franny" and "Raise High the Roof Beam, Carpenters" (1955), "Zooey" (1957), "Seymour: An Introduction" (1959), and "Hapworth 16, 1924" (1965). The first four also reappeared in book form. These stories are populated exclusively by the Glasses, a fictional family consisting of two retired vaudeville performers and their seven precocious children, all of whom had starred on the fictional radio quiz show *It's a Wise Child* (Teddy is their precursor). In a sense, the Glass saga starts with "A Perfect Day for Bananafish", which narrates the final hours in the troubled life of oldest child Seymour and hints at the extensive family history that Salinger was to piece together meticulously over the next two decades (and beyond – who knows what Glass material lies in the executor's files?). But in another way, this early story is the endpoint, as the later work all points to Seymour's death, the defining moment in the family narrative.

Perhaps predictably, all the Glass children we meet are interested in Zen Buddhism and the Hindu concept of Vedanta, the goal of which is a state of cosmic consciousness that cannot be described in language. Paradoxically, the more deeply Salinger explores this concept, the longer and more convoluted the stories become, culminating in the twenty-six-thousand-word "Hapworth 16, 1924" (the story made up an entire issue of *The New Yorker*), which purports to be a letter home from summer camp by a wildly precocious seven-year-old Seymour and which the novelist Jay McInerney described as "an insane epistolary monologue, virtually shapeless".

The elaborate history of the Glass family is accompanied by a retreat into formal experiment and radical self-reference. "Raise High the Roof

Beam, Carpenters", "Seymour: An Introduction" and "Zooey" are narrated by Buddy Glass, the second oldest child in the family, who suggests at points in these stories that he is also the author of "A Perfect Day for Bananafish", "Teddy" and even *The Catcher in the Rye*. Critics usually suggest that Buddy is Salinger's alter ego, but Buddy's claims make more sense as examples of postmodern self-reflexiveness. The inward-looking, highly self-conscious sense of form reflects the solipsism of the Glass family itself and the rarefied atmosphere of the stories they inhabit.

More relevantly, these characters and their stories also betray Salinger's own alienation. The fiercer his rejection of the world at large, the more complex and hermetic his fictional world – and his place within it. And the world was playing its role as if scripted. As Salinger took longer and longer to produce each story, straying further from the narrative qualities that marked his best work, the assault on his privacy reached absurd proportions. The fame created by *The Catcher in the Rye* had mushroomed as the book moved from simple bestsellerdom to cult status, propelled by growing media consciousness of fifties teenage rebellion. "Between 1956 and 1960," Hamilton noted, "no fewer than seventy pieces (on *The Catcher in the Rye* alone) appeared in American and British magazines … Salinger had a new version of himself to cope with. He had originally chosen Cornish as a retreat. From now on it would seem to him more like a fortress."

In the early sixties, *Newsweek*, *Time*, *Life* and the *New York Post* sent investigative journalists to Cornish. Their sleuthing, and the features that resulted, established a pattern for decades to come: Salinger would refuse to be interviewed; the journalist would speak to townspeople, take photographs of Salinger's jeep or mailbox, or peer over the six-and-a-half-foot fence around his property; the interviewer might get as far as speaking to Salinger's wife, Claire, or even meeting the recluse himself, only to be rebuffed; a story would follow that described Salinger's shopping routine or eating habits and speculated about the reasons for his seclusion. The interest was anything but literary, and the tone was gossipy and hypocritical – just the thing to entrench Salinger in his anti-social attitudes.

Salinger's last published story, "Hapworth 16, 1924", gives us a peculiar snapshot of his self-conception at the point where he abandoned publishing. In his long letter from camp, seven-year-old Seymour prophetically describes his brother Buddy working in the present day – that is, 1965 – in a surrounding much like Salinger's skylight-topped study in Cornish:

> It is all his youthful dreams realized to the full! ... He will be overjoyed when he sees that room, mark my words! It is one of the most smiling, comforting, glimpses of my entire life, and quite possibly with the least strings attached. I would far from object if that were possibly the last glimpse of my life.

And with this badly written passage readers have been left with their last glimpse, so far, of Salinger as a working writer. In the long, blank years to come, the eccentric defence of his privacy became the sole reason he was in the public eye, from his legal action against Hamilton in 1986 to the teasing agreement in 1997 to have "Hapworth" reprinted by a small literary press (the book never materialised) to his attempts in 2009 to prevent publication of an unauthorised sequel to *The Catcher in the Rye* by Swedish publisher Fredrik Colting. The evolution from writer to recluse was complete. Nothing happened in the last twenty-two years of his life to modify Hamilton's concluding words on Salinger's fiction:

> In 'Hapworth' the reader is blithely disregarded: 'Take it or leave it' is Salinger's unmistakeable retort to any grumbles from the nonamateurs among his audience and he seems fairly certain (indeed makes certain) that most of them will leave it. The boy Seymour really is writing to his family. The Glass family has, in this last story, become both Salinger's subject and his readership, his creatures and his companions. His life is finally made one with art.

Salinger's fear of publicity was intensely personal. His metafictional techniques are not, as they are in other American novelists who have moved beyond realism, a means of exploring a world where media saturation, technology and consumerism have, in their view, debased language and compromised the ability of traditional fiction to depict contemporary culture with the force and incision great art demands. The wariness of Pynchon and DeLillo with the media is a direct expression of their unhappiness with the destruction of meaning in advertising, popular entertainment and reportage, which in turn fuels their search for fictional forms that challenge those versions of reality.

Their reluctance to be interviewed or otherwise filtered relates directly to their vision of what fiction should achieve. In a different way, much of Philip Roth's formal experimentation, his blurring of fact and fiction, arises from his oft-expressed belief that because America's reality is so bizarre its writers struggle to construct fictional worlds that allow us to suspend disbelief (though Roth has never been shy around the media). For these writers and many others like them, criticism of contemporary culture is a component of the intellectual energy that drives their work.

Salinger, on the other hand, consistently took the media's bait. At times manipulative himself, he was in turn manipulated, and his response to this fruitless give and take was often counterproductive. In the end we have to ask if his quest for privacy, his narrative choices and his long silence did not spring from a single personal source: his Holden-like distrust of all adult behaviour and his ambiguous relationship with society. It was fate's cruel joke to make the writer of *The Catcher in the Rye* the kind of person least able to deal with its success. A man who was frightened of his own ambition.

In the long story "Franny", Salinger subjects Franny Glass to a trial by fire when she visits her boyfriend, Lane Coutell, at his college. Over an interminable lunch, their conversation unveils an unbridgeable gap between Lane's bluff worldliness and her impending spiritual crisis. Much of Franny's argument sounds like Salinger rationalising his own overwhelming tendency to withdraw from the conventional arenas of success:

'All I know is I'm losing my mind,' Franny said. 'I'm just sick of ego, ego, ego. My own and everybody else's. I'm sick of everybody that wants to get somewhere, do something distinguished and all, be somebody interesting. It's disgusting – it is, it is. I don't care what anybody says.'

Lane raised his eyebrows at that, and sat back, the better to make his point. 'You sure you're just not afraid of competing?' he asked with studied quietness. 'I don't know too much about it, but I'd lay odds a good psychoanalyst – I mean a really competent one – would probably take that statement – '

'I'm not afraid to compete. It's just the opposite. Don't you see that? I'm afraid I will compete – that's what scares me. Just because I'm so horribly conditioned to accept everybody else's values, and just because

I like applause and people to rave about me, doesn't make it right. I'm ashamed of it. I'm sick of it. I'm sick of not having the courage to be an absolute nobody.'

This passage, like many others from Salinger's late work, raises an essential question: was his long silence an act of courage to be a nobody or a failure of courage to be famous, not for shunning fame, but for writing fiction? Maybe the unpublished stories, if they ever see the light of day, will help us find an answer.

Mean Street USA

The Cambridge Companion to American Crime Fiction
by Catherine Ross Nickerson (ed)
Cambridge University Press | 208 pp | ISBN: 978-0521136068

A FEW bald generalisations first. If we were asked to say what was the hallmark of English fiction, the chances are the answer would be that it's very concerned with manners – good manners, that is; with the types of behaviour permissible under an agreed code which combines prescriptions and expectations and which reinforces, often through the implementation of social rituals, a realm (for the reader, perhaps, a fantasy) in which consensus rules and which does not allow for very much room outside the consensual.

Even Dickens, no stranger to crime or related doings in the dark of night, remains convinced that his characters can be retrieved from permanent outsider status by showing up in the drawing room's morning light, models of comportment and saying the right thing. This type of outcome is familiarly read as sentimental, and Dickens makes no apology for being a three-handkerchief writer. But it's not too difficult to see that emotionally affecting as those retrievals are, there is also a compulsory element to them, a kind of enforced social logic whereby doing right and thinking right have to be embraced. All else is wilful selfishness and leads to a bad end.

American fiction is very different. Certainly, there are American novelists of manners, first and foremost Henry James who, bless his cotton socks, depicted the course and consequences of many a deadly sin within interiors not far removed from Dickens's bleak houses. These very settings, and the accompanying sense of uprooted American characters enduring their dislocated destinies in other than their places of national origin, rarefy and circumscribe James's cast of characters and their sphere of action. They are at one remove from the *demos*, as James showed himself to be in *The American Scene*, his somewhat appalled report on the unmannerly state of the Union. But then American civic life has had, from the word go, a built-in "we the people" element, leading to much general aggro as the people tried and tried again (and are trying still) to find out who exactly they are. This type of public environment is not conducive to good manners or to manners in the consensual sense being much on people's minds. Needless to say, American culture tends to reflect the various ways in which striving thrives. It's not really so surprising, then, that rather than the novel of manners, à la James, American literature has produced the novel of bad manners. And the crime novel, in its modern form an American invention, is the last word in bad manners.

American crime fiction is not merely a matter of mean streets and jaded gumshoes. From Nathaniel Hawthorne to Flannery O'Connor, crime is a central preoccupation among the great American novelists, violent crime for the most part. Literary movements such as American naturalism would be nothing without sensational homicides, as Frank Norris's *McTeague* and Theodore Dreiser's *An American Tragedy* show; even *The Great Gatsby* needs a gun; and as is pointed out in passing in this *Cambridge Companion*, Norman Mailer, Don DeLillo and Thomas Pynchon have murder very often on their minds, while Joyce Carol Oates (strangely overlooked by *Companion* contributors) goes a Gothic step further. Crimes against the person are given a typically unexpected configuration by Toni Morrison, though funnily enough American fiction retaining ethnic traces can take crime or leave it alone. Bellow, Roth and Malamud do very well without the benefit of thuggery and its melodramatic baggage. Ditto novelists of Chinese, Vietnamese and Indian origin. Irish-America's own James T Farrell has more than his share of punk-infested mean streets, but his work gives the overall impression that it's America itself that's criminally violent, its national image not that of Lady Liberty but of a cold and distant father whose upraised hand keeps home in constant shadow.

All this fictional blood makes one wonder if we are not seeing in such a degree of imaginative interest in violent crime a return of the repressed. Living in America, it's always strange to see how poorly events so fundamental to the securing of the nation and the maintenance of the Union – the Indian wars, slavery, the struggles of labour, the civil rights struggle – are publicly discussed and represented. America, to repeat a banality, prefers to look to the future. Looking back is a downer – unless a sanitised version of what's back there is available (for Civil War read *Gone with the Wind*). As though unconsciously aware of these omissions, the parts that are not adequately addressed in forms of public speech such as, let us say, schoolbooks, seek out a language and form of their own, well and truly breaking the consensual silence not only by means of gunfire, sirens, screams and fleeing footsteps but by a barbed, aggressive lingo whose iconoclastic idiom treats interlocutors as though they are anything but partners in consensus. This language is free speech with a vengeance. As such it suits very well the contrarian identity assumed by the dick, the shamus, the gumshoe, and is consistent with his (and, for quite a few years now, her) other characteristics – unorthodox righteousness, alertness to and indifference to social class, male sexism, often allied to prudishness and self-denial, and the notion of citizenship as a kind of crusading. Such traits come across as a rebuke to various prevailing notions of collective behaviour and experience, a self-consciously oddball set of variations on American exceptionalism, a critique both of the inert presence of mass life and its tawdry accoutrements as well as of an individualism which can only validate its worth in terms of power and exploitation.

As the *Companion* makes clear, in comparison with other kinds of related novel – such staple sub-genres as the country house mystery, the spy story and the Sherlockian puzzle in particular – the *roman noir* is America's most striking and most resonantly modern contribution to crime writing. On the other hand, as we learn here, true crime narratives make up a distinctly, if not uniquely, American genre whose popularity has increased, though with all due respect to *In Cold Blood* and *The Executioner's Song*, it's hard to see why it's a genre that belongs in a companion to crime fiction. Speaking of Holmes, he was a great hit in the States, though it's interesting that no home-grown smartass was produced to compete with him, especially given that he has his origins in Edgar Allan Poe's Dupin, the first crime-buster to claim that the dark side could be kept at bay through the operation of reason alone.

But perhaps American crime is something more than a puzzle, an event which brings into play much more than reason. The setting, tone and the nature of the criminal activity with which noir – which is the definitive American crime scenario – deals (the typically unthinkable consequences for family, fame and fortune threatened by a missing family member for instance), all bring to the fore feelings of insecurity, helplessness, lack of confidence and fear for the future. Such feelings are hardly unusual, but crime novels in general highlight them by indicating that they typically supply the preconditions for murder. In American noir, outraged fortune takes on a dystopian colouration, as though there's something especially unAmerican about threats to the given order of things, an order often thought of by those in command of it as a realisation of the access to power and plenty that makes America God's own country.

Thomas Jefferson's well-known nostrum that the price of freedom is eternal vigilance is given two mutually incompatible interpretations by the private eye and his client, with the former, in effect, airing the small man's democratic doubts about the structures of privilege even as he chooses – often against his better judgment – to be employed in their defence. That is, if "employed" does not understate the nature of the ensuing social contract: the aggravation, exhaustion and incidental injuries the work entails smack of a more medieval type of servitude. And obviously the fact that the work in question takes place on the fringes of the law not only dramatises a conflict between justice and self-interest, embodied by employee and employer respectively, but tacitly explores the limits and orientations of the much vaunted freedom of the individual, which of course is one of America's more myth-inducing promises to its citizens.

Dashiell Hammett is probably the American crime writer who, thanks to his firsthand knowledge (as a former employee of the Pinkerton detective agency) but also to his ideological outlook, has the best sense of the dark and what it can disclose. More sceptical, or if you like, less romantic than Chandler, he was closer in spirit to the version of the foul rag and bone shop on show in the pulp magazines from which noir evolved (the *Companion* has some useful potted history about this evolution, about the celebrated *Black Mask* magazine and its mainstay contributor, Carroll John Daly).

His left-leaning politics gave Hammett a sensitivity not only to the dystopian milieux in which his characters were trapped but also to the self-deceiving utopian pursuits which are synonymous with wrongdoing. Remember the Maltese falcon, and all the blood and tears it caused? The most memorable thing about it is that in the end it proved to be a fake. Given his politics, and the fact that he was writing in the wake of the 1929 crash, Hammett's work risks being classified as a knee-jerk reaction to a time when the raw deal, rather than the new deal, was the norm. But this is too facile and overlooks his contribution to the writing of urban America, to the establishment of California as a distinctive fictional realm where the dystopian is in a uniquely tense relation to the utopian, and to modern rearrangements of the artistic balance between thought and action, all of which have had a lasting influence that reaches well beyond crime writing and which was also decisive in fashioning from the low cultural life of pulp fiction a new literary idiom and method.

At the same time, though he brought a new conscious awareness to the dystopian dimension of the American dream, neither Hammett nor any other crime writer actually invented that dimension. It was always there, even if in its pre-twentieth century reality it was marked by repression or conversion rather than by the forms of authentication modern crime writing accorded it. In their commitment to establishing "a city on a hill", a utopian vision of a community easily defensible from outside attack but also in need of defending from internal corruption, Puritan Americans elaborately codified and confidently abjured the evil that men do, never mind the kinds of thing non-men – women and slaves – could get up to.

One useful and popular instrument of propaganda in maintaining the desired degree of order was the execution sermon. These are not the exercises in self-criticism carried out on the scaffold by those about to die but texts composed by the clergy which turned the criminal case into a teachable moment, not only drawing the sting of execution but subsuming the reality of crime into an alternative framework of order.

The *Companion* does have something to say about these sermons as early forms of crime writing, without fully entering into their ideological dynamics, by means of which the puzzle and threat of crime is solved by Christian understanding, in which dark deeds can only be publicly discussed as preludes to seeing the light and the frailties which inevitably challenge the totalitarian ambitions of utopia are pretexts for disciplining both the malefactor and the order his misdeeds impinged upon. The sermon's inevitable rhetorical magnification of a given crime makes sin seem like a surprise, or perhaps something in the nature of a sneak attack, such as those to which the community believes itself to be prone to from those "others" outside the walls – the natives. For its ideal character to be consistent, the city on a hill should be spotless, its standing as a beacon undimmed. Hill street blues are bound to follow such willed acts of communal sublimation – though the reality of those blues is likely to be denied too.

I don't suppose anyone much remembers *Hill Street Blues*, but it is mentioned in passing in the *Companion*'s chapter on television crime shows (though the inclusion of that form of crime fiction and not film is one indication of how disappointing the book is, with most of the contributions amounting to not much more than annotated bibliographies). Those discussed, however, are all cop shows. And true enough, it's the cop who is the mainstay of crime fiction these days – another large generalisation, admittedly, made with all due respect to E Leonard, S Paretsky and many more. Numerous as private eyes still are, they are currently heavily outnumbered by cops, and nowhere more so than on television. Even in the supposedly depressed book business, there's not a state in the union that doesn't have a sleuthing cop to call its own, which perhaps goes to show that the city is everywhere now, its manners, opportunism and anxieties the stuff of the everyday from Vermont to the Navajo nation. No doubt noir crime fictions had an element of the procedural in them. Thus was conveyed its sense of work. But the pace and style of that work were quite different from police procedurals (a fairly late arrival on the American crime writing scene, incidentally; Ed McBain's 87th Precinct sets up shop around the time that the 1950s Organisation Man – who turned out to be principal consumer of cop attention – arrived on the scene).

The always strong class component of crime writing changed. Murder turned suburban and white flight and other body blows to the inner city took their toll. Police procedurals have a different tempo from private eye novels. Verisimilitude has something to do with that. The cop's working conditions are almost directly the opposite of a gumshoe's, the former working in a bureaucracy with all that entails – colleagues, superiors, lousy coffee. Such a workplace also of course reflects the increasing corporatism of the postwar world with which most readers of *policiers* will be only too familiar. But the tempo is also stodgy (and the books fatter) because of the cop protagonists themselves, who typically find it difficult to get on with the job, burdened by the personal cost of long hours and little recognition, the labyrinthine ways of the legal system in which they are entangled and a good deal of free-floating doubt as to the meaning of their mission and the value of their commitment, a state of mind which is not theirs alone but which receives an added emphasis when embodied by somebody in the front line of public service.

In certain respects, cops like Michael Connelly's Harry Bosch, say, are rogue cops, but in ways that reverse the conventional meaning of the term. Ordinarily a rogue cop is the one who takes bribes, resells the drugs from the bust, has a record of brutality and in general uses the badge to conceal his own lawless nature. These days, though, rogue cops are more likely to question authority, give back chat to their superiors, and do their best work while suspended from the job or under investigation by the department. Such figures are not new – see William P McGivern's *The Big Heat* (1953); but there does seem to be an increasing number of them. Fans of James Ellroy, especially his early stuff, will recognise the type. Their wayward conduct expresses a lack of faith in their profession's claims to righteousness, impartiality, honesty. Sooner or later they discover that they cannot go by the book, ownership and interpretation of which is in the hands of uptight and self-serving administrators (the Puritans, as it were). They have an interesting, unstated kinship with that real-life antagonist of the corporate superego, the whistleblower.

In their doggedness, isolation, outspokenness and strong taste for crap-cutting and improvisation, they recapitulate what makes the private eye stand out, even if what they're up against tends to suffer from noir deficiency, except in Ellroy's case, where it's laid on thicker than a stripper's mascara. As both part of the problem, thanks to their badge, and part of the solution, thanks to their resistant behaviour, these cops are very like the rest of us in the current condition of civil society, and in that way maintain the intriguing status of crime fiction as cultural barometer. Their manners would not please Henry James, but that's probably a good thing.

CAROL TAAFFE | 2011

Behind the Curtain

All a Novelist Needs: Colm Tóibín on Henry James by Colm Tóibín

Johns Hopkins University Press | 176 pp | ISBN: 978-0801897795

MANY OF the essays in this collection begin with raids on Henry James's letters and notebooks. Some provide hints of how his most famous stories began, while others have traces of those which were never written. In his private papers, James is shown worrying about exposure upon the publication of his sister's diary, or giving instructions for personal letters to be burnt, or – following the very public failure of his play *Guy Domville* – firmly directing himself back to the work in hand: "I take up my own old pen again – the pen of all my old unforgettable efforts and sacred struggles. To myself – today – I need say no more."

Again and again, this collection uncovers a fascinating tension between the work and the life, the public and the private. Colm Tóibín explores how the life made its way into the fiction, but in a slantwise fashion. James is shown enjoying the effects of his fame, but also guarding his solitude. For all their scholarship and insight, the essays respect the reticence and subterfuge at the heart of Henry James's work.

All a Novelist Needs brings together Tóibín's writing on James over the past decade, most of it published after the appearance of *The Master* in 2004. In effect these pieces lay bare the elements that went into making that novel because they are also explorations of the writer at work. And for that reason, they are as likely to be read for insight into Tóibín's working methods as for those of James himself. Some are essays, some reviews of the newer biographies of James and his family, others originated as introductions to recent editions of the novels. Because they were written for different occasions they vary in depth and attack, and certain ideas sound as keynotes throughout the collection. But as a whole they are never less than fascinating, together pointing the reader to central preoccupations in Tóibín's dialogue with Henry James.

The Master was an audacious novel, focused on only four years of James's life following the spectacular failure of *Guy Domville* on the London stage in 1895. But time in the novel is fluid, and just as Tóibín's writer is haunted by family and loss, the echoes of Jamesian images and patterns in *The Master* also look forward to the achievements of his later years. Condensing the life and the work, Tóibín's book inhabits the writer in a way no biography ever could, and this collection provides an intriguing complement to the novel.

The *Master* opened with some interesting byways to Henry James, one being his escape to Ireland after the *Guy Domville* debacle. This collection takes the same route, beginning with an essay on Henry James and Ireland, and ending with a story based on one of his encounters with Lady Gregory. The Irish connection might be an unimportant side route in Jamesiana, as some critics have complained, but it provides Tóibín with a useful key to the lock of the writer's imagination.

"Henry James in Ireland" gathers up all those disregarded Irish connections. James's paternal grandfather grew up on a farm in Bailieborough, Co Cavan and joined a wave of Presbyterian emigration to America in the 1790s. There he became friends with Thomas Addis Emmet, brother of the doomed rebel, and the memory of Robert Emmet would remain venerated in the James family – Henry James Snr was adept at reciting the speech from the dock. But his novelist son had little sympathy for Ireland. When his sister's diary was printed two years after her death, he remarked how the years which Alice spent in England had revealed her to be "really an Irishwoman! ... in spite of her so much larger and finer than Irish intelligence".

Needless to say, James did not share what he regarded as her atavistic passion for Home Rule. At the opening of *The Master*, Tóibín has him holed up in Dublin Castle as a guest of the lord lieutenant, one of a number imported from Britain since the castle's social season was being boycotted by the Anglo-Irish. Discomfited by the squalor of the mere Irish outside the gates, bored by his courtly hosts, he broods on his recent failure. The Dublin setting highlights a strange coincidence – that *Guy Domville's* disastrous run was cut short by the launch of Wilde's *The Importance of Being Earnest*, which played on with the same actors and manager. As Tóibín suggests, the disappointment was made all the more bitter for James since he had little respect for Wilde's work. But if the brilliant success of *Earnest* obscured his own shattering failure, those positions would soon be reversed.

Tóibín's interest in Henry James and Ireland has led him to a suggestive juxtaposition of two very different writers. The secrecy, almost subterfuge, that was habitual to James's life obviously resonates with the various masks of Oscar Wilde. Where Wilde's sexuality was scandalously exposed, James's remained private and ambiguous. Where Wilde was too flamboyantly Irish (as Tóibín has James think), the other writer kicked over all traces of his Irish heritage. Both were artful writers, both taken with the style and architecture of their work. James used his to plumb psychological depths; Wilde played brilliantly on surfaces. Both were exiles who reinvented themselves in English society. One preserved the space and solitude to write; the other, disastrously, did not.

In those first chapters of *The Master*, Tóibín shows what a novelist can make of a momentary intersection of two very different lives. Without leaning too heavily on a minor historical coincidence, he sets in motion a train of association and suggestion that helps form the architecture of his Jamesian personality. And one of the most fascinating features of that novel is Tóibín's dramatisation of the same process at work in the mind of Henry James. From a novelist's point of view he recreates the indirect processes of the imagination, tracing the gradual manifestation of a story's pattern and design. It is a novel laced with hints and suggestions of what will later work itself out in James's fiction. Also laced with Jamesian phrases and paraphrases, *The Master* reads as a subtle echo-chamber of his work. Moving from that novel to Tóibín's essays and reviews on Henry James feels a little like stepping behind the wizard's curtain. But then *The Master* is itself a novel that celebrates the writer's ingenuity as much as his powers of illusion.

In a fascinating essay, "A More Elaborate Web: Becoming Henry James", Tóibín gives his own account of the imaginative process that is staged at one remove in his novel. He chose to focus *The Master* on the years 1895 to 1900, he writes, because it was then that Henry James "was building up the images and figures that would constitute the three masterpieces he was gathering all his strength to write". This essay illustrates the same process in the development of Tóibín's novel. It sketches the genesis of *The Master* from his first reading of Henry James on a college holiday in Wexford to the day the writing finally had to begin (when "no matter what happened it would become the opening of my novel"), and the accumulation of images and patterns that followed. Through a combination of accident and research, snatching inspiration from artworks and Venetian scenes and moments in James's fiction, the novel took shape. And as in *The Master* itself, the line between autobiography and fiction was constructively blurred:

> By the end of *The Master* I simply did not know if certain moments of the book took their bearings from things that were important for me or were merely inventions, images made to satisfy the pattern I was making in the book, or images made in my own likeness. In the time I was writing the chapter on James and Oscar Wilde, I was hearing stories about priests whom I had known personally going to court for sexual abuse of minors. A few days I was like James himself, sitting at home writing a book, waiting curiously for a phone call to keep me informed about the case against Father X. But maybe this had nothing to do with the Wilde chapter; maybe the book needed such a chapter, whether I needed to tell the story or not.

Though *The Master* shows Tóibín "riffing" on James, as he puts it, there is also a sense in the novel that one writer inhabits the other. The central figure he creates in that book is both himself and Henry James (and also, of course, neither himself nor Henry James). And a similarly mysterious conjunction of the work and the life in James's writing is a recurrent theme of this collection.

In many of these essays and critical introductions Tóibín marks the traces of James's cousin Minny Temple in Daisy Miller or Isabel Archer, or how the streets he walked with the American novelist Constance Fenimore Woolson found their way into *The Portrait of a Lady*, or how its drama was staged in the rooms of his friends in Florence. But these were not simply transcriptions from life; instead, what a youthful summer with Minny Temple offered, for example, was a "set of configurations" that captured James's interest and imagination. It is a subtle critical observation that Tóibín makes in a number of essays, and one he dramatised in *The Master*. In that novel, patterns develop in the writer's eye that then seem to manifest themselves everywhere he looks. *The Turn of the Screw* might have its main source in a story told by the Archbishop of Canterbury of two children left in the care of servants in an old country house, but it also evokes the plight of the James children themselves, shuttled around Europe, or Oscar Wilde's sons, separated from their father's disgrace and taken off to Switzerland. As Tóibín writes of such patterns:

> This is all a novelist needs, nothing exact or precise, no character to be based on an actual person, but a configuration, something distant that can be mulled over, guessed at, dreamed about, imagined, a set of shadowy relations that the writer can begin to put substance on.

This may be all the novelist needs, but what about the biographer? This collection also brings together Tóibín's reviews of recent James biographies, his prodigious research giving him impeccable credentials in this area. But it is the working insights of the writer that again give him the edge here. One casualty is Sheldon Novick, whose interpretation of some erotically charged letters is found to be a bit "literal-minded". In contrast to the controversy raised by Novick's reading of Henry James's homosexuality, Tóibín renders his sexual life both more ambiguous and perhaps less essential to his version of the writer. Similarly, his repeated praise for the brilliance of Lyndall Gordon's book (on Henry James, Minny Temple and Constance Fenimore Woolson) is tempered by his own wish not to pass judgment on James's relationship to these women, but to replicate the sense of moral complexity in his fiction:

> Someone who, in another novelist's hands, could be presented as a villain was, once captured by James's all-embracing and all-forgiving and oddly ironic gaze, a trapped heroine until terms such as 'villain' and 'heroine' melted into meaninglessness.

Perhaps where the biographer aims to reveal, to assess and to pass judgment, the novelist is equally drawn to ambiguity and concealment. Tóibín marks how Henry James's letters home show him to be "manipulating his family with slow doses of conceit". In James's fiction, language is "both mask and pure revelation; he played with the drama between circumlocution and bald statement". Even in the prefaces to his books, Tóibín notes, James freely described the systems and form of his novels while at the same time concealing their roots in life.

In *The Master*, Henry James is often presented standing at a window, a lone figure watching. Or perhaps that is just the overriding impression left by the novel, because throughout it he is always observing those around him – reading a story in the smallest gesture, tracing the lineaments of the unspoken. In Tóibín's sketch of the author, those powers of observation seem sharpened by James's own awareness of what he is capable of withholding. There is a central reticence in his work which Tóibín's novel masterfully captures. So it is fitting that this collection of essays on James, which does so much to uncover the workings of fiction, closes with a reminder of how fiction can be shrouded in silence and enigma.

Henry James once recorded in his notebook a story told to him by Lady Gregory about a clergyman who abandoned his wife on their wedding night, having found a letter to her from an old lover. He sent her home to her parents, though he finally ended by taking her back to live with him, but never as his wife. James did not use the story, but Tóibín does. He imagines Gregory's relief at spinning it out to the understanding novelist – a heavily disguised version of her own love affair with the poet Wilfred Blunt, her marriage to the much older William Gregory. The anecdote had grown, as Tóibín remarks elsewhere of fiction, out of something that mattered to the hidden self, though on finishing the story Gregory realises "she had said as much as she could say, which was, on reflection … hardly anything at all". And so this illuminating collection of critical essays on Henry James closes with an image of fiction as a series of Chinese whispers, a brilliant exercise in "coded disclosure". Tóibín's editor, Susan M Griffin, notes that with this last piece in the collection he declines to sum up an argument about Henry James – instead he gives us a story. But that story is argument enough.

Lost in the Funhouse

Vladimir Nabokov's Lolita *was first published in 1955 in Paris by Olympia Press. It was later published in 1958 in New York by GP Putnam's and Sons and in London by Weidenfeld & Nicolson in 1959.*

It should be, and probably has been, told to a psychoanalyst, and it has been elaborated into a novel which contains some wonderful writing, but it is overwhelmingly nauseating, even to an enlightened Freudian. To the public, it will be revolting. It will not sell, and it will do immeasurable harm to a growing reputation ... It is a totally perverse performance all around ... I am most disturbed at the thought that the writer has asked that this be published. I can see no possible cause could be served by its publication now. I recommend that it be buried under a stone for a thousand years.

AS REJECTIONS go, this one – from an early reader of *Lolita* for an unidentified publisher – is fairly emphatic. It's not clear whether the verdict was ever shown to Vladimir Nabokov, but the combination of scorn and disgust here might have been expected to provoke second thoughts in any writer. Luckily for us, Nabokov was not just any writer and by the mid-1950s, when he was carefully trying to usher *Lolita* into print, he was not a fragile first-time novelist but a respected academic at Cornell University and a seasoned literary campaigner with an impressive repertoire of fiction, criticism and translation to his name. The production of *Lolita*, published fifty-five years ago in the United States, was a long and sometimes tortuous one requiring all the reserves of literary credit the writer had built up since fleeing with his family from France in 1940.

The novel's composition was equally protracted. The idea of a man who marries a dying woman as a means to obtain the young daughter he lusts after had first appeared in an unpublished short story from 1939; it was the early 1950s before Nabokov took up the plot again in earnest, taking notes on the same index cards he used for research on his lovingly-collected butterflies. He struggled with the work, and at one point, according to his later statements to interviewers (separating Nabokov's self-mythologising from fact is a tricky business), his wife, Véra, had to prevent him from burning his pile of cards in frustration. His biographer Brian Boyd describes how, during one of the many cross-country summer trips Nabokov and his wife took in their battered car in search of new lepidopterological specimens, the novelist would escape the draughts and noise emanating from the thin-walled motel rooms in places like Dolores, Colorado by retiring to the back seat of his car, where he would scribble plot notes on batches of cards.

Over the following months, Nabokov juggled his research for the novel – reading gun catalogues, newspaper reports of sex crimes, Girl Scout manuals – with his lecturing load at Cornell, and to a friend he wrote the plaintive lament of the modern fiction writer: "I am sick of teaching, I am sick of teaching, I am sick of teaching." The novel would develop in sporadic bursts over the subsequent years, a pattern imposed not only by Nabokov's academic duties but by the huge amount of work he had taken on; he was also composing poetry, planning his next novel, *Pnin*, translating Pushkin into English and his own English-language novels into Russian, as well as finding the time to drive thousands of miles to chase butterflies in Arizona. However, in the winter of 1953, *Lolita* entered the home stretch: Nabokov spent sixteen-hour days poring over the typescript (while the indefatigable Véra marked his exam papers) and before long the novel was finally complete.

Lolita's form and plot – a long confessional monologue by Humbert Humbert, a killer, abductor and rapist (the accuracy of this last term is still argued over by critics) describing his crimes in detail – made it not only *risqué* but, as the reader above noted, potentially ruinous to anyone involved in its production. Nabokov seems to have been well aware of this, and to have expected little in the way of commercial success from the novel. He knew that *The New Yorker*, which had published extracts from several of his works (and to which he was obliged to show it first) would never touch it, and he was not only prepared to accept a relatively low royalty rate for any edition but even hoped to publish the book anonymously (an idea he gave up when advised that it was unlikely to work). Boyd describes how, when leaving Cornell for his 1954 summer holidays, he locked the typescripts in a box, hid the key in another locked box, and then locked the office itself. All of the major publishers and several friends who initially viewed it kept their distance: Simon and Schuster's editors described the book as "sheer pornography" while even sympathetic friends at New Directions felt that it was too big a gamble. Nabokov was soon searching abroad for a publisher, and the book ended up in the hands of the Olympia Press.

This Parisian imprint was run by the enterprising Maurice Girodias, whose opportunistic and undiscriminating editorial policy involved publishing experimental and occasionally salacious literary works (Miller's *Tropic of Cancer*, Burroughs's *Naked Lunch*, Donleavy's *The Ginger Man*) alongside less ambitious "dirty books" with titles like *Until She Screams*, *The Sexual Life of Robinson Crusoe* and *There's a Whip in My Valise*. Nabokov knew little of Girodias's business (he could not foresee the later dispute that would arise due to the publisher's equally cavalier attitude to copyright procedures and royalty payments) and was eager to publish, provided readers could be made to understand the book's literary status: "You and I know that *Lolita* is a serious book with a serious purpose. I hope the public will accept it as such. A *succès de scandale* would distress me."

The first months of Lolita's early reception were in fact relatively quiet: the first spark of significant public attention was its selection as one of Graham Greene's books of the year – despite it being available only in France – in the Christmas 1955 edition of *The Sunday Times*. Nabokov's fears would soon prove to be well-founded, though: the editor of the *Sunday Express* expressed the view that "without doubt it is the filthiest book I have ever read" and a controversy was born. Attempts to publish the book in the anglophone market gathered pace, and the reaction among publishers was similarly polarised. Copies of the novel (many of which had, like early editions of *Ulysses*, been smuggled through customs in the bottom of suitcases) began to circulate among British and American editors and while many recognised its merits, the opinions of those who mattered tended to be unfavourable. Most agreed with Viking Press's Simon Covici that anyone who took it on would risk a jail sentence.

When a publisher was eventually found, the promotional strategy for the novel revolved around the possibility of court action (not to mention Nabokov's anxieties about a possible threat to his continued employment at Cornell). Jason Epstein of Doubleday proposed a carefully stage-managed publication process by which the novel would be gradually rendered respectable through critical approval and carefully selected extracts; the only way to avoid ruining its chances, he thought, was by surrounding the book "with academic praise and high critical authority, letting her peep out of the pages of the *Anchor Review* until eventually, little by little, the country gets used to her".

The *Review* was a literary journal connected to Doubleday, and its 1957 issue printed a number of long excerpts along with an introductory critical essay by a literary scholar and a defensive afterword by Nabokov himself. The strategy would prove to be a winning one, and it was later copied by George Weidenfeld when the book was on its way to publication in Britain as he encouraged eminent literary figures like VS Pritchett, Stephen Spender and Iris Murdoch to write to *The Times*, invoking *Ulysses* and *Madame Bovary* in their defence of literature and of the novel's right to exist.

It is worth remembering that the novel needed its defenders. In France, *l'Affaire Lolita* exploded in 1956 as the French ministry of the interior – spurred by the British home office's alarm at the thought of British tourists bringing dirty books home from their holidays – banned it, prompting legal action from Girodias and a press debate about artistic freedom. Problems also persisted behind the scenes: the book would, in fact, eventually be published by Putnam's in the US as Girodias's excessive royalty demands caused Doubleday to withdraw from negotiations. Meanwhile, Australian federal police were raiding the Sydney *Nation* in search of the copy of the book from which the paper had published an extract. Nigel Nicolson, (one half of the UK publishing firm whose publication of *Lolita* would make its name) would soon lose his seat as Conservative MP for Bournemouth, partly as a result of the furore surrounding the book. Véra, however, seemed less worried about the potential for scandal than her husband and was perhaps more aware of the potential benefits, noting that the novel was creating "a lovely row in the French press".

Lolita contains, to a greater degree than most novels, a built-in awareness of the problems inherent in its own interpretation. The narrative is surrounded by several framing devices, the first a foreword from the novel's ostensible editor, a vaguely ludicrous individual identifying himself as "John Ray, Jr., PhD" who purports to transmit Humbert's story. JR Jr, a psychologist, dispenses questionable facts and platitudes and admits Humbert's "moral leprosy", while defending the narrative as "a great work of art". In addition, we have Nabokov's own commentary "On a Book Entitled *Lolita*", originally written for the *Anchor Review*, which subsequently became an afterword to the book we read today. It is a strange, impressive and sometimes contradictory piece of work, seeming to swat away any foolish anxieties and misconceptions the reader may have with an arrogant wave of the hand as Nabokov defends the aesthetic function of fiction and declares morality to be irrelevant in art: "no writer in a free country should be expected to bother about the exact demarcation between the sensuous and the sensual". He claims that the novel is "fantastic and personal" and argues that "it is childish to study a work of fiction in order to gain information ... about the author", but still makes sure to put some distance between himself and the narrator, assuring the reader that "there are many things" in which he disagrees with Humbert.

This pseudo-critical apparatus and defensive, distancing posturing cannot simply be put down to the prudery of an earlier time. Humbert Humbert is one of the trickiest narrators in all of literature, and the reader who opens the first chapter of *Lolita* will immediately be faced with his complicated wordplay:

> Lolita, light of my life, fire of my loins. My sin, my soul. Lo-lee-ta: the tip of the tongue taking a trip of three steps down the palate to tap, at three, on the teeth. Lo. Lee. Ta.
>
> She was Lo, plain Lo, in the morning, standing four feet ten in one sock. She was Lola in slacks. She was Dolly at school. She was Dolores on the dotted line. But in my arms she was always Lolita.

The magnificent opening passage contains the book's technique in microcosm: the masterful prose style, with its elegant variations and irresistible alliterative lilt; the contrast between lyrical sensuousness and precise detail; the skilful implication of the reader in the story's telling (try reading this passage without saying the name yourself); and the stealthy way in which disturbing, creepy hints (loins? four foot ten? school?) are threaded throughout the perfectly crafted sentences.

Not the least of the tricky questions facing the reader is this: what type of book is *Lolita* exactly? Is it a "poignant personal study", as JR Jr promises us? We are teased at the outset with the prospect of a neat Freudian unresolved-childhood-issue case study as Humbert reminisces over his unconsummated love for a doomed childhood sweetheart (the origin, he claims, of his obsession with "nymphets"). Humbert refers to the narrative as his "sinister memoir", and the book begins with pseudo-autobiographical reminiscences about his French childhood, but the odd glimpses of dark humour strike a different tone: "My very photogenic mother died in a freak accident (picnic, lightning) when I was three." Boyd observes that the book is structured as an inverted detective story: Humbert confesses to being a murderer in the opening pages – "you can always count on a murderer for a fancy prose style" – and the suspense of the plot consists in identifying his victim.

Is the novel perhaps a satire on bourgeois American values, as we might begin to suspect during the comic fish-out-of-water situation that develops when reserved European Humbert unexpectedly finds himself lodging with a suburban New England mother and her prepubescent daughter? Much of the first third of the book is a very dark and very nasty joke at the expense of Dolores/Lolita's mother, the unsuspecting and hopelessly aspirational Charlotte, described as "the rather ridiculous, though rather handsome Mrs Haze, with her blind faith in the wisdom of her church and book club" (words which also hint at Nabokov's contempt for bad or lazy readers). Indeed Charlotte fails utterly to "read" Humbert's designs and soon we find him suffering his way through a sham marriage, contemplating murder in the midst of home improvements and dinner parties while the real object of his lust is away at summer camp (it is Humbert's great success as a narrator that he portrays himself as a helpless victim "on the rack of joy" and manages to make his dilemma amusing and even sympathetic). Another freak accident – Charlotte runs in front of a car after reading Humbert's shocking diary entries, an early sign of the powerful relationship between words and action that Nabokov would soon explore further in *Pale Fire* – leaves the narrator's new wife dead and the road to realisation of his evil designs free of obstacles.

Humbert now finds himself as his stepdaughter's sole guardian, and takes full advantage. After bringing her from camp to a hotel, another convenient twist of fate saves him from having to take responsibility for his plans. He insists that "it was she who seduced me" and in another uncomfortable inversion, portrays his child victim as his corruptor: "Sensitive gentlewomen of the jury, I was not even her first lover." The following portion of the book takes the form of a depraved road trip, as Humbert spends his days in "guilty locomotion" and enjoys his newfound power in a series of motels. The couple's relationship oscillates between one of co-conspirators – Bonnie and Clyde on the run from the law – and one of terrorist and hostage. Their "extensive travels all over the States" could be read as a dark reflection of the classic American road narrative and their "wild journey" a sinister counterpoint to Kerouac's *On the Road*, written and published more or less contemporaneously with *Lolita*. Humbert's grip on reality seems to loosen here as his prose stretches into rhapsodic reveries and ecstatically aestheticised paeans to the "quick-silverish water and harsh green corn", the "mysterious outlines of table-like hills, and then red bluffs ink-blotted with junipers, and then a mountain range, dun grading into blue, and blue into dream ..."

Humbert, showing a creepily fastidious concern for his captive's "formal education", eventually decides to settle in a small college town where Lolita can return to school. There is more queasy domestic comedy here as Humbert plays the dual roles of jealous lover and disapproving dad struggling to prevent his increasingly assertive "daughter" from going on dates and taking part in the school play. Soon they decide to hit the road again, and this is where the plot really thickens; the novel mutates into an extended paranoid chase scene as obsessive, gun-toting Humbert, whose lust has by now deepened into an obsessive and doomed urge for control (Martin Amis described the novel as "a study in tyranny"), starts to become aware of a mysterious presence trailing, tracking and perhaps even pre-empting his movements. We sense that we may be leaving the expected confines of the realist novel here, and several questions begin to present themselves. Who is the enigmatic playwright Quilty, and why does he seem to have an almost supernatural status in the plot? Is Lolita making a break for her own freedom, or is this all the work of Quilty, who may be even more malign and depraved than Humbert? What do we make of the metafictional hints dotted here and there, and why does our narrator feel that he is a character in "the ingenious play staged for me by Quilty"? And why is Quilty in league with the enigmatically (and anagrammatically) named Vivian Darkbloom? As the mirror imagery multiplies and Lolita's world fractures, we realise we have wandered into the centre of the funhouse.

Nabokov would later profess total contempt for Humbert and name Lolita as one of the characters he most admired in his own work. Not all readers have arrived at the same interpretation though, and many of the book's early readers assumed that the narrator and author were interchangeable. Nabokov's French agent reported, disturbingly, that Girodias "finds the book not only admirable from the literary point of view, but he thinks that it might lead to a change in social attitudes toward the kind of love described in *Lolita*, provided of course that it has this authenticity, this burning and irrepressible ardour". Nadezhda Mandelstam (writer and wife of Russian poet Osip) told a critic that in her mind "there was no doubt that the man who wrote *Lolita* could not have done so unless he had in his soul those same disgraceful feelings for little girls". These may seem like simplistic readings that break one of the basic tenets of criticism, namely the recognition of the division between author and fictional narrator (was Anthony Burgess a closet sociopath? Is it fair to suspect Bret Easton Ellis of plotting serial murder?); however, the novel itself makes this division difficult, and many critics have found themselves under Humbert's spell.

Humbert is considered to be one of the great examples of the unreliable narrator in literature. The real problem for interpretation, however, lies in the fact that while he may be unreliable – not to mention criminal, reprehensible and possibly insane – he is the only narrator we've got. He tells the story from start to finish (even when we begin to question his control of it); more confusingly, he is also charming, funny and entertaining. It is hard not to enjoy his blatant, playful invention of names, supposedly altered for legal purposes (Harold D Doublename, Miss Opposite); the cruel humour in the choice of words in "the man having a lavish epileptic fit on the ground in Russian Gulch State Park"; and the subtlety in vivid observations such as

"Mrs Haze gently touched the silver on both sides of her plate, as if touching piano keys". Humbert's obsession is so lovingly detailed, so suffused with authorial craft, that the reader can't help taking pleasure in his world: while the means by which he achieves his moments of bliss are repellent, his depiction of that bliss is so poetic ("I dissolved in the sun, with my book for fig-leaf, as her auburn ringlets fell all over her skinned knee, and the shadow of leaves I shared pulsated and melted on her radiant limb") that we are carried unwillingly along with him. As Lionel Trilling noted, our recognition of the fact that Humbert's joy is doomed helps him to play on our sympathies, making the novel – at one level – a story of unrequited and impossible love. Humbert runs up against one of the last taboos left (not to mention the natural time limit imposed by his obsession with "nymphets"), and our understanding that an inevitable comeuppance is on the way lends an air of twisted romance to his passion.

Humbert condemns himself before we can, describing himself as a "monster", a "brute" and an "ape", constantly professing his depravity and brutality in an effort to pre-empt judgment. He wheedles his way towards our sympathy, asking again and again for our understanding, using every rhetorical trick to get us on his side: "Please, reader: no matter your exasperation with the tenderhearted, morbidly sensitive, infinitely circumspect hero of my book, do not skip these essential pages! Imagine me; I shall not exist if you do not imagine me ..." He presents himself as a cultured aesthete in the grip of passions too refined for ordinary mortals (alluding to Keats, Dante and Virgil among many others) and enlists literature itself as his defence witness: "the gentle and dreamy regions through which I crept were the patrimonies of poets – not crime's prowling ground". He admits the presence of alterations and evasions at key points in his narrative, which makes it hard for critics even to agree on whether he can be trusted: Craig Raine contends, in disagreement with Boyd and others, that Humbert "is not an unreliable narrator and his distortions, when they occur, are acknowledged". Humbert argues that "fate" has dictated events and that he was helpless to control them ("I am nature's faithful hound") and as the bizarre events and coincidences multiply in the unfolding of the increasingly cryptic plot (the identical room numbers, the odd verbal echoes and mirroring of characters), it becomes dangerously easy to agree with him.

Lolita's relentless refusal to settle on a clear moral tone in relation to its subject matter makes it hard to pin down; critic Benjamin Widiss argues that it refuses to allow the reader to comfortably make the distinction between author and narrator and, ultimately, to "feel safe in enjoying the book". Early reaction seems to have focused on the novel's right to depict sex, without always stopping to worry about the specifics of the plot; Michael Wood points out that the way in which the novel's title has entered our language – its definition in most dictionaries is "a sexually precocious young girl" – shows, when applied to the novel, an inherent sympathy with Humbert's point of view rather than that of his victim. This not only hints at the rather schizophrenic nature of the modern view of child sexuality, but suggests that an entire culture may be guilty of misreading Nabokov's book.

Lolita, of course, would go on to sell tens of millions of copies, and in a far shorter space of time than *Ulysses*. Popular tastes had become a little more receptive to modernist fiction over the preceding decades and the victory for Allen Ginsberg's "Howl" in its 1957 trial for obscenity surely did Nabokov's cause no harm in legal or cultural terms. In the US, outrage was sporadic and local, and failed to prevent widespread cultural acceptance. An LA city official complained about the book's presence in a public library (causing an inevitable sales spike) and the Texas town of Lolita considered changing its name; meanwhile, though, Nabokov was receiving invitations to lecture at universities, his students were asking him to sign copies of the book as Christmas gifts for their parents and TV hosts and comedians were making the book and its title character a household name (Groucho Marx: "I've put off reading *Lolita* for six years, till she's 18."). Nabokov finally achieved widespread commercial success for his writing, with the sale of movie rights (to Stanley Kubrick) and paperback rights for a hefty sum; as Véra's biographer Stacy Schiff notes, one of the great ironies of *Lolita*'s success was that it allowed the author to resign from the teaching job he had been so afraid of losing in the event of any scandal. His reaction to the news that his book was becoming a bestseller was typically self-confident and dismissive: the book, he noted in a letter to his sister, was an "unbelievable success – but all this ought to have happened thirty years ago".

Lolita would return in popular culture over the coming decades, sometimes in strange guises. Kubrick's heavily censored (and very loose) film adaptation had a mixed reception; Edward Albee's 1982 Broadway adaptation flopped badly (as had, less surprisingly, a mystifying 1971 attempt to turn the story into a musical), highlighting the difficulty of translating Nabokov's famous prose into another medium. The novel remains widely read and influential – its traces can be found, for example, in John Banville's *The Book of Evidence*, as Eoghan Smith noted in the previous number of this series of rereadings in the *drb* – and it places high in almost any list of great twentieth century novels you will find. Its subject matter, though, continues to present a problem for modern readers.

While the dirty bits of *Ulysses*, for example, now seem relatively tame in our own moral climate – descriptions of sex, masturbation and desire on the page are no longer argued over – *Lolita* can still shock. The idea of adolescents as sexual beings is perhaps less surprising than it was in the 1950s and the right of artists to depict disturbing and taboo activities is now rarely challenged, but the presence of a narrator who gleefully describes sexual encounters with a twelve-year-old girl, using only the most thinly-veiled figurative language ("every movement she made, every shuffle and ripple, helped me to conceal and to improve the secret system of tactile correspondence between beast and beauty – between my gagged, bursting beast and the beauty of her dimpled body in its innocent cotton frock") is still unsettling. Humbert describes how any passer-by would, by peering in his window, "obtain a free glimpse of things that the most jaded *voyeur* would have paid a small fortune to watch", an observation that makes us uncomfortably aware of the implications of following his story.

Our heightened twenty-first-century awareness of the pervasive and destructive nature of child abuse also makes its representation, if anything, more of a taboo. As recently as 1997, Adrian Lyne's film adaptation (with Jeremy Irons and Melanie Griffith) had trouble finding an American distributor despite its relative tameness. The idea of an artist reading studies of the physical development of schoolgirls and conducting interviews with his friends' daughters in order to write a novel such as this one seems more problematic in our hyper-vigilant times, and the recent cases of Pete Townsend (cautioned by police in 2003 after they accepted his explanation that he accessed child pornography for research purposes) and Will Self (who wrote angrily in August of this year about his experience of being stopped by police while walking in Yorkshire with his son) suggest that this might, strangely, be more dangerous territory for artists today than in the comparatively innocent 1950s.

Critics agree that *Lolita* still demands to be read, but don't quite reach a consensus on how exactly to read it. An entire book (*Approaches to Teaching Vladimir Nabokov's* Lolita) has been published with the stated aim of providing classroom strategies (the blurb notes that the novel's "particular mix of narrative strategies, ornate allusive prose, and troublesome subject matter complicates its presentation to students"). Critic Peter Rabinowitz describes a recent debate during which he found himself defending the novel from the charge that it uses a high-art modernist veneer to excuse pornographic pleasures, making it "an elaborate display of smoke and mirrors aimed at tricking intellectuals into defending smut", an excuse for illicit fantasy as well as a joke on Nabokov's most devoted readers. Widiss defines the novel as "an endless hall of mirrors" and a "deliberate provocation"; even the afterword, he argues, is a "full-blown literary performance, as complex and convoluted as the novel it accompanies", and the difficulty of identifying the author's own position is precisely the point.

"Faced with a Nabokov novel," Zadie Smith writes, "it's impossible to rid yourself of the feeling that you've been set a problem, as a chess master sets a problem in a newspaper." Certainly, while Humbert asks the reader "not to mock me and my mental daze", the suspicion is that the power dynamic in his tale is a little different. A Nabokov reader, perusing an intricate surface of sculpted prose, literary allusions and intertextual links, is apt to feel in a similar position to Humbert's hapless neighbour:

> In my chess sessions with Gaston, I saw the board as a square pool of limpid water with rare shells and stratagems rosily visible upon the smooth tesselated bottom, which to my confused adversary was all ooze and squid-cloud.

Lolita, as much as any other work in modern literature, illustrates the pleasures and the stakes involved in agreeing to play the game.

Mind Games

Beatlebone by Kevin Barry

Canongate | 272 pp | ISBN: 978-1782116134

IN 1967 John Lennon and Yoko Ono bought Dorinish, one of the cluster of small islands in Clew Bay, Co Mayo. Their plan to make a home there never came to pass, and instead John allowed a New Age community known as "The Diggers" to use the island for a number of years, thus creating a piece of what Kevin Barry calls "the as yet unwritten radical history of the west of Ireland".

Beatlebone imagines Lennon returning – or trying to return – to the uninhabited island in 1978. He wishes to spend three days alone there to engage in the therapeutic practice of Screaming (or screaming, to you and me), as taught by alternative psychologist Dr Arthur Janov of California. But what John is really after is an experience intense enough to lift him out of his creative funk, his inability to write – "His words are fucked and all over." He finds it.

Sort of. Lost and alone in the Mayo dark, John wanders into a cave where he has a series of revelatory visions, and his magnum opus takes shape in his mind:

> It will have nine songs, and it will fucking cohere, and it will be the greatest fucking thing he will ever fucking do. … This is the one that will settle every score. This is pure expression of scorched ego and burning soul. … Heard once it will haunt you fucking always.

But it will turn out that the actual task of making – the long slog in the recording studio – remains the hardest part.

This is Barry's fourth book, after two excellent collections of short stories and the Impac-winning novel *City of Bohane*. Those books established his name as one of the most exciting and bold writers of our time; this book enhances that reputation. *Beatlebone* is a work of technical brilliance by a wonderful literary talent in virtuoso mode.

Barry's Lennon is recognisably the man of his songs and TV interviews; the wit, sting and rhythm are captured by a writer with a terrific ear. The narrative is not clogged with biographical details: there are no nights in the Cavern, screaming teenage girls or squabbles between Yoko and Paul. With Lennon, the oedipal interpretation is there for the taking: he adored his mother and was traumatised by her early death; he remained angry with his father, a failure who resembled John in many ways and abandoned the family. Barry follows this line, but his exploration of Lennon's inner workings is far from simplistic, an achievement of empathetic imagination.

John is accompanied by local man Cornelius O'Grady, who has been employed to help him get to the island without attracting press attention. Much more than your average chauffeur, Cornelius becomes John's counsellor, spiritual adviser, father-figure, and, in passages, the real star of the novel. He is a wonderful, hilarious creation. There is something of a loveable Buck Mulligan about him: plump and confident, given to declamatory statements about the landscape and the sea, a calm foil for the anxious, troubled artist at his side; Barry suggests the comparison adjectivally during an outdoor shaving scene: "He slaps his face to get the blood back in. The blood comes hotly in a rush to enliven the stately face." (And isn't there a Joycean touch to those sentences, the commaless run of them, the repetition of "blood"?)

There's also a touch of Flann O'Brien's eponymous third policeman in both the gentle rural cadence of Cornelius's speech and his peculiar blend of straightforward simplicity and occult knowledge. A bundle of contradictions that somehow add up to a plausible whole, Cornelius is both the epitome of down-to-earthness, trying to talk common sense into his half-mad charge, and possessed of a kind of pagan, otherworldly earthy wisdom. He explains to John how places in the landscape retain and transmit the feelings of humans. (After four books we can say that this notion is one of Barry's major themes and chief preoccupations.) He delivers this and other strange nuggets as though he were commenting on the price of petrol. The effect is, to reuse a word, hilarious.

It wouldn't do to say here whether John makes it to his island, but, inevitably, it is the journey which is the real destination – as John remarks toward the end, "Turns out the thought of it's the thing." The stopping-points on that journey include a pub where John poses as Kenneth, a cousin of Cornelius; Cornelius's house, where John puts on Cornelius's father's old suit, and his experience briefly mingles with that of the father's ghost (the book is full of ghosts); and an abandoned hotel on Achill now occupied by a cultish New Age threesome, where Cornelius leaves John overnight while some unwanted press attention dies down.

This group is presided over by a charismatic leader with nobody's best interests at heart. Their therapy of choice is not Screaming but ranting – they "get the rants on", they "go in hard" – which resembles real alternative psychological practices of the twentieth century in which, in the belief that suffering is caused by keeping it all bottled up inside, participants ritualistically verbally abused each other in order to strip away the layers of the ego.

Such theories have largely been rejected in the decades since – what goes out comes in, and it turns out that raging fuels rage as violence begets itself – but John's encounter with the Achill freaks does provide a kind of catalyst for his subsequent inspiration. If there is a psychological theory behind *Beatlebone* it is that sometimes, at least for the artist, it is necessary to push the mind to its limits. As John explains: "What's it about? Fucking ultimately? It's about what you've got to put yourself through to make anything worthwhile. It's about going to the dark places and using what you find there."

What *Beatlebone* is about, "fucking ultimately", is the creative process and the difficulties of making. In fact it tells the journey of two artists: for the length of a chapter, the narrative voice switches to the first person and describes the author's experience of writing the novel. He "drifted into a paranoid sea of numerological speculation". He went to Clew Bay and encountered ghosts (more on that later). He found a cave which was eerily similar to one he had already written from imagination.

The book's nine chapters mirror the nine songs planned for John's new album, also titled *Beatlebone* (John was obsessed with the number nine –

think the Beatles' "Revolution 9"). The question then, with the narrative interrupted by a fourth-wall-breaking chapter, is: does it "fucking cohere"? It bloody does. The author-narrator and John's experiences are in many ways parallel. And throughout the other eight chapters, Barry employs a variety of technical tricks to make this a novel about its own making. He eschews inverted commas and employs italics in such a way as to blur the borders between John's voice and the third person narrator. John's creative block, his struggle to find the right words, becomes the narrator's difficulty ("How to explain these fucking things?"); and when an appropriate word is struck on, a voice which is the narrator's but might also be John's remarks with satisfaction, "there's a word". At the very end, John takes over (or is it the author?), the narrative voice switching to the first person.

The effect is that the text seems to shift, alive as something in the process of being made. And all this is, as you see, difficult to describe ("How to explain these fucking things?"); suffice it to say that Barry shows us the workings so that *Beatlebone* becomes both a meditation on and demonstration of the creative process. It is quite a feat, in which form and content and praxis are interwoven at the surface level. Barry is showing off, of course, and he is a performative writer, thrilling the reader with his acrobatic skill.

It remains to mention the dead – and "The Dead". The west, the land of the setting sun, has long been associated in the mythic imagination with the land of the dead. Joyce surely had that, as much as the cultural idea of Connacht as the home of romantic Ireland, in mind when he had Gabriel Conroy gaze out a window in Dublin, reflecting on the living and the dead and realising that "The time had come for him to set out on his journey westward."

Beatlebone picks up this association and runs with it. Cornelius describes paradise to John (it is a field sloping to the sea), concluding: "Certainly, John, it is in the west of Ireland." And on his journey westward – a journey in search of personal resurrection – John, haunted by his dead parents, encounters a number of spectral presences. So does the author (or the first person voice we take to be his), and part of the difficulty of making *Beatlebone*, he realises, will be "an old, old question: how do you bring up the fact of ghosts in reasonable company? Especially in the reasonable company of one's readers?" The answer is: straightforwardly. Barry approaches occultish subjects with an unapologetic matter-of-factness that wins the reader to his side.

Beatlebone was to be John's album "where he breaks the fucking line". Barry here is breaking borders of form, opening new ground. The language throughout is richly poetic, the sentences finely crafted – not a word speaks out of turn – yet they unroll themselves before you with apparent ease. In its selection of *Beatlebone*, the case has been strengthened for the Goldsmiths Prize as the most astute and relevant literary award around.

Europe and
Beyond

After reading a study of the founders of French Existentialism, Simone de Beauvoir and Jean-Paul Sartre, LARA MARLOWE *concludes that it is hard not to think they were dreadful people: politically and morally reprehensible, and unwashed and smelly into the bargain.*

Sartre and Beauvoir tended to talk up their – virtually non-existent – role in the French Resistance, but as SEAN O'HUIGINN *points out in an essay on how artists and intellectuals reacted to Occupation, they were not alone in their lack of heroism. As Jean Guéhenno wrote in his diary in 1940: "The species of the man of letters is not one of the greatest human species. Incapable of surviving for long in hiding, he would sell his soul to see his name in print."*

The Nazis called it the "Night of the People's Indignation" but the 1938 attack on German Jews that we now know as Kristallnacht had nothing reactive or spontaneous about it. It was, writes JOHN SWIFT, *a highly organised pogrom designed to further the campaign to expel Jews from Greater Germany, and eventually from Europe.*

One of the great anti-war novels of the twentieth century, All Quiet on the Western Front, *received the ultimate accolade from the Nazi regime, writes* DEREK SCALLY, *when it was thrown onto a raging bonfire outside Berlin's Humboldt University in 1933. Its author, Erich Maria Remarque, was beyond the regime's reach, having left Germany on the day after Hitler took power, but the Nazis took revenge on him anyway by executing his sister.*

PÁDRAIG MURPHY *is impressed by a study of life and death in Moscow in 1937, the year in which the secret police's "Operational Order 00447" decreed the arrest of 260,000 people and the execution of 75,950. In fact the quotas were overfulfilled and by the time the operation ended, in the following year, 386,798 people had been shot.*

After less than a decade of respectable economic growth, in 1958 the Chinese authorities launched the Great Leap Forward, a misconceived campaign designed to greatly accelerate industrial production. It was to lead, writes CORMAC Ó GRÁDA, *to many millions of deaths: the Great Leap famine was, in terms of the number of victims, the greatest famine ever.*

The historical episode known as the Paris Commune was essentially a civil war between a radicalised Paris and the rest of France. Paris was to lose and the Communards were dealt with savagely in bloody repressions. Even using the lowest estimate for killings, writes HUGH GOUGH, *there were more deaths in Paris in ten weeks than the French revolutionary terror achieved in eighteen months.*

Enfants Terribles

A Dangerous Liaison by Carole Seymour-Jones

Century | 574 pp | ISBN: 978-1844138227

IN THE preface to her brilliant, devastating biography of Existentialism's terrible twins, Carole Seymour-Jones writes that "It would be wrong ... to suppose that my admiration for both Beauvoir and Sartre ... has been in any way eroded."

The statement may have been a sop to Sylvie Le Bon de Beauvoir, Simone de Beauvoir's adopted daughter and companion for the last twenty years of her life. As Seymour-Jones acknowledges, the book could not have been written without Le Bon's help. To a detached reader, however – and all the more so to one whose French literature professors lionised the couple – *A Dangerous Liaison* dismantles another twentieth century icon. After reading Seymour-Jones's impeccably researched and documented portrayal of the founders of Existentialism, it is hard not to conclude that they were dreadful people: politically and morally reprehensible, and unwashed and smelly into the bargain.

Seymour-Jones seems to be saying that Sartre and Beauvoir's hypocrisy, lack of scruples, self-obsession, lying, and what by today's standards could only be labelled child abuse do not lessen the considerable impact of their work, or the literary quality of a masterpiece like Sartre's autobiographical *Les Mots*. Doubtless their respective *oeuvres* stand as great works of twentieth century literature. But at the end of this riveting book you are disgusted with both of them, and annoyed with yourself for being so puritanical.

Most reviewers have concentrated on the couple's wild sexual lives (of which more later), but their political stupidity arguably ranks higher in the scale of immorality. Until the Second World War, both of these future champions of engaged literature were curiously uninterested in politics. During a stay in Berlin in 1933, Sartre managed to totally ignore the rise of Nazism. Neither of them cared less about the Spanish Civil War or the election of the left-wing Popular Front government in France in 1936.

Sartre and Beauvoir loved American jazz and cinema, but hated the US government. Soviet culture bored them, but they didn't have the common sense to figure out that their judgment was flawed. Beauvoir wrote in the early 1930s: "Paradoxically, we were attracted by America, though we condemned its regime ... while the USSR, the scene of a social experiment which we wholeheartedly admired, nevertheless left us quite cold."

The behaviour of Sartre and Beauvoir during and immediately after the Second World War is probably the greatest stain on their reputation. Sartre knowingly took a plum teaching post at the Lycée Condorcet when it was vacated because Henri Dreyfus-le-Foyer (a great-nephew of Captain Alfred Dreyfus of the Dreyfus Affair) was sacked under the Vichy regime's laws against Jews. "Careerist to the bone, it was his hunger for fame which led him to step over Dreyfus," Seymour-Jones writes.

Far from opposing Vichy's laws, Sartre took advantage of them. Though he denied it after the liberation of Paris, he wrote for the collaborationist weekly *Comoedia*. Jean Guéhenno, one of the principled writers who refused to publish during the occupation, wrote of Sartre and those like him: "Incapable of living a long time hidden, he would sell his soul in order to have his name appear. A few months of silence, of disappearance – he can't stand it."

Sartre submitted his play *The Flies* to German censors and socialised with German officers who came to see it. When Simone de Beauvoir lost her job in 1943 for teaching the works of the homosexual writers Gide and Proust, Sartre got her a post at French national radio, which was by then part of the German propaganda machine.

Sartre and Beauvoir compare badly with Albert Camus, who was their friend for less than a decade. Camus risked his life by writing anti-Nazi articles in the Resistance newspaper *Combat*, and by using his office at the Gallimard publishing house as a mailbox. Yet he was always modest about his role. Not only did Sartre reject every opportunity to play a part in the Resistance but when the Americans arrived in Paris he considered them to be invaders, like the Germans. "The arrival of the American army in France seemed to many people, including myself, like a tyranny," he wrote. Shortly after the Liberation, he added: "Never were we more free than under the Germans." It was meant to be a *boutade* or witticism, signifying that freedom had to be a deliberate choice, especially under oppression.

Sartre nonetheless performed an amazing flip-flop, becoming a postwar spokesman for the Resistance. As Olivier Todd wrote: "The less they themselves had resisted, the more certain people wanted to punish others for having collaborated." On principle, Camus – a true member of the Resistance – opposed the death sentence for the collaborationist newspaper editor Robert Brasillach, while Sartre and Beauvoir refused to sign a petition asking for a pardon. Brasillach was executed. Years later, Sartre mendaciously wrote that he had "taken an active part in the Resistance on the barricades". As Seymour-Jones comments in a rare ironic moment, "By then he probably believed it." The philosopher's fame as the founder of Existentialism spread to the US, where the *Atlantic Monthly* claimed he had "devoted himself to underground activities with sublime courage, organising illegal publications [and] representing the most brilliant tendencies of postwar French literature".

Abhorrence of the treatment of blacks in America was one of the few things Sartre got right, in the late 1940s:

> In this land of freedom and equality, there live 13 million untouchables. They wait on your table, they polish your shoes, they operate your elevator, they carry your suitcase, but they have nothing to do with you, nor you with them ... They know they are third-class citizens. They are Negroes. Do not call them 'niggers'.

Yet even when he was arguably right – about independence for Algeria, the Vietnam War or the May 1968 riots – his extreme views undermined his position. In 1961, during the Algerian war, he advocated murdering Europeans in his preface to a book by the Martinican psychiatrist Frantz Fanon: "In the first days of the revolt you must kill: to shoot down a European is to kill two birds with one stone, to destroy an oppressor and the man he oppresses". He made a similar apology for violence in May 1968:

> These young people don't want the future of our fathers – our future – a future which has proved we were cowardly, worn out, weary ... Violence is the only thing that remains, whatever the regime, for students who have not yet entered into their fathers' systems ... The only relationship they can have to this university is to smash it.

Sartre and Beauvoir were wilfully blind to the evils of the Soviet Union. They broke with Camus in 1952, in part because he condemned Sartre's support for Stalin, pointing out the older writer's "taste for servitude". Jealousy and spite were also factors in the spectacular literary break-up: Camus had rejected sexual advances by Beauvoir, and he seduced one of Sartre's mistresses, Wanda Kosackiewicz. Sartre asked an underling to demolish Camus's book *The Rebel* in a review in *Les Temps Modernes*.

On returning from one of many trips to the Soviet Union in July 1954, Sartre said: "*La liberté de critique est totale en URSS*" ("There is total freedom of criticism in the USSR"). "He later admitted this was a lie, saying "Obviously it's not true yet. But if you want it to become so, you have to help them." Little wonder Solzhenitsyn later refused to shake his hand. Sartre had an excuse, however poor: he was besotted by Lena Zonina, a Soviet agent who served as his interpreter on his Russian visits. Zonina became his mistress and dutifully reported everything he said to the KGB. Jealous as she was of Zonina, Beauvoir, like Sartre, was also a "fellow traveller" and propagandist for the USSR. In 1962 she claimed that the Gulag of Soviet labour camps were "really rehabilitation centres", adding that the internees they met approved "in principle" of the system.

It was Sartre's admiration for the USSR which led him to refuse the Nobel Prize for literature in 1964, though Beauvoir warned him: "People are going to think that you're refusing it because Camus got it first." He refused the prize, he said, because it "appears to be a distinction reserved to leaders of the Western bloc and rebels of the Eastern bloc." He reprimanded the jury for having given the award to Boris Pasternak, disapproving of the fact "that the only Soviet work to be honoured should be a work published abroad and banned at home".

By the time he turned down the Nobel Prize, Sartre was supporting five women (not including Beauvoir) and he needed the prize money. "You're spitting on 26 million (old francs)!" Wanda Kosackiewicz reproached him. In 1978, two years before his death, frail, diabetic and blind, Sartre boasted of having nine women in his life – not counting Beauvoir and her companion Sylvie Le Bon. The extended, incestuous "family" (as Sartre and Beauvoir called it) of mistresses and lovers was the end result of their famous pact, concluded on October 14th, 1929, which the couple celebrated for the next fifty years as if it were a wedding anniversary.

Sartre wanted to marry Beauvoir, whom he'd met that year at the École Normale Supérieure, but having witnessed her parents' miserable marriage, she refused. Instead, they swore to maintain their "essential" love but allow other "contingent" loves on the side, on condition that they never lie to one another. Though infidelity has for centuries been a hallmark of French marriage, the idea of "transparency" was new and would become a model for changing mores in the 1970s and 80s. In her memoirs and interviews, Beauvoir, however, lied about the relationship, claiming she had never even kissed a man on the mouth before Sartre, and minimising her "contingent" loves, in particular her relationship with Jacques-Laurent Bost, one of Sartre's students, with whom she had a long affair.

In fact, Beauvoir's first lover was René Maheu, a married fellow student at the École Normale who gave her the lifelong nickname of Castor, the French word for beaver, which resembled her surname. Within ten days of the initiation of her pact with Sartre, Beauvoir was reunited with Maheu, and rejoiced in her journal at having him "in my bedroom ... this enchanted room ... How I love him!"

There was a basic imbalance in the relationship since while Beauvoir bordered on the nymphomaniac Sartre was not very interested in sex. Both had passed the daunting *agrégation* in philosophy that year. He was ranked first, she second. Sartre was assigned to a teaching job in Le Havre, Beauvoir to Rouen. In Rouen, she established a pattern she would repeat at least three times. She seduced an immigrant, teenage female student, in this case Olga Kosackiewicz, had a lesbian affair with her, then tried to pass her on to Sartre.

Sartre was suffering from depression provoked in part by a "bad trip" on mescaline, and Beauvoir dispatched Olga to Le Havre in the hope of cheering him up. She was annoyed by his breakdown, writing: "Psychology is not my strong suit. He had no right to indulge such whims when they threatened the fabric of our joint existence." Though Olga always refused to sleep with Sartre, two girls later seduced by Beauvoir, Bianca Bienenfeld and Nathalie Sorokine, succumbed to his advances. Seymour-Jones documents his fetish with watching women make love. Both Sartre and Beauvoir confessed to a preference for virgins. When the couple did not share lovers, they wrote to each other in sadistic detail of their conquests.

For a man who did not enjoy sex, Sartre consumed an incredible number of women, who were attracted by his fame. Bianca Bienenfeld recalled that "Sartre was very ugly, with his dead eye. He was small, but with a big tummy." Bianca was only seventeen when Sartre lured her to the Hotel Mistral in Paris, where he lived at the time. As they went to his room, he remarked: "The hotel chambermaid will be really surprised, because I already took a girl's virginity yesterday."

Beauvoir's early stay in Rouen was particularly sordid. She and Olga settled in a seedy hotel:

Le Petit Mouton, with its tarts and pimps and fist fights, provided endless entertainment. [Beauvoir] had often resented sacrificing her adolescence to academic toil; now Olga enabled her to live out all her fantasies. The hotel was even more squalid than the Rochefoucauld [where they had lived earlier]. In bed, after a hasty supper of ham eaten from its greaseproof paper wrapper, Beauvoir would wake to the sound of rustling as mice dragged the wrapper from the waste-paper basket into which she had tossed it. At night she felt tiny paws pass over her face, although during the evening, when Simone and Olga played chess and drank cherry brandy, the rodents remained behind the wainscoting – not that the pair would have noticed. So drunk was Olga one evening that she rolled down the stairs and spent the night asleep at the bottom, until one of the tenants kicked her awake.

Olga was the first victim of Sartre and Beauvoir's sexual adventurism. Seymour-Jones suggests that she "may have been violated by Beauvoir" and knew about Sartre's rape fantasies, because he had written about them. The young woman began to mutilate herself. Sartre and Beauvoir recounted Olga's self-mutilation in graphic detail in their fiction. In Beauvoir's *She Came to Stay*, Françoise (Beauvoir) and Pierre (Sartre) watch Xavière (Olga):

> In her right hand she held a half-smoked cigarette which she was slowly moving towards her left hand. Françoise barely repressed a scream. Xavière was pressing the glowing brand against her skin with a bitter smile curling her lips. *C'était ... un sourire de folle*, it was the smile of a mad woman ...

The older couple watch speechlessly as Xavière/Olga continues:

> With her lips rounded coquettishly and affectedly Xavière was gently blowing on the burnt skin which covered her burn. When she had blown away this little protective layer, she once more pressed the glowing end of her cigarette against the open wound. Françoise flinched ...
> 'That's idiotic,' she said. 'You will burn yourself to the bone.'
> 'It doesn't hurt,' said Xavière.

Sartre called Olga "Ivich" in his novel *The Age of Reason*. In a scene in a nightclub, Ivich grabs a pocket knife and someone shrieks:

> Mathieu [the Sartre character] looked hurriedly at Ivich's hands. She was holding the knife in her right hand, and slashing at the palm of her left hand. The flesh was laid open from the ball of the thumb to the root of the little finger, and the blood was oozing slowly from the wound.
> 'Ivich!' cried Mathieu. 'Your poor hand!'

The Sartre-Beauvoir love triangles sold well as fiction. Bianca Bienenfeld, the Jewish girl they abandoned at the beginning of the Second World War because she became too demanding, and Nelsen Algren, Beauvoir's American lover, pleaded not to appear in their novels, to no avail. After he read Beauvoir's *Force of Circumstance*, Algren wrote:

> I've been in whorehouses all over the world and the woman there always closes the door ... but this woman [Beauvoir] flung the door open and called in the public and the press ... I don't have any malice against her but I think it was an appalling thing to do.

When Albert Camus's friends urged him to respond to the unflattering portrait Beauvoir painted of him in *The Mandarins* he refused, saying: "You don't discuss things with a sewer." Yet doubtless the most scathing critique of a Beauvoir novel (*She Came to Stay*) was recorded by the poet Jean Cocteau in his diary: "She's a bitch who recounts the lives of dogs, who gnaw at bones, who take turns to piss on the same lamp post, who bite and sniff each other's bottoms".

Sartre and Beauvoir were revolted by the idea of children, but both legally adopted young women with whom they had had affairs. Their "daughters" became the executors of their respective literary estates. Sartre probably gave Beauvoir the idea. He adopted Arlette Elkaim, an Algerian mistress who was thirty-two years his junior, in 1965. Seymour-Jones implies that another Sartre mistress, Evelyne Lanzmann (the sister of Beauvoir's lover Claude Lanzmann), committed suicide because she was so upset by the adoption.

Sartre, and especially Beauvoir, portrayed their partnership of a half-century as exemplary. But it quickly ceased to be a sexual relationship and did a great deal of damage to their "contingent" lovers. Sartre proposed marriage to at least three women other than Beauvoir; it is doubtful if their partnership would have survived his marriage. Though their sexual behaviour appeared predatory, Sartre and Beauvoir rarely broke off with members of their extended "family". He in particular felt a duty to provide financially for his mistresses.

Both had unhappy childhoods, which go a long way to explaining the way they lived. "Childhood decides everything," wrote Sartre, whose father died when he was just a year old. The boy enjoyed an almost incestuous love with his mother until he was twelve, when she remarried. Sartre identified with the poet Baudelaire, who also felt outraged and abandoned when his widowed mother found a second husband. "When you have a son like me, you don't remarry," Baudelaire wrote. For his part, Sartre said his stepfather, Joseph Mancy, "was perpetually the person I wrote against. All my life. The fact of writing was against him."

The hatred was mutual. When Sartre finally succeeded in publishing his first collection of short stories in 1937, his stepfather particularly objected to "The Childhood of a Leader", a vicious attack on the far right and Charles Maurras's Action Française. "My little one, Uncle Jo has asked me to return your book ... he is outraged," Sartre's mother, Anne-Marie, wrote to him.

She admitted she hadn't read the story herself. "But why do you write such unseemly things? ... My little one, try to regain a little purity."

All his life Sartre delighted in provoking the hated bourgeoisie from which he came. By the time he met Beauvoir at the École Normale in 1929, he'd earned a bad reputation:

> She'd heard that he'd gone naked to the student ball, that he and his friend Pierre Guille had dropped water bombs from the roof of the École Normale on to the heads of the dinner-jacketed guests below, shouting, 'Thus pissed Zarathustra!' It was common knowledge that he had vomited drunkenly on to the feet of the principal of the Lycée Henri IV on passing his *baccalauréat*, and performed in drag in *La Belle Hélène*.

His years as a *lycée* teacher in Le Havre inspired Sartre to write *Nausea*, in which the Existentialist anti-hero, Roquentin, is sickened, among other things, by the local bourgeoisie looking at paintings in an art gallery. Seymour-Jones describes the sensation Sartre created at prize day at the *lycée* where he taught:

> The rebellious teacher, supported on the platform by two colleagues, was too drunk to speak, and made a hasty exit through the emergency exit, where he could be heard vomiting. A rumour ran round the hall that his condition was due to having spent the previous night in a local brothel with his students.

Beauvoir too was a rebel. Her mother, Françoise, was a banker's daughter whose dowry was never paid because the bank went bust. Despite his aristocratic-sounding name, her father, Georges, was a dandy who was too lazy to finish law school and frittered away his money on mistresses and prostitutes. As the Beauvoir family grew ever poorer, they were forced to move to a fifth floor walk-up flat without a lift, bathroom or running water. The plight of her mother, trapped in a loveless marriage and doomed to drudgery, made the young Simone determined to escape and prefigured her most successful book, the feminist manifesto *The Second Sex*. In her diary, Beauvoir recorded:

> Every day lunch and dinner; every day washing up; all those hours, those endlessly recurring hours, all leading nowhere: how could I live like that? ... No, I told myself, arranging a pile of plates in the cupboard; my life is going to lead somewhere.

Sartre's physical ugliness was another determining factor. His grandfather had "Poulou's" golden curls shorn when the child was seven: "His mother's reaction was unexpected. She shut herself in the bedroom, weeping. Not only had her little girl been changed into a little boy, but his ugliness had been revealed."

Anne-Marie would accompany Jean-Paul to the Luxembourg Gardens, where other children refused to play with him. As an adult, he would be only five foot two and a half inches tall; one of the attractions of Beauvoir was that she was only an inch taller. As a boy, he was tiny in size, and already had a squinting cross-eye. "Shall I speak to their mothers?" Anne-Marie would ask, and the little boy shook his head No. He was, he wrote, "ever pleading and ever rejected", an experience he said he never recovered from. But he did learn to befriend little girls with a Punch and Judy theatre his mother gave him. He reconciled himself to his ugliness, and learned that intelligence is the greatest seduction: "I should have hated anyone to love me for my looks or my physical charm ... What was necessary was for them to be captivated by the charm of my ... plays, my speeches, my poems, and to come to love me on that basis."

When Sartre and Camus initially became friends in 1943, the two writers chased women together in St-Germain-des-Prés: "'Why are you going to so much trouble?' asked Camus, as Sartre showed off to a pretty girl. Sartre replied, 'Have you taken a look at my face?'"

Despite their rebelliousness, Sartre and Beauvoir shared a hunger for praise and success. In the 1930s, both suffered from repeated publishers' rejections. But both had decided in childhood that they would be writers. Beauvoir was fifteen when she answered the question in a friend's album: "What do you want to do in later life?" with the words "to be a famous author".

"I was born from writing," Sartre wrote. "By writing, I existed, I escaped from the grown-ups; but I existed only to write, and if I said: me – that meant the me who wrote." Writing was their shared passion, the glue that kept them together. Sartre often quoted Dostoevsky: "If God does not exist and man dies, everything is permissible." With a little help from Kierkegaard, Heidegger and Hegel, he and Beauvoir spun out the philosophy of Existentialism: simply stated, that we must strive to create meaning in an absurd, Godless world. Few readers mastered the complexity of Sartre's Existential treatise on *Being and Nothingness*. Now their flawed lives risk overshadowing whatever meaning they created.

Getting By

And the Show Went on: *Cultural Life in Nazi-occupied Paris* by Alan Riding
Duckworth | 432 pp | ISBN: 978-0715640678

WE HAVE a "near past", as the Russians have their "near abroad", a zone whose very familiarity can mask dimensions of strangeness which mean the "near abroad" is still essentially abroad and the "near past" is still another country, where they do things differently.

The Second World War is a period close enough to feel almost contemporary. We regularly see its newsreels and films, hear its sound recordings and to dress in its fashions would leave us looking merely "retro" rather than in fancy dress. It takes a corresponding effort of the imagination to understand how much separates us from a time where the future of Europe, and by extension the world, was open-ended to an extent that has never been the case since, and where the antique laws of military conquest were still seen as a valid basis for political structures. It looms large for many reasons, not least for its extraordinary dramatic and epic qualities, as if the gods who had produced the First World War had decided to outdo themselves in the second act of their tragedy. The sweep of the conflict, the unprecedented depth of evil of the Holocaust and its other atrocities, the morbid fascination of Hitler, who came closer than most mortals to tasting, however fleetingly, the pinnacle of social omnipotence, are crystallised in historical retrospect. But our past was still the future for those who lived then and we who view these events backwards will always be at a remove from those who had to live them forward, in all their as yet unresolved fluidity.

That corrective lens is particularly necessary in the case of occupied France, the theme of Alan Riding's fine book. We experience occupation in our time generally as an asymmetric matter, as in, say, Iraq or Afghanistan. Modern occupations are usually presented as mere temporary expedients to serve a higher purpose, greatly to the benefit of the occupied if these latter will only summon up the necessary insight and patience. The occupation of France was grounded unapologetically on the traditional rights of military conquest. It involved no even aspirational time limits. It was an engagement between two societies of broadly comparable levels of progress at the forefront of social and technical modernity. Under the exceptional circumstances of the Occupation, France became to some extent a social laboratory, and it is one of the many fascinating aspects of Riding's book to trace how the unwilling French subjects of the experiment reacted to the unprecedented stresses and dilemmas imposed on them.

The fall of France, after a German attack so risky that even the arch-gambler Hitler was dubious, neutralised in just under a month the largest army in Europe and reset to zero all political and military calculations on the continent. It ended whatever precarious equilibrium had flowed from the capacity of France and Germany to wound each other so deeply as to inhibit, if not prevent, aggression, and it seemed all too possible that Hitler had inaugurated, if not exactly a thousand-year Reich, at least an era of prolonged German hegemony in Europe.

The France which fell so suddenly and catastrophically had long been a deeply fractured society, a fracture reflected in the political volatility of the Third Republic, often referred to in the unlovely language of the hard right as *la gueuse* (the tramp, in all pejorative female applications of the word). The fault line between a strongly conservative and Catholic-oriented France and the France of the revolutionary tradition – to simplify two complex rival social and political tendencies – remained unbridged throughout the history of the Third Republic, which was almost equally unloved on the left. Sartre, burnishing, or some might say inventing, his Resistance credentials, invoked the reluctance to suffer or die "for a disgusting France, corrupt, inefficient, racist, anti-Semite, run by the rich for the rich" – until the French understood that the Nazis were worse.

The German occupation of France was unique in that it allowed a more complex interaction between conqueror and conquered than was tolerated in other German zones of occupation. Hitler's dominant motivation was to make conditions safe for his eastward expansion by neutralising France. *Mein Kampf* makes clear he could contemplate no partnership with the French arch-enemy, which had to be punished for its inveterate hatred of Germany and its past sins and denied opportunity for the future. His more concrete intentions remain uncertain. He once spoke of reducing France to its borders of the year 1500 and reincorporating the ancient kingdom of Burgundy into the Reich. It is probable that had he prevailed France would indeed have been reduced to some such rump state, carefully rendered harmless by the preponderant Reich and oriented to its purposes. In the shorter term it made sense to run the Occupation on the basis that required the least expenditure of precious German manpower, while a vagueness as to ultimate intent kept the French motivated by the hopes of some better accommodation with the Reich. If the same goal was served by some indulgence of France's decadent ways, then French decadence, as Hitler jovially pointed out to Speer, was so much the better for Germany.

For the French, the search was for some equilibrium in the bewildering circumstance of their sudden and utter defeat. As long as Marshal Pétain incorporated that hope he was idolised to a degree which would be hard to credit were not the evidence so conclusive at every level. The newsreels showing endless processions of schoolchildren being beamed at or having their chins chucked by the marshal were obviously propaganda, but there is no doubt that he, rather than de Gaulle, had the overwhelming support of the French population at the outset (it is ironic that in the wake of the greatest military catastrophe in the history of France it fell to two military figures to embody the nation's contradictory hopes for salvation).

The growing brutality of the Occupation and the ever more voracious demands of the Reich on France's wealth and manpower made it increasingly obvious, even in Vichy, that this devil's pact of collaboration was a one-sided affair – as such pacts tend to be. The increasing military pressure of the war on the Reich robbed it of its initial aura of invincibility and further swelled the ranks of the *résistants* and enhanced the role of de Gaulle.

Riding rightly emphasises the outstanding cultural achievements of France in the early modern period, and the particular prestige it accorded to its writers and artists. Through the prism of culture he encompasses the demeanour of French society as a whole, which, like Caesar's Gaul, he usefully divides into the three elements of *collaborateurs*, *résistants* and *attentistes* (the great mass of fence-sitters prepared to wait and see). Decades before the Occupation, the writer Jacques Rivière claimed that great writers could not be great moral characters, because their necessarily self-centred natures made them poorly equipped for devotion and sacrifice, and since they had to distance themselves from their feelings in order to see them, these were never as genuine as other people's. Jean Guéhenno, a writer free of any taint of collaboration, wrote in his diary in 1940: "The species of the man of letters is not one of the greatest human species. Incapable of surviving for long in hiding, he would sell his soul to see his name in print."

Not very much happened during the Occupation to refute these bleak views. Few writers were to be found in de Gaulle's entourage in London. Honourable exceptions such as Albert Cohen and Joseph Kessel were less than stellar names in the world of literature (although Kessel and his nephew, the future writer Maurice Druon, gave the Resistance its hugely resonant anthem *Le chant des Partisans*). For the most part, the luminaries of the French artistic world devoted themselves to personal and artistic survival in the treacherous new world into which they found themselves transported as if by a malevolent spell. Some even tried to use the new circumstances to advance their feuds, as when the painter Maurice de Vlaminck used his good standing with the Occupation to launch a spiteful attack on Picasso.

For writers who stayed in Paris, the circumstances of the Occupation were as strange physically as they were morally. It is harder to imagine a greater contrast than that presented then by Europe's two great capitals. London was convulsed by the nightly inferno of the Blitz, an interlude which remains a powerful heroic component in British myth and self-image. Paris became a kind of ghost town. Genet thought it was a kind of Pompeii, "a city a burglar dares dream of". Ernst Jünger, serving with the occupying forces, called it "a dead planet". The curfew confined night life to those privileged to have passes, leaving the city eerily empty. By day petrol rationing gave the streets back to pedestrians and to bicycles, rickshaws or horse-drawn conveyances which seemed to have materialised from the previous century, lending the city an unwonted stillness. Food rationing led to a novel urban agriculture, with chicken coops, rabbit hutches and vegetable beds appearing in incongruous places. The curfew also led to all-night clubs and parties, including "fiestas" fondly recalled by Sartre, which enabled revellers to make it through the night until the curfew was lifted next morning.

It was common ground between Vichy and the Germans that France's cultural life should flourish, Vichy wishing to promote one of the few dimensions of French life where an assertion of French glory was still possible, the Germans to demonstrate the normality of occupation. Naturally each envisaged this under their own particular conditions. Vichy, in accordance with its motto of *travail, famille, patrie* (work, family, fatherland), was determined to present France's plight as the result of social and political decadence rather than military failure and introduced a range of new moral legislation, for example limiting divorce, tightening the ban on abortion and criminalising homosexuality in France for the first time since the Code Napoléon had, by enlightened omission, abolished legal penalties for it almost a century and a half earlier. These measures were buttressed by a pervasive censorship, or more accurately a system of editorial prescription, combined with a control of printing, drawing all the mass media under a preventive control. German concerns related primarily to negative presentations of the Occupation and to the role of the Jews. In some other areas they were sometimes inclined to take a less censorious view than Vichy, occasionally permitting books and productions the collaborationist government wanted banned.

Disgracefully, the treatment of the Jews was not an issue which caused any particular tensions between Vichy and the Germans. Riding does full justice to this shameful dimension, where, incidentally, Catholic writers such as François Mauriac and Paul Claudel and even the frivolous Jean Cocteau emerge with greater credit than Sartre and de Beauvoir, who carefully avoided any protests on the subject which might have damaged their careers. It is no longer disputed that the notorious deportations of the Jews to the Reich were organised and executed by French people. Indeed the efficiency of the French security apparatus exacerbated the problem. Its register of enemy aliens compiled at the outbreak of the war later served as an excellent database to round up the large Jewish component of German nationals living in France. As with so many other aspects of collaboration, Vichy officials probably saw themselves as opting for the lesser evil, believing that a propitiatory offering of non-French Jews to the Reich would give some space for less savage treatment of French-born Jews, of whom about a quarter of a million survived the war. As in Germany, banal bureaucratic considerations often played an incongruous role. Pierre Laval's notorious decision to deport Jewish children with their parents was probably intended to plump up the quota but also to avoid the administrative headache of dealing with thousands of parentless children.

Rather as abusive relationships are said to be most paralysing for the victim when cruelty coexists with some measures of kindness, the German occupation could also show an amenable side, the better to entice influential artists and intellectuals into its orbit. Francophiles such as the German ambassador Otto Abetz (married to a French wife) and Gerhard Heller, the influential head of the literature department of the Propagandastaffel (the 1,200-strong bureaucracy intended to make French opinion fit for Joseph Goebbels's purposes) fancied themselves in the role of patrons of French culture. They were helped by the official German acceptance that there was a role for French culture, even if it was to be culture of the frivolous kind, to which the manly seriousness of the Reich would offer an edifying contrast. The protection of Abetz or Heller was often crucial for French writers and the benefits of their patronage could include supply of the vital ration of paper necessary to print a book or, on a less basic level, luxury fare at dinners and receptions, greatly coveted in a half-starved Paris. The intricacies and paradoxes of their interaction with French cultural life are a fascinating part of Riding's narrative, although it would take another Balzac or Proust to do the story full justice.

Riding's book goes beyond the purely cultural remit of its title and examines the impact of the Occupation on almost all sectors of French life, with many fascinating sidelights. He recounts that the theatrical hit of the entire Occupation was, improbably, Claudel's *Soulier de Satin* (The Satin Slipper), a Wagnerian-scale epic of eleven hours dealing with redemption through renunciation in baroque Spain. Jean-Louis Barrault, who directed and acted in the play, browbeat the very reluctant Claudel into reducing the Comédie-Française production to a mere five hours, overruling aesthetic objections with the imperative of the last Metro. In spite of its demands on the endurance of the audience the play had seventy-seven sold-out performances in 1944, garnering the plaudits of occupier and occupied alike.

Riding's account of French cinema under the Occupation is no less interesting. Motivated perhaps by the desire to eliminate the Jewish role in the art form and to ensure influence on such a popular medium, the Germans were the improbable patrons who enabled and in some cases financed several masterpieces of French cinema, including *Le Corbeau* (The Raven), *Les Visiteurs du Soir* (The Evening Visitors), and *Les Enfants du Paradis* (The Children of Paradise). French cinema in those years clearly benefited from the elimination of its Hollywood competitors. In spite of the double censorship of the Germans and of Vichy (it was the latter who took the scissors to what would have been French cinema's first nude shower scene, featuring Arletty and an outsize sponge) the popular nature of the art shielded it from the crasser forms of pro-German content which would have repelled French cinemagoers and allowed for at least subtexts which were assertively French, even bordering on resistance.

In terms of the behaviour of individual artists, great narcissists such as Colette and Cocteau, or the dancer Serge Lifar, remained great narcissists, treating the Occupation as just another backdrop to the central drama of their personalities but making the necessary adjustments. Colette had to hide her Jewish husband in the attic (a Jew who doesn't know he is one, as she described him). Cocteau benefited from his association with his touchingly loyal former lover Jean Marais, then taking his first steps towards stardom as a popular film actor, an association which helped to balance his insouciant networking with Germans such as Arno Breker, Hitler's favourite sculptor, whose Paris exhibition in 1942 was the high point of Franco-German cultural cooperation. For the most part the "great beasts" of French culture remaining in Paris continued an existence which remained enormously privileged – even if in reduced circumstances – compared with what was endured by their compatriots.

Riding deals also with prominent Frenchwomen who had difficulty in grasping the difference between the French and German subsets of the male tribe. Coco Chanel had always had a decidedly horizontal component to her business strategies, and she merely adapted this tried and trusted approach to the new challenges of the Occupation, sharing a suite in the Ritz with a Wehrmacht officer thirteen years her junior and probably deploying her charms also on Hitler's foreign intelligence chief Walter Schellenberg. (Her attempt to exploit Aryanisation measures to recover control of her firm from the Jewish Wertheimer family was thwarted, as they had prudently installed an "Aryan" owner, but that saga ended happily in a reconciliation after the war, when the Wertheimers' retailing clout made Chanel one of the richest women of her time.) The actress Arletty also became notorious for her German lover. Her famous defence that her heart was French but her ass international is probably apocryphal but entirely typical of her sassy style. In fact her affair with her German "Faun", as she called him, was a genuinely passionate one, and even survived the war. Her career never recovered, although her head was never, as popular legend would have it, shaven. Her lover went on to become German ambassador to the Congo, where he drowned in a swimming accident in 1960.

Riding's book is a comprehensive overview rather than one which breaks new ground. The watershed in that respect was Max Ophüls's 1969 film *Le Chagrin et la Pitié* (The Sorrow and the Pity) which demolished the myth cherished by both the Gaullist right and the communist left that France had been overwhelmingly a nation of *résistants*, whose indomitable spirit had been temporarily eclipsed by German military might. Sartre too showed the same deep need to conjure dignity from an essentially inglorious interlude. In a text which is as eloquent as it is implausible, he wrote:

> We were never more free than during the German occupation … Because the Nazi venom seeped even into our thoughts, every accurate thought was a conquest … Thus, in darkness and in blood, a Republic was established, the strongest of Republics. Each of its citizens knew that he owed himself to all and that he could count only on himself alone. Each of them, in complete isolation, fulfilled his responsibility and his role in history. Each of them, standing against the oppressors, undertook to be himself, freely and irrevocably. And by choosing for himself in liberty, he chose the liberty of all. This Republic without institutions, without an army, without police, was something that at each instant every Frenchman had to win and to affirm against Nazism. No one failed in this duty, and now we are on the threshold of another Republic. May

this Republic to be set up in broad daylight preserve the austere virtue of that other Republic of Silence and of Night.

Riding's book makes all too clear that the austere virtues of Sartre's ideal were not so prevalent but Ophüls's film features the wise observation of Sir Anthony Eden, which Riding quotes and which to some extent serves as the epigraph for his book: "If one hasn't been through the horrors of an occupation by a foreign power, you have no right to pronounce upon what a country does which has been through all that."

In retrospect it is clear that few of France's first rate cultural talents were decided collaborators. Writers such as Robert Brassilach and Pierre Drieu la Rochelle were zealous converts rather than opportunists, and they were in a minority. Riding's book has its share of villains, and its share of heroes, such as the inconspicuous Rose Valland at the Jeu de Paume museum, who meticulously and at considerable risk chronicled the art the Nazis were looting. For the most part, the French intelligentsia was guilty of accommodation rather than collaboration, and in fact developed a rough and ready code of behaviour of its own, on a spectrum from writing for a French collaborationist publication (an unfortunate professional necessity) to a promotional visit to Germany (decidedly reprehensible).

After the liberation, the sins of France's cultural elite arguably received more scrutiny and censure than those of many other even more collaborationist strands of French life, such as the business sector, but it was the obverse side of the coin to their prestige. De Gaulle, on being congratulated on drawing a massive rally of support so soon after Pétain had been able to muster his own enormous crowds, was supposed to have remarked "Ils sont les mêmes" (They are the same people). Much as de Gaulle felt his "noble lie" about resistance was a necessary therapy for France, he was also wise enough to realise its fragility, and he used his influence to keep the settling of scores within reasonable bounds. (The post-liberation exchanges between Mauriac and Albert Camus on the issue of forgiveness remain a document of permanent value, Camus ultimately conceding that Mauriac, the champion of forbearance, was right.)

After the war, the cultural leadership once exercised by France, like the political leadership exercised by Britain, was assumed by the New World, perhaps relativising in the broad sweep of history the very diverse experiences and roles of the two countries in the war. No amount of revisionism could make the Occupation anything other than an inglorious interlude in French history, but Alan Riding's book is a salutary reminder that this strange period had its splendours as well as its miseries and the human resilience he chronicles cautions us against summary judgments.

Jean Paulhan, the influential critic who used his impeccable credentials as a *résistant* to oppose the witch-hunts of the Liberation perhaps came nearest to anticipating the likely future French consensus on the Occupation, when, in defiance of all the prevailing rhetoric, he allowed a role to both "the resistant and the obedient: the first to save our principles, the second to save, as far as possible, the people and land of this country". *Hypocrites français, nos semblables, nos frères!*

JOHN SWIFT | 2013

The Barbarians Strike

The Night of Broken Glass: Eyewitness Accounts of Kristallnacht

Uta Gerhardt and Thomas Karlauf (eds)

Polity Press | 360 pp | ISBN: 978-0745650845

The Shoah is a crisis of human history. These memories are an ethical, historical and spiritual ... warning to us. They remind us that this happened and could happen again.

Romano Prodi at Auschwitz

First, they came for the Communists and I did not speak out because I was not a Communist. Then, they came for the Jews and I did not speak out because I was not a Jew. Then, they came for the trade unionists and I did not speak out because I was not a trade unionist. Then, they came for me and there was no one left to speak for me.

Martin Niemöller

A JUNIOR German diplomat, Ernst vom Rath, was shot by Herschel Grynszpan, a German-born Polish Jew, in Paris on November 7th, 1938; vom Rath died on November 9th. Hitler and Goebbels organised a fierce pogrom against Jewish persons and property, which took place on the night of November 10th and 11th and over the following days. The declared rationale was that the assassination of vom Rath had been organised by "world Jewry" with a view to disrupting the easing of international tensions brought about by the Munich Agreement in September. The real reason was to further the existing campaign to expel all Jews from Greater Germany and ultimately from Europe. The official government name for the pogrom was *Nacht der Volksempörung*, that is, "Night of the People's Indignation". The name *Kristallnacht* is a Berlin witticism. In English it is known as the Night of Broken Glass.

In the pogrom, about four hundred Jews were killed, while a very large number were arrested, publicly humiliated and physically abused, some forty thousand being sent to concentration camps, the majority to Dachau, Buchenwald and Sachsenhausen, where they were detained for at least a month in atrocious conditions. Synagogues all over Germany were burned and desecrated; Jewish homes, shops and businesses were attacked, their owners insulted and terrorised and their contents systematically and meticulously destroyed; Jewish schools, orphanages, cemeteries, youth clubs and cultural institutes were vandalised, damaged or desecrated. The reactions of non-Jewish Germans ranged from scorn, mockery and abuse, through indifference, real or feigned, to active sympathy and covert support for the victims.

The events of *Kristallnacht* fitted into a coherent package of racial theory, hate campaigns, and an increasingly severe series of anti-Jewish legal enactments. The Nuremberg Laws of 1935 had, among other things, made German Jews stateless refugees in their own country. Measures taken in 1938 included higher tax rates for Jews in February; confiscation of Jewish passports in March; compulsory registration of all Jewish assets worth over five thousand reichsmarks in April; cancellation of the rights of Jewish persons to own real property or run businesses in July; special identity cards for Jews the same month; a Jewish Emigration Office under Eichmann in August; and the withdrawal of the licence to practise from Jewish doctors and lawyers in September. Poland withdrew citizenship from all Polish Jews living abroad for more than five years in October; before the end of that month, Germany expelled sixteen thousand Polish Jews at a few hours' notice and dumped them on the Polish frontier in extremely adverse conditions.

Following *Kristallnacht*, a conference was held to discuss plans to complete the exclusion of Jews from German civic and economic life. All the key ministers, ministries and state agencies attended. Hermann Göring proposed a one billion reichsmarks "atonement levy" on Jewish assets, which was agreed and speedily passed into law. Jewish owners would have to repair the damage caused to their property at their own expense but all insurance payments were to be handed over to the state. Ghettoes and special identity marks for Jews were discussed. Other measures came into force before the end of the year, including a ban on Jewish children attending secondary schools and the expulsion of all Jewish students from universities. As pointed out by Fritz Rodeck in this volume, on the economic side this combination of specific levies and fees, special and excessive taxes, bans on ownership of or participation in business or certain professions, together with thefts, extortions, forced "Aryanisation" of businesses and the installation of provisional managers and the nullification of all legal protections amounted to a barely concealed confiscation by the state of all Jewish assets and the reduction of German Jews to beggary.

Not surprisingly, these measures produced results. According to figures quoted by Karlauf, in January 1933 about half a million Jews lived in Germany. By early March 1938 their numbers had fallen to 360,000. The *Anschluss* of that month added another 190,000 Austrian Jews, of whom 170,000 lived in Vienna. Around 19,000 Jews left Germany in the first half of 1938; in the second half of the same year, and in spite of the failure of the thirty-two-nation Évian conference in July to agree to take in substantially increased numbers of Jewish refugees, Jewish emigrants numbered 100,000 from Germany and a further 100,000 from Austria.

The core of the book under review comprises volunteered accounts of *Kristallnacht*, and the weeks and months which followed, by twenty-one victims and eyewitnesses. The accounts are organised in three sections of seven chapters each, under the headings "The Terror", "In the Camps" and "Before Emigration". They were all written within eighteen months of the events described, by persons who had managed to leave Germany. They make for vivid but grim, painful, even harrowing reading. The contributors are varied: men and women (eight of the writers are women) from different parts of Germany and Austria, including Berlin, Vienna and provincial capitals, mostly Jewish and middle class (one rabbi), mostly middle-aged or elderly, with a bias towards the professions (doctors, lawyers and teachers) and businessmen. Inevitably, there is repetition and some blurring of the stories and their impact, but the skill of the editors and the varied approaches, styles and content of the writers keep such negative effects to a minimum. The two-page foreword by Saul Friedlander (author of *The Years of Extermination: Nazi*

Germany and the Jews, 1939–1945), and the lengthier introduction by Karlauf and afterword by Gerhardt, are valuable and add interesting commentary and context. The footnotes are helpful, though perhaps too brief. An index would have been useful. Translation from the German by Robert Simmons and Nick Somers is fluent. In all three sections, some views and arguments are repeated and make a particularly forcible impression.

There was nothing spontaneous about this "boiling over of the people's wrath". The National Socialist Party organised everything but took pains not to appear as the instigator. The principal activists were young SA and SS men, often drunk. The police were involved only to the extent of ensuring that the pogrom was conducted and controlled in an orderly fashion; the fire services were instructed to take care that fires did not spread to non-Jewish property. Property was destroyed but generally not plundered; thefts and looting were small-scale and probably locally inspired. Publicity in newspapers and on radio was orchestrated in detail; a building up of tension but no hard information in advance, followed by a stress on popular anger and damage to property but little coverage of the public humiliations, assaults and murders. Then the publicity tap was turned off to minimise negative impact abroad.

What is most sickening in these stories is not the brutal savagery inflicted on defenceless people but the different perverse refinements of cruelty, some planned in detail in advance, others perhaps dreamed up at the last moment. As reported by Alice Barwold, one old lady whose apartment had been invaded had a hammer put into her hand and was forced, herself, to destroy all her delicate and valuable belongings, her porcelain, mirrors and clothes. Elderly men, arrested in Vienna or sent to Buchenwald, were not only subjected to wanton humiliation and brutality, but were forced to alternate physical exercises beyond their capacity with standing upright for between twenty-four and thirty-six hours, without food or drink, prevented from sitting or lying down (reported by Siegfried Merecki, Karl Schwabe and Rabbi Rosenthal). This may not have been extreme torture but the physical and psychological effects, then and later, can easily be imagined.

Similarly, in the camps, inmates were sometimes denied spoons or forks and forced to eat like animals; and of course the sanitary conditions for those under detention were frequently indescribable, with widespread dysentery adding to the organised horrors. For many of the middle-aged and elderly prisoners, it was clearly an additional burden and source of despair that many of their worst tormentors were young men whose minds had been captured and corrupted by a perverted and senseless set of beliefs. In the generational war, even schoolchildren were enrolled, to sing hate-filled songs outside Jewish homes, or, in Vienna, to loot Jewish shops.

The different accounts and analyses by women collected here are particularly compelling because the authors were prepared to express their emotions directly and cogently. Margarete Neff reports on the emotional impact of seeing her husband's coat, among others, at the police station: "The old, worn-out coat was not an ordinary piece of clothing; it was something that had belonged to a person and had been taken away, just as arbitrarily as he himself had been, defenceless and mistreated." She also reports on her feelings when she saw her husband, a lawyer, for the first time after his arrest: "I hardly recognised him – a helpless-looking creature in a dirty suit, with shirt collar unbuttoned, looking as if he could not move – uncomprehending, dismal, helpless." Her description of the terror felt by women whose husbands or sons had been taken away, without prior notice or subsequent news, is riveting: "they ran from one acquaintance, one official, one possible source of help to another, fear running with them and before them, torment and agony, blood freezing in the veins, wearing down reason, making mouths dry and breasts pound to the point of bursting".

What is striking is the extreme thoroughness with which everything, literally everything, in Jewish homes and properties was broken, vandalised and left smashed beyond repair. Sofoni Herz, who ran a Jewish orphanage in Dinslaken, reports that when they returned there they found every last article of their possessions destroyed; windows, mirrors, chairs, tables, cupboards, dishes, cutlery, stairs, banisters, suitcases and the piano; she was however assured by party officials that the orphanage cow would continue to be fed. Her prompt action in evacuating the premises meant that at least her young charges were not, unlike those reported on in Königsberg by Alice Barwald, turned out into the night on their own in their pyjamas. This universal and perverse meticulousness in destruction is surely another proof, if one were needed, of the planned, organised nature of the pogrom.

Not only Jews but those who dared to show kindness or support to Jewish friends suffered. Marie Kahle relates what happened to herself, her husband

and sons in the days following *Kristallnacht*. Her husband was a professor at Bonn University, her son Wilhelm, aged nineteen, was also studying music there. The family activities were publicised as a "betrayal of the people" in the *Westdeutscher Beobachter* of November 17th; their house was painted red to mark them as "Jew-lovers"; while Marie was sheltered by Catholic nuns and supported by the Catholic professor of theology at the university, only three other colleagues showed any signs of sympathy or support. Wilhelm was dismissed from college and denied credit for his semester's work. A three-man university court in December, upon which sat the rector, Professor Dr Schmidt, charged that Wilhelm had found it "justifiable" to enter a Jewish shop after the given incidents and "help the Jewess put her merchandise back on the shelves"; this action was judged "thoroughly reprehensible" and the court found it had seriously "endangered the reputation and dignity of the University". It is difficult to rid oneself of the notion that universities would hold themselves to higher standards of behaviour.

The section "In the Camps" covers much that is familiar from other sources but offers in addition details and personal perspectives. By reputation, Sachsenhausen was a "better" camp than Buchenwald. The testimony of the physician Kurt Lederer regarding the dirt and disease, casual brutality and death in Buchenwald is particularly compelling. He blames canned whale meat goulash for the widespread dysentery, which added to the indescribable stench and excrement-encrusted filthiness of his washhouse "hospital for the insane". He started with a few dozen patients, some of whom had to be restrained with wire, and ended with one hundred and thirty-five at the peak, including some volunteer assistants who could not cope with the conditions. There were no medicines, except a little Luminal; the physically sick got no treatment and died; a guard who was irritated by an old Jew's sobbing and praying gave the doctor a few minutes to calm him down, and when his efforts were not immediately successful, the old man was beaten and kicked in the head and died within a few hours. Estimates in this book of the death rate in the different concentration camps vary but could have been around 10 per cent in the two months following November 1938. Rabbi Rosenthal says that he only realised later that the extreme, gratuitous and incessant brutality was all part of a planned, thought-out wearing-down process.

There were, of course, other moments when friendship triumphed over imposed "duty"; or when complete strangers went out of their way to show sympathy and help as much as they could; or when camp elders, often political prisoners, sometimes Jehovah's Witnesses, spoke words of encouragement, to reassure prisoners that the worst was now over and to appeal for steadfastness and solidarity. After a very bleak day in Sachsenhausen, as reported by Rabbi Rosenthal, an elder produced an old harmonica and this wretched attempt at music and song was treasured afterwards as a sign that all was not hell and brutality in the camp and that the voice of humanity still existed. Notwithstanding this, there were some fresh bodies (suicides) on the electric fence the following morning.

The differing accounts show how the reactions of those abused varied. The sustaining power of religious faith and belief in the values of compassion and decency (in spite of all the evidence to the contrary) helped some. But others reacted differently. On the day after *Kristallnacht*, Hertha Nathorff, until then head physician in Charlottenburg Hospital in Berlin, reported that "Today, in me, a sacred fire has been put out – the belief that people are fundamentally good."

The rationale for the final section, "Before Emigration", is unclear since it includes much material similar to that in the earlier sections. What is new are the descriptions of the bureaucracy involved for Jews leaving Germany and the efficiency with which they were stripped of their remaining assets by an exhaustive and coherent legal process before they were allowed to do so. Karl Schwabe, a shopkeeper, reports that he had to visit the passport office, police, customs investigation office, currency exchange bureau, his city treasury, the emigrant centre and the registry office before departure.

A number of these agencies, especially the currency exchange and the tax office, had particularly nasty reputations for harassment and delays. Everything was charged, often surcharged (Schwabe had already paid seven thousand reichsmarks for cleaning up his own shop after the "day of wrath"). The final legal necessity was for an export permit for all assets which were being taken abroad; according to Rodeck, currency exchange officials were allowed to tax all such assets in excess of two thousand reichsmarks at punitive rates of between 50 per cent and 100 per cent, at their discretion. One extreme case of an "extra payment" was the man charged for the price of the petrol used in burning his local synagogue, home and father's business. Siegfried Wolff, another physician witness, concludes that if civilisation begins when strangers are guaranteed hospitality and safety, as the nineteenth century Prussian doctor, prehistorian and anti-racist Rudolph Virchow had argued, then Germany had sunk below the starting point of civilisation, and he no longer had a fatherland.

The first point made in Saul Friedlander's foreword is that much of the testimony assembled here is based on the presumption that November 1938 and its sequel marked the height of Nazi barbarism and the biggest imaginable breach with modern Western civilisation. In fact it was but the faintest of preludes to what was about to happen. But some could read the signs of the times. Writing in January 1939, a full two years before the Wannsee conference, Fritz Rodeck ended his account with the prophetic insight that the Nazis were not simply pursuing a policy of expulsion; their basic aim was *Juda verrecke* (Death to Jews), not just *Juda verreise* (Jews must leave); and he also foretold that when there were no more Jews left in Germany and Austria, the Nazis would turn against the Jews of Czechoslovakia, Poland and Russia.

These accounts were first written in response to an essay competition organised by three Harvard academics in August 1939 on the theme "My life in Germany, before and after 30 January 1933". The essays were to be authentic eyewitness accounts of life in Germany and guidance was given on length, style and presentation. Relevant quotation from contemporary documentation, personal and official, was welcomed. The organisers were Sidney Fay, professor of history, Gordon Allport, professor of psychology, and Edward Yardell Hartshorne, lecturer in sociology; the moving spirit behind the enterprise was probably Hartshorne. The deadline for submission was fixed for April 1940. More than two hundred and fifty submissions were received, from which Hartshorne eventually picked thirty-four, focused on *Kristallnacht*, for a book to be called *Nazi Madness – November 1938*. The book was never published. From Hartshorne's original selection of thirty-four essays, the editors of the present volume have chosen twenty-one. Curiously, although Hartshorne included the essay originally awarded the second prize in the competition, that by Gertrud Wickerhauser Lederer, neither he nor the present editors included the winner of the first prize of $1,000, Carl Paeschke, a journalist from Upper Silesia. Hartshorne's manuscript for "Nazi Madness" eventually ended up in Berkeley, California; here it was seen in 2008 by the editors of the present volume and prepared for publication.

Hartshorne, born in 1912, was an activist anti-fascist academic from 1936–37 and was particularly influenced by his previous mentor at Harvard, Talcott Parsons. He studied also at the University of Chicago, which pioneered the "life-history" approach to political and sociological problems, and this influenced the form of the essay competition. While he shared the approach, he disagreed strongly with the conclusions of Theodore Abel's 1935 study, *Why Hitler came into Power*. He spent six months in Berlin in 1935–36, partly in the home of the historian Friedrich Meinecke. A book based on his doctoral thesis, *The German Universities and National Socialism*, was published in 1937. He wrote on the fascination of Nazi master race theories for German young people, Hitler's strategy of terror and the Führer complex. He also criticised the "psychic inertia" of German Jews in refusing to take Hitler's threats seriously and believed this pushed Hitler into organising the November 1938 pogrom. One of the reasons why his planned book, *Nazi Madness*, was never published was that he joined the US security services in September 1941, working successively for the Co-ordinator of Information, the Office of Strategic Services, the Office of War Information and the Psychological Warfare Division. His final posts were with the postwar American zone in Germany, where he had responsibilities for denazification programmes in German universities and in Bavaria.

In August 1946, for reasons which remain obscure, Hartshorne was assassinated in Bavaria. Uta Gerhardt speculates that his murder may have been connected to the murky internal politics of the Counter Intelligence Corps of the US military government in Germany, which was responsible both for the denazification programme and, from earlier in 1946, for a highly secret "hotline" used to smuggle high-ranking national socialists to Latin America, including some coming out of the Soviet zone. From what we know of Hartshorne's convictions, it is probable that he would have been vehemently opposed to this.

The remoteness of 1938 Ireland from events in continental Europe, even in a year of crisis and with the threat of a renewed general war looming ever larger, should not be minimised. But Ireland also received the British media; it had a small but significant Jewish community of about four thousand people; it played its part in the international community, not least as a member of the League of Nations since 1923; and it participated in the Évian conference of July 1938. Since 1933, it had been represented in Berlin by minister plenipotentiary Charles Bewley.

The background to the Évian conference, held from July 1st to 13th, 1938, was not propitious. The United Kingdom did not wish to increase the numbers of Jews arriving in Britain or in Palestine. (In 1939 immigration to Palestine was capped at 75,000 over five years). The United States was embarrassed because it was not at that time filling its immigration quotas, especially the British-Irish quota, but it did not want to take in more Jews either. (Incidentally, the contrast between pre-war US and European states as regards their attitude to Jews is sometimes overstated. It is not mentioned in this book, but a US poll measuring public views on immigration and refugees, taken in December 1938, one month after the "Nazi madness", showed that opposition to higher immigration quotas had increased, not decreased, in the meantime). At Évian, France claimed "saturation" as regards refugees and Australia said it did not wish to import racial tensions. South Africa and Canada were equally reticent and only the Dominican Republic made a relatively generous offer. According to Christopher Sykes, even the Zionist organisations were slow to press other countries for increased quotas for fear of slowing up emigration to Palestine. Chaim Weizmann had observed two years earlier: "The world seems divided into two parts – places where Jews cannot live and places where Jews cannot enter."

In the circumstances, while the conference was rich in expressions of sympathy and willingness in principle to help, it was substantially a failure in not increasing significantly the existing numbers of entry visas. Ireland formed part of this minimalist consensus. Apart from expressing sympathy and the hope that other countries could help, Ireland's representative, Francis T Cremins, in a brief intervention, limited himself to pointing out that Ireland was primarily an agricultural country and did not have enough land for its own people; that emigration from Ireland continued to be significant and therefore it could not help with refugee settlement; and that we were oversupplied already in the medical and other professions. All of this was of course true but it was hardly generous. The most positive interpretation is probably that a country which had long exported its population and which had become (partially) independent only in 1921 found it difficult to conceive of significant immigration in the 1930s.

In the fraught economic and political circumstances of the late 1930s, the Irish administration shared a view common among European states that immigrants, and especially refugees, represented additional and burdensome problems which should be avoided if possible. But against this European trend, de Valera gave significant recognition and protection to Jewish beliefs before World War II, in Article 44 of the 1937 Constitution. By asserting human and civil rights for Jews in a constitution adopted by popular vote, the Irish prime minister made it more difficult for any successor government to abolish them, as the Nazis, and some central and eastern European governments, had done. Enshrining the rights of a small minority in this way was an important symbolic gesture.

In 1943, during the war, de Valera responded positively to a request from his friend Rabbi Isaac Herzog by agreeing to grant Irish visas to a group of Jews stranded in Vichy France, who hoped to escape to South America; this and other attempts to help Jews of Italian, Dutch, Hungarian and Slovakian background were all unsuccessful as the German authorities were unwilling to let such groups go to Ireland or leave occupied Europe under Irish auspices. In 1948, after the war, he also intervened to overrule the opposition of the Irish Department of Justice to having one hundred and fifty Jewish children brought to Ireland. In face of the scale and intensity of Jewish suffering in the 1930s and 1940s, these might be seen in retrospect as pitifully small gestures, and essentially sporadic and reactive; but they were an attempt to help by a small neutral country in circumstances where consistent, larger-scale practical assistance was not possible.

In response to a specific request, Charles Bewley sent a closely typed report of twenty-seven paragraphs to the Department of External Affairs on December 9th, 1938, one month after *Kristallnacht*. On the reasons why the governments of Germany, Italy, Czechoslovakia, Hungary and Poland had adopted policies of discrimination against Jews, he said that discrimination was enforced because Jews were not loyal and refused to assimilate to their country of residence; they were not patriotic and did not fight; the chief supporters of communism in Russia and Central Europe were "almost inevitably" Jews; Jews had acquired such a dominating position in the financial world, the learned professions and the universities that they could almost control public opinion and public policy; they were never labourers or farmers but often financiers, frequently fraudulent; they demoralised society by indulging in and promoting moral degradation – the white slave traffic, pornographic papers, abortion etc; they were criminals and assassins, and international Jewry always defended criminal actions by Jews.

On measures taken by Germany and other countries against Jews, Bewley outlines the measures taken before and after *Kristallnacht*, up to and including Göring's "atonement levy". On the November events, he acknowledges only "an organised movement to smash the windows and in some cases, the fittings of Jewish shops". He points out that Catholic clerical regimes – those of Msgr Tizo in Slovakia and Msgr Woloschin in Carpatho-Russia – also had such exclusionary regimes and indeed that the Vatican had previously operated a raft of similar measures. He ends this section by stating that judgments on whether the measures adopted were necessary would not apply in cases of deliberate cruelty, but "I am not aware of any such towards Jews on the part of the German government". He adds: "There has been no episode in connection with Jews in Germany which could even remotely be compared with the atrocities of the Communists in Spain or Russia, or of the British in Palestine." On press reports and public opinion, he stresses that the international news agencies are in the hands of Jews (Reuters, Exchange Telegraph, etc); that these "Anglo-Jewish" agencies are partial in highlighting stories favourable to Jewish interests and suppressing the contrary. Newspapers in Ireland, "like the rest of the English press", take these stories at face value, so public opinion in Ireland is naturally corrupted by forces bitterly opposed both to "Irish Nationalism and to the Catholic Church".

Bewley may have had impeccable German but he was a hopeless diplomatic representative. He failed in a primary duty of ambassadors, to keep his authorities informed regarding what was happening in his country of accreditation. Getting information about what was happening in Nazi Germany was not always easy, but it was possible. Talking to some German Jews would have been a good, if obvious, starting point. On the main point, "deliberate cruelty to Jews", he was either lying, or being disingenuous ("I am not aware"), or he did not know what he did not know. In general, he echoed the senseless and poisonous tissue of ideological prejudices broadcast daily by the German Ministry of Propaganda and did not even begin to analyse it in terms of probability or innate contradictions (Jews as both communists and financial leeches?)

As regards what happened on *Kristallnacht*, he was just plain wrong, as Gerhardt and Karlauf's book makes abundantly clear, and the "Anglo-Jewish agencies" were essentially right. His enthusiasm for national socialism, his antisemitism and his suspicion of all British views and policies combined to blind him to the truth. During his six years in charge of the Berlin embassy, fewer than one hundred resident visas for Ireland were granted to German Jews. He should have been dismissed from his post long before 1939.

Irish public opinion and Irish politicians in the 1930s were certainly not antisemitic in the Nazi "scientific racism" sense. Most Irish people then did not share Bewley's active dislike of and prejudice against Jews. But, as elsewhere in Europe, there existed in Ireland a degree of passive antisemitism which contributed to the lack of concern with which reports of the persecution of Jews in Germany and elsewhere were received. As regards the components of this prejudice, I believe three separate elements can be distinguished.

First, there was the cluster of images inherited from the nineteenth century and perhaps from much earlier which saw Jews as treacherous and grasping. As portrayed by Father Creagh in Limerick in 1904, the Jews were a stubborn and impious people who had rejected and betrayed Christ; they were usurers sucking the blood of the poor; they were freemasons, in league with enemies of the church; they were taking over the local economy and sold inferior goods at inflated prices; they were middlemen who took and took, and contributed nothing. At a different social level, these attitudes could be reinforced by the casual disdain of certain literary figures or the exclusivity of golf and rugby clubs.

Second, less than twenty years after independence, there was still a very narrow line in Ireland between the generous inclusive nationalism which, on the whole, typified the 1916 Rising and the War of Independence and a corrosive, narrow-minded chauvinism which by definition rejected all foreigners as "others" and sought to maximise ethnic, political and cultural "purity". Joyce disliked and mistrusted this strident combination of nationalism and prejudice; in *Ulysses*, the Citizen denied Jews the right to call themselves Irish; it is evident that he would also have had grave suspicions of

Wolfe Tone, Parnell, Synge, Douglas Hyde, Erskine Childers, Lady Gregory and Samuel Beckett. I understand that the *Catholic Bulletin* dismissed Yeats's Nobel Prize of 1924 as an award to "a member of the English colony in Ireland". One key strand in this cultural mix was an unhappy combination of national chauvinism with religious fundamentalism. Views expressed by Arthur Griffith and DP Moran, at least at certain times, opinions expressed in the *Catholic Bulletin*, the activities of Fathers John Creagh and Denis Fahey and their supporters attest to this. From the Catholic side, the influence of French right-wing anti-Dreyfusards seems to have been particularly strong and long-lived, in defiance of the facts.

Third, there was the Catholic church, at home and abroad. In pre-Vatican II, pre-ecumenical days, relations between Catholicism and Judaism were characterised, at best, by coldness and distance. When Frank Duff founded the Pillar of Fire Society in Dublin in 1942 as a forum for dialogue, Archbishop McQuaid of Dublin saw it as a place for explaining Catholic doctrine to Jews. He feared that Jews would see it mainly as a channel which could be used "to stave off persecution or expulsion". He wrote: "Their purpose, however it be marked by an appearance of suavity or accommodation is and will remain material." The coldness and lack of human sympathy in this comment, more than three years after *Kristallnacht* and in a year when the first rumours were already circulating in diplomatic circles of "deportees being sent to death by various methods in places specifically prepared for this purpose" is striking. Archbishop McQuaid may not have been typical of the Irish ecclesiastical hierarchy but his views on ecumenical dialogue, especially when conducted by lay people, were widely shared.

Such coldness may have been an echo of attitudes at the highest levels of the church. Much modern writing on the record of the church and the Vatican in the 1930s and 1940s is sensationalist and of tabloid quality. But the fact that many big questions on that record are still open, three-quarters of a century later, puts the attitudes of the Irish church and the Irish people in the 1930s into a different, and larger, perspective; it suggests at least that a balance between self-questioning and condemnation is desirable.

The Nazi policy of terrorising certain groups in Germany – the Jews, first and foremost, but also left-wingers, gypsies, homosexuals, the handicapped, Jehovah's Witnesses et cetera – may be analysed in different ways. It was, of course, flagrantly cynical and unjust but also irrational and self-contradictory in the arguments used to justify it; blaming "World Jewry" for the assassination of a middle-ranking German embassy official, the declared cause of *Kristallnacht*, makes as much sense as blaming all Poles, or all Grynszpans, or all seventeen-year-olds. But scapegoating the Jews had already been planned, and in Nazi terms it was successful in the short term. It strengthened internal policy (reinforcing unity through accelerating Jewish emigration, increasing support from convinced racists and frightening waverers into acquiescence), as well as confirming the identity of external hostile forces and states. Seventy-five years later, it also poses some uncomfortable questions for us.

Those born in Europe in the late nineteenth or twentieth centuries who did not personally experience total war or brutal totalitarian dictatorship have much to be thankful for. Sensitivity to that good fortune should involve both the suspension of facile judgments on those who did and a willingness to face the hard questions. In an earlier age, the question was often put: "Where were the good Germans?" In other terms did the quiescence displayed by the great mass of non-Jewish Germans show indifference and "passive complicity" or is it evidence of a self-protecting distance from a regime under which all public opinion was staged, controlled and manipulated by the state under threat of the most absolute of sanctions? For those of us who are not German, that is for others to answer. But the hardest questions are for us: how would I have behaved in Nazi Germany? Would I have kept my head down or would I have had a tipping point to declare myself in word or deed against the regime? If so, where would my tipping point have been? Would it have been sufficient to be another Sophie Scholl (the young anti-Nazi resister executed in Munich in 1943) and lose oneself apparently for a simple declaration of other values, or would I have felt compelled to fight? How would I have conducted myself, especially in those grey areas of part opposition, part compromise referred to by Primo Levi and recalled in the foreword to this volume by Saul Friedlander?

Reading and reflecting on these gripping accounts of *Kristallnacht* has made me think differently of two incidents in my own life. In 1979, my twelve-year-old daughter was treated very roughly by a Greek doctor in Rhodes. Because she was fair, and wore her hair long in plaits, he thought she was German. His manner changed the following day when he learned she was Irish. His error was not in mistaking her nationality but in imposing a kind of collective punishment, in punishing one member of a supposed group for the perceived misdeeds of others of the same collectivity, a practice which lay at the heart of Nazi treatment of the Jews on *Kristallnacht*. He had not yet discovered the wisdom of Martin Freudenheim, the grace to pray repeatedly, "no hatred, no hatred; hatred strikes inward".

In the late 1980s, I had the opportunity to visit Auschwitz-Birkenau but I said no. I was afraid that such a place of horror would overwhelm me, that I would not be able to cope with my emotions and the emotions of other people there. After reading this book, I now think of Auschwitz, and Buchenwald, Dachau and Sachsenhausen and the other concentration camp sites not just as places of gross inhumanity and evidence of the worst potentialities inherent in human nature but as witnesses to human endurance, courage and wisdom, and the triumph of the human spirit.

The Word from the Trenches

Im Westen nichts Neues was first published serially in the Vossische Zeitung Berlin daily in November and December 1928 and by Propyläen Verlag, an imprint of the Ullstein publishing group, in 1929.

THE ONLY remarkable thing about my otherwise unremarkable street in Berlin is Remarque. High on the wall of my apartment complex, a dark metal plaque reads: "In this building Erich Maria Remarque lived until 1929 and wrote 'All Quiet on the Western Front'. Born 22.6.1898 Osnabrück. Died Locarno 25.9.1970."

It was from here – looking out at the cream-and-green Bauhaus facades, smelling the fragrant linden trees – that Remarque returned to the horrors of the Belgian trenches he had experienced a decade earlier. His journey paid off and *Im Westen nichts Neues*, as it's known in the German original, is now considered a classic of twentieth century literature.

As the WWI centenary approaches, and Great War fatigue begins to set in, this great anti-war novel is a reminder of the terrible fate that befell millions of soldiers in 1914. On its publication in 1929 the book became that rarest of beasts: a simultaneous literary and commercial success. Critics hailed it for its skewering of Germany's military establishment and the carnage they had triggered a decade earlier. The country's conservative elite retaliated by savaging book and author, which only served to further pique reader interest and boost commercial success. Eventually, *All Quiet* was to receive that most notorious of German literary honours when, on May 10th, 1933, Nazi-supporting students tossed it, alongside the works of the Mann brothers and Erich Kästner, onto the raging pyre opposite Berlin's Humboldt University.

Unlike Kästner, Remarque wasn't there to see the blaze. After years of public pillorying, he had left the country on January 31st, a day after Hitler's ascent to power. His life in Germany had ended. It had begun with the birth of Erich Paul Remark in Osnabrück in Westphalia on June 22nd, 1898, the son of Anna Maria and Peter Maria Remark, a bookbinder. He went to school in Osnabrück and then on to the University of Münster. At eighteen he was drafted into the army and, after six months' training, sent to Flanders on June 12th, 1917. He was wounded five times in the course of a month on the western front, the last during the third battle of Ypres, when artillery fire struck his right arm and throat. Recovering in a military hospital in Duisburg until October 1918, he began writing about his own experiences and supplemented them with those of other convalescing soldiers.

His first draft from 1917, reprinted in a new critical edition of the book published by Kiepenheuer & Witsch, plunges readers into the immediacy of bunker warfare: "The barrage of fire swelled up once more. The shelter shuddered. The dirt fell in spray in the stillness between the impacts."

Even in this early draft, the writing style is already apparent: short, punchy sentences that Ernest Hemingway would later employ to similar effect – and develop into his literary trademark – starting with his own war novel, *A Farewell to Arms*. Remarque's book was more a farewell to dreams. An injury to his right hand robbed him of the dream of becoming a musician and when he returned home from his lengthy convalescence his mother had died. His return to civilian life was problematic. He continued the teacher training that had been interrupted by his call-up but saw he was not cut out for the classroom. Instead he spent most of the 1920s in odd jobs, beginning as a copy-writer for the Continental Tyre company magazine and, later, as a journalist at a sports magazine. By the end of the decade, in a manner typical of his "lost" war generation, he was drifting and depressed. He used writing as self-analysis and identified his suppressed war experiences as the source of his depression. Pulling out his 1917 manuscript, he reworked it in three successive drafts, offering the last to the publishers S Fischer in 1927. They rejected the work, arguing that, a decade on, no one was any longer interested in the war.

Editors at Ullstein's Propyläen imprint however liked the book but asked for a rewrite. Remarque set to work on the manuscript, which he abbreviated in correspondence to I.W.n.N, either striking out or relativising references to the pointlessness of the war. It first appeared in serial form in the popular *Vossische Zeitung* daily from November 10th to December 9th, 1928, beginning with a note from Remarque to readers: "This book should be neither an accusation nor avowal. It should be the attempt to report on a generation that was destroyed by war – even if it escaped the grenades."

In a departure from his earlier drafts, Remarque opens his first chapter far from the trenches. His narrator, Paul Bäumer, shows us soldiers chatting among themselves, satisfied with double portions of stew and cigarettes. Then, in a slow reveal, Remarque explains how the field cook ordered food and prepared for 150, but only 80 soldiers from Bäumer's company have returned from the front. At a leisurely pace, Bäumer takes readers through his generation's dehumanising process at the hands of their morally bankrupt elders: "For us 18-year-olds they were supposed to be interpreters and leaders to the grown-up world," he writes. "The first dead we saw demolished this conviction. We had to realise that our age cohort were more honest than theirs, they were ahead only in adroitness and phrases."

During training Bäumer grows indifferent to his superiors' bullying and soon realises he is being "prepared for heroism like a circus pony". A new reality has been forced on him, he realises, where "a polished button is worth more than four volumes of Schopenhauer". Transported to the front, he watches the centrifuge of death and violence pull in his comrades, transforming them from "cranky or good-humoured soldiers" into *Menschentiere* – "humanimals".

"The front is a cage where you have to wait nervously for what will happen," he observes. "Chance and coincidence is what makes us apathetic. Every soldier only stays alive through a thousand coincidences. And every soldier believes and trusts coincidence." He learns to recognise the signs of death "working its way out from the inside" of comrades, and eventually realises that war kills all, even those it leaves alive. The only difference, he notes, is that the dead know they are dead whereas those left alive aren't sure what they are any more. "We don't know if we are still alive," he writes. "We are feelingless dead men who through a trick, a dangerous conjuring, can still run and kill ... I am just 20 years old but I know nothing of life but doubt and death." A century after the events described, the book's power lingers, less in Remarque's digressions into the inhumanity of war as an abstract concept than in his chilly, spare description of its pointless reality. WG Sebald once declared that "the present tense lends itself to comedy", but there is nothing to laugh at – and plenty to rage at – in Paul Bäumer's present-tense monologue. His voice, spare but stinging, was what made the book so powerful – and dangerous – in 1929.

Some time after he handed in the manuscript and before the book's explosion onto the market, Ullstein decided that Remarque's work – which he had subtitled *Roman* (novel) – would sell better as a pseudo-memoir. Remarque, on the other hand, saw his work as an "anti-memoir", an attack on the scores of war-glorifying volumes flung onto the market after 1918. But his publishers were determined the book should strike the right tone with readers and ordered substantial rewrites that transformed Remarque's anti-hero from conscientious objector to resigned foot soldier.

A day before the newspaper serialisation began, on November 9th, 1928 – a decade after the armistice – the *Vossische Zeitung* published a front page piece that reads today like an overwrought publisher's press release: "This is no war novel and no diary. It is life lived and yet set apart through the creative power, the personal experience without artifice, without distortion ... The memorial for the 'unknown soldier' has been created ... stronger than stone and more permanent than ore."

In interviews to promote the book, the divergence between author and publisher are clear. Remarque told the *Literarische Welt* newspaper in 1929 that his book was about the "shadow of war" hanging over his generation. "We all were – and often still are – uneasy, without goal, one moment exulting, the next apathetic, at heart unhappy," he said. But his original intentions were reshaped during Ullstein's substantial reworking and recasting of the book as a non-fiction "true" image of war. Their overeager editing and marketing would deliver ample ammunition for Remarque's powerful critics, anxious to play the man as much as the ball. They questioned the book's veracity, pointing out that he had served "only" a month at the front before being injured. Remarque insisted that his work was a literary reworking that conflated many war fates into one. The controversy did no harm to sales, but it weighed heavily on the author. For the rest of his life, Remarque often spent as much time answering questions about the book's provenance as its content.

In a 1946 interview he admitted that it was a "best-of collection of war stories", written with the intention of earning money and, with it, financial independence. It did that, but financial success brought him no peace as a writer. In a private diary entry in 1951, he wrote: "Thought. When did my complexes became more strong? After I.W.n.N. The fear. The feeling of being a swindler ..." But he kept his doubts private, telling a 1963 interviewer he was "extremely surprised by the political effect" of the book. The criticism of its anti-war message, he felt, missed the point of a book that he said addressed the psychological consequences of war for its survivors. "My real theme was a human theme, suddenly presenting death to 18-year-olds, who should be confronted with life – and what would happen to them," he said. "This is more a postwar book in which the question is asked, 'what became of these people?'"

The controversy rolled on into the next year when the 1930 US film version of the book, directed by Lewis Milestone, won two Oscars. Its highly anticipated Berlin premiere was a debacle thanks to Joseph Goebbels, then NSDAP *Gauleiter* in Berlin. He organised a crowd of six thousand to protest against the film on Nollendorfplatz while, inside the cinema, Nazi plants booed while the future propaganda minister threw stink bombs and released white mice into the auditorium. The screening was cancelled, police cleared the cinema and the government, shocked by events and under "pressure from the street", demanded significant cuts to a film they said "endangered German reputation and injured German (national) feeling". On taking power three years later Hitler banned the film, the book and all other works by Remarque. All the while the Nazi rumour mill worked overtime, suggesting that the author's birth name, Remark (his grandfather dropped the French spelling), was actually an anagram of his real, Jewish, name: Kramer.

The campaign against the author continued even in his absence. On December 16th, 1943 Remarque's sister Elfried, a staunch anti-Nazi, was sentenced to death in the infamous *Volksgerichthof* (people's court) for undermining the war effort. "Your brother is beyond our reach," said the court president, Roland Freisler, "but you will not escape us." She was beheaded and the bill – 495.80 reichsmarks – sent to her sister, Erna.

By this stage Remarque was far away from the Nazis' reach. His first marriage, to actress Ilse Jutta Zambona, ended after five years in 1930. They had fled together to Switzerland in 1933 and eventually remarried five years later to prevent her forced return to Germany. Tall, blonde and handsome, Remarque was in great demand during the war period in the United States. A literary celebrity, he had affairs with all of Hollywood's great European leading ladies: Marlene Dietrich, Hedy Lamarr and Greta Garbo. He was stripped of his German citizenship by the Nazis in 1939 and became a naturalised US citizen in 1947, dividing his time between the US and Switzerland. He divorced Zambona in 1957 and got married again a year later to Paulette Goddard, former wife of Charlie Chaplin and Burgess Meredith.

Alongside the colourful private life, the novels continued to appear: *Spark of Life* (Der Funke Leben) in 1952 and *Zeit zu leben und Zeit zu sterben*, published in English as *A Time to Love and a Time to Die*. It was filmed in 1958 by fellow German émigré Hans Detlef Sierk, known in Hollywood as Douglas Sirk. Other novels followed – *Heaven Has No Favourites* and *The Night in Lisbon* – as well as several screenplays and a stage play. None of his later works achieved the runaway success of *I. W.n.N.*, though most, if not all, achieved respectful reviews for Remarque's talent for using narrative – rather than explicit moralising – to explore and develop his pacifist views.

Remarque invested his royalties in modern masters – Matisse, Klee, Picasso – and what began as an investment eventually became a passion – and an antidote to the horrors he had witnessed decades earlier. A despairing Paul Bäumer, watching the slaughter before his eyes, declares "how senseless everything that was ever written and done, that something like this is possible". His generation will "become superfluous to ourselves, we will grow, some will conform, others comply and many others will be perplexed".

Remarque survived the First World War, rose above a full-frontal attack by the German conservative establishment that had helped trigger it and escaped the Nazis, who started a second one. His posthumous novel *Das Gelobte Land* (The Promised Land) suggests he found peace as an author and art lover by the time of his death in Switzerland in 1970 aged seventy-two. In the novel, the narrator sits before "still pictures, in the dying summer". "The pictures were a window into infinity," he writes. "They were the best things that people had created in a time of the worst things people were capable of."

A Tearless People

Moscow, 1937 by Karl Schlögel, translated by Rodney Livingstone

Polity Press | 650 pp | ISBN: 978-0745650760

ON MARCH 13th, 1988, one Nina Andreeva published an article in *Sovetskaya Rossiya* taking issue with Gorbachev's glasnost and perestroika as unconscionable transgressions of received Soviet dogmas. It was not quite clear who Nina Andreeva represented. On the face of it, she was a Leningrad teacher outraged at the sacrileges against what until recently had been regarded as the Holy Grail of Soviet socialism. There was more than a suspicion that she was a stalking horse for more powerful established interests.

Gorbachev had to react. He confronted the challenge in a number of meetings of the Central Committee. In the course of one he said:

> It was another question when we did not know what was going on. But when we learned and continue to learn ever more, that is another question. Stalin was a criminal lacking all morality. Three million were sent to the camps, where they were left to rot. Whole roll-calls of the best were knocked out. And this is not taking into account collectivisation, which killed still more millions. If we are to proceed on the logic of Nina Andreeva, we will come to a new 1937. Do you want this? You, members of the Central Committee? You have to think deeply of the fate of the country.

Gorbachev could depend on his listeners' understanding that 1937 represented an unprecedented descent to the depths in the sorry chronicle of Stalinism.

Karl Schlögel rightly seconds this view. His comprehensive overview of this fateful year in Moscow is prefaced by situating it as "one of the key settings of European history" and "a fault line of European civilization". His focus is Moscow. Given the extreme centralisation that was characteristic of the Stalin system, this focus is valid for the policy decisions that affected the whole Soviet Union at the time. It is, he says, "an attempt to capture, as in a prism, the moment, the constellation, that contemporary witnesses to the events of the time always deemed 'historically significant'". The book represents then a prism with many facets, or a constellation of perspectives on a city at a particular time. The result is impressionistic to a degree, but by the end the reader has a profound overall view of what it was like to live in such a crucial place in such a crucial year.

The book begins with one of the main literary productions of the era, Bulgakov's *Master and Margarita*. This was practically completed by October 1937, but not published in full until long after the author's death, in 1967, and then not in the USSR but in Paris. Publication in full in Russia had indeed to wait until 1973. Even then, Bulgakov's work did not cease to exercise the Soviet powers that be. Yuri Lyubimov, the director of the Taganka Theatre, adapted it and brought it to the stage in Moscow in 1977. The adaptation, among other theatrical provocations – as they were seen by the authorities – caused all his productions to be banned. Lyubimov was stripped of his Soviet citizenship and left the country, not to return until after perestroika in 1989.

Schlögel's chapter on the novel manages to give a sense of contemporary Moscow, including from the air – in Margarita's flight – as well as the tight limits within which an artist like Bulgakov could work. For instance, the account of a series of police raids, in which "people vanished from their apartments without trace", is clearly an account of what was actually being carried out by the NKVD in Moscow at the time. The eerie atmosphere of the novel, which recounts a visit to Moscow by the devil, involves a pact with the same devil and recounts Pilate's trial of Jesus, is an essential part of the picture of the city at the time. The novel also provides an insight into the extremely restrictive living conditions that prevailed, in the view that Margarita gets from the air. The *komunalkas*, rooms in which whole families were housed, sharing one kitchen and one bathroom, will feature later in *Moscow, 1937* as typical of contemporary conditions in the city.

As Schlögel puts it: "Almost all the themes that go to make up the mysterious nature of the year 1937 can be found in the book: the utter confusion, the blurring of clear distinctions, the shockwaves created by the irruption of the unknown, anonymous forces into the lives of ordinary people, the fear and the despair. Almost all the locations that form part of the drama of Moscow 1937 are referred to: the glorious city and the awfulness of communal housing; the public places filled with hysterical choruses; the setting for the show trials; the place of execution; but also the retreats in which the individual could find happiness."

In a work so titled, Schlögel must give a comprehensive account of what life was like in the Moscow of the year in question. This he does, acknowledging fully the work of Sheila Fitzpatrick, whose *Everyday Stalinism* is such a ground-breaking work in this field. And so we learn of the *Moscow Directory* of 1936, an analogue of *Thom's Directory*, with the additional piquancy in the case of Moscow that this information-filled publication was a last issue for the – long – time being. (It is of some interest that, by way of contrast, the equivalent publication, Вся Москва, is today an iPod app.) We are told the story of the famous "House on the Embankment", made famous by Yuri Trifonov's novel of the same name, essentially a gated community for party bigwigs, and of the toll that the repression of these years took of such members of the *nomenklatura*. Lion Feuchtwanger, who came to Moscow from December 1936 to early 1937, figures as a then eminent – now largely forgotten – visitor from abroad who was used by Stalin as a "useful idiot", just as Shaw and so many others were.

Feuchtwanger was a German novelist obliged to leave his homeland by the Hitler regime. Schlögel has the sensitivity to realise that his perspective was determined by his perceived impotence against fascism as well as by a consciousness of relativism, that is, his sense that the USSR was completely different from the West, and that the standards of the West could not be applied. His naivete appears, however, in his statement that "what I have understood is excellent, from which I conclude that what I have not understood is also excellent". Those who had met him or were refugees in Moscow from his time in Munich – Feuchtwanger had been in Munich during the short-lived radical socialist *Räterepublik* in 1919, and had many friends among the radicals – had no occasion for naivete: Schlögel gives a full list of the large numbers of them who were shot or sentenced to long periods of camp detention after Feuchtwanger left.

Stalin's regime recruited the preeminent Russian poet, Pushkin, on the two-hundredth anniversary of his death as part of an effort to gain national credibility. The party sought to bask in his prestige as a great Russian cultural figure and notably the effort was extended to all constituent republics of the USSR, and, indeed, to the world in general. Papers were published on "Pushkin and World Literature" and on "Pushkin in Georgian Literature". Schlögel rightly speaks of "the Pushkin industry" and points out that the jubilee was celebrated between the second great show trial and the Plenum of the Central Committee, which would set off the Great Purge.

Schlögel gives an account of Soviet participation in the Paris International Exposition of 1937, remarking on the inspiration it gave to Albert Speer, the designer of the German pavilion, which was just across from the Soviets. Both pavilions were indeed completely in accord with the spirit of the age, which can still be seen, for instance, in EUR, near Rome, or indeed, in the buildings of the League of Nations in Geneva. The Soviet pavilion was the USSR's own view of itself, something that subsequently became the cliché of "socialist realism". It did not content itself with what was there, Soviet communism being a vision of a glorious future. Thus it contained a painting by Aleksandr Deineka of the then planned, but never to be built, Palace of the Soviets in Moscow.

The parade of physical culture adepts through Red Square is described, partly through the eyes of Joseph Davies, the rather naive American ambassador. Davies enthuses: "It was flaming youth. And a very beautiful youth it was – all bareheaded and tanned to a deep brown, for the most part wearing only white shorts and coloured jerseys." The coincidence of this phenomenon with the contemporaneous cult of the body in Nazi Germany cannot be overlooked, nor is it by Schlögel, even if one could challenge his view that "Fizkul'tura (the Soviet cult of physical fitness) was the first fitness movement in history and therefore a characteristic phenomenon of the emerging mass society." This would be to reckon without "Turnvater Jahn", the early nineteenth century originator of the physical fitness movement in

Germany, this too having been consciously aimed at promoting a sense of identity, this time national identity, against Napoleon.

When it comes to the "glorious city", Schlögel gives a full account of Stalinist ambitions to engineer a new world – "to quite literally remake the world and create a new landscape". As Stalinist communism had the ambition, in the words of the title of Josef Škvorecký's novel, to be the engineer of human souls, so too physical planning was approached in the mode of modelling with infinitely plastic material. The preeminent exemplar is the plan to construct a pharaonic Palace of the Soviets on the site of the Cathedral of Christ the Saviour, a recurring theme in the book. The cathedral, planned as a memorial of the defeat of Napoleon in 1812, was not in fact dedicated until 1883. It was a prominent feature of the Moscow landscape and, as such, given that it was a Christian monument, a standing reminder that Moscow also had another history. It was therefore demolished, and, as Schlögel puts it, "the competition for the Palace of the Soviets sought to close the gap in the skies that had been opened up". The new project was envisaged as a building of the future, appropriate to a new society, "a true laboratory of the architecture of the twentieth century". It was heavily influenced by monumental American and European architecture of the time, the reason, no doubt why Frank Lloyd Wright deemed it "grandomania of the American type" and called on the architect, Boris Iofan, to stop work on the building.

As it turned out, the project did not go according to plan, progressing no further than excavation of the foundations, and the German invasion of the USSR in 1941 finally put paid to it, as it did to the reconstruction of Moscow in general. Khrushchev's deStalinisation finally gave it the *coup de grâce* and the empty foundation became an open-air swimming pool, before the new Cathedral of Christ the Saviour was built on the site between 1995 and 2000. Ironically, the rebuilding took place during another spasm of Moscow reconstruction, sometimes rather bombastic, under Mayor Yuri Luzhkov. Luzhkov gave the commission to reconstruct the cathedral to Zurab Tsereteli, one of the more controversial architects/sculptors at the time – there are many who dismiss his work, including the restored cathedral, as kitsch. Luzhkov was accused of turning contracts in the direction of his wife, Elena Baturina, who became one of Russia's richest women, and he was eventually dismissed by then President Medvedev in 2010.

By the mid-thirties there were already fifty-seven large cinemas in Moscow and hundreds of other places where films could be shown. The party was very well aware of the propaganda potential of film, and generous provision was made for cinemas in the general plan for the city. Naturally, the medium was not untouched by the omnipotent party hand. Sergei Eisenstein was forced to withdraw his film *Bezhin Meadow*, a dramatisation of the tale of Pavlik Morozov, an apparently apocryphal fable of an odious child who shopped his own father to the authorities and was then murdered by his family. Eisenstein went on to redeem himself in Stalin's eyes by producing *Aleksandr Nevskii*, a panegyric of Russian greatness, the following year. The Soviet film industry was very productive, and not all this production was propagandistic.

In music, the USSR could show some outstanding talents, and these were the years when David Oistrakh and Emil Gilels, subsequently to achieve world fame, came to public notice. After a lively debate, *Pravda* declared authoritatively that there was a place for proletarian Soviet *dzhaz*. Its main exponent was Leonid Utesov, who rose through the cabaret scene to become one of the most popular Soviet musicians. A typically "Soviet" form of light music was provided by Isaak Dunaevskii, prominent as the writer of the score for Soviet musicals such as *The Jolly Fellows*. The most famous Soviet musician at the time was of course Shostakovich. His opera, *Lady Macbeth of the Mtsensk District*, had been denounced by *Pravda* in January 1936 as "chaos instead of music". He spent 1937 working on his Fifth Symphony, which was premiered in Leningrad to great acclaim in November of that year.

As for refuges from the dreariness of the workaday life – and Schlögel mentions their existence – they can be hard to find. There was, of course, the perennial Russian recourse to talk *na dushakh*, or soul-to-soul, around vodka at the kitchen table. But the prevalence of *komunalkas*, where the kitchen table had to be shared by many families, made that problematic. There was, of course, no recourse to shopping. André Gide remarked on the Soviet version of the Potemkin village, where goods appear to be available in abundance but are in practice unattainable, and this indeed was a feature of Soviet life right to the end. Gorky Park, which Schlögel calls Arcadia in Moscow, was a real refuge and a serious effort was made to provide public facilities of this sort for relaxation. But even in Arcadia snakes cannot be avoided: Betty Glen, the longstanding director and "soul of the park", was arrested in June 1937, accused of having placed a bomb under the visitors' stand during a visit to the park by Stalin. She spent almost seventeen years in prison and exile.

The population of Moscow had doubled within a decade. While the Stalinist general plan for Moscow envisaged a grandiose city for the glorious communist future, the reality was quite different. There had been huge immigration from the countryside, especially to the factories, which needed working hands so badly they asked few questions and demanded few or no qualifications. The workforce of the main Moscow car factory grew from 1,798 in 1928 to 19,329 in 1932 and was 37,000 in 1937, to reach 40,000 in 1940. These rural immigrants were housed in wooden houses at best, often in jerry-built barracks, and sometimes even in holes dug in the ground. Schlögel remarks on "the outbursts of rage, despair, hatred and desire for revenge that were common occurrences in the works meetings of 1937". The divisions were fanned by party paranoia, urging the rooting out of Trotskyists, Bukharinites, counter-revolutionaries of all stripes, all of this being urged on immigrants who were largely illiterate and had no idea what Trotskyism or any of the other isms might consist of.

The year was, of course – if one brings in the immediately preceding period – preeminently that of the show trials of precisely these Trotskyists, Bukharinites and others. In August 1936 it was the turn of Kamenev and Zinoviev. Schlögel devotes much thought to the dynamics of these trials which have intrigued many then and since – they are, for instance, the main theme of Arthur Koestler's novel *Darkness at Noon*. While a certain mysteriousness remains about how it all functioned, Schlögel does, in the course of the book, succeed in laying bare much of the psychology behind the process. The trials aimed at rooting out what was called "double dealing", a term which covered those who allegedly maintained a mental reservation to the party line. They thus aimed at "disciplining ordinary members of society – indeed, society itself – especially those acting in and around the Party". There was a distinction between former members of the exploiting classes, and indeed foreign experts, many of whom had been dealt with in repressions before now, and members, or former members of the party, including foreign Comintern activists resident in Moscow, all of whom now became targets. Here a dynamic of public declaration of fault and a supposed cleansing punishment came into play.

The cleansing property of punishment, in the shape of imposed hard labour, had supposedly been demonstrated in such spectacular projects as the building of the White Sea Canal, in which brigades of men condemned to forced labour were deployed. Many had died in the process, but this did not prevent Maxim Gorky, to his eternal discredit, hailing it as one of the great achievements of Stalinist communism. Schlögel explains:

> Whereas members of the exploiting classes could be accused of unrelenting hard-heartedness, the courts relied on improvement and re-education in the case of 'people of one's own kind'. An admission of wrongdoing and the readiness to make 'a courageous, open confession of the error of one's ways' were the preconditions for the return to cooperation on equal terms and complete rehabilitation. What was looked for was an 'honest admission of guilt', the product of enlightenment, admonition, the helpful criticism of colleagues and comrades, and self-criticism, in which the accused proclaimed that they grasped the implications of their responsibility and guilt. These procedures were the order of the day in the Bolshevik Party.

This punitive reflex was already part of the party's, and hence the authorities' approach before 1937. However, the climate of paranoia which it evidenced was made more acute in that year because of international developments and domestic ones. To take the latter first, collectivisation had been forced through in the previous decade, at great human – in the sense of human lives lost – and psychological cost. The party was uneasily aware of much seething resentment in the country, particularly in the countryside, which, if it managed to coalesce, could be a vital threat to the viability of the revolution. Internationally, there was Spain, where Stalin saw potential gains threatened by Nazi Germany and Italy, with Britain and France standing by. Even more threateningly, Hitler had consolidated his position in Germany and it was clear that his *Lebensraum* objective would not stop at reuniting the German *Volk* in the Reich.

Even further indeed, Hitler had made no secret of his ambitions to destroy Bolshevism. The Plenum of the Central Committee of the Party met in Moscow in February–March. At that plenum, Stalin had urged the NKVD to realise that everything should be seen in the context of encirclement by capitalism and the growing threat of war. Schlögel shows from the transcripts of the plenum how "the discourse of a ruling elite merges into a collective readiness to kill. We are witnesses of a plan to salvage that elite's own positions of power at any, absolutely any, price. Even at the price of destroying the Party as it had existed hitherto and the literal murder of members actually present at the Plenum." The members referred to were Bukharin and Rykov, the former characterised by Lenin in his time as "the darling of the Party". At the conclusion of the plenum, both were arrested and led away to the Lubyanka prison by the NKVD.

Bukharin and Rykov were not to be the only victims. Another contributing factor to the gathering paranoia was the adoption of the new constitution, known as the Stalin Constitution, in December 1936. At the height of the previous repression, a group of about four million "former people", that is to say, members of the old ruling class, what was called the bourgeoisie, former White Army combatants, Orthodox clergy and kulaks were discriminated against. Under the Lenin Constitution of 1918, these people were disenfranchised and had lost their right to homes, work, schools and universities. They were free game for informers and the authorities, being in effect outlaws. At every election, they were registered as such all over again. Under Article 135 of the new constitution all were guaranteed the right to vote, and this discrimination was thus due to end. The first elections under the new constitution were scheduled for December 1937. As the date approached, the authorities became more and more nervous at the prospect of all these "former people" making effective use of the franchise. As well as this, in many places those expelled from the party outnumbered actual members. The solution found was the single list, established by the party, and affecting to include those outside the party, in reality fellow travellers. Thus was established the practice which prevailed throughout the Soviet time: no choice, but massive electoral support, usually of more than 90 per cent.

Nikolai Ustrialov was one of the most prominent representatives of the Russians in exile. He returned to Russia in 1935, clearly intent on seeing the Bolsheviks as engaged in the promotion of a new and great Russia. He listened enthusiastically to Stalin's presentation of his new constitution on the radio in December 1936, writing:

Our country is the machinery of state of a Eurasian power at a critical juncture in world history. It is not led by an old-style expert in English constitutional law. We need a talisman, we need STALIN to set the steam pistons, the valves and cogwheels in motion, these systems of systems made by men for men and which are essential to rescue our state, to reconstruct it, to make it great and to secure the victory of socialism, to consolidate it and to extend its influence.

Six months later, Ustrialov was arrested in Moscow, and on September 14th, 1937, under Articles 1a, 8, 10 and 11, he was condemned to death by firing squad by the military division of the Supreme Court of the USSR. The court found him guilty of treason, terrorism, propaganda and agitation to bring about the fall of Soviet power, and of having organised preparations for activities detrimental to Soviet power. The sentence was carried out immediately.

Schlögel provides full documentation of the horror-filled shooting range at Butovo, near Moscow, documentation available thanks to the persistent efforts of Memorial, the Russian NGO dedicated to investigating the crimes committed in the Soviet period, and the Russian Orthodox Church. (It is not, unfortunately, without significance that Memorial should now be among the NGOs being harassed by the Russian government on the basis of the allegation that it is foreign-funded.) One hundred and twenty-six persons were shot in Butovo in July 1937; 2,327 in August. What had happened in the meantime? On July 2nd, the politburo published a decree "On anti-Soviet elements". On the following day, a telegram composed by Stalin was sent to the secretaries of the party organisations of all regions and republics. It read:

It has been observed that a large number of former kulaks and criminals deported at a certain time from various regions to the North and to Siberian districts and then having returned to their regions at the expiry of their period of exile are the chief instigators of all sorts of anti-Soviet crime, including sabotage, both in the collective farms as well as in the sphere of transport and in certain branches of industry. The Central Committee of the CPSU recommends to all secretaries of regional and territorial organisations and to all regional, territorial and republic representatives of the NKVD that they register all kulaks and criminals who have returned home *in order that the most hostile among them be forthwith administratively arrested and executed by means of a three-man commission* and that the remaining, less active but nevertheless hostile elements be listed and exiled to districts as indicated by the NKVD. The Central Committee of the CPSU recommends that the names of those comprising the three-man commissions be presented to the Central Committee within five days, as well as the number of those subject to execution and the number of those subject to exile. (Italics mine.)

This was followed by Operational Order 00447 of July 30th by the NKVD, signed by Yezhov, the head of the organisation: in effect, the specification in detail of how the telegram instruction of July 3rd was to be implemented. The order provided for the arrest of 260,950 people, of whom 75,950 were to be shot. Because of the lack of any sense of legality, not to speak of due form, inevitably the numbers increased in the course of the operation. By the time it ended in November 1938, 767,397 people had been sentenced, 386,798 of whom were shot; in other words, over half of those sentenced were executed. Schlögel rightly characterises Operational Order No 00447 as a key document for 1937 "and no doubt also for the twentieth century as a whole".

The effects of this on a population already traumatised – from revolution, civil war, collectivisation and previous repressions – would be difficult to overestimate. One of the great Russian poets of the twentieth century, Anna Akhmatova, lived and suffered through it all. Her husband, Nikolai Gumilev, was executed in 1921 following accusations of participation in a counter-revolutionary plot. Between 1933 and 1945 her son was arrested four times on false charges and not freed from labour camps and rehabilitated until 1956, in the course of deStalinisation. In the introductory remarks to her great poem *Requiem*, she says, under the heading "In Place of a Foreword":

During the terrible years when Yezhov was Commissar of the Interior I spent seventeen months in queues of prison visitors. One day, someone recognised me in the middle of just such a queue. Then the woman standing behind me, who of course had never actually heard of me, roused herself from the torpor which was so much a part of every one of us, and with lips that were blue with the cold whispered in my ear (we all talked in whispers there):

'And can you describe all this?'

'I can,' was my reply.

Then something like a smile slipped over what had once been her face.

Bukharin is only one of the hundreds of thousands who found their death in the Great Purge initiated in this year. But his case is unusually interesting for what it shows of the dynamics whereby the victims themselves and the whole Soviet system accepted their fate. On March 2nd, 1938 a group of eighteen defendants arraigned before the military tribunal of the Supreme Court of the USSR were sentenced to death. They included Bukharin, Rykov and Krestinskii, all three of whom had been members of Lenin's politburo. One of them had been an ambassador. They included Yagoda, former head of the NKVD and three former People's Commissars. They were charged with "treason, espionage, sabotage, terrorism, wrecking activities, subverting the military power of the USSR, and provoking a military attack on the USSR". Appeals for mercy were rejected, and the eighteen were shot on March 13th, 1938. Bukharin was an old-fashioned intellectual, well versed in Marx and his filiation in German philosophy. He must, to have survived in the party up to 1937, also have been a subscriber to the thesis that one cannot make an omelette without breaking eggs, but there remained something of the naive theorist in him. In his last plea before the court on March 12th, he said:

For three months I refused to say anything. Then I began to testify. Why? Because while in prison I made a revaluation of my entire past. For when you ask yourself: 'If you must die, what are you dying for?' – an absolutely black vacuum suddenly rises before you with startling vividness. There was nothing to die for, if one wanted to die unrepentant. And, on the contrary, everything positive that glistens in the Soviet Union acquires new dimensions in a man's mind. This in the end disarmed me completely and led me to bend my knees before the Party and the country. And when you ask yourself, 'Very well, suppose you do not die; suppose by some miracle you remain alive, again what for?' … And at such moments, Citizen Judges, everything personal, all the personal accretions, all the vestiges of rancour, pride and a number of other things, fall away and disappear. And, in addition, when the reverberations of the broad international struggle reach your ear, all this in its entirety does its work, and the result is the complete internal moral victory of the USSR over its kneeling opponents ... World history is the court of world justice.

The last phrase is striking. It is a direct translation of Hegel's famous statement that *die Weltgeschichte ist das Weltgericht*, a phrase that Bukharin, who of course spoke German, had internalised like a quotation from sacred scripture. Indeed, the whole performance amounts to a declaration that he is dying as a willing martyr for the sacred cause.

Bukharin went on to cite Hegel specifically:

There emerged what in Hegel's philosophy is called an unhappy consciousness. This unhappy consciousness differed from the ordinary unhappy consciousness only by the fact that it was also a criminal consciousness. The might of the proletarian state found its expression not only in the fact that it smashed the counter-revolutionary gangs, but also in the fact that it undermined its enemies from within, that it disorganised the will of its enemies. Nowhere else is this the case, nor can it be in any capitalist country.

Here we have a man who has convinced himself he is dying for a cause which has a sound philosophical basis, seemingly unaware that the whole cause is that of the supreme cynic, Stalin, who has manipulated both the cause and its devotees in the interest of promotion of himself alone. In submitting himself to this, Bukharin not only went apparently meekly to his death, he also endured the vilification of the prosecutor, Vyshinskii, who, in his final summing up, characterised him as "a hybrid, half fox, half pig". In his confession, Bukharin makes even clearer his sense of his role as that of a martyr. He assumed responsibility for the "sum total of actions taken", "irrespective of whether or not I knew of, whether or not I took direct part in, any particular act". Even more extraordinarily, he writes to Stalin from prison that he does not intend to recant anything, nor does he plead for mercy. "Standing on the edge of a precipice, from which there is no return," he writes, "I tell you on my word of honour that I am innocent of those crimes to which I confessed during the investigation." All this, he emphasises, is for Stalin's personal information only. The conclusion must be that he is informing Stalin as, for him, the personification of the party, that he is consciously sacrificing himself for the sake of the progress of history as led by the party.

This surely is part of the answer as to why so many party members played their curious role in the show trials: they had internalised the Leninist doctrine formulated on the basis of Marx, who himself derived in this regard from Hegel, to the effect that the Communist Party played the leading role, that of a midwife, in a way, in progressing history along its destined path. All individual sacrifices seemed of secondary importance in this perspective. Under Stalin, these individual sacrifices did not cease while he was general secretary of the party. In total, they undoubtedly come to several million.

Schlögel closes his book with a short chapter entitled "Instead of an Epilogue". In it he argues persuasively that an epilogue is inappropriate in that this history has no neat conclusion. Apart from the many more deaths due to the direct action of Stalin's regime, he adverts to the Second World War, to draw the conclusion that the massacres of 1937–38 were followed by human sacrifices whose numbers were estimated at the end of the Soviet Union to be twenty-seven million. The only worthwhile comment is again that of Anna Akhmatova. In the distich, dated 1922 – and we remember that her husband was shot in 1921 – to her 1961 poem *Native Land*, devoted to the earthy qualities, in every sense, of Russia, she writes: "There is not in the world a people more tearless, more proud nor more simple than we."

CORMAC Ó GRÁDA | 2014

Leaping Into Darkness

Forgotten Voices of Mao's Great Famine, 1958–1962 by Zhou Xun

Yale University Press | 288 pp | ISBN: 978-0300184044

THE LAST few years have seen a spate of books on the Chinese Great Leap Forward famine of 1959–61. They include Ralph Thaxton's *Catastrophe and Contention in Rural China* (2008), Frank Dikötter's *Mao's Great Famine* (2010), Yang Jisheng's *Tombstone* (2012), Zhou Xun's *The Great Famine in China, 1958–1962: A Documentary History* (2012) and Felix Wemheuer's *Famine Politics in Maoist China and the Soviet Union* (2014). Two of these – Dikötter's and Yang's – became bestsellers. A famine that was both "hidden" and ignored for several decades is finally getting the scholarly attention that it requires.

After less than a decade of economic recovery and respectable growth in the wake of liberation, in 1958 the Chinese authorities launched the Great Leap Forward, a reckless and misconceived campaign aimed at greatly accelerating economic development. The perceived need to catch up with the capitalist West – Mao hoped that China's industrial output would match Britain's within fifteen years – was a primary motivation. The policy shift had much in common with Stalin's Soviet first Five Year Plan of 1928–32. Both sought to place the burden of faster growth on a backward agricultural sector: where else was the requisite investible surplus to come from? Both relied on collectivisation to generate the food required to sustain helter-skelter industrialisation. And both resulted in massive excess mortality, almost all of it in the countryside.

Of course there were differences too: communal dining halls, backyard furnaces and the campaign to eradicate sparrows were distinctively Chinese. In China the downside risk of failure was even greater than in the Soviet Union, and the cost in lives accordingly much greater, both in relative and absolute terms. The combination of disastrous harvests and excessive requisitioning for urban consumption resulted in a massive, if regionally uneven, famine that lasted between 1959 and 1961. Estimates of excess mortality remain controversial; they range from the implausibly (indeed, ridiculously) low two or three million recently proposed by some neo-Maoist scholars in China to the fifty or sixty million suggested by some of Mao Zedong's most severe critics. The Great Leap famine was, in terms of numbers of victims, the greatest famine ever.

All the works cited above make important contributions and underline the catastrophic dimensions of the famine, although much about its causes and incidence remains unresolved. Apart from Thaxton's, all are based largely on the public record. Zhou Xun's *Forgotten Voices* is different, being the first book-length oral history of the catastrophe.

Forgotten Voices is based on interviews with "nearly a hundred" famine survivors, organised around eight themes such as "the tragedy of collectivization", "starvation and death" and "surviving the famine". Zhou, it would seem, selected her informants in a rather haphazard fashion. She chose a woman selling herbs on a village street in western Sichuan; a chef encountered by accident at a street market near Chengdu, the capital of Sichuan; a woman "sitting against a wall and petting rabbits in a basket" just west of Chengdu; another whom she "ran into by accident in a small market town not far from Pengshan"; a shy man encountered at a roadside café in Anhui who became talkative after "a few cups of alcohol and a hot meal"; "an old neighbour of my family"; her father; and so on. An anthropologist friend recommended some of the others. A majority are what Zhou describes as "illiterate peasants" – and keep in mind that in China as recently as 1980 nearly half of adult women were illiterate – but they also include several who were students at the time, as well as a few former teachers and medical practitioners. Some still lived in poverty in the 2000s; a few had made it, as emigrants in Hong Kong and London.

A disproportionate number of the narrators – about half of them – live (or were living) in Zhou's own province of Sichuan in western China. The famine hit Sichuan very hard, though its impact across that vast province was uneven.

Very often her informants were in remote, almost inaccessible places: "farther up in the mountains" of northern Sichuan; "a mountainous village in eastern Shandong province"; "deep in the mountains of Liangshan". Whether people living in such remote areas were more or less likely to suffer during the famine remains a moot point, not broached by Zhou: although they did not escape collectivisation, their very remoteness may have shielded them more than people in other places against the worst of the grain procurement campaigns (as Anthony Garnaut argues in his essay "The Geography of the Great Leap Famine"). Or, alternatively, those campaigns may have come as a particular shock in hitherto isolated communities.

Some of Zhou's narrators were mere toddlers or young children in 1959–61; some were already in their forties. Zhou does not dwell on the traps laid by autobiographical memory, nor on the evasions and silences and chronological confusions associated with oral history as a source. Dropping her original plan to have all her informants answer the same set of questions, she simply invited them to talk. This turned out to have been a wise decision, and her sorting of their reflections by theme is effectively done.

It all sounds rather random and unscientific. And still, serendipitously, it works. On nearly every page the obscenity of the famine is brought home in the depictions of its deaths, its cruelties, its insanities and horrors. True, many of these cameos, especially those describing survival strategies, could apply to any major famine. Stories of how famines turned children against parents and the strong against the weak, and made liars and thieves and (*in extremis*) even cannibals of decent people have been told about other famines, in China and elsewhere. But there is much that resonates of China in the 1950s too. And the anecdotal, autobiographical character of the narratives lends these accounts a compelling potency and immediacy.

After brief introductions, Zhou lets her informants speak for themselves. She has the knack of getting complete strangers to reveal very personal stories of hardship and loss. Her sources trusted her – often breaking down in her presence – and her decision in turn to conceal their identities is a measure of her respect for them. The overall impression is of convincing and sincere accounts.

Nearly one-third of the book is taken up with collectivisation and the propaganda and pressures associated with the Great Leap Forward. This focus on context matters, since the consequent diversion of labour and grain from the countryside was a key factor behind the famine. The tragic accounts of communal dining halls without adequate food, of slaving long hours, of the expropriation of cooking utensils and domestic furniture and of incessant pressure from party cadres are compelling. Sections on unnatural disasters and on death follow. The rest of the book is concerned with the impact of the famine on the cities, survival strategies, and memories of the famine.

The quest for survival was reflected in the search for substitute foods (insects, earth, chaff, tree bark, poisonous plants etc), in anti-social behaviour and in migration. The oral record, significantly, is silent on organised resistance and food riots, though individual actions of defiance were common. The role of migration as a path to survival is a recurring theme. Some were fortunate enough to be able to escape to Macau and Hong Kong, but Zhou also mentions migration from Gansu to Henan, from Shandong and Henan to the northeast and from Hunan in central China to Yunnan in the far southwest. One narrator fled with his brother from Fushun county in southern Sichuan to Liangshan Yi autonomous region in 1959, exaggeratedly claiming to have covered "more than one thousand kilometres" on foot in a week. Cities were also magnets for those seeking food and work. Those who managed to leave survived; "they were all very capable people, but there were very few of them"; "if I had not run away, I'd have starved to death too". Some deserted dependents in fleeing. That so many found it possible to escape despite the efforts of the authorities to stop them is in itself telling.

Most of the evidence on party cadres is very negative. They were "real tyrants"; they were "fearsome" and "brutal"; they stole food; they were "like slave owners"; "they only cared about themselves". Some narratives, to muddy the water, spin a more positive tale: "cadres were under a lot of pressure in those days"; they "had to be fierce, or else no one would follow their orders"; they risked being purged for underperforming; "my father [a cadre] was an honest man"; cadres saved a camp labourer's life by having his stomach pumped out. As local agents, cadres were caught between a rock and a hard place; either to bow to the "Wind of Exaggeration" fanned by the Great Leap or to risk getting beaten up for telling the truth. Here are some examples:

I remember during those years no family produced any new babies except for the families of cadres, because there was no food to eat ...

My parents were cadres, so they received extra meat coupons. That's how we got to buy canned ribs ... My mother was a cadre at the Beijing municipal government ... Even there a lot of cadres suffered from edema. I remember that my mother's legs were all puffed ...

[Cadres] took away all our pots and pans to make iron and steel ... and they even destroyed our stove. They went as far as pulling down the four walls of our house in order to make fertiliser.

It would be tempting to infer a narrator's experience from mention of the loss of family members in the famine. Thus in mountainous Langzhong county in northern Sichuan, Wei Dexu watched people die, though not members of his own family. Another distanced reference to deaths comes from an informant in Sichuan's Renshou county, who says that "you could see people drop dead while walking". However, moving and vivid reports of deaths of siblings and parents and near relatives are all too frequent:

My father starved to death in 1961. It's really hard for me to talk about that time. [Crying] In those days there weren't even any coffins for those who died. The bodies were just covered up with some earth, and their feet were often exposed outside ...

I had nine children, and two starved to death during the time of the famine. In those days even adults couldn't get enough to eat, and it was even worse for children ... Cry? I am a man, I could bear it. But it's different for women. My wife wept. How did I feel? What could I do? They were my own children ... Their little bodies were thrown away. The best we could do was to ask some people to cover up their bodies with earth ...

In those days there were no roosters crowing any more. In the end, the head of the militia went to the canteen and got a handful of rice from the staff there. He put it in my hand. I ran home ... My father died while I was feeding him. It was in 1959. He was only in his forties. [She wept at this point.]

Zhou provides plenty of evidence straight out of the "grey zone" inhabited by those living through famines (on which see Breandán Mac Suibhne's masterful "A Jig in the Poorhouse", *Dublin Review of Books*, Issue 32). Discord over food within families is a recurrent theme. An in-law of one of Zhou's informants in Sichuan refused to feed a weak grandson. When remonstrated with about this refusal, her reply was "Why don't you feed him yourself?" The little boy died shortly afterwards. Stealing communal food was also endemic. In Sichuan's Pengshan county "thieves constantly came across other thieves". When there was nothing left to steal, some engaged in cannibalism: with no dogs or cows left, "people had to fill their stomachs with something".

The evidence is not always consistent. So at the construction site of the Xichong reservoir in Yunnan's Luliang county "many people died", whereas at the site of the Banqiao dam in Henan's Suiping county "no one died", that is, the dying were moved elsewhere lest a government inspection team discover the truth about conditions on the ground. On the whole the role of the weather is discounted, but in Huang county, Shandong "it rained savagely" in 1960 and 1961 while in Gansu "there were sandstorms all the time". But in Renshou county food was scarce, not because of the weather, but because "all the young and strong labourers were sent to make iron and steel" and "the crops were left to rot in the fields". Zhou makes much of the environmental damage caused by the Great Leap Forward. Certainly, some of it was immediately obvious; what is less clear is whether the losses resulting from dust storms and alkalisation of water were widely predicted at the time or would have been already a problem by 1960–61. Today, the warnings of hydrologist Huang Wanli against the construction of gigantic dams during the Great Leap are universally acknowledged as brave and prescient, but Huang's warnings were more about silt and sedimentation than salinisation and alkalinisation (see Judith Shapiro, *Mao's War Against Nature*). On this, Zhou's narrators may have the advantage of hindsight over the madcap enthusiasts for big dams and small backyard furnaces during the Great Leap.

While Mao's personal, genocidal culpability is central to accounts such as Dikötter's *Mao's Great Famine* and Jasper Becker's *Hungry Ghosts* (1996), he is quite a remote – though hardly sinister – figure in Zhou's narratives. One informant notes that "militarization was Mao's idea", another that he stressed the need for "self-reliance"; one remembered Mao's visit in 1958 to the village of Xushui, iconic for its communistic feats, but he "couldn't see him"; another, Barber Feng of northern Sichuan, referred to the head of his brigade as a crook, "the type of person that Mao once warned us about". But that is about it. Moreover, to Zhou's evident surprise, Mao's memory was revered almost everywhere she went. In Henan's Suiping county, devastated by the famine, "in almost every home there was a portrait of Chairman Mao", while an old neighbour of Zhou's in Chengdu claimed that "if it wasn't for Chairman Mao, who liberated us, we would not be able to enjoy today's good life". An old villager, wondering why Zhou was dwelling on the past, explained that while under Mao people learned to appreciate life by eating bitter food, "these days life is not too bad for many people". Zhou does not attempt to resolve the "disconnect" between the follies of the Great Leap Forward, the violence, and the deaths, on the one hand, and Mao's role, on the other.

Had Zhou interviewed her subjects a generation ago, would their verdict on the part played by Mao in the famine have been the same? Oral history, like all history, often tells us as much about the present as the past. Its strength lies in the searing anecdote and the local detail, not in sophisticated analysis of political decision-making at the top. The Chinese poor were as remote from Mao and Beijing in the 1950s as the Irish poor were from Lord John Russell and London in the 1840s. The willingness of Zhou's witnesses to let Mao off the hook in the 2000s, though important, hardly resolves the extent of Mao's culpability in the 1950s. That issue remains controversial. For some (like, say, Frank Dikötter or Jasper Becker) it is enough to declare the famine "Mao's Famine" – and Zhou's subtitle also echoes this sentiment. For others (like, say, Tom Bernstein or Stephen Wheatcroft or Felix Wemheuer) the famine was the result of an ill-conceived and reckless attempt at forcing a desperately backward economy to catch up. To compound the disaster, when the Great Leap imploded China lacked what Yang in *Tombstone* dubs "negative feedback": thanks to the form of "closed" governance they had created, Mao and his circle seem to have discovered "destruction on a scale few could have imagined" rather late in the day – although this issue is controversial and is one on which Yang and Dikötter, for instance, disagree.

Forgotten Voices closely complements Zhou's earlier and shorter *The Great Famine in China, 1958–1962* (2012), a collection of famine-related documents surreptitiously copied in provincial Communist Party archives. Acknowledgements in the two books overlap, and both cover much common ground from different perspectives. Indeed, Zhou seems to have conducted her interviews between visits to the archives in connection with the earlier book.

Readers of the *Dublin Review of Books* may wonder how the material in *Forgotten Voices* compares with oral evidence on the Great Irish Famine. Like the material collected by the Irish Folklore Commission between the 1930s and the 1950s, the Chinese evidence also focuses on the local and the anecdotal. Just as the Irish material is silent on the likes of treasury undersecretary Charles Trevelyan, the Chinese material is silent on provincial party secretaries such as Wu Zhipu of Henan or Li Jingquan of Sichuan, who feature prominently in written histories of the famine. However, the Chinese oral record is more explicit and more immediate in its accounts of violence and death.

The Irish evidence is doubly vicarious in that the narrators related second-hand information from people who very often described the sufferings of third parties who fared worse during the Famine than themselves. Indeed, hardly anywhere in the IFC archive do we encounter an informant who admits that somebody in the immediate family of their own forebears suffered a Famine-related death or that one of their own people entered the workhouse as an inmate. And whereas in Ireland there is much on workhouses and soup kitchens and evictions and shopkeepers, in China the emphasis is on cadres and state violence and propaganda and communal dining. This is not the place for a systematic comparison between themes in Zhou's narratives and Cathal Póirtéir's excellent compendia (*Famine Echoes*, 1995; *Glórtha ón Ghorta*, 1996), but such a comparison would be a worthwhile exercise.

Forgotten Voices comes at a time when debate about the 1950s is heating up in China itself, with President Xi Jinping sounding more positive notes about Mao's legacy than his immediate predecessors, and Chinese mathematician Sun Jingxian claiming that the Great Leap Forward famine claimed only 2.5 million lives, against estimates of specialist demographers who reckoned that it was eight or even ten times that. Sun's claims are also music to the ears of some younger left-wing activists in China, nostalgic for an era when the party – in their view – was pursuing a Marxist path. At the same time, critical voices such as those of Yang Jisheng, author of *Tombstone*, and Shanghai-based demographer Cao Shuji (whose advice is acknowledged by Zhou) have not been silenced: both they and Sun Jingxian gave as good as they got at a conference on the famine in Wuhan in early July 2014. It is to be hoped that the debate and the research continue, and that voices like those recorded by Zhou are an important part of the story.

White Terror

Massacre: The Life and Death of the Paris Commune of 1871 by John Merriman

Yale University Press | 384 pp | ISBN: 978-0300174526

ON JANUARY 11th, over a million people marched through the streets of Paris in solidarity with the journalists of *Charlie Hebdo*, the two police and four Jewish civilians, victims of the Kouachi brothers and Amedy Coulibaly in their jihadist killing spree. It was a powerful demonstration of respect, sympathy, and support for the principles of press freedom and *laïcité*. There were no political or trade union banners and no slogan-chanting: just sporadic renderings of the *Marseillaise* and bursts of applause for police along the route.

It was the largest Parisian street demonstration since the Liberation in August 1944 and followed a three-pronged route, from the Place de la République to the Place de la Nation: one section going up the boulevard de Ménilmontant and past the Père Lachaise cemetery, another following the boulevard Voltaire through the Place Léon Blum, and a third going down the boulevard des Filles du Calvaire past the Place de la Bastille. The Place de la République, Père Lachaise, boulevard Voltaire and the Bastille formed four fitting symbolic spots for republican solidarity, indelibly linked to the republican image of Marianne, the Enlightenment's championing of free speech, the Commune's *mur des fédérés* and the people's victory in the 1789 revolution. The end point of the march, the Place de la Nation, has less symbolic power: formerly known as the Place du Trône, and the site where over 1,300 people were guillotined during the French Revolution, it was renamed the Place de la Nation in the 1880s and now has a giant statue of the Triumph of the Republic as its centrepiece.

Symbolism is important in French politics. Republican demonstrations tend to use the artisanal eastern areas of the city as their focal points, whereas the right wing favours the Champs Élysées in the more prosperous west. The artisanal east embraces the faubourg Saint Antoine, the eleventh arrondissement and Belleville, which was a rapidly developing industrial zone in the mid-nineteenth century. All were also focal points of the Paris Commune, which John Merriman brings vividly life in this detailed and action-packed narrative. Merriman is a leading historian of nineteenth century France, of the revolutions of 1830 and 1848, of mid-century Limoges and of the anarchist activity of the 1880s and 1890s. As befits a historian of revolution, his heart lies on the left and this compelling narrative is written very much from ground level within the *communard* side, providing a counterbalance to Robert Tombs's analysis of the Commune as seen from Versailles.

The Commune was essentially a civil war between a radicalised Paris and the rest of France, following French defeat in the Franco-Prussian war of 1870–71. After Napoleon III's capture at Sedan his Second Empire collapsed and a republic was proclaimed from the traditional site of the balcony of the Hotel de Ville. A government of national defence was hurriedly patched together to carry on the war but Paris was put under siege by the Prussian army, the military situation proved hopeless and in late January a truce was signed with a united Germany. The historic French aim of keeping Germany divided, stretching back to Richelieu but fatally compromised by Napoleon I's hubris, had finally collapsed.

During the siege, political radicalism had grown in Paris with the emergence of clubs, newspapers and democratic structures around the National Guard. However, elections that were held in February to a new Assembly, with the authority to negotiate a permanent peace with Germany, produced a right-wing assembly dominated by conservatives and royalists. It appointed the veteran politician Adolphe Thiers as prime minister, a man who came originally from Provence and had been politically active since the 1820s. Thiers was a conservative republican, determined to impose order and bring the capital to heel, and he quickly ended the moratorium on the sale of goods in pawn shops, made all overdue bills (including rent) payable immediately and moved the seat of government to Versailles on the grounds that Paris was too dangerous. These were direct blows at a population that was suffering mass unemployment since the previous summer and the final straw proved to be his order to remove cannon from the National Guard in Montmartre on March 18th. The central committee of the National Guard stepped in, Thiers pulled back all troops from the city and within days Paris was in revolt.

What followed was over ten weeks of innovation and revolution, marked by vibrant political debate and social welfare reform that included the opening of workers' cooperatives and collective workshops to provide work and subsistence for the needy and the poor. Politically, the Commune was multipolar and decentralised, with only a very flimsy central authority, initially provided by the central committee of the National Guard and then by a municipal government, or Commune, elected by universal male suffrage in late March. Yet relations between the two, as Merriman points out, were always strained and there was a great deal of autonomy at *arrondissement* level as well. The Commune's activists tended to be men and women in their twenties and thirties, most of them literate although few had had a secondary education. Two-thirds had been born outside Paris, and then sucked into areas like La Villette, Belleville and Saint-Denis by the building and industrial boom of the 1850s and 1860s. Many were unskilled labourers, but most activists were artisans, skilled workers, clerks and shopkeepers, with a scattering of intellectuals and artists such as Gustave Courbet the realist painter. Merriman provides a comprehensive picture of their involvement, and also welcome attention to the role of women, who supplied around fifteen per cent of the membership of political clubs; some of them, like Elisabeth Dmitrieff, established the Union des Femmes to build barricades while others like Louise Michel were active and vociferous in clubs and workshops. Although Versailles deliberately exaggerated their importance, several hundred foreigners were also involved, attracted by the potential for a full-blown working class revolution.

Yet that potential was never there, for the vast majority of the communards had little interest in attacking private property and were instead a product of the rich ideological diversity of the French left. Jacobins looked back to the 1789 revolution for their ideal of a centralised democratic republic; Proudhonists had their roots instead in the July Monarchy and looked for a decentralised structure of self-governing cooperatives and communes, of which Paris would just be one. To their left, followers of Auguste Blanqui, who spent the entire Commune in prison, insisted on shelving the social question until they had consolidated the political foundations of the revolution. Almost no one subscribed to Marx's ideal of a socialism founded on the abolition of private property.

If the Commune's social and political aims were fluid, its religious aims were not and its prime target was the Catholic church, which had firmly attached itself to the conservative and royalist right since 1789. After the death of Archbishop Christophe de Beaumont on the barricades in June 1848 the church had become one of the major props of the Second Empire, benefiting in return from an almost total monopoly of the educational system. Largely due to Catholicism's persistent habit of cosying up to the political right, anticlericalism had become a feature of popular radicalism and exploded into life as the Commune began: church schools were closed, state and church separated, religious orders dispersed and churches used as shelters, refuges and political clubs. When the Versailles government executed several captured prisoners in early April, Archbishop Darboy was taken hostage, along with several dozen priests, and imprisoned in the Conciergerie, which had held victims waiting for the guillotine during the French revolutionary terror. He was eventually executed on May 24th after Thiers refused to barter prisoner exchanges, the third Parisian archbishop to die a violent death since 1848.

What began as festival ended in tragedy. There was no realistic hope of the communards either fragmenting the French state into self-governing units or persuading the provinces to rally behind them. Without outside support their fate was inevitable. Thiers quickly mopped up mini-communes in Lyon, Marseille, Toulouse and elsewhere. Even leading republican politicians like Clemenceau, Gambetta or Victor Hugo refused to swing behind the Commune, opting instead for an unsuccessful attempt to negotiate a compromise.

Thiers then was able to methodically put together an army that badly needed a morale boost after its drubbing at the hands of the Prussians, and gradually move on Paris from the west. It remorselessly reconquered the capital, suburb by suburb and street by street as the communards fought a long and bloody rearguard battle. The army neutralised barricades by outflanking them through side streets, or firing from high buildings, while the communards delayed their advance in a desperate rearguard resistance that included the appalling tactic of setting fire to major buildings. The Tuileries palace was badly damaged, along with the Ministry of Finance and the Palais Royal, while the Hôtel de Ville was totally gutted (today's building is just a faithful replica). The fighting ended in Belleville, and in the tenth and eleventh *arrondissements*, climaxing in a final massacre in the Père Lachaise cemetery on Sunday, May 28th at the spot now known as the *mur des fédérés*. Thiers's forces of order were no sabbatarians, the Commune was well and truly over and much of Haussman's Paris in ruins.

The exact death toll will never be known. Communards themselves later claimed a figure of more than thirty-five thousand. Merriman goes for a lower figure of seventeen thousand, while Robert Tombs, who studied the conflict from the Versailles side, opts for less than half that number, around eight thousand. Even using the lower death figure, the Commune had almost four times more Parisian deaths in ten weeks than the French revolutionary terror achieved in eighteen months. Yet statistics alone will never reflect the intensity of the conflict and Merriman rightly emphasises the importance of the class hatred that shaped the attitude and behaviour of the political and military authorities both during and after the event.

Several army units slaughtered opponents without authorisation, interrogation or reprimand. A *Te Deum* was later celebrated in Notre Dame for the murdered Archbishop Darboy, but none for the thousands of communard dead, whom Pius IX later called "men escaped from Hell". The Catholic church went on to clarify its attitude by constructing the basilica of the Sacré-Coeur in Montmartre as an act of penance for the sins that had brought Prussian defeat and civil war. Like Père Lachaise cemetery, it has since lost much of its symbolic significance and became just another stop on the tourist trail.

Yet history has ironies to match its bathos and one of the short-term results of Thiers's victory over the Commune was the belief that a republic could guarantee order as effectively as a monarchy or empire. As Thiers remarked, "the republic will be conservative or it will not be". A return to kings was unnecessary –just as well, as the rival Orléanist and Bourbon candidates fell out over who should reign first – and the Third Republic was consolidated in the 1870s, to create the model on which successive republics have been founded. Another consequence was the devastation of the French left as, besides the dead, over four thousand communards were deported to the Pacific island of New Caledonia. By the time an amnesty allowed thousands to return in 1880 the republic was firmly established: Bastille Day became an official celebration for the first time that year. It was also the year when the first commemoration was held at the *mur des fédérés* in Père Lachaise, a tradition that continues until now on every May 1st. The communards are dead but their legacy was important and Merriman's study is the best point of departure for anyone wanting to know the idealism, violence and tragedy involved.

War and
Revolution

The high politics of the "Irish question" in the years 1910–1922 is fairly well-trodden ground, writes FRANK CALLANAN, *but Ronan Fanning's book on the period builds on previous work, offering a graceful marriage of informed reference to secondary sources and a grasp unrivalled among contemporary Irish historians of the mainly British primary sources, all delivered with aplomb in strikingly fluent prose.*

The most persistent argument put forward in recent years in favour of commemorating the Great War, writes PÁDRAIG YEATES, *is that we should remember all the Irishmen who served in the British army and who were subsequently forgotten. The reality, however, is that they were not forgotten, at least by their own. And what values are we commemorating? Beyond the concept of heroic sacrifice, writes Yeates, it is difficult to think of any.*

ROY FOSTER *reviews an original and suggestive new study of the Irish Protestant experience since 1795, which does not have much to say about the well-worn topics of Big Houses or decayed estates. Instead it concentrates on the little people, their associations, how they consorted together, their dogged faith and their reaction to the threats of violence and expulsion which hung in the air during the Troubles.*

FRANK CALLANAN | 2013

The Road to Partition

Fatal Path: *British Government and Irish Revolution 1910–22* by Ronan Fanning
Faber & Faber | 448 pp | ISBN: 978-0571297399

RONAN FANNING has contrived to write a fresh and sparkling narrative of the course of Irish history from the Irish party gaining the balance of power at the election of January 1910, and retaining it in December 1910, to the establishment of the Northern Ireland and southern Irish states. This is no mean feat.

The high politics of the "Irish question" in this period is fairly well-trodden ground, in general or thematic works, and occupies daunting chunks of the biographies of the main players. While the end dates vary, the focus strikingly tends to narrow to the extraordinary thirteen-year period Fanning chooses. This saw the long-deferred prospect of the attainment of Home Rule with the enactment of the Parliament Act in August 1911 and the introduction of the third Home Rule Bill in April 1912 (just over a quarter-century after Gladstone introduced the first) turn to ashes, and the turmoil that ensued in nationalist politics, leading to the foundation of the Free State in 1922 after the establishment of the Northern Ireland state by the Government of Ireland Act 1920.

The two-state outcome was engendered in circumstances of extraordinary political drama: the seemingly imminent triumph of the Irish parliamentary party under John Redmond's leadership, to which nationalist Ireland prematurely adjusted its expectations; the emergence of a grimly formidable leader of Irish unionism in the person of Edward Carson in February 1910, coupled with the election of an implacably resolute defender of Ulster, Andrew Bonar Law, as leader of the Conservative party in the following year; the rise of marshalled resistance to Home Rule in Ulster abetted by the leadership of the Conservative party; the convulsive political crisis that ensued in British as well as Irish politics; the outbreak of the Great War, followed by the enactment of a suspended third Home Rule Bill in September 1914; the 1916 Rising; the death of Redmond in March 1918; Sinn Féin's defeat of the Irish party at the general election of December 1918; the first meeting of Dáil Éireann on January 21st, 1919, with on the same day the killing of two policemen in an ambush at Soloheadbeg in Tipperary that marked the inception of the War of Independence; the enlistment of British recruits in the Royal Irish Constabulary (the "black and tans"); "Bloody Sunday" on November 21st, 1920; the opening of the Northern Ireland parliament by George V in June 1921; the truce between the IRA and the British army in July 1921; the Anglo-Irish conference in London in October and December 1921 that issued in the signing of the treaty; the approval of the treaty by the Dáil in January 1922; the pact election of May; the IRA incursions into the Pettigo-Beleek triangle of Fermanagh; the assassination of Field Marshal Sir Henry Wilson in London by the IRA; the deaths successively of Griffith and Collins in the autumn, eight months before the ending of the civil war in April 1923.

Nicholas Mansergh's magisterial *The Unresolved Question: The Anglo-Irish Settlement and its Undoing* was published in 1991. Ten years ago, Alvin Jackson's *Home Rule: An Irish History 1800–2000* appeared. Jackson deploys the paradoxical concept of the Ulster Unionist embrace of a form of Home Rule. Fanning characterises Ulster unionist resistance to Home Rule as a revolution. It says much of the shifting sands of the period – sands that have not ceased to shift – that both approaches are valid. George Dangerfield published his engaging *The Damnable Question: A Study in Anglo-Irish Relations* in 1976, a coda to his incisively elegiac *The Strange Death of Liberal England*, a post mortem in which Ireland featured prominently.

Much much more has been written, and it is one of the outstanding merits of Fanning's work that he draws with elegant succinctness on the scholarly writings touching his subject. The net is cast wide into the depths of British high politics. What he has perfected is the graceful marriage of reference to secondary sources to his grasp unrivalled among contemporary Irish historians of the mainly British primary sources. His syncretic method cannot be overpraised, a late efflorescence of the extraordinary school of history at University College Dublin, a university now in infuriatingly self-inflicted institutional crisis. It is a monument to that school, one hopes not funerary. For a graduate of UCD of my generation one can see distantly filtering through the text the faint and slightly dropsical smile, with drooping cigarette, of TD Williams. Williams, who died in 1987, brought to the history of modern Ireland a scepticism sharpened by his immersion in European interwar diplomacy.

Ronan Fanning's prose is strikingly fluent, and his characterisations of the usually remote and untreated figures on the British side exemplary and entertaining. It is a recurrent feature of history of this type that, the main players apart, characters are often left unexplored, so that the Irish (or perhaps at this stage any) reader is left to invest their names with this or that imagined characteristic, as we may perhaps imagine an unfamiliar destination emblazoned on the front of a London bus, or a tube train destined for the further reaches of the underground. Fanning resolutely sets out to correct this in a glittering sequence of vignettes. His analysis of the strikingly inept design of the Parliament Act is masterly, and works as a kind of prelude to the substantive politics of Home Rule and Irish independence in which neither side was exempt from the laws of unintended consequences.

If a dominant theme emerges, it is the cynicism of the post-Gladstonian Liberal leadership in relation to Home Rule, and what Fanning sees as the culpable gullibility of Redmond and Dillon. The portrayal of Herbert Henry Asquith, Liberal leader and prime minister in the crucial years 1910–16, who tends to be given the benefit of the doubt in sanguine moderate nationalist readings of the period, is biting, and will endure. If there is a hero in this determinedly anti-heroic narrative, it is Lloyd George, whom Redmond's successor, John Dillon, came morosely to believe had set out purposely to destroy the Irish party. He "solved the Irish question in the form in which it had bedevilled British politics since 1886". His statement to the House of Commons in December 1919 provides the book's epigraph, and its title: "There is a path of fatality which pursues the relations between the two countries and makes them eternally at cross purposes." Lloyd George's haunting observation goes to show that politicians, at the height of their utterance, are as serenely exempt as poets from the ordinary laws of expression.

The reservations I have in relation to *Fatal Path* derive in part from the constraints that inhere within the genre of close high political analysis, and in part from what Prof Fanning has to say in his introduction, which is rendered down in the publisher's blurb from Faber. As to the limitations of the genre, even though Ronan Fanning provides an introductory chapter entitled "Gladstone's legacy" it is necessarily an abbreviated prelude. Close analysis of 1910–22 unavoidably occludes what went before. The Parnell era, and the catastrophe of his overthrow, is relegated to a distant political time. In one sense the Parnell era was in the weirdly accelerated temporality of Irish nationalism already remote, but its legacy and the fall-out of the split continued to be of consequence. The Irish party emerged from the ten-year split 1890–1900 institutionally enfeebled in Ireland, and tightly locked into the logic of the Liberal-nationalist alliance with sharply diminished leverage. Somewhere along the way, whether as a result of the split in Parnell's lifetime or by insensible steps thereafter, the party had compromised its independent agency.

Astringently high political analysis abstracts from how parliamentary nationalism got to where it was, and from politics on the ground. There are hazards in an aphoristically judgmental, ex post facto mode of analysis. The Irish party, in its heavily laden post-split trajectory, failed and failed dismally. It is however somewhat facile to couple that failure with Liberal private and public admissions of a kind of negative opportunism in relation to Home Rule, which Fanning collates to devastating effect, to deride the judgment of the party leadership. In the position in which it found itself, having trumpeted the imminence of Home Rule for a quarter-century, the party had to wager all on the game, something of which Asquith in particular was cruelly conscious.

It is true that the tide was going out on Home Rule since before Gladstone's retirement, and Margaret O'Callaghan has argued forcefully that it was already in trouble by the time of the Special Commission before the Parnell split. The Irish party was nevertheless dealt an unexpectedly good hand in 1910 and played that initial hand with competence and resolve. It was impotent in the face of the organised resistance of Ulster, sustained by the leadership of the Conservative party, which, however extra-constitutional, the Liberal government was not prepared to face down. The Irish nationalist electorate was wholly unprepared for partition, but the Irish party might have survived a partitionist Home Rule settlement in a time of peace. Its grip was radically undermined by the Great War, and Redmond's improvident advocacy of enlistment, and the Easter Rising marked less the beginning than the middle of the end.

The unpalatable truth is that the main lines of the narrative were indelibly inscribed from the outset, and aggravated by the war. However one characterises the actions of the Ulster Unionist and Conservative leaderships, those actions were undertaken on the correct premise that in British politics the "coercive" inclusion of the northeast in a Home Rule Ireland was unacceptable, easily presented by unionist publicists as a dismemberment of the United Kingdom and a dagger pointed at the heart of the British empire. One struggles to see where, had the Irish party played a different hand, it would have significantly affected the outcome, to identify the decisive moment where history could have engaged a different thread.

No matter how sternly realistic one tries to be, the remorseless course of adverse events from an Irish perspective, its ghastly rolling inexorability, remains extremely exasperating and profoundly depressing. At times the Irish question in its final parliamentary phase resembles a vast deserted asylum whose last inhabitants are its historians, who come to fear, in the manner of *The Magic Mountain*, that having arrived as visitors they are now confined as inmates.

Fanning is far too good a historian to blame Redmond's Irish party for partition, though he does occasionally get a little carried away, writing of the personal amity of Lloyd George and Bonar Law that "the full flowering of that fellow-feeling swiftly smothered antagonism in Lloyd George's coalition government and provided the bedrock for the partition of Ireland". His basic point is that the IRA campaign in the war of independence was necessary to move Lloyd George's Conservative-dominated government to a settlement beyond the confines of "the 1914-style limitations of the Government of Ireland Act of 1920". Mansergh expressed an essentially similar view a quarter of a century ago. The paradigm of an Irish settlement that derived from Gladstone's conception of Home Rule was already obsolete, post-Versailles. The establishment of a Northern Ireland parliament introduced an asymmetry that could not be sustained.

The demand for legislative independence across forty years from Parnell to Sinn Féin was unequivocal. From the British perspective, there was a void in which there had to be an Irish settlement, and it was given a significant further push by the IRA campaign. There is a strange sense in which the violence could be said to have conformed to the needs of the British government. A settlement could only be politically with Sinn Féin and militarily with the IRA. It is hard to disagree with Fanning's view, in part because events had reached a point that did not admit of counterfactuals. With whom else on the Irish side could there have been a settlement?

In relation to the conduct of the treaty negotiations themselves there is a supplement of asperity in Fanning's criticisms of Arthur Griffith in particular. It is odd how many historians for one reason or another disesteem the much misunderstood Griffith, indicted successively for being too narrow-mindedly obdurate and not inflexible enough.

In his introduction, Fanning has a side-swipe against revisionists, using the term in its Irish political sense. Enlisting a quotation from (curiously enough) Bernard Lewis, he states "there is no better description of how and why throughout Northern Ireland's long war the British and Irish political establishments sought to control the presentation of the history of 1912–22 in order to buttress and legitimise their own authority while at the same time denying legitimacy and authority to the Provisional IRA and other paramilitary forces". This seems to me trite and faintly offensive, but it does enunciate the prevailing historiographical wisdom. History unceasingly evolves, never more so than on what was in British politics called "the Irish question". Later events force one to reconsider earlier events, and to suggest otherwise is an exercise in a kind of strange temporal political correctness.

Conor Cruise O' Brien (not mentioned by name, in itself a feature of the primness of the current academic orthodoxy) certainly questioned the necessity for the IRA campaign in the War of Independence, but he did so primarily in the context of querying the destructive consequences of anti-partitionist rhetoric in southern politics and the exaltation of political violence. It is moreover a travesty of politics in the Republic to imply that it was felt necessary to repudiate the proximate origins of the state in the War of Independence to condemn the campaign of politico-sectarian murder prosecuted by the IRA in the Troubles. (The striking resurgence of Michael

Collins as an Irish popular hero in recent years does not suggest that most Irish people are discomfited by the War of Independence, or have difficulty distinguishing between the IRA of that war and the IRA of the Northern Ireland Troubles. Perhaps historians who share Fanning's view will suggest that the memory of Collins would not have made its contemporary ascent if it were not for the Good Friday agreement. Though absurd, this would at least have the merit of consistency.)

If one accepts that partition in some form was inevitable, the principal casualty of the course of events expertly chronicled in *Fatal Path* was Irish nationalist self-confidence, which seeped into statehood. Majoritarian support for the treaty and pride in the establishment of an independent Irish state weirdly coexisted with a sense of betrayal and defeat, fortified by an unassuageable sense of guilt provoked by the feeling that Southern nationalists had abandoned their Northern brethren to their fate in the deeply inhospitable institutions of the Northern Irish state. With Fianna Fáil's entry into the Dáil and government this complex became inextricably woven into the fabric of Irish party politics. The pall of woundedness was not dispelled by the achievements of the independent Irish state under successive governments and had profoundly retrograde consequences. It endured into the late 1950s and was not then quickly dispelled.

That sense of despair, and the curious combination of passivity and mystical nationalist elan to which it conduced, had its origin in the escalating setbacks sustained by the Irish Party in the 1910–18 period. Irish nationalists had been nurtured since Parnell's time on the promise of unitary Home Rule. Whatever the inevitability of a two-state outcome, the manner in which it unfolded to 1918 – the militaristic marshalling of resistance in Ulster followed by a series of stepped compromises at Westminster in which the Irish party found itself constrained to acquiesce – was catastrophic. It is difficult to conceive of a script more wounding to nationalist self-belief.

It is arguable, at least in the extended and perhaps artificial hindsight of the history of the early decades of independence, that the better course would have been for the Irish party to have made a virtue of its impotence and held aloof from ratifying the successive concessions to Ulster unionism. It could have gone further and effaced itself at the 1918 election in favour of Sinn Féin. That of course is not how political parties tend to behave, but it is an option that John Redmond's brother William, who alone of the older cadre of the Irish party retained something of the imaginative resilience of his Parnellite youth, contemplated in the interval between the 1916 Rising and his death on the western front in June 1917. He is unlikely to have been alone. The momentum of the great party of Parnell had turned alchemically to lead. The Irish party remained in any event adamantly opposed to Sinn Féin's doctrine of parliamentary abstentionism, and at the 1918 election retained a much higher level of electoral support than its exceedingly meagre haul of seats might suggest.

My principal disagreement with Ronan Fanning relates to some of the sentiments expressed in the introduction which I happen to find provoking but which do not inform the mordant assuredness of his narrative. *Fatal Path* is an admirable centennial accretion to the quite short shelf of indispensable works on the tormented decade or so in the crucible of which the modern Irish state was formed.

PÁDRAIG YEATES | 2014

No Poppy, Please

LAST YEAR I was heavily involved in commemorating the Great Dublin Lockout of 1913. I was involved, as were a lot of other people, not just because it had been largely forgotten about but because of the values it encapsulated – social solidarity, the right to equality of treatment no matter who or what you are, the right to freedom of association, the right to representation, the right to be in a trade union, the right to decent pay and conditions, the right to a roof over your head.

We commemorated the lockout because the issues at stake were as important and as relevant – and as contested – today as they were a hundred years ago. But I look at the centenary of the Great War and I have to ask myself what values are we commemorating. Beyond the concept of heroic sacrifice I can't think of any, and if we are remembering heroic sacrifice, heroic sacrifice for what? The vast majority of combatants were mobilised by Hohenzollern Germany, Tsarist Russia, the Austro-Hungarian, British and Ottoman empires to fight and die for them. None of these exist any more.

The most persistent argument I have heard put forward in Ireland in recent years for commemorating the Great War is to remember all the Irishmen who served in the British armed forces and were subsequently forgotten. The reality is that they were not forgotten, by their own at least. There were mass commemorations every year on the Sunday nearest Remembrance Day until long afterwards. You only have to look at the newspapers in the 1920s and 1930s to see them.

Up until 1932 Free State government ministers attended commemorations each November in Whitehall, as well as in Dublin. When Fianna Fáil came to power official Ireland ceased honouring the Great War dead but it did not prevent commemorations from taking place. Numbers attending fell, but so did the number of survivors and more current events were crying out for public attention. One of them was the Spanish Civil War, which erupted in the summer of 1936.

Nevertheless, in November of that year a thousand Catholic ex-servicemen formed up behind the British Legion flag in Beresford Place, outside Liberty Hall, and marched to the Pro-Cathedral for a commemorative Mass, while their Protestant counterparts formed up in St Stephen's Green and marched to St Patrick's Cathedral. The Old Contemptibles Association, the Royal Irish Fusiliers Old Comrades Association, the Irish Horse Old Comrades Association and the Royal Dublin Fusiliers Old Comrades Association all attended these services and some firms, such as the GSWR and Guinness, held ceremonies to commemorate their own war dead at Broadstone, Kingsbridge and James's Gate. The old IRA Association objected to these events, as it usually did. In 1936 it called on the president of the Free State executive, Eamon de Valera, to "prohibit these imperialistic displays".

Eighteen years after the end of the First World War, fifteen years after the end of the War of Independence and thirteen years after the end of the Irish Civil War, "old comrades" were still fighting old conflicts, not just here but across Europe. Three years later a new generation was fighting in the second act of the great European civil war. It is hard to kill a bad thing, but while it might be argued that the First World War was a war that should never have been fought, the Second World War was one that had to be fought if European civilisation was to survive, however mutilated by the process.

The European Union and that apparent aberration, the Russian Revolution of 1917, were among the most significant products of the Great War. The former sought to reconcile nationalist aspirations with the notion, to paraphrase Winston Churchill, that "to jaw-jaw is always better than to war-war". The Russian Revolution sought to replace competing nationalisms with a universal brotherhood, and sisterhood, of the human race based on the emancipation of the working class.

The Soviet Union has disappeared, as have most of its satellite states. The much younger European Union survives, but it is currently struggling to contain the aggressive nationalist tendencies of the right-wing parties in power across many of its newer member states in eastern Europe. Nationalism has been the driving ideology behind most wars on this continent since the French Revolution. The last major conflict was in the Balkans, where two nations, Serbs and Croats, who speak the same language but subscribe to two slightly different varieties of Christianity, saw power-sharing as a zero-sum game. Does that remind anyone of a conflict nearer home?

I am old enough to remember the start of the current Northern troubles. I was in Belfast the week internment was introduced in August 1971. The British army behaved brutally and often without restraint and yet I have to say that without its presence in Northern Ireland in the 1970s I think we would have had our own Srebrenicas and Sarajevos. Hopefully the current conflict in the Ukraine can be contained without developing into a full-blown war, but it is a reminder that there are still contested zones and identities across Europe, from the Basque country in the south to the Baltic states in the North. Added to the old identities are pockets of ethnic Russians, the residue of the old Soviet empire, planters, who are the "Orangemen" of our era.

It is depressing to have to recall that the First World War broke out because the political elite that ruled Europe after the Congress of Vienna in 1815 failed to keep pace with the social, economic, technological and cultural changes that transformed European civilisation in the following century. In the summer of 1914 three of the key decision-makers were Franz Joseph of Austria Hungary, who had been emperor since the failed revolution of 1848, Nicholas II of Russia and Kaiser Wilhelm II of Germany. All of these men were inadequate to the challenges that confronted them in the summer of 1914. The armed alliances that each relied upon as a guarantee against war ultimately had the opposite effect. The ruling elites could not prevent a couple of shots fired by a dissident Serb nationalist from plunging Europe into a war that resulted in millions of people dying.

Would Ireland have been spared war if the great powers had resolved their differences in 1914? It seems unlikely. By the summer of 1914 the

100,000-strong Ulster Volunteer Force had assembled perhaps as many as 60,000 weapons to resist Home Rule by force and militant nationalists were belatedly beginning to arm. John Redmond was still the undisputed leader of nationalist Ireland but his political capital was rapidly dwindling. His offer to accept partition as a temporary expedient in 1914 seriously wounded him. Important figures such as William Martin Murphy, owner of the *Irish Independent* newspaper empire and the key political strategist of the Catholic church, Dr William Walsh, archbishop of Dublin, never forgave him and lost faith in his capacity to deliver on the nationalist agenda.

Would the faltering Liberal government have held the ring when the low-level sectarian conflict already taking place in the North had evolved into something more serious? Probably, but it almost certainly would not have prevented it. We might well have witnessed something similar to the events that emerged in the War of Independence or the more recent Northern Ireland Troubles on a much greater scale. And we should not forget that the seeming inevitability of serious conflict in Ireland was a contributory factor to the German decision to risk British involvement in the First World War by its violation of Belgian neutrality in August 1914.

However, I would argue that, paradoxically, the outbreak of the war allowed the conflict that did emerge in Ireland to be much less violent and politically regressive than might otherwise have been the case. For a start, the outbreak of war saw tens of thousands of potential combatants enrolled in the British army – 50,942 from Belfast and 28,268 from Dublin alone. For another, the failure of the Easter Rising saw the Irish Volunteers disarmed. They would never recover from those losses sufficiently to pose a serious military threat to unionists or the British in subsequent years.

Also, if the Great War united the fractured British establishment to confront militant Irish nationalism in a way that was inconceivable beforehand it also created the space in which more original, radical nationalists could challenge the deeply conservative Home Rule consensus. A whole host of writers and propagandists, including four signatories of the 1916 proclamation, Patrick Pearse, James Connolly, Thomas MacDonagh and Joseph Mary Plunkett, put forward new and often original concepts of Irish nationality.

The proclamation itself was a wonderful document. It could not have been written anywhere in Ireland except Dublin and it could not have been written at any other time except during a war when Britain was involved in a life and death struggle. The Democratic Programme of the First Dáil was the other outstanding political legacy of this period. (I think we could include Sean O'Casey's Constitution of the Irish Citizen Army, from which the proclamation draws some of its inspiration.) I don't think it is pure coincidence that the last comparable outburst of imaginative political thought within Irish nationalism came during a similar cataclysmic conflict, the French Revolutionary and Napoleonic Wars. The real possibility of throwing off British rule opened new intellectual horizons for the United Irishmen as it did for the generation of 1916. The proclamation declared "the right of the people of Ireland to the ownership of Ireland". It guaranteed "civil liberty, equal rights and equal opportunities to all its citizens", including women – the half of the population that Redmondism could not bring itself to enfranchise. The proclamation also resolved to pursue the happiness and prosperity of the whole nation "oblivious of differences".

The Democratic Programme went even further, promising "to resume possession of the nation's wealth ... whenever the trust is abused", to aim at "the elimination of the class in society which lives upon the wealth produced by the workers of the nation" and "to make provision for the physical, mental and spiritual wellbeing of the children, to secure that no child shall suffer hunger or cold from lack of food, clothing or shelter, but that all shall be provided with the means and facilities requisite for their proper education and training as Citizens of a Free and Gaelic Ireland".

I would argue that from 1913 until 1921 Dublin was the political, cultural and conceptual capital of Ireland from which most of the fresh and original ideas flowed. Traditional currents of thought were temporarily subverted by the uncertainties and possibilities created by the war and the Easter Rising provided a platform on which novel new ideas could be debated. It would take some time for the traditional, Catholic nationalist consensus to reassert itself. In that it was helped by some aspects of militant nationalism, the most significant of which was the Belfast Boycott. If Redmond conceded the principle of partition, Sinn Féin and the IRA built the wall that divided North and South – albeit provoked by the Belfast pogroms. (It is hard to envisage any sane person looking forward to that centenary.) The task of reining in radical nationalism to conform with the dominant ethos in the South gathered pace after the truce. The general election of June 1922 marked the end of the one-party Sinn Féin-IRA state. The Civil War that followed ultimately ushered in the return to normality of Irish politics, when the parish pump resumed its traditional primacy, albeit in rather violent and convoluted ways.

Similar things were happening across Europe. Revolution, civil war, inter-state and ethnic conflicts were the norm in many places after 1918. There were more men under arms in the early 1920s than at the outbreak of the First World War. Boundaries changed dramatically. Hungary shrank, Romania expanded, Poland re-emerged as a nation, new countries such as the Baltic states, Czechoslovakia, Yugoslavia, and above all the Union of Soviet Socialist Republics emerged. There were huge transfers of population, with 1.2 million Greeks alone forced to leave the ancestral homes they had occupied in Anatolia for over two and a half thousand years and resettle in their Greek "homeland". But large ethnic minorities remained captive within the new so-called nation states, of which the most fatal to European peace would ultimately prove to be the Sudeten Germans.

It may not be much consolation to people who believe that veterans of the Great War were unjustly forgotten afterwards but the same thing happened in Britain and, I suspect, further afield, especially after the Second World War, when people had fresher and even more terrible experiences to get over. I think it was forgotten because many people who lived through the first half of the twentieth century wanted to forget it. The power of the Russian Revolution to capture the imagination of millions was based on the hope, misplaced as it ultimately was, that the system that created the Great War could be changed: that the emperors, the capitalists, the bloodsuckers in all their guises could be overthrown and ordinary people could inherit and enjoy the wealth they had created. It was only when the fiftieth anniversary of the Great War occurred in 1964 that it resumed a central place in the British public memory with a welter of books, magazine series and TV programmes. These provided a largely sentimentalised version of events. It was informed by greater awareness of the wider suffering the war inflicted, but the military core of commemoration remained intact. Within that core was a militarist culture that I believe still exists today and, increasingly since the Falklands War, the poppy has been used by the British establishment to support foreign military adventures.

I must say I have difficulty dealing with these conflicting legacies myself. Several members of my own family served in the British armed forces, including my grandfather and father. I never knew my grandfather and I have no idea what he thought about anything but I do know that my father, who served in the British army in the Second World War had no time for the British establishment. I suspect that his time in the army were the best years of his life but he loathed the values of its officer class and despised the barrack room culture that appealed to the basest human instincts and prejudices. His attitude was common among men I met who had served in the British armed forces during the Second World War; and we should not forget it was the servicemen's vote that put Churchill out in 1945.

By the way, whatever unit my father served in as a member of the Pioneer Corps he was dubbed "Paddy" as soon as he opened his mouth. In early 1943 he was awarded the George Medal for saving the lives of other soldiers in North Africa and, like other servicemen granted a major gallantry award, he received it from King George VI at the war's end. When the king shook his hand and said "Congratulations Paddy" he replied "Thanks Kingy", for which my mother never forgave him. However crass his reply, it was his way of saying he was not fighting for king and country, to save the British empire or to keep his betters in the manner to which they felt entitled. He never wore a poppy, never joined the British Legion or attended a Remembrance Day commemoration. Like tens of thousands of other Second World War veterans he became a convinced socialist as a result of his wartime service and began fighting for a better world. The ranks of the labour movement in Britain after the Second World War were filled by these men.

Some of the legacy of the welfare state these men built has survived, such as the NHS; more of it has been thrown away in the name of deregulation and the unfettered pursuit of profit. It is perhaps fitting that we are commemorating the Great War in such an ambience because it certainly reflects the world and values of 1914 rather than 1945. If we only look at the past with a sentimental eye, it is not only a waste of time but a dangerous illusion. We should be as careful about what we remember as we should be about what we wish for.

Feeling the Squeeze

Descendancy: Irish Protestant Histories since 1795 by David Fitzpatrick

Cambridge University Press | 282 pp | ISBN: 978-1107080935

THIS CONCENTRATED, original and suggestive book packs a punch which outweighs its modest length, but that is only to be expected. Forty-odd years ago David Fitzpatrick's *Politics and Irish Life*, a close-up study of Co Clare during the revolutionary decade, set a benchmark which later historians of Ireland have been aspiring to ever since: an exploration of mentality, history and society which illuminated the psychology of those years (and of Co Clare) in a completely new way.

His work since then has branched out in several new directions. It includes a classic and profoundly moving account of emigration to Australia, a rather quizzical biographical study of Harry Boland, a survey of "the two Irelands" in the twentieth century, and most recently, a remarkable and empathetic biography of Bishop Frederick MacNeice, father of the poet. There has also been a stream of seminal articles on the geography of Irish nationalism, the disappearance of the Irish agricultural labourer and other key Irish sociopolitical issues in the nineteenth and twentieth centuries. When he is described on the jacket of his new book (by Alvin Jackson) as "one of the most gifted, original and influential historians of modern Ireland", it is no more than the truth. He is out on his own, and you are never quite sure where he is going next.

Invariably, Fitzpatrick ploughs his own furrow. His latest work deals with aspects of the Irish Protestant experience, and like everything else he has written it conceals a faintly contrarian angle behind an urbane and judicious style. The title tells us what to expect, suggesting that the declining fortunes of Ireland's Protestants will be surveyed; but there is nothing here about Big Houses and decayed estates, nor about the possessor bourgeoisie alleged by Fergus Campbell to have held the reins of privilege well into the twentieth century.

Fitzpatrick is interested in the little people, their associations, how they consort together, their dogged faith and their reaction to the threats of violence and expulsion which hung in the air during the Troubles. Accordingly, his sources are not the diaries, memoirs and estate records of landlords and ladies; instead he has plumbed the archives of the Grand Orange Lodge and of the Methodist Historical Society, the minutiae of census returns and church records, memorials of long-forgotten preachers and the highways and byways of genealogical websites such as ancestrylibrary.com. His work (particularly in the closing chapters) also shows the rich social history to be extracted from the files of compensation claims lodged with both the British and Irish governments after 1922 – as recently demonstrated in Gemma Clarke's absorbing book on interpersonal violence during the Civil War.

It is a rich and suggestive mix, and the picture that emerges is in some ways a surprising one. Implicitly invoking David Trimble's memorable phrase about Catholics in Northern Ireland, Fitzpatrick points out that the minorities he surveys "became expert at keeping themselves warm in cold houses", and the picture that emerges suggests that – in the twentieth century at least – intercommunal tension owed more to land hunger and historic grievances than sectarian animosity. His picture of Irish Protestant life at the demotic level investigated here reminds us of some salient facts, obvious but often implicitly ignored. One is that Irish Protestants were far from universally a middle or upper class elite – especially before the 1920s. Another is that, before independence, and partition, a Protestant presence – at all social levels – was distributed more widely throughout the island than later commentators often assume. And a third important fact is that for many Irish Protestants, partition presented itself as a worse evil than the prospect of all-island Home Rule. The recognition may have come belatedly, but it came nonetheless.

As late as the 1960s, the ecclesiastical architecture of provincial Irish towns and cities featured not just the elegant spires of the Church of Ireland, but a surprising variety of modest meeting-places dedicated to Methodists, Presbyterians, Baptists, Congregationalists – and often a "Protestant Hall" used by all varieties for social purposes. Rural congregations were more scattered, but still hung on tenaciously in places like Co Cork, the subject of much of Fitzpatrick's research. His early chapters, however, dealing with the Orange Order, necessarily concentrate on Ulster, all nine counties of it (there is much interesting material on Monaghan, as well as a wide gallery of Belfast activists). The origins of lodges are related to an Enlightenment moment, though their idea of "civic and religious liberty" differed from that of the freemasons, with whom their rituals had much in common. The rebarbative ideology of Orangeism widely infiltrated the army and yeomanry, a process carefully traced in this book; this led to serious issues regarding conflicts of loyalty and instability of allegiance, which came into sharper relief when Orangeism emerged as equally dominant in paramilitary organisations.

At the same time Fitzpatrick draws attention to the alternative tradition of less predictable Protestant politics represented by luminaries such as the Home Ruler JB Armour, and the part played in Dáil politics by Border Protestants with Orange tinges. But overall, the gloomy image of a subculture of teetotalism, meat teas and dreary assemblies in damp fields persists. Fitzpatrick injects some energy into the subject by drawing out statistical patterns and, as ever, looking for the unexpected and treasuring exceptions; this perhaps lies behind his enduring affection for Bishop MacNeice, who though not the Home Ruler his son claimed him to be, was nonetheless a liberal, thoughtful and percipient figure.

MacNeice's refusal to sign the Covenant in 1912 is given detailed treatment here, along with other non-Covenanters; while those who did sign are profiled by intensive use of a fascinating contemporary survey conducted by the *Daily Mail*, along with a battery of material culled from biographical and church sources. The non-Covenanting Protestants include not only the perennially interesting Armour but also the clergyman Arnold Harvey, incumbent at Portrush during 1912, later bishop of Cashel: his liberal opinions might perhaps be traced back to his friendship with

Lady Gregory's family at Gort, where he tutored the young Robert Gregory and forged a lasting friendship with Jack Yeats (who sketched him rowing on Coole Lake).

Harvey had been rector at Lissadell, and another avenue which Fitzpatrick prospects in his determined quest to shine a new angle on the subject concerns WB Yeats, and the Orange connections of his Sligo forebears (Yeatses no less than Pollexfens). The poet's slightly devious and evasive use of the theme in his memoirs is carefully anatomised, and related to his later political attitudes (one is reminded that Fitzpatrick long ago wrote a pioneering article on Yeats's Senate speeches). More might perhaps be made of Yeats's refusal to sign a 1912 manifesto on behalf of Irish Protestants, which claimed that they had no fear of Catholic bigotry; and, indeed, his remarkable defence in 1926 of the "Cromwellian" tradition in Irish life. ("He had been told the previous night that he was a Cromwellian, and there was a valuable part of Ireland – the Cromwellian part – which had its own patriotism. It was chosen, and it had great qualities.") Yeats the Protestant remains something of a no-go area in Yeats studies, and elsewhere; years ago my description of him as a *déclassé* Protestant was furiously contested by a senior figure in RTÉ: "You can't talk about Yeats like that! He was as Irish as I am."

Protestantism and Irishness intertwine in odd ways, as this book shows: never more so than in the subculture of Irish Methodism, which – as the book goes on – seems to preoccupy Fitzpatrick more and more. (So much so that he sometimes takes an explanation of terms such as "circuits" and "colporteurs" for granted.) This is partly due to the exceptional richness of Methodist records, for the purposes of demography and biography fully exploited here. Fitzpatrick also pays close attention to the sociology of Methodism in Ireland. They appear as "something of an occupational and educational elite", overrepresented (like Ireland's Jews) in the professions and shopkeeping, while among the third of the Methodist population working in agriculture, most were farmers occupying relatively large holdings, with very few farm labourers or servants.

Before the revolution in West Cork, an area of especial interest for Fitzpatrick, though a small minority they were a well-organised and active community linked by Sunday schools, temperance associations and Christian Endeavour societies. There were twenty-nine chapels and 151 halls and homes where services were held – all this for fewer than two thousand adherents. (Each "circuit" kept intensive records both of financial organisation and of personnel, enabling the detailed reconstruction provided in this book.) Good social relations were preserved, not only with fellow Protestants of other denominations, but apparently with Catholic neighbours as well – though intermarriage was, in Fitzpatrick's words, "abhorred by both communities", a reflection which, while depressing, is certainly accurate.

All this forms the background to Fitzpatrick's close and absorbing delineation of the decline and exodus of the Methodist population from about 1920, and how far it was precipitated by what he calls the "unsurpassed ferocity and frequency of attacks against Cork Protestants". His general conclusion (which is shared by previous commentators) is that the unrest between 1916 and 1923, while it may have accelerated the decline of Protestant communities in the rural south, did not inaugurate it. The last two chapters in the book discuss the process with the aid of huge and complex batteries of statistics, concluding that the general picture of low nuptiality and fertility, the effects of *Ne Temere*, and the failure to enrol new members provide most of the explanation for the decline in numbers: though he admits that "statistics … reveal little about the mentality or emotions of the people lurking behind the numbers".

With this caveat in mind, he turns to the actual events and memories of those West Cork Methodists who were targeted and threatened during the Troubles. It is clear that some of the events, such as the killing of British soldiers attending a service at Fermoy Methodist church, however traumatic, were directed at combatants rather than Protestants; the same could be argued for the killing of Methodist farmers entrapped into giving information to IRA members disguised as Auxiliaries (an episode recounted in what Fitzpatrick calls "chirpy detail" by one of Tom Barry's flying column members for the Bureau of Military History).

The subsequent contest for the farms involved suggests a longstanding antagonism over tenure, traced back in one case by Fitzpatrick to alleged "landgrabbing" in the early 1880s. The killings of three Methodists, tagged as "spies", by July 1921 was accompanied by a far larger number of threatenings, woundings and pressure to emigrate; the circumstances are vividly recorded in compensation claims. Boycotts and intimidation featured heavily in subsequent efforts to sell the farms of those who had left the country. "Sectarian animosity was compounded by festering agrarian or political resentments, which often outweighed issues of religious affiliation." Fitzpatrick also draws a picture of temporary withdrawal from the area by local Protestants at times of heightened insecurity, returning when things quietened down – as indeed was the case with the relics of some of those who emigrated to Britain.

But the Truce was not the end of it, and the terrible "Bandon Valley massacre" of April 1922, in which a dozen Protestants (including two Methodists) met their deaths and more were wounded, created a real sense of panic. It is vividly and horribly conveyed in a letter from the widow of the murdered 81-year-old James Buttimer to her solicitor:

> My dear husband was holding my hand at the time, as he was so frightened. He said 'Surely, boys, you would not harm an old man like me?' Then by light of the candle behind us I saw several faces turn from each side of the door and aim at him and he fell down by my side and was soon lying in pools of blood. His teeth were scattered all over the place as his jaw was smashed in and he was riddled with bullets.

Sons (who had long left home) in the British army may have had something to do with it, but this cannot explain the generalised attack on other Protestants; the killing of a local anti-Treaty republican may have precipitated the attacks, but their genesis remains veiled in uncertainty. Local feeling was apparently strongly against the killers, but the psychological impact was deep, and emigration –while not amounting to a dramatic exodus – was certainly accentuated. The progress of these "displaced families" is carefully logged by Fitzpatrick, who concludes that "violence and intimidation did not necessarily lead to a panic-driven, unplanned, terminal and irreversible exodus". The spectre of extermination had been raised, but – in his view – the response was an effort to rebuild communities and to come to terms with life in the Free State. That electric phrase "ethnic cleansing" is not applicable.

This seems a judicious and convincing conclusion, but a certain fear and constraint must have remained among the people whose lives had been threatened and who had been frightened from their farms. Such fears and memories are transmitted to posterity in half-unspoken ways, though the relations of Protestants to the Free State were to some extent eased by the public determination of the Cumann na nGaedheal government that they should see the new dispensation as fully representing them (indeed, in the Senate, somewhat overrepresenting them). The escalating pietism and unofficially theocratic inclinations of future governments form a counternarrative, but it is not part of this book.

It is hard to disagree with Fitzpatrick's restrained and judicious conclusions, but it is also important not to airbrush the undertone of sectarian animosity out of this history. As Yeats said in his response to that Protestant Home Ruler manifesto in 1912, "there is intolerance in Ireland, it is the shadow of belief everywhere, and no priesthood of any church has lacked it". This is equally applicable to the Orange tradition explored in the earlier part of the book. But above all, the dispassionate exploration of these themes, intimately woven into Irish history, is essential; and not the least value of *Descendancy* is the manner in which it is written, which contrasts markedly with the strident, pompous and self-regarding language adopted by some contributors to the discussion of the historical problems dealt with here. Ideally, it should help lower the hectic and accusatory tones in which the issues of Protestant depopulation in the Irish revolution have come to be treated. But I somehow doubt that it will.

Contemporary Controversies

Earlier dystopian visionaries like George Orwell, MICHAEL CRONIN *writes, saw totalitarian governments as the villains, subjecting us to constant surveillance and direction and eradicating privacy. But as it has turned out it is the banks, the insurance companies, the pension funds, and above all low-cost airlines, the raucous cheerleaders of deregulation, which enervate and stupefy their customers with a network of complicated rules.*

One of the root causes of the current crisis in cancer care, writes SEAMUS O'MAHONY, *is sentimentality. Family members will often say that their stricken relative is "a fighter" but in fact this kind of subjectivist thinking about ageing, disease, death and other unavoidable biological realities is both unhelpful and wasteful of resources.*

In law, everyone is presumed innocent until proven otherwise. But this, writes ADRIAN HARDIMAN, *seems a hard thing for some people to accept, particularly in sexual cases, even very old ones, where there is a tendency to think there should be a different presumption: that the accuser is to be believed.*

It is extremely difficult to forecast the future, and those who attempt to do so should remember that it is a fraught business. Unfortunately, writes TOM HENNIGAN, *cautious modesty is not the usual modus operandi of a successful newspaper columnist, and few are more successful than Fintan O'Toole, arguably Ireland's leading public intellectual.*

MICHAEL CRONIN | 2013

The Meaning of Ryanair

A CHRISTIAN Brothers primary school in Mullingar in the late 1960s. A young boy has been forced to sit under the teacher's desk for failing a spelling test. Every time he makes a mistake he receives a further kick. Was this abuse? Not in the view of the CEO of Ryanair, Michael O'Leary, who was that little boy. In an interview with Siobhán Creaton for her 2007 book on Ryanair, he claimed: "I was only seven years old but I don't think of myself as an abused or battered soul and I certainly got my spelling right the next day."

He helpfully added that if he had children and a teacher asked him if he could slap one of them, he would say: "Go right ahead." Nothing like a good kicking to make sure you get your ABC right and, as every Ryanair passenger comes to realise, sparing the rod can spoil the bottom line. The states of fear that provided the formative milieu for the young O'Leary have been profitably transferred to the airline which has developed a specialism in corporate punishment.

What you have you can no longer hold. The first intimation that fear is the order of the day is the policing of the weighing scales. The suitcase is lifted with a faint crackle of anxiety onto the belt and the digits illuminate the verdict. The shame of being outed for being overweight and ordered to leave the queue, like some errant Oliver being refused another bowl. Here is your moment in the stocks, the disinterred contents of your suitcase subject to the mocking gaze of onlookers who quietly savour the *Schadenfreude* of the moment, that vaguely condescending triumph of the rule-obeyers, craftily weighing bags on bathroom scales to enjoy the warm compliance of the Ryanair forcing house.

The queues. This is another sign that you are entering a world where new rules apply. The queuing starts long before the gate opens. Initially, there is the animated conversation as the passengers join the queue for the unallocated seats, but quickly the initial excitement of departure gives way to the silent, sullen hostility of the long wait. Penned in like unhappy cattle destined for foreign meat markets, the passengers have that fretful anxiety of deportees alert to any rumour of delay or departure. Here is where the black and white realities of coercion begin to leak from the past into the present. The photographs of those people in a line in Warsaw, Leningrad, Vilnius, Prague, queuing for a living. Waiting hour after hour for the goods that might or might not make it to the counter and past the reproachful glare of the Konsum hireling. State communism and advanced capitalism converge in this lining up of subjects. The same sense of frustrated expectation, the fretfulness of losing one's place, the inner stiffening as the officials in uniform pass by checking entitlement, examining the size of bags, according the random grace of privilege (it's a bit over but it's OK). A queue becomes not just a means of saving money – there is no need to allocate seats – it becomes a way to order lives.

Giorgio Agamben has captured a sense of this experience in the notion of "apparatus". For Agamben, in *What is an Apparatus and other essays*, the apparatus is anything which has the capacity to capture, orient, determine, intercept, model or control the gestures, conduct, opinions or discourse of living beings. Thus the apparatus is to be understood not only in the Foucauldian sense of prisons, confession boxes, factories, hospitals but also the pen, writing, literature, philosophy, agriculture, the cigarette, computers, mobile phones and indeed language. He sees a fundamental dichotomy between living beings and the apparatuses to which they are subject, a division between the ontology of creatures and what he calls the *oikonomia* or organised system of the apparatuses which determine and govern their lives. Agamben argues that traditionally each apparatus brought with it its own form of subjectivity.

An apparatus only became effective when one willingly complied with its demands and took on the role of the model prisoner or the good student; otherwise the only way the apparatus could be enforced was through pure violence. In our present era, however, Agamben argues that what we are increasingly experiencing through various kinds of political and technological apparatuses is a form of desubjectivisation. In other words, rather than the apparatus giving rise to a new form of subjectivity, it leads to the loss of subjectivity or the reduction of the subjective to larval or spectral forms. Hence, the increasing difficulty of thinking of contemporary politics in terms of traditional subjectivities and identities such as the working class, bourgeoisie and so on, or the eclipse of major policy differences between parties of the left and right so that politics becomes reduced to a mere matter of technical governance. The much vaunted era of the individual becomes the age of the vanishing subject. The apparatus of the queue becomes both the instrument and the showcase for this diminished sense of self.

There are of course not one but two queues. The early rhetoric of emancipation (low-cost travel for all) gives way to more brutal distinctions. Priority Q and Other Q. The delicate euphemisms of other airlines, Coach or Economy, hint at a certain exercise in differentiation, a desire to flag difference without dismissal. "Other", however, in a satirical bow to the postmodern, as in so much in late capitalism, brings to mind an undifferentiated mass not worthy of distinction. The adjective is not even granted the escort of a determiner, a "the" that might hint at specification. No, only the Other, an empty receptacle for those who are not considered a Priority. It is these numberless Others who must compensate for an absence of privilege with an excess of patience. As George Orwell repeatedly noted, the one thing the poor need and the rich lack is time. As they stand and wait in the Other Q, passengers are reminded that it is the indistinct, like taxpayers subsidising bankers, who are constantly prey to the cost of Distinction.

When boarding begins, just as it seemed as if the plane had been grounded in an eternity of cussedness, the scene makes for poor viewing. More shambolic senior infants' race at a school fair than thoroughbreds bursting from the gates at Fairyhouse, the passengers hurry in a nervous, windblown dash to the waiting craft, a primal fear of being left behind giving way to an aggressive wish to be ahead, a civilised veneer of docility fading to a red in tooth and claw quickstep. This is reality TV for those grounded in reality. The Apprentice Travellers learn that it is all about the survival of the fastest. In the bargain basement Darwinism of Low Cost, there is no room for the encumbered or the halt of limb, as the meek are jostled off the steps to the plane by the neo-liberal *Übermensch*. The Weakest Link is to be despised, not pitied, in this new moral order that plays itself out on the middle passage between the departure gate and the aircraft door. Zarathustra is on this stretch of tarmac, proclaiming for our post-democratic age the inalienable rights of the strong and the uncaring.

In order to ensure an on-time departure, please vacate the aisle and take up the seat nearest to you. The endless harrying in broken English over the intercom – the crew like fretful collies bringing their flock to higher ground. The suitcase will not, of course, fit into the overhead locker and the overfull bag will not go under the seat. As the tone on the intercom becomes harsher, the image darkens and you begin to imagine bullwhips, arc lights and the frenzied barking of Alsatians. The thin ridge of apprehension over your shoulders tightens and sweat pools in your armpits as you struggle with the untameable bulk of your belongings and the bustling impatience of your fellow passengers. Time is money. Or more correctly, less time for you means more money for Ryanair. As the flight attendants and the pilots deal with the bullying compression of time under the starting pistol of the "quick turnaround", the baton of anxiety is passed to the passengers fumbling with coats and bags in the elbow-strewn gulch of the aisle. In the new regimen of time, a dogged rudeness is the sign of an evolved species.

Something's the matter. Knees pressed hard against the fast food plastic. Elbows hustled off the narrow armrests by an indifferent neighbour. The unlovely cartoon of a battery hen farm in flight. Discussing the changing relationship to space during the period of the Reformation, Iain McGilchrist, in *The Master and his Emissary*, notes that "[w]here the Roman church encouraged and incorporated movement, walking and processing, the new Church's chairs are everywhere the most visible feature of the Reformed interior, enforcing stasis and system". The focus shifts from the altar to the pulpit, whose panoptic gaze takes in the heads and souls of the faithful, ranged below in rigid, geometric order. McGilchrist intimates that "this is something we can all recall from personal experience: in a congregation seated neatly in rows, one feels like an obedient subject, one of the masses, whereas standing in a crowd, as one would have done in a pre-Reformation church, one is part of a living thing, that is that community of living human beings, there and then". Filleting space for profit, shaving off those inches of leg room, makes for ever more obedient subjects, trapped in the rabbit hutches of incapacity.

In one of the more tasteless metaphors that crop up in Michael O'Leary's account of his education at Trinity College Dublin, he talks of how he and his fellow business students "just wanted to go out and 'rape the world'". His time at Trinity "was about meeting girls and drinking alcohol". In the world of tabloid travel, booze and birds are locked in the unfond embrace of the stag flight. The inflight magazine offers passengers an opportunity to buy the Ryanair calendar, featuring Ryanair flight attendants in bikinis. In the cynical wedding of prurience and philanthropy, young women (not men, of course) take their clothes off. But it's OK. It's for a good cause. The fratprat sexism has the silky alibi of charity. Philanthropy becomes the new form of indulgences, no sin too great (no tax dodge too artful, no wage too low, no working hours too inhuman) to be absolved by the Peter's Pence of the charity ball or the generous donation. For every successful tycoon busy relocating a tax base or stripping workers of pension entitlements, there are the persistent, healing rumours of quiet, unstated acts of personal generosity, as if at the heart of advanced capitalism lay the reassuring horizon of a feudal regime of seigneurial largesse where absolutism (don't talk to me about unions) walks hand in hand with absolution.

Free trade, of course, is one of the forces that is routinely identified as bringing down the feudal order. Free trade. Free competition. Freedom becomes increasingly just another word for nothing much left to lose. As the pilots sip the water they have bought themselves and the flight attendants hurry along the aisles in the uniforms they have paid for out of their own pockets, barking curt, dismissive orders at the bewildered and the non-compliant, the Free World begins to feel remarkably like the world on the other side of the Wall.

WARNING 1 CABIN BAG ONLY 55 X 40 X 20 CM (MAX 10 KG) HANDBAG, BRIEFCASE, LAPTOP, SHOP PURCHASES, CAMERAS ETC. MUST BE CARRIED WITHIN YOUR 1 CABIN BAG. Extra/oversized cabin baggage will be refused at the boarding gate, or where available, placed in the hold of the aircraft for a fee of £/€50. If you are unsure, check at the Bag Drop desk before going through security. N.B. There is no baggage allowance (cabin or checked) associated with the purchase of an extra seat.

This is a world of border signage. Of block capitals and underlining and dark emphasis. The Free World is fenced in with prohibitions and refusals. In the negative poetics of the neo-liberal, modal verbs of obligation ("must") and adverbs of restriction ("strictly") police the channels of communication and exclamation marks are inserted for the hard of reading:

IMPORTANT REMINDERS! Please read

- Each passenger must present their valid photo ID (as specified as accepted in our General Conditions). Driving licences are not accepted.
- Passengers with prebooked special assistance must present this boarding pass at the airport special assistance desk and again to assistance staff at the arrival airport.
- Bag Drop desks close strictly 40 minutes before the scheduled flight departure time.

The hyperbole of coercion has a viral quality and soon spreads to other "carriers" ("to tamper with the smoke alarm is a criminal offence and may result in prosecution"). Alexis de Tocqueville, contemplating the future of democracy in America, suspected a new kind of servitude was on the cards in the land of the free. Society would develop a novel form of enslavement which

> covers the surface of society with a network of small complicated rules, through which the most original minds and the most energetic characters cannot penetrate ... it does not tyrannise but it compresses, enervates, extinguishes, and stupefies a people, till each nation is reduced to be nothing better than a flock of timid and industrious animals, of which government is the shepherd.

Whereas earlier dystopian visions such as Orwell's *Nineteen Eighty-Four* had seen totalitarian governments as the wicked shepherd leading the flock to certain destruction, now it is banks, insurance companies, pension funds and low-cost airlines, the raucous cheerleaders of deregulation, that routinely enervate, extinguish and stupefy their customers with a "network of small complicated rules".

Stupefaction comes early. Booking a ticket on the website is like dealing with a snickering ticket tout ever alert to the foibles of the gullible or the inattentive. The future passenger is forever on guard against a kind of digital cute-hoorism so that she does not end up with a Samsonite suitcase she never wanted, travel insurance she never asked for and a car she never intended hiring. Concealed in the thicket of drop down menus are the pass keys out of the labyrinth of algorithmic disorientation and the pop-up messages are video game villains which must be swatted down if the future passenger is to arrive safely at the destination of payment, where more inexplicable charges await the unwary. Being charged for the privilege of printing your own boarding pass is perhaps one of the most inexplicable. This version of paying others for work you do is at the heart of the present moment of market capitalism, where low cost increasingly means, to the producer at least, no cost.

Intending passengers are obliged to print out their boarding passes in advance. This implies that passengers have access to the equipment (computer and printer) and internet connection which allow them to enter the necessary details and print out the pass. Both the equipment and the connection are a cost to the passenger or to the entity that has made these available to the passenger. There is the further opportunity cost of the time spent accessing the site, filling in the details and printing out the pass. During this time, of course, the passenger could have been doing something else. In short, what were formerly production costs for the airline – paying someone to prepare and print out your boarding pass and thereby creating a job – now become consumption costs for the passenger.

In the upsidedown world of transferred or devolved costs, the labour is done by the passenger, not by the airline operator, so that the surplus value accrues not to the passenger but to the airline. In the snap, crackle and pop of the ads on board for lotto tickets, train tickets, car hire, you know that there is no hope that you too could be a Ryanair millionaire. You are too busy making Ryanair millionaires and know at some unspoken level that taking the flight is in every sense being taken for a ride.

Milton Friedman once observed that the beauty of the free market was that affections did not count. You did not have to like somebody to buy or sell something to or from them. Emotions did not enter the equation. Or maybe they do. In the adept way that modern capital has espoused the lifestyle totems of the counter-culture, the CEO of Ryanair wears the open-necked shirt and juggles with locker-room expletives (Buzz, another low-cost airline, failed because "It got saddled by KLM with the shittiest set of aircraft in the fleet, flying to shitty airports"), playing the part of the thorough Bad Boy who boldly takes on public authorities and vested interests. The rough and ready machismo of the corporate cowboy means that the rhetoric of the hard-done-by David can always be pressed into the service of the financial Goliath. In this Nietzschean revaluation of all values, the strong appear weak while the weak appear not so much strong as inept. The CEO of the most profitable airline in Europe knows that the media-friendly rough talk of his anti-regulatory soundbites will not remind most of his listeners of why deregulation has led to the one of the worst economic crises of modern times and impoverished millions but will comfort them in their understandable suspicion of all forms of established authority. As the tone rises so do the share values.

The bugle sounds as the plane bumps along the tarmac announcing another on-time Ryanair arrival. The children applaud and the adults smile uncertainly, unsure if the joke is on them. This brief parenthesis of communal hilarity is out of spirit with the presiding genius of the individual. The Lingus in Aer Lingus, an anglicised version of *loingeas*, is the word for a fleet, a collective entity. Ryanair is named, of course, after an individual, Tony Ryan. If Aer Lingus was the flagship project of a young nation finding its footing in the chorus line of national aviation companies, Ryanair is the highly profitable instrument of the Ryan family and associated shareholders. In this shift from the collective to the individual, it is the lone traveller, the unattached, unencumbered foot soldier of liquid modernity who comes closest to Ryanair's Platonic Idea of the Perfect Passenger. Minimum baggage. Minimum fuss. Minimum space. Maximum gain.

As you arrive at the departure gate in Terminal One in Dublin Airport and set off on the interminable trek to passport control and the luggage carousel, you wonder again at those queues. Why are we waiting in those queues? Because there is no alternative. Why the abject docility? Because there is no alternative. If the strained harp rather than the windswept shamrock has come to dominate European airspace, it may be because Michael O'Leary learnt much under that table in Mullingar about what the world would look like if the main purpose of post-democratic governance was to give populations a good kicking. The states of fear that were once seen as the monopoly of strap-wielding Christian Brothers have not so much disappeared as being displaced. The disciplinary apparatus of low-cost air travel is a routine example of how stridently free markets make for remarkably unfree subjects. Taking to the skies with Ryanair is to be reminded not so much of what we have left behind but of how much baggage we still carry with us.

The Big D

Mortality by Christopher Hitchens

Atlantic Books | 106 pp | ISBN: 978-1848879218

CHRISTOPHER HITCHENS had been a prolific journalist and public intellectual for more than three decades when he finally achieved the global fame he so richly deserved following the publication of *God Is Not Great* in 2007.

"Hitch" had been a swaggering figure in literary and political circles for many years before this. He was a brilliant prose stylist who savaged the reputations of Henry Kissinger, Bill Clinton and Mother Teresa. A formidable speaker and debater, he had the gift of the immediate and apposite retort. He moved to the United States in the 1980s, and it was rumoured that the character of the drunken journalist Peter Fallow in Tom Wolfe's *Bonfire of the Vanities*, was based on him. Charismatic and good-looking in a slightly battered way, he was part of a close-knit coterie of writers which included Martin Amis, Salman Rushdie, Ian McEwan and James Fenton. After the success of *God Is Not Great*, he joined the premier league of celebrity atheist intellectuals. Richard Dawkins was perceived as arrogant, humourless and hectoring, but even Hitchens's opponents admired his wit, his preternatural fluency and his cheek. Although wildly inconsistent and self-contradictory, he never confessed to a moment's doubt.

When, in 2010, he was diagnosed with oesophageal cancer, it came as no great surprise, the major risk factors for the condition being smoking and heavy drinking, both of which Hitchens cheerfully admitted to: "In order to keep reading and writing, I need the junky energy that scotch can provide, and the intense short-term concentration that nicotine can help supply." Although he managed to quit smoking briefly in 2007, it was too late. "Knowingly burning the candle at both ends and finding that it often gives a lovely light ... I have now succumbed to something so predictable and banal that it bores even me."

His "rackety, bohemian life" finally caught up with him in June 2010 when, during a tour to promote his memoir, *Hitch-22*, he was taken acutely ill in his hotel bedroom ("feeling as I were actually shackled to my own corpse"), whisked off to the nearest emergency room and diagnosed with Stage Four oesophageal cancer ("the thing about Stage Four is that there is no such thing as Stage Five"): the cancer had spread, or metastasised, to his lungs and the lymph nodes in his neck. Following this diagnosis, he wrote a number of articles about his illness for *Vanity Fair*, where he had been a contributor for many years. These articles have been collected, edited and book-ended by moving tributes from his wife, Carol Blue, and his editor, Graydon Carter. This little book is simply called *Mortality*.

I am intrigued by *Mortality* for one main reason, which is this: Hitchens's beliefs about his advanced cancer and its treatment were, for a man whose fame rested on his scepticism, uncharacteristically optimistic. I hesitate to use the word delusional, as he admitted that he would be very lucky to survive, but it is clear that he steadfastly hoped, right to the end, that his particular case of advanced cancer might lie on the sparsely populated right side of the bell-shaped curve of outcome statistics. He famously mocked religious folk for their faith in supernatural entities and survival of the soul after bodily death, yet the views expressed in *Mortality* are just as wishful and magical. "The oncology bargain [oncology is that branch of medicine which deals with the treatment of cancer]," writes Hitchens, "is that in return for at least the chance of a few more useful years, you agree to submit to chemotherapy and then, if you are lucky with that, to radiation or even surgery." Years? I must now confess to a professional interest. I am a gastroenterologist in a large acute hospital, and I have diagnosed many patients with oesophageal cancer. "Years" is a word not generally used when discussing prognosis in Stage Four oesophageal cancer, "months", in my experience, being a more useful one.

Although bracingly dismissive of the absurd notion of "battling cancer", he is an ardent admirer of modern American oncology: "For example, I was encouraged to learn of a new 'immunotherapy protocol', evolved by Drs Steven Rosenberg and Nicholas Restifo at the National Cancer Institute. Actually, the word 'encouraged' is an understatement. I was hugely excited." He contacts Dr Restifo (I would imagine that American oncologists are keen on celebrity patients), who responds enthusiastically: "Some of this may sound like space-age medicine, but we have treated well over 100 patients with gene-engineered T cells, and have treated over 20 patients with the exact approach that I am suggesting may be applicable to your case." His hopes are dashed, however, when it turns out that his immune cells do not express a particular molecule (HLA-A2) which must be present for this pioneering treatment to work: "I can't forget the feeling of flatness that I experienced when I received the news."

His hopes are raised again when he is emailed by "perhaps fifty friends" about a television programme called *60 Minutes*, which "had run a segment about the 'tissue engineering', by way of stem cells, of a man with a cancerous esophagus. He had effectively been medically enabled to 'grow' a new one." His friend Francis Collins, molecular biologist and devout Christian, "gently but firmly told me that my cancer had spread too far beyond my esophagus to be treatable by such a means". Collins evokes ambivalent feelings in Hitchens:

> Dr Francis Collins is one of the greatest living Americans. He is the man who brought the Human Genome Project to completion, ahead of time and under budget, and who now directs the National Institutes of Health. He is working now on the amazing healing properties that are latent in stem cells and in 'targeted' gene-based treatments. This great humanitarian is also a devotee of the work of C.S. Lewis, and in his book *The Language of God* has set out the case for making science compatible with faith.

Ironically, it is the Christian who has to lower the expectations of the sceptical atheist. Hitchens proposes to Collins that his entire DNA, along with that of his tumour, be "sequenced", "even though its likely efficacy lies at the outer limits of probability". Indeed. Collins is circumspect, conceding that if such "sequencing" was performed, "it could be clearly determined what mutations were present in the cancer that is causing it to grow. The potential for discovering mutations in the cancer cells that could lead to a new therapeutic idea is uncertain – that is at the very frontier of cancer research right now." Diplomatically put, Dr Collins. He also points out a more prosaic reason for Hitchens not having his genome "sequenced", namely that "the cost of having it done is also very steep at the moment". Although this is not mentioned in *Mortality*, his tumour DNA was eventually sequenced, and showed a mutation for which a known chemotherapeutic agent already exists, and Hitchens was duly started on this drug.

Hitchens was strongly encouraged in his optimism: "An enormous number of secular and atheist friends have told me encouraging and flattering things like, 'If anyone can beat this, you can', 'Cancer has no chance against someone like you'; 'We know you can vanquish this.'" More alarmingly, however, his wife and his closest friend, Martin Amis, shared this optimism. Amis, interviewed some months after Hitchens's death, answered a question about his reasons for moving to New York:

> Just over two years ago, my mother died, and within a week, the prognosis for Christopher Hitchens was available. That got us to thinking about mortality and my wife's mother and step-father. We thought, 'They're not going to be around forever'. At this point, it looked as though Christopher might well live for *five or ten years more* (my italics) and those two considerations were enough.

Mortality closes with an "Afterword" by his wife, who writes: "Christopher was aiming to be among the 5 to 20 percent of those who could be cured (the odds depended on what doctor we talked to and how they interpreted the scans)." I wonder how his doctors could have given a man with Stage Four oesophageal cancer such expectations of long-term survival, let alone a one in five chance of cure (which is about the survival chances for all oesophageal cancers, the lucky ones being those with very early, localised disease, not those with metastases in their lungs and lymph nodes). A quick glance at the website of the American Cancer Society would have informed Hitchens that five-year survival for Stage Four oesophageal cancer is 3 per cent (surprisingly high, I thought, as I have never seen a single patient with advanced oesophageal cancer survive five years). She continues: "Without ever deceiving himself about his medical condition, and without ever allowing me to entertain illusions about his prospects for survival, he responded to every bit of clinical and statistical good news with a radical, childlike hope."

When Hitchens died at the MD Anderson Cancer Center in Houston, Texas, his wife was clearly not prepared: "The end was unexpected." In *Mortality* she describes how Hitchens, still intubated after a bronchoscopy, and therefore unable to speak, scribbled notes for her, such as: "I'm staying here [in Houston] until I'm cured. And then I'm taking our families on a vacation to Bermuda." Interviewed on Australian television after his death, she said:

> Well, first off it was not clear to his doctors or to us that he was dying. His very radical state-of-the art medical treatments had proved quite successful and the cancer was in abeyance ... the oncologist said he was in the one per cent of people who could have been alive then and we hoped that he would either go into a long remission or certainly have quite a bit more time. He caught a very, very virulent pneumonia, a hospital pneumonia, one so powerful that everyone who came to visit in the hospital in the last few days had to wear gowns, masks, gloves and were told it could be spread outside the hospital. So even though he's been sick for some time and we understood the seriousness of his condition, the ending was quite a shock to him and to me. I don't think we actually knew that he was gonna die till maybe 20 hours before ...

Asked by her interviewer whether Hitchens considered at that time that "it might be the moment to let go", Blue answered:

> No, not at all, actually, because he's been given such a prognosis. When they did the follow-up scan basically it was black; no cancer was showing, so ... and as I say, he was ill for quite some time, but the actual ... diagnosis of his very virulent hospital-acquired pneumonia and then ... the course it took over the last few days was quite a surprise so it was almost like, you know, hearing the news that your beloved had been in a car crash. So it was kind of odd. It was not really expected at that moment at all, so that was very, very hard.

Mortality contains vintage Hitchensian demolitions of such received wisdoms as "battling cancer": "People don't have cancer: They are reported to be battling cancer. No well-wisher omits the combative image: You can beat this. It's even in obituaries for cancer losers, as if one might reasonably say of someone that they died after a long and brave struggle with mortality. You don't hear it about long-term sufferers from heart disease or kidney failure." He recalls the absurd quixotic optimism of the Nixon-era "War on Cancer", when America, fresh from conquering the moon, decided that the "big C" was next. He quotes a wickedly funny line from Updike's *Rabbit Redux*, where Mr Angstrom Sr declares: "they're just about to lick cancer anyway and with these transplants pretty soon they can replace your whole insides".

He is assailed with well-meaning suggestions: "in Tumortown you sometimes feel that you may expire from sheer advice". He is wonderfully dismissive of "natural" therapies: "I did get a kind note from a Cheyenne-Arapaho friend of mine, saying that everyone she knew who had resorted to tribal remedies had died almost immediately, and suggesting that if I was offered any Native American medicines I should 'move as fast as possible in the opposite direction'." A correspondent from an (unnamed) university advises Hitchens to have himself "cryogenically frozen against the day when the magic bullet, or whatever it is, has been devised". (This particular nonsense is a rather spooky modern echo of the Christian belief in resurrection, a parallel which Hitchens surprisingly fails to spot.) Inevitably, somebody as well-connected as Hitchens will be advised to see the Top Man (or Woman): "Extremely well-informed people also get in touch to insist that there is really only one doctor, or only one clinic." (A contemporary equivalent to the medieval visitations to holy shrines and relics?) He admits that he did take up this advice: "The citizens of Tumortown are forever assailed with cures and rumors of cures. I actually did take myself to one grand palazzo of a clinic in the richer part of the stricken city, which I will not name because all I got from it was a long and dull exposition of what I already knew."

He ponders on the moment of death, and reminds us of what he wrote in *Hitch-22*: "Before I was diagnosed with esophageal cancer a year and a half ago, I rather jauntily told the readers of my memoirs that when faced with extinction I wanted to be fully conscious and awake, in order to 'do' death in the active and not the passive sense. And I do, still, try to nurture that little flame of curiosity and defiance: willing to play out the string to the end and wishing to be spared nothing that properly belongs to a life span." When the end came, however, Hitchens had the modern cancer death, comatose for the last day or so. There were no Jamesian profundities or Voltairean *bons mots*.

Mortality contains heartbreaking accounts of the sheer awfulness of cancer: for Hitchens the loss of his voice is the cruellest blow: "Deprivation of the ability to speak is more like an attack of impotence, or the amputation of part of the personality. To a great degree, in public and private I 'was' my voice." We are spared no chemo-related detail: "the pathetic discovery that hair loss extends to the disappearance of the follicles in your nostrils, and thus to the childish and irritating phenomenon of a permanently runny nose". An admirer of Nietzsche, he comes to realise that the dictum "that which doesn't kill me makes me stronger" is nonsense: "In the brute physical world, and the one encompassed by medicine, there are all too many things that could kill you, don't kill you, and then leave you considerably weaker." He introduces the concept of "cancer etiquette": "my proposed etiquette handbook would impose duties on me as well as upon those who say too much, or too little, in an attempt to cover the inevitable awkwardness in diplomatic relations between Tumortown and its neighbours".

Only a man with Stage Four cancer himself could, with impunity, skewer the sickly sentimentality of the late Randy Pausch's *The Last Lecture*. Pausch, a professor of computer science at Carnegie Mellon University, was diagnosed with terminal pancreatic cancer and became an internet sensation after his lecture was posted on YouTube. The lecture, delivered to a standing ovation at his university, was called "Really Achieving Your Childhood Dreams", and included such fridge-magnet aphorisms as "we cannot change the cards we are dealt, just how we play the hand". Hitchens was unmoved: "It ought to be an offense to be excruciating and unfunny in circumstances where your audience is almost morally obliged to enthuse."

The late philosopher Sidney Hook is Hitchens's anti-Pausch. Hook, taken seriously ill in old age, "began to reflect on the paradox that ... he was able to avail himself of a historically unprecedented level of care, while at the same time being exposed to a degree of suffering that previous generations might not have been able to afford". Hook, suffering from heart failure and a stroke, asked his doctor "to discontinue all life-supporting services or show me how to do it". His doctor denied this request, and Hook survived: "But the stoic philosopher, from the vantage point of continued life, still insisted that he wished he had been permitted to expire. He gave three reasons. Another agonizing stroke could hit him, forcing him to suffer it all over again. His family was being put through a hellish experience. Medical resources were being pointlessly expended." Hook's essay "In Defense of Voluntary Euthanasia" is the perfect antidote to Randy Pausch: "Having lived a full and relatively happy life, I would cheerfully accept the chance to be reborn, but certainly not to be reborn again as an infirm octogenarian." Hook coined the phrase "mattress graves of pain" to describe the suffering of those similarly afflicted, and concluded his piece with a quotation from the Roman Stoic Seneca: "The wise man will live as long as he ought, not as long as he can."

Clearly, Hitchens did not adopt Hook's non-interventionist stance. It could be argued that his approach to his cancer treatment was at odds with much that he previously professed to believe (or not believe) in. In *God Is Not Great*, he coined the withering phrase "the tawdriness of the miraculous". He summarised the views of David Hume approvingly:

> A miracle is a disturbance or interruption in the expected and established course of things. This could involve anything from the sun rising in the west to an animal suddenly bursting into the recitation of verse. Very well, then, free will also involves decision. If you seem to witness such a thing, there are two possibilities. The first is that the laws of nature have been suspended (in your favour). The second is that you are under a misapprehension, or suffering from a delusion. Thus the likelihood of the second must be weighed against the likelihood of the first.

He backs this up with Ambrose Bierce's definition of "prayer": "a petition that the laws of nature be suspended in favour of the petitioner; himself confessedly unworthy". His wife, his friends and his doctors might wish to remind themselves of what Hitchens wrote in *God Is Not Great*: "Those who offer false consolation are false friends." In his memoir, *Hitch-22*, he was scathing of such wishful thinking: "I try to deny myself any illusions or delusions, and I think that this perhaps entitles me to try and deny the same to others, at least as long as they refuse to keep their fantasies to themselves."

As far back as 1993, Hitchens wrote about biogenetics in *Vanity Fair*: "One need not be Utopian about biogenetics, which like any other breakthrough can be exploited by the unscrupulous." When I was a junior research doctor in the late 1980s, my colleagues used to joke that inclusion of the phrase "genetic polymorphism" in the title was enough to get any scientific paper published. Since the 1980s, molecular biology/genetics has been the dominant force in laboratory medicine, and has been lavishly funded by government agencies. There is now, however, a grudging acceptance in the scientific and medical communities that despite all the advances in genetics, including the sequencing of the entire human genome, there have been precious few applications for treatment of cancer and other serious diseases. Steve Jones, emeritus professor of genetics at University College London, admitted as much in 2009, when he wrote: "We thought it [genetic research] was going to change our lives but that has turned out to be a false dawn." He went on to suggest that too much money had been spent on genetic research and that such scarce funding would be better spent elsewhere. Many took issue with Jones's nihilism, but most agreed that genetics had not led to the advances we had hoped for. Most common diseases are a complex mixture of genetic and environmental factors, and only a minority of conditions are caused by a single, identifiable gene mutation.

Why did Hitchens harbour such unrealistic expectations? It is clear that his oncologists (he would appear to have consulted several) actively encouraged his misplaced optimism. Oncologists prefer the word "hope" to "delusion". Over the years, I have witnessed many cancer patients, after protracted (and ultimately futile) therapies, facing death with all the preparedness of Carol Blue and Christopher Hitchens. These patients often experience a sudden deceleration in medical intensity from high-tech, invasive intervention to a side room, the morphine infusion and the chaplaincy service. Oncologists naturally tend to emphasise the positive, concentrating on the good news flashes, such as the "clear" scan. Most doctors will only impart the cold, bare facts when cornered and directly questioned, usually by patients with the necessary medical knowledge. As a profession, we are loath to appear "blunt" and "uncaring". Giving cancer patients a truthful and realistic prognosis is not done with the intention of taking hope away, but rather to give that person a framework around which they can plan their remaining time and conclude their affairs. My experience, sadly, is that patients and their families for the most part actively resist such an honest engagement.

Even those within oncology, or the "cancer community" as they sometimes call themselves, accept that the current model of cancer care in developed countries has now become unaffordable and unsustainable. The *Lancet* Oncology Commission (not exactly a cranky fringe group but a gathering of the great and the good of modern oncology) produced a lengthy report in 2011, a few months before Hitchens died. They pointed the finger squarely at "over-utilisation" and "futile care". "One factor driving over-utilisation in oncology," says the report, "is time. It is sometimes quicker and easier to discuss a plan of treatment than to discuss why treatment might not be indicated." "Do something" is the default setting of modern oncology; indeed, it is the default setting now of all modern medicine. Futility is at the core of the problem: "Many forms of cancer are currently incurable and patients will eventually die from their disease. If we could accurately predict when further disease-directed therapy would be futile, we clearly would want to spare the patient the toxicity and false hope associated with such treatment, as well as the expense."

One of the root causes of this crisis in cancer care is sentimentality. I am often told by well-meaning family members that their stricken relative is a "fighter", by which they mean that the known biological statistics appropriate to other, lesser souls, do not apply in this particular case. The psychologist Bruce Charlton has written about the sentimentalising of medicine: "There is a whole school of subjectivist thinking about ageing, disease, death and the other unavoidable biological realities, that downplays the inevitable and the intractable, and instead asserts that for every health problem there 'must' be an answer – somewhere, somehow, if only you fight hard enough, shout loud enough, travel far enough – and shell out enough money." To his credit, Hitchens dismisses this notion of struggle: "the image of the ardent soldier or revolutionary is the very last one that will occur to you. You feel swamped with passivity and impotence: dissolving like a sugar lump in water."

Only those faced with such a diagnosis know how they will react. Although the great majority of oncologists I have encountered have been fine, caring doctors, I am an oncology apostate. I hope that my medical knowledge and bitter experience will spare me the delusions of the layman. Perhaps,

perhaps not; some medical acquaintances of mine, diagnosed with cancers as advanced as Hitchens's, harboured hopes as unrealistic as their lay brethren, but mostly, doctors undergo far less treatment for incurable conditions than do lay folk. An American physician, Ken Murray, wrote a piece called "How Doctors Die", just a few weeks before Christopher Hitchens died in 2011:

> Years ago, Charlie, a highly respected orthopedist and a mentor of mine, found a lump in his stomach. He had a surgeon explore the area, and the diagnosis was pancreatic cancer. This surgeon was one of the best in the country. He had even invented a new procedure for this exact cancer that could triple a patient's five-year survival odds – from 5 percent to 15 percent – albeit with a poor quality of life. Charlie was uninterested. He went home the next day, closed his practice, and never set foot in a hospital again. He focused on spending time with family and feeling as good as possible. Several months later, he died at home. He got no chemotherapy, radiation, or surgical treatment. Medicare didn't spend much on him.
>
> It's not a frequent topic of discussion, but doctors die, too. And they don't die like the rest of us. What's unusual about them is not how much treatment they get compared to most Americans, but how little. For all the time they spend fending off the deaths of others, they tend to be fairly serene when faced with death themselves. They know exactly what is going to happen, they know the choices, and they generally have access to any sort of medical care they could want. But they go gently.

We should be wary of mocking beliefs which we do not share. One man's delusion and folly is another's "radical, childlike hope". As news of Hitchens's cancer diagnosis first became widely known, evangelical Christians speculated on the internet about whether his illness would lead to a religious conversion. In *Mortality*, Hitchens scoffs at the notion. But in his time of "living dyingly", he did find a kind of faith. This was not a return to the Anglicanism of his upbringing, or the Judaism of his mother's family. Hitchens, the arch-mocker, the *über*-rationalist, the debunker of myth, found solace and consolation in the contemporary rites of genetics and oncology. Reviewing *Arguably* (Hitchens's final prose collection), the philosopher John Gray observed: "That Hitchens has the mind of a believer has not been sufficiently appreciated."

Kafka on Thames

Love, Paul Gambaccini by Paul Gambaccini

Biteback Publishing | 448 pp | ISBN: 978-1849549110

Thus the unfacts, did we possess them, are too imprecisely few to warrant our certitude … if it be true that any of those recorded ever took place for many, we trow, beyessed to and denayed of, are given to us by some who use the truth but sparingly …

James Joyce, *Finnegans Wake*

PERHAPS WE expect too much of the law. Childhood murder mystery games – Colonel Mustard, in the library, with a candlestick – and detective stories from Wilkie Collins to Stieg Larsson have created an expectation of simple justice, scientific resolution and finality. But life's not like that, or not any more.

Now we live in the era of the ten-part Netflix sensation *Making a Murderer* and the world's most popular podcast, *Serial*. Both expose to the world the shaky nature of justice even in some very ordinary cases in the United States and the role which malice, incompetence and self-protection can play in the theoretically scientific process of detection and trial. Each case is subjected, in the works mentioned, to saturation analysis, but the process ends only with enhanced doubt.

Strictly speaking, that is not a problem for the law. Every person is presumed to be innocent, so if an investigation or trial simply fails to resolve the issue beyond reasonable doubt the suspect or defendant is entitled to the benefit of the presumption. But this can be a hard thing for some people to accept. In sexual cases particularly, even very old ones, such people seem inclined to think that there should be a different presumption: that the accuser is to be believed. Thus Hillary Clinton in January 2016 declared that every accuser was entitled to be believed. Asked whether this entitlement extended to the women who had made allegations against her husband and, in at least one case, against herself, she amended her statement orally, at a raucous election meeting, to "Everyone is entitled to be believed at first until they are disbelieved ... [after?] evidence." The intervening words are not clearly audible. Mrs Clinton is a lawyer of some experience.

This conflict of feeling, which is shared by far more people than Mrs Clinton, has radically undermined the presumption of innocence and has given rise, even in a thoroughly civilised country like Great Britain, to a climate of opinion in which some people, and some institutions, postpone or forsake the idea of bringing an accused person to trial, which carries the possibility of an acquittal, preferring instead to use the powers of the criminal law to subject them to public shaming so intense that it can destroy their lives. This provides all the stigma of a conviction with none of the risks of a trial. A disproportionate number of the victims are elderly white males. The book under review provides a brilliant account of this process from the point of view of one unlikely victim.

This remarkable book, written mostly in diary form, tells the appalling story of how a well-to-do, well-educated, well-known and widely respected sixtysomething media personality was all but destroyed by a sophisticated and apparently concerted campaign of leaking by the police and harassment by the media in 2014/2015. He was never convicted of, or even charged with, any offence, but he was sentenced by the police/media coalition to what an English academic criminologist reviewer of his book has called "social death". The effect on his professional activities amounted to "economic calamity". He was "shunned" (this word is used like a technical term) by various individuals who had previously courted him. He was ostentatiously abandoned by various organisations to which he had devoted time and money, not least Ed Miliband's Labour Party.

Paul Gambaccini, now sixty-six, was something of a national treasure in England, a status achieved through his remarkable career over the forty years preceding October 29th, 2013, the day he was arrested. An American by birth, he was educated at Dartmouth College, New Hampshire, before coming to Oxford on a Fulbright scholarship. He never left England after that. After a short period in journalism (for *Rolling Stone*) he became a radio disc jockey with the BBC. His remit broadened over the years into that of a more general cultural commentator: he is said to have been the only man to have had programmes running simultaneously on BBC One, Two, Three and Four. In August 2013, to mark his fortieth anniversary in broadcasting, the BBC honoured him with a tribute programme, in which the four preceding decades were dubbed *The Gambaccini Years*. And so they were, for music fans.

Paul Gambaccini has for many years been an openly gay man, now living in London with his husband, whose parents, decent and respectable people who move in a quite different world from his, were among his bravest and most loyal supporters. He was associated with a great many groups and organisations and in particular was a lifelong supporter of the Labour Party. Ed Miliband's first fundraiser following his election as leader was held in Gambaccini's London flat. He was a member of an exclusive Labour financial supporters' group, the Thousand Club. But the events of a few days in late October and early November 2013, and their sequel, made him an untouchable in Labour circles and far beyond.

On the first of those dates Gambaccini was arrested in his London flat at 4.38am by Metropolitan Police officers who were part of "Operation Yewtree". This was an operation set up in 2012 when the Met's abject failure to detect or interrupt the activities of Jimmy Savile had become public knowledge. Yewtree, apparently in an effort to redeem the force's reputation, concentrated on historical inquiries against celebrities, mainly from the worlds of show business and politics. Gambaccini had publicly criticised both the police and the BBC over Savile.

There were other victims besides Gambaccini. The octogenarian former Tory politician Lord (formerly Leon) Brittan QC died in January 2015 with an open Yewtree investigation apparently outstanding against him, even though a decision that there was no evidence to prosecute him had actually been taken long before he died. But this was concealed and never admitted or announced during his lifetime. Brittan's family eventually received a full apology, but only after it was too late for him. Gambaccini also received a belated apology, for all the good it did him.

Still more recently, on Friday January 15th, 2016, a ninety-two year old D-Day veteran and former chief of the defence staff, Field Marshal Lord Bramall, also received an apology of sorts from the Metropolitan Police for the appalling hounding he had been subjected to after being involved in a leaked Yewtree inquiry into very old allegations. He too was the subject of a dawn raid on the flat where he lived with his dying wife, conducted by no fewer than twenty police officers, who stayed for seven hours. It is hard to view this as anything but an exercise in throwing the Met's official weight about and hoping to garner some good publicity. The eventual apology was grudging in the extreme and blamed the media for Lord Bramall's ordeal. There is, of course, a denial that the police leaked Bramall's name, a denial believed by absolutely no one, just as in Gambaccini's case.

Gambaccini's diary of events begins, with a nod to James Bond, on the day of his arrest, with the phrase "My name is Kafka. Franz Kafka." And indeed his story has many of the hallmarks of Kafka's surreal novel of persecution *The Trial*. He describes being immediately plunged into a world where arrests happen at times like 4.38am, to ensure that the suspect is likely to be home, but also to disorient him, to justify holding him in a cell (for four hours in this case) before he is interviewed by the police, or before he can consult his solicitor. A cell, incidentally, with an unscreened toilet but with no toilet paper. It is a world with which his family solicitor of many years was absolutely unfamiliar, being a lawyer dealing mostly in "leases and wills"; where the criminal lawyer to whom he is hastily referred instructs him, when asked to sign a routine police document, to draw squiggly lines below his signature to prevent anything else being added; and worse.

The very worst is that, though he is arrested only for questioning and is never charged, the police immediately leak that fact of his arrest and detention, thereby destroying his career and reputation. He knows they will do this because it had become their practice to do so in other Yewtree arrests (he was the fifteenth person arrested). It catapults him into an unreal world, a world where a posse of journalists takes up residence outside his apartment building; where the *Sun* editorially complained that it could not name him (yet); where his relatives abroad, in Europe and the US, are systematically doorstepped; where he enters and leaves his apartment block under a blanket in the back of a car and where he is quite systematically "shunned" by people and organisations from whom he deserves nothing but good and for whom he has done much good in the past.

The first calls from the media were received at Gambaccini's home while he was actually still in the police station. He realised that, as he feared: "The police have leaked my name." He has to make contact with various personal and professional associates before they read the news in the redtops because "it only takes a couple of hours to realise that this arrest is one of the worst kept secrets in police history". The next day a female journalist, equipped with shopping bags to suggest she is a resident, manages to tailgate a bona fide caller into his building and is found later hiding in the basement. Shortly after this he has to cancel the first of a sequence of social or charitable events: he was due to host a yearly charity dinner but "I cannot be associated with charities for young people until I am cleared. My string of MITES (a music industry charity) dinners ends at fourteen."

Gambaccini's employer, the BBC, "makes it clear … that I will continue on air until I am named or charged". This is because "the corporation wants to cover its backside against possible accusations of employing a person suspected of sexual offences". Reality closes in in other ways too: a friend, a high executive in the BBC, offers to introduce him to her own "reputational lawyer", who comes accompanied by a "reputational PR". Both of these professional men, it must be said, give sterling service but this is the third set of advisers he has been forced to employ: his family solicitor, the criminal lawyer and the reputational team. There is then discussion, leading to Gambaccini taking on a new solicitor, from the well-known firm of Bindmans, about what counsel to retain. He concludes: "'Taking silk' sounds like indulging in some sort of polite drug. However, if I have to go to court, I will be sure to be represented by someone who has taken silk."

All of these numerous professionals who come into Gambaccini's life after his arrest give him great service. But he has had to employ them just at the time when his source of income has dried up, as was absolutely predictable when the police leaked his name. Hence the "economic calamity" he describes.

The individuals and organisations who were significant in Gambaccini's life varied a good deal in their reaction to his difficulties. Some friends were heroic in their refusal to shun him and a few organisations were brave as well. But mostly the organisations come out much worse than the individuals, turning away for fear of being tainted. The reaction of the Labour Party is not unlike that of other groups. He had already, before his arrest, been invited to the "Thousand Club" 2013 Christmas drinks, by his friend Charlie Falconer, a party grandee, the former Labour lord chancellor Lord Falconer of Thornton; "warmly invited" too, according to the card. Two days after the arrest an assistant of Falconer's (the party's "donor stewardship officer") asked by text for a number on which she could speak to him confidentially. When she rings it is to disinvite him to the Christmas drinks. They hate doing this, of course, but: "You know what the Press are like."

Thus, just a few years after he very publicly hosted a Labour Party fundraiser, held, at the party's request, in his home, he is persona non grata. This is the subject of one of the saddest passages in the book: he severs his relationship with the Labour Party, reflecting: "It has obviously not occurred to anyone in Labour that something more than manners is at stake here. An injustice is occurring in its own House, yet it turns away from the victim for fear of taint ... the heroism of leaders from Clement Attlee to Neil Kinnock has yielded to cowardice."

There follows a long, sad account of the depth and length of Gambaccini's connection with the party, going back to the days of former prime minister Jim Callaghan. It all counts for nothing now. Falconer later apologised. Shortly after this apology Gambaccini found that his bowling club of twenty years had removed his "pin" from their display of the pins of celebrity members.

The allegations made against Gambaccini are so old and so vague that they were virtually impossible to make any useful comment about, other than strong denial. They involved two individuals. Because of the terms of the UK Sexual Offences (Amendment) Act, 1976, about which he has been warned, he is not entitled to identify the two complainants or give any detail of what they said that might identify them. In other words these people are guaranteed absolute anonymity, a basic protection which the police quite deliberately stripped from Gambaccini himself. But it is possible to say that the allegations related to a six-year period between twenty-nine and thirty-five years before his arrest.

Each of these accusers, who are known to each other, allege that they engaged in homosexual activities with Gambaccini in premises belonging to a neighbour of his at a time when he lived in a quite different area of London. It is important to reiterate that no evidence was found to support these allegations and they were not made the subject of a prosecution. But because the accusers alleged they were teenagers at the relevant time, and because the leaks about Gambaccini came from Operation Yewtree, it allowed the worst of the tabloids to apply the paedophile label: one reported his detention near a photograph of a different event, in which a sign saying "Burn the Paedo" was clearly visible. All Gambaccini's misfortunes are due to the fact that, as the criminologist reviewer quoted above put it in the *Times Literary Supplement*, "The paedophile label is so toxic that it leads to a form of social death" (Professor Eugene McLaughlin).

Gambaccini had been, as we have seen, an early and very public critic of Jimmy Savile and the Savile investigation. As a result of the leaks from Operation Yewtree he suffered the ultimate and ultimately damaging fate of having his photograph appear next to Savile's in certain newspapers. A coincidence?

A very important aspect of criminal procedure in the United Kingdom is that, when the police have arrested a person for questioning, they can release him on police bail without the need to go to court, binding him to turn up for further questioning at a later date. This can be repeated several times and was repeated in Gambaccini's case for over a year. Each re-bailing was leaked to the media before he or his solicitor were informed, with the consequence that there was no possibility that the scandal would simply fade away: it was regularly and very publicly stoked. And this publicity also carries the risk that it may lead other people – fantasists, people interested in selling their story, or deluded individuals who actually believe they were abused by a particular person – to make further allegations.

Gambaccini's story, together with that of Lord Brittan, Lord Bramall and, a little earlier, Sir Cliff Richard, lead me to wonder whether presumption of innocence can survive in a legal system which permits the police and the media to destroy a person's reputation in advance of any trial. Paul Gambaccini is a man with many advantages of wealth, fame, intelligence, reputation and extraordinary courage and resilience. If this can happen to him one wonders how a less favourably situated individual could possibly survive.

On March 3rd, 2015, Gambaccini gave forty-five minutes of evidence to the House of Commons Home Affairs Committee. A fortnight later the committee advocated major reforms of the police bail system. More important to Gambaccini, it affirmed his innocence and instructed the Crown Prosecution Service "to write and apologise to Mr. Gambaccini explaining why the case took long when the original police investigation was dropped for insufficient evidence a month before he was even arrested". The reforms the committee proposes are set out at the end of Gambaccini's book. They include a strong assertion of a suspect's right to anonymity, the need for any police communication to the media to be formally done, and the need for there to be "zero tolerance on the police leaking information on a suspect in an unattributed way". Whether the committee's recommendations will have any significant effect of course remains to be seen.

Miscarriages of justice on a mass scale have historically been linked with periods of public hysteria, such as the Salem Witch Trials, the McCarthyite persecutions in the United States, the decades of show trials in the Soviet Union or the cases of the Birmingham Six, the Guildford Four and the Maguire Seven at the height of the hysteria generated by IRA violence in Britain. There is evidence that well-informed opinion in Britain is appalled by the excesses of Operation Yewtree. On January 19th, 2016, the warden of Wadham College, Oxford, Sir Kenneth McDonald QC, who is also a former director of public prosecutions in England, reacted to the case of Lord Bramall as follows:

> The police need urgently to face up to the shameful possibility that in their concern to atone for past mistakes they have allowed themselves to be fooled by manipulative fantasists.
>
> The alternative is there for all to see: the cruel, public humiliation of an impeccable old warrior and mealy-mouthed apology from a police force unable to see that it has done anything wrong.

A few days later, on January 21st, 2016, the journalist David Aaronovitch in the London *Times* gave a detailed explanation of the murky origins of many of the Yewtree allegations. He concluded:

> I have no doubt that criticism of the authorities over cases such as Janners's [Greville Janner, a long-time Labour MP] and Jimmy Savile has

led to the police losing a sense of perspective and sometimes even basic commonsense, and to some journalists thinking that any public figure – alive or, preferably dead – is fair game so long as they can find someone – anyone – prepared to make an accusation.

The police bail system has no equivalent in Ireland: if the gardaí wish to rearrest a person for questioning they must get a court order to do so. (See Section 10 of the Criminal Justice Act 1984. The detention periods may be "suspended" until another date in the case of certain theft and fraud offences under Part 2 of the Criminal Law Act 2011.) This does not, of course, prevent leaking. But one would have thought it hard to imagine that a well-known person in Ireland could have the fact that allegations had been made about him leaked to the media before he was even questioned.

Despite the grim subject matter, and the numerous personal and professional humiliations which Gambaccini recounts, the diary reads well, like the production of a person who manages to maintain both his dignity and his cheerfulness in very difficult circumstances. The dominant themes are those of total conviction of innocence, coupled with terror, bewilderment and a massive sense of injustice at how he has been treated. He reiterates several times his love for England, a love which perhaps only a migrant can feel so intensely. But he concludes:

> Imagine how much I loved this country. Imagine my disappointment when it betrayed, psychologically tortured and abandoned me. My unqualified love for Great Britain has been qualified … There is a greater loss. I have lost my faith in the British justice system.

Against that background it is inspiring to read that at his very darkest moments he took comfort in WE Henley's poem "Invictus", which also consoled Nelson Mandela and other victims of injustice. He sets it out in full, commencing:

> Out of the night that covers me,
> Black as the pit from pole to pole
> I thank whatever gods may be
> For my unconquerable soul.
> In the fell clutch of circumstance

I have not winced nor cried aloud.
Under the bludgeonings of chance
My head is bloody, but unbowed.

Most readers will hope they could do so well.

TOM HENNIGAN | 2016

The Analyst as Eeyore

OPINION WRITER might be the dream job of many reporters who instinctively sense readers breezing past their bylines to read the star columnists. Nevertheless the position has its own challenges. For a start there is the relentless demand, week in week out, for opining, a task the bar bore might think easy enough, though his captive audience knows otherwise.

To be properly engaging, one's opinions should be fresh, enlightening and stimulating, but in the age of ready availability of online archives the search for engagement must be set against the need to maintain some intellectual coherence with one's previous body of work. One does not want to relentlessly hammer out the same pet ideas forever using just one key, but neither would anyone with an ambition to be taken seriously plan to start out a Blueshirt and end up a Trotskyist, all for the sake of a good argument.

Then there is the reality, even at old-fashioned newspapers holding out against modern culture's drive to reduce everything to bullet points, that the canvass provided is a small one while the subjects opinion writers tackle are complex, and sometimes vast. And increasingly these subjects must be tackled in real time with an authority that readers seeking to make sense of a convoluted present find useful or reassuring. This can be treacherous, because events and their outcomes are unruly and rarely tidy enough to be convincingly analysed in a thousand words or (increasingly) less. This is especially so at moments of heightened instability in the affairs of humans. Traditionally opinion writers are better at spotting the historical nature of a particular moment than explaining what it means for the future and what our reaction to it should therefore be.

Back around the start of the decade, Ireland's disastrous crash, which left it a ward of the troika, had been prominently covered in Brazil's media and the wider financial crisis affecting richer nations left many Brazilians, possessed of bitter memories of dressing downs after their own experiences with economic calamity, with a wholly understandable sense of *Schadenfreude*. Confidence was then coursing through Brazil's society and the country had become the darling of the global investor class thanks to the dramatic 7.5 per cent economic expansion of 2010, a result of the bold counter-cyclical policies that its government implemented following the 2008 global financial crisis. It is almost totally forgotten now but Brazil's economy crashed in the immediate aftermath of the black September of 2008 but underwent a whiplash revival once flooded with state credit.

From this Brazilian perspective Ireland's surrender to austerity looked like an act of self-harm and many others, at the time and since, have agreed with that analysis. But now the roles have been reversed. After years of pain Ireland currently has the fastest-growing economy in Europe while Brazil experiences its worst recession since the Great Depression. Its government's financial firepower almost exhausted, it is now paralysed, caught between implementing brutal austerity and allowing the country to drift towards the rocks of debt and stagnation.

Last year Ireland's economy surpassed its pre-crisis level, leaving it set fair to undo some of the social harm caused by the crash. Meanwhile Brazil is locked into a dramatic contraction. Its industrial base, the main beneficiary of all that counter-cyclical spending, is on course – if it is not already there – to be smaller than it was on entering the 2008 crisis. Having previously rejected austerity on economic and ideological grounds, the Workers Party administration of President Dilma Rousseff is loath to implement it now but has not yet come up with a convincing alternative bar half-hearted suggestions of a rerun of the counter-cyclical policies that preceded its current plight.

Workers Party intellectuals and those on Brazil's broader left argue that this time it will be different. But the country's ability to tread the same path again is compromised by the fact that its starting position is now far less favourable than it was at the end of 2008. In this vacuum the party's supreme leader, Lula, has warned that all the social advances made since he came to power in 2003 are now at risk. Despite a fiscal deficit of ten per cent of GDP, public services are being slashed by stealth and millions raised out of poverty during the Workers Party's time in power have already been dumped back into it as the economy sheds jobs at a furious pace.

The point of these two sorry tales is not that austerity is preferable to its anti-austerity opposite but rather that outcomes are slippery affairs. It is exceedingly difficult to forecast the future and those who do so should always keep in mind that it is a fraught and possibly futile business. Unfortunately a cautious modesty is not the usual modus operandi of a successful newspaper columnist and in Ireland few are more successful than Fintan O'Toole of *The Irish Times*, arguably the country's leading public intellectual.

For many of us whose first ever vote was cast for Mary Robinson, O'Toole was a formative influence. In a society politically dominated by two populist conservative parties and an arrogant, authoritarian Catholic church, he appeared not just as a pathfinder towards a more liberal, pluralistic society but also as a scourge of those forces that fought against its emergence, most thrillingly dissecting the real state of Irish republicanism by detailing the corruption clustered around Fianna Fáil.

But O'Toole's long career detailing the crookedness of Irish political life, along with his Europhilia, an article of faith among most of the liberalising class, gave him a skewed understanding of Ireland's economic crash. This is most clearly evident in *Ship of Fools*, his 2009 screed about "How stupidity and corruption sank the Celtic Tiger". The book is an excellent retelling of the story of the graft and cronyism that infested Ireland's political-business power nexus, which O'Toole had done so much to expose in the 1990s and into the new millennium. But its economic analysis is wanting, overlooking as it does the fact that Ireland's crash took place in a wider global context in which states happily not under Fianna Fáil rule also saw their economies implode, some of these more, some less corrupt than Ireland, according to Transparency International.

Ship of Fools skips past the crucial fact that shaped the Irish crisis, not the country's supposed land hunger, or the moral vacuum left by the disintegration of the Catholic church, but rather its membership of the euro. Of course economies outside the single currency were also skittled by the crisis, perhaps the best proof that 2008 was nothing more than another of the characteristic destructive spasms of capital that have been with us since at least the tulip mania of the seventeenth century. But the extraordinary inflation of the Irish economy and then the state's inability to navigate an independent path out of the mess when the bubble burst took place within the context of membership of the euro.

Corruption in Irish political life has existed since the foundation of the state, though on a smaller scale than in some of our near European neighbours. This is not to deny the pernicious impact it had or the fact that this worsened under Fianna Fáil after CJ Haughey rose to prominence. But it is hard to argue that any of it equalled the damage done to the country by its membership of the euro, which allowed a previously unimaginable flood of cheap credit in until it eventually destabilised the ship of state. Rather than corruption, it is arguable that it was wishful economic thinking, rooted in our Europhilia, that caused the crash. And Europhilia was rampant at the time of joining the euro, when disdain for the UK's decision to keep out was paraded as a badge of some sort of Irish superiority rather than an example of the naivety of a newcomer.

At the time of the Maastricht referendum, O'Toole was cementing his reputation by reporting on the beef tribunal and perhaps did not have the time to subject the proposal to rigorous analysis. But the desire to join was the result of a national groupthink that meant the only major party in the state which can now look back and say it opposed membership of the single currency is Sinn Féin. The benefit of being in the euro was an article of faith that united conservatives and modernisers. For the former it helped advance the project of shifting the state out from under the economic shadow of the old colonial master across the Irish Sea. For the latter, Europe was viewed as a font of social good thanks to the mixed market economy that O'Toole eulogised.

If *Ship of Fools* paid little attention to the European context, O'Toole has since gone some way towards making up for the oversight, but without ever taking the time to wonder if ardent pro-Europeans like himself had been wrong about the nature of the EU project, preferring instead to argue that a group led by Angela Merkel betrayed it. The crash resulted in Ireland's first serious falling out with the idea of Europe and O'Toole's response to the EU-brokered deal that provided the state's citizens protection from a brutal experiment in autarky was to thunder against the community's mean-spiritedness. "European ideals and values have been exposed as window dressing," he wrote in the immediate aftermath of the bailout, ignoring the fact that treaties entered into by the EU's democracies, such as the one creating the euro, specifically ruled out any such bailouts:

> Yesterday's bailout of broken and delinquent Ireland is much more Versailles than Marshall. There is no sharing of the burden. There is no evidence of a single thought for the consequences of mass unemployment, mass emigration and war on the most vulnerable. There is no European solidarity. And there is not even a genuine sense of self-interest. The sadistic pleasures of punishment have trumped the sensible calculation that an Ireland enslaved by debt is not much use to anyone.

O'Toole predicted that the bailout would fail given that it shoved one of its members "into a vicious downward spiral of depression and debt", calling the programme "a punitive, short-sighted and utterly unsustainable deal that will not solve the Irish crisis and that reduces the EU to the status of a banker's bailiff".

Fintan O'Toole is rightly praised for his penetrating insights into Irish culture and society. But as a forecaster, like most opinion writers, he has a decidedly dodgy track record. After Fianna Fáil's victory in the 2002 general election he wrote:

> Fine Gael, in other words, is finished. For the foreseeable future, the party will not be what it has been for 70 years: the core around which any alternative government could be organised.

Adding that not even Labour could save it, he told us that "the two-and-a-half party system is gone".

Five years later, with the economy already on the precipice, he was fighting manfully for a fairer redistribution of the wealth being generated by the Celtic Tiger. "That task of integrating economic progress and social justice is the fundamental job of our society for the next decade," he wrote before Bertie

Ahern's third election victory. After Ahern fell short of an outright majority O'Toole was back facing the durability of the two-and-a-half party system he had declared finished five years before. Amazingly he recommended that Labour, the political party that then most closely represented his political philosophy, enter into coalition with the man whose corruption he had spent years denouncing in his columns. Such a deal opened up long-term perspectives for O'Toole:

> Barring a catastrophe, Fianna Fáil and Labour can be practically certain of at least a decade in office. They could look forward confidently to the respective heirs of Patrick Pearse and James Connolly occupying the GPO for the 2016 celebrations.

Of course catastrophe was already under way and Labour's refusal to follow O'Toole's advice and thus find itself in government when the storm broke probably saved its political bacon, leaving it well-positioned to enter coalition with Fine Gael less than a decade after O'Toole had declared that party finished.

This mixed track record in forecasting did not prevent him from making dire predictions as Ireland signed up to the punitive terms of the bailout. As well as forecasting that this would fail he also warned that the EU itself would now be subject to a crisis of legitimacy for its failure to mutualise its crisis resolution. Here he might yet be proved correct if austerity helps deliver power to anti-EU parties. But this possible outcome should not distract from the fact that the EU's opting for austerity was in part a response to the reluctance, enshrined in treaty, among voters in the EU core to bail out the periphery. For it to have gone ahead anyway and done so might have been the morally satisfying path but could well have provoked a very different crisis of legitimacy rooted in the union's own democratic deficit that might have led to disintegration anyway. History rarely presents leaders with a set of clear binary options, no matter how much columnists pretend otherwise. One might say that the solutions are not always as obvious as the problems, or at least those that seem obvious should be treated with suspicion.

In this binary framing of choices, usually between good and bad, O'Toole and those like him who draw clear moral lines downplay the difficulty of navigating a path out of crisis for a supranational organisation built on top of multiple democracies, all to one extent or another wedded for better or worse to a model of turbo-charged global capitalism whose unruly energy is rapidly transforming our global society in ways that are contradictory and fiendishly difficult to predict.

O'Toole's analysis consistently seeks to exclude the broader economic and geopolitical forces in play. His analysis of Germany's role in the Irish bailout exists only to provide a villain for his story rather than involving any serious engagement with the complex realities and conflicts within that country. In O'Toole's view, if the deal was morally wrong then it could not work. But when his predictions of failure were proven to be off the mark he had his answer ready, writing at the end of 2015 that "all of the things that have rescued the Irish economy from disaster are strokes of fortune".

Contrasting this analysis with the one he provided on the causes of the crash exposes a double standard. When things go wrong in Ireland it is the fault of our corrupt political class, while external factors (which from abroad look suspiciously like determining factors) are relegated to the footnotes. When things go right, disproving his own predictions that they could not, then the role of the Irish state and behind it the sacrifice of the population in turning things around is to be ignored. Instead it is all down to "cheap oil, cheap money, the ECB's belated reversal of policy, the strength of the US and British economies and the weakness of the euro. Luck, by definition, is about the things you can't control and, for us, those things have turned out spectacularly well."

Of course international factors have played a role in the recovery, just as they did in the crash. But behind the contradiction in O'Toole's analysis lurks the suspicion that he cannot reconcile himself to the reality that the process of Irish modernisation with which he is centrally identified has so far failed to break the old Fianna Fáil-Fine Gael duopoly on power and that having led the country into disaster this stale double act is now leading it out of it. His frustration at the country's peculiar political features is a familiar one among Irish progressives: "Having two big right-of-centre parties gives Irish conservatism both belt and braces. It can manage the dramatic gesture of whipping off the belt to whip Fianna Fáil's behind, knowing the braces will ensure it is not exposed."

No credit can ever be given to this system, which he has spent his whole career denouncing and exposing but which despite all the changes in Irish society in recent decades remains entrenched, even if increasingly frayed at the edges. At the height of the crisis O'Toole called for the replacement of the democratically elected Fianna Fáil government by "a non-party technical administration" and for the country's response to the crisis to be decided by plebiscite. "Sovereignty belongs, not to the State, or the government, but to the people. We have outsourced it for too long to an incompetent, amoral and self-serving elite. Now we face the starkest of choices: use it or lose it."

There is a Rousseauistic thrill to such language but a cooler head might spy in it an unintended door through which demagogy might sneak through. It also hints at a desire to find a path around the glaring failure of those among the roughly half of Irish society who now reject the traditional duopoly to build a viable political alternative, the chief culprit here being the political organisation that best represented O'Toole's beliefs, the Labour Party, with its fondness for subaltern roles in right-wing-dominated coalitions.

It also overlooks the problem that any "collective decision" by the sovereign Irish people would in no way be binding on foreign interlocutors. As Greece was later to learn under Syriza, a sovereign people might vote for something entirely different but still be left with a choice between austerity and a crude autarky that, as the debt crises of Latin America demonstrate, is usually the most brutal form of austerity of them all.

Of course Ireland did not go down the path sketched out by O'Toole, leaving him to label voters "timid", in the week before they voted in 2011, for their refusal to embrace his rejection of EU-imposed austerity and plans for a radical reordering of Irish democracy and instead giving over half their votes to the old duopoly. That timidity might now instead be seen as good sense when one looks at the relative fortunes of Ireland compared with, say, Greece. This is not to enter into a moral debate with O'Toole on the evils of austerity relative to its alternatives but rather to point out that given the seriousness of the situation, the relative balance of forces in the field, the best evaluation of what was available beyond the bailout and the uncertainty surrounding the outcomes offered by such alternatives, Irish voters demonstrated an unheroic but quite sound sense of realpolitik.

O'Toole's early analysis of Ireland was rooted in its own realpolitik, that is the ability to look behind the rotting edifices erected by the church and Fianna Fáil to the actual reality of the country rather than the official version, which no longer matched the experience of most people, if indeed it ever had. But dissecting the 2008 crisis and its aftermath has demanded skills beyond dissecting the ills of Ireland's elite. And O'Toole, in undertaking this task, has settled instead for curating a certain type of liberal discourse (redux: "austerity is bad") that does not allow or even have need for uncertainty.

The irony is that the voters are with O'Toole when it comes to social liberalisation, as the marriage equality referendum proved. But they do not yet trust him with their money. He thinks this a result of the historical cultural repression experienced by Irish society but a look around Europe would indicate that much of the continent has long favoured long stretches of conservative or Christian democratic government even as it evolves into a more socially pluralistic place. O'Toole has written reams on wealth redistribution but seems little concerned with its creation. It is hard to remember a tax or social benefit he has come across that he does not approve of.

But governing and deciding who governs us is not just a question about how to distribute wealth in the interests of social justice. It is a debate about where to strike the compromise between wealth creation, and the often unpalatable measures needed for this, and distribution. There is an inherent tension in this debate that has nothing to do with the moral superiority of the redistributionist agenda (or looked at from the opposite point of view, held by some Goldman Sachs bankers, the superiority of those wealth-creating titans carrying out God's work). Most voters would sign up to no poverty, but they have the right to ask at what cost to themselves or to the future prospects of their children this would come. Opinion writers who acknowledge this tension will not only leave their readers better informed but will also find themselves better engaged with one of the central issues that voters have grappled with for decades in Western societies.

This could benefit O'Toole, who has confused the anger of the citizens with an appetite for radical measures when in fact much of the Irish electorate remains, in common with much of the European one, intrinsically conservative, a fact he should be more aware of having brilliantly engaged with it reporting from the frontlines of the country's cultural wars.

In a complex and changing world calls for new republican beginnings, greater social justice and wider European solidarity might provide a rallying point for some of those uneasy about the direction of events. But no matter how desirable these things might be there is a risk that, once reduced to pieties and disengaged from the complex realities of modern societies coexisting in an integrated global economy, they will in the emerging century become for more and more voters practically irrelevant no matter how often politicians of all stripes pay them lip-service. However dispiriting this may be, conservative caution is as likely a reaction to troubled times as revolutionary action.

The recent election results bear this out. Rather than being evidence of the breakdown of Ireland's "imaginary consensus" as described by O'Toole, political scientists might in years to come wonder how after a corruption-tainted crash and punishing years of austerity Fine Gael and Fianna Fáil, once their unruly former members running as Independents are counted in, retained over half the vote, leaving Micheál Martin, after an apology and five years on the opposition benches, rehabilitated and in the running to become taoiseach.

O'Toole's deep disdain for the enduring pattern of Irish politics, and behind it the conservativeness of the "timid" voters who sustain it, has seen an increasingly sarcastic tone enter his writing in recent years. One might speculate that this could be the cost of an intense personal engagement with the realities of public life over three decades. But dangerously the sarcasm comes with a flip-side, an increasingly unshakable belief in the superior virtue of his own positions, which should be a warning light for any commentator. There has also been something of a narrowing of horizons, necessary in order to avoid engaging with the fact that perhaps the Irish voter, unhappy as he is with the status quo, will not risk anything too radical in the current climate of global uncertainty. O'Toole is a surprisingly provincial writer for one whose influence on Irish public discourse is so great. A stint in China has left almost no apparent trace on his thinking of how the economic re-emergence of this global behemoth is reshaping our world. His engagement with Merkel's Germany reads as if conducted from a desk in Dublin.

Of course O'Toole once famously considered greater direct engagement in politics himself, having toyed with the idea of running for the Dáil as an Independent in 2011. One of the features of this year's general election has been the rise of the independent TD, yet bar a few exceptions, this is a conservative expression of growing discontent with traditional politics, narrowing as it does the voter's gaze further from the national to the local or single issue. Looked at from one angle, the rise of the Independents might be read as the electoral arming of the citizenry against a self-serving political class. But considering the damage this does to the party system, how will greater accountability of the deputy – another piety we all seem to agree on – in the Irish context not just aggravate the tyranny of parish pump politics at the expense of the serious business of national governance?

The dream of a republican citizenry taking over from the professional politicians also overlooks the evolutionary role of parties in democracies. They exist because history shows people tire of permanent political mobilisation. It is why they delegate rather than leaving their fate in the hands of the most committed, too often synonymous with the most aggressive. In explaining his decision not to run in 2011, O'Toole wrote:

> What if it were possible to stand, in every single constituency, someone not currently involved in party politics, but with a track record of civic achievement in business, in the arts, in community and voluntary activity, in sport, in single-issue campaigns? What if they could be united on a small core of big questions, while retaining their independence, so they could bring some free thought to the Dáil?

Some might spy in that idea the genesis of a new party. O'Toole, however, might find the debate involved in drawing up "a small core of big questions" instructive as to the difficulties of party politics and why it is an inherently disappointing system. After all, most broad-based parties are not conspiracies against the citizens of a state but rather a working compromise between groups of them. Countries that have flirted with new movements bent on ending corrupt political systems (such as Argentina's Que Se Vayan Todos – Kick Them All Out – movement which followed the 2001 economic implosion) have quickly come to realise that while political parties may often be reprehensible institutions they still constitute the most practical method of mediating disputes across regions, classes and generations within a democratic polity. We can all be for more accountability within our democracies but achieving it is no easy thing or it would have been accomplished long ago. The brush with running for office seems to have brought some of this messy reality into focus for O'Toole. His article explaining his decision not to stand ends: "If nothing else, to misquote Karl Marx, I've been reminded that analysing the world is a lot easier than changing it." It is a pity that his commentary since then seems to have ignored this lesson.

O'Toole's narrow gaze also allows him to portray the cockups and conspiracies and now "cockspiracies" of Irish public life as a reflection of something deeply amiss, one could almost say uniquely so, in our society. His closely cropped view allows him to denounce Ireland's public services as "squalid". But squalid compared to what or to where and at what cost in the places where they are not squalid? Such language feeds a persistent belief among many Irish people that their country is little more than a banana republic, a term O'Toole largely avoids using, though the rest of his language lends significant ammunition to those who do. Suffice it to say that anyone who thinks Ireland is a banana republic should visit a real one to properly understand how the state they live in is not unduly burdened with intractable political disputes among corrupt elites governing masses bereft of hope.

Here is where O'Toole's reluctance to widen his gaze is limiting. Which country would he have Ireland be more like? One might assume from his writings one of the Scandinavian monarchies (though without that region's increasingly influential xenophobes). But such a forthright declaration would have to acknowledge the progress the Irish state has made to have such an ambition in sight and to accommodate the admission that there are fewer countries left to emulate thanks to that progress.

When he does venture a comparison in his columns it is usually to highlight some statistic that proves the country's failings. Low wages, lack of social spending, lack of investment. But statistics are adaptable. If O'Toole wanted to understand the enduring power of the country's conservative parties he might consider that, according to the United Nations, Ireland is the sixth best country in the world to live in, tied with Germany. Or that according to Eurostat, Irish inequality is close to the mean on what remains, even after the recent crisis, the most socially just continent on earth (again tied with Germany).

It is of course within a columnist's remit to highlight what is wrong and what could be done better. And in Ireland there is much that could be done better, but this is a view that is shared by utopians and realists alike. For all the failures, the modern Irish state has also delivered successes. A sense of realism – and proportion – are thus the most likely means to prove effective in driving forward debate and winning adherents to one's side.

O'Toole's writing in recent years, however, has been moving in the opposite direction. He has responded to the crisis with the urgency the situation demands but his moral indignation has not been allied to the forensic grasp of detail he demonstrated when laying bare the cronyism in Irish public life. Instead there has been a retreat into liberal pieties, placing him squarely in a wider trend towards the ideological siloisation of public discourse (hugely driven by the Internet) involving a failure to engage with both wider social, political and economic contexts and the innate conservativism of a majority of Irish and other European citizens. Instead his work is veering off into calls for a new republic, as if this will somehow prove more successful than the present model. France is on its fifth republic but it is hard to discern the advantages of regularly retooling the state. One is entitled to ask if this type of commentary continues to add to public debate or now serves rather to divert us away from the ground where key issues will be resolved.

As ever, future events will help resolve that question. And as ever, the events keep coming, constantly reshaping our understanding of the world and testing our values. Angela Merkel, the scourge of the Greeks and author of Ireland's austerity, is suddenly politically vulnerable because of her morally correct and widely praised decision to admit one million Muslim refugees from the wars in the Middle East. Meanwhile the euro zone crisis awaits its next flare-up while broader markets are in turmoil. China's long transformative boom might have ended in a glut of overinvestment, useless spare capacity and bad debts. The US's recovery remains underwhelming and is still doing little for long-stagnant workers' incomes just as it enters an election process that seems to signal its gathering transformation into an outright plutocracy. Against this background, in an Ireland now accelerating away from the crisis of recent years, Fine Gael and Fianna Fáil once again dispute the right to lead the state. Meanwhile, in Brazil, genuinely squalid public services are worsening by the day as the government holds out against a final surrender to austerity.

In the Post

This final section features a selection of shorter pieces on a variety of subjects ranging from aspects of intellectual and social history in Dublin to miscellaneous reflections on literature, culture, publishing and European history and politics.

How, in a post-religious society, do we understand the work of a poet like Czesław Miłosz, who warned readers that "all my intellectual impulses are religious"? Miłosz himself was to offer an agnostic admirer an interesting analogy for the Christian idea of heavenly bliss.

In the twentieth century English was to replace French as the lingua franca and the Russian revolutionary VI Lenin was one who felt he should learn a little of the language. Did he speak it though with a Rathmines accent, and if he did would this have been better than a Drumcondra one?

Some people find Jane Austen's novels a little too decorous, but there was nothing particularly decorous about the author herself, who liked to throw back a few glasses of wine and then get out on the dance floor.

Joseph Sheridan Le Fanu is remembered chiefly as an accomplished writer of Gothic and horror fiction. But he also took a keen interest in politics, which is reflected too in some of his historical novels, where he never quite managed to square his human sympathy for the downtrodden with his ingrained social conservatism.

The poet James Clarence Mangan became, towards the end of his short life, an opium addict and would wander round the streets of Dublin with green tinted glasses, a massive cloak and a large conical hat, attracting to himself the attention, and the persecutions, of street urchins. Yet he still found time to fall in love, unhappily of course.

An extract from The Christian Examiner of 1827 gives an account of a Sunday stroll through Dublin's Thomas Street, Meath Street and Patrick Street, where the author found much to displease him in the open shops and the patrons of the public houses, full of "dirty, degraded creatures", reeling forth onto the street much the worse for wear yet "still recklessly resolved to continue under the excitement of ardent spirits".

Can Europe be cured of its ills, as the German sociologist Ulrich Beck suggested, by the healing properties of the Mediterranean lifestyle: sunshine and blue skies, beauty, food, wine and joie de vivre? It is a tempting thought, and by no means a new one. But addressing the European Union's problems and its current stasis may require a less dreamy and more practical approach.

An altercation that ensued after a Dublin middle class matron followed her son into a picture house in the company of a married woman ended up in court. The mother was righteous in her anger, convinced her son had been bewitched by a Jezebel. But the married woman stood her ground and the court found that she had been wronged and awarded her fifty pounds in damages.

A well-known tall tale purporting to be about Lord Mandelson, and a series of archaeological finds in Roman and pre-Roman Britain, each teach us some lessons about how negatively "sophistication" can be viewed and the English public's deep attachment to narratives which portray the island race as always standing sturdily alone.

The phrase "sexual harassment" might have been unfamiliar to James Joyce, but it refers to a phenomenon that certainly existed in early twentieth century Dublin, and one which he would have been familiar with and which features in his work.

Miłosz in Heaven | 2011

CYNTHIA L HAVEN wrote in a recent *Times Literary Supplement* essay about the wave of commemorations and celebrations that attended the hundredth anniversary this year of the birth of the great Polish poet Czesław Miłosz. At the same time she emphasises the difficulties that many will have in understanding the now largely vanished world of religion and ideology in which he was formed:

> There were centenary events in Warsaw, Vilnius, Krasnogruda, Moscow, St Petersburg, Novosibirsk, Madrid, Bucharest, Paris, Rome and across the United Kingdom [and in Dublin too – *drb*] throughout the year. The fever was naturally less acute in the English-speaking world, but here the divide may indeed be more generational than linguistic. Miłosz's former assistant Natalie Gerber, now a professor in New York, described the perils of presenting the poet's work to her undergraduates in *An Invisible Rope: Portraits of Czesław Miłosz* (reviewed in the *TLS*, April 8th, 2011): 'Few have much experience with verse, and almost none have read poetry that overtly wrestles with conscience and historical circumstance, as does Miłosz's, or, for that matter, poetry that requires its reader to work as hard as his does to understand both its literal meaning and its ethical import ... [They] don't presume that the morally complex and personally engaged stances taken by the speakers in Miłosz's poems are even possible.'
>
> At the conference in Cracow, Artur Sebastian Rosman, a doctoral student, recalled a discussion at the Elliott Bay Book Company in Seattle, devoted to Miłosz. 'All, and I mean all, of the Americans there were convinced that Miłosz was most likely a postmodern spiritual seeker, probably much like them, possibly fascinated by archetypes, certainly spiritual, and definitely not religious.' Had Miłosz been there, said Rosman, he might have repeated his claim that his readers don't 'take into account a particular, quite fundamental fact: all my intellectual impulses are religious and in that sense my poetry is religious'.

But what does that mean? An Irish Catholic, or at least one whose schooling goes back a few decades, may have some idea of what is going on with Miłosz's great interest in the taxonomy of sin, even if, as is normally the case, he or she is more or less "lapsed", but what of an American brought up without any religious education? Haven recalls that the poet Brenda Hillman, wife of Miłosz's translator Robert Hass, once asked him: "What is heaven? What is it like?" To which the poet replied decisively: "Brenda, heaven is the third vodka." A fine answer, but one wonders if it would be much use to Seattle's postmodern spiritual seekers, who, one suspects, would on the whole find just one vodka quite enough thank you.

Could it also be that Miłosz, a man who from time to time worried about his own drinking (though he lived well into his nineties), was unconsciously echoing the more worldly *bon mot* of James Thurber, who once described "that third martini feeling" as occurring "when you are beginning to feel increasingly sophisticated, but can no longer pronounce it"?

The Rathmines Accent | 2012

THE EXCELLENT website of Dublin life and lore Come Here To Me! embarks on a discussion of that now vanished phenomenon "the Rathmines accent", prompted by the (not, it must be said, enormously well vouched) idea that Vladimir Ilyich Lenin was taught English by an Irishman – in fact a native of Leinster Road in Rathmines.

The phrase seems to have been a simple shorthand term for posh or anglified speech, which then as now tends to rub many ordinary citizens up the wrong way. Still, the accent had its uses, it seems: in 1942 "a married woman" and "a married man" (not married to each other, one assumes) were able to gain admission illicitly to one of Mr Paddy Belton's licensed premises by saying they were from Rathmines. They were, in fact, from Santry and were fined 5/- each for the imposture at Kilmainham District Court.

One memorable comic use of the figure of the Rathmines toff which the Come Here To Me! post does not mention is O'Casey's in *The Plough And The Stars*.

A "fashionably dressed, middle-aged, stout woman" comes upon Fluther, the Covey and Peter, who are looking to profit from the confusion caused by the uprising to do a bit of looting.

> *Woman*: For Gawd's sake, will one of you kind men show any safe way for me to get to Wrathmines? ... I was foolish enough to visit a friend, thinking the howl thing was a joke, and now I cawn't get a car or a tram to take me home – isn't it awful?
>
> *Fluther*: I'm afraid, ma'am, one way is as safe as another.
>
> *Woman*: And what am I gowing to do? Oh, isn't this awful? ... I'm so different from others ... The mowment I hear a shot, my legs give way from under me – I cawn't stir, I'm paralysed – isn't it awful?
>
> *Fluther*: (moving away): It's a derogatory way to be, right enough, ma'am.

One public figure whom we do know to have been taught English by an Irishman was the interwar leader (regent) of Hungary, Admiral Miklós Horthy – an authoritarian figure of the right and thus very much an enemy of Lenin. It seems unlikely that the two men ever met, but if they did English would have been a language they had in common.

But would the Rathmines-accented Vladimir Ilyich have been able to understand Admiral Horthy, who took in some lessons from James Joyce when the latter was briefly teaching at the Berlitz school in Pola/Pula on the Adriatic (today in Croatia) before he moved to Trieste? Joyce of course lived all over Dublin, but his accent may well have been a Northside one, at least if we are to judge from a line in the *Portrait*: "It [a funnel] is called a tundish in Lower Drumcondra, said Stephen, laughing, where they speak the best English." Cf Bertie Ahern.

Lenin, of course, as Brian Earls has informed us in a recent *drb* essay on Russian jokes, spoke with a rather strange high-pitched voice, which many citizens found funny, though perhaps most were shrewd enough not to laugh in public. He also had considerable difficulty pronouncing the letter "r", so we can perhaps imagine him, on being congratulated by Comrades Zinoviev and Lunacharsky on his good English, confiding that he had learned it from an excellent Iwish chap from Wathmines.

Friday Night and
the Lights are Low | 2013

JOHN MULLAN, author of the splendid *What Matters in Jane Austen*, writes in *The Guardian* (May 4th) on the significance in her novels of dancing and balls in a piece written to link to a forthcoming BBC2 programme, *Pride And Prejudice: Having a Ball*.

"The ball," he writes, "was the occasion for a couple to perform together in front of others. It was their opportunity for physical intimacy." These things of course being relative: "They could not clinch each other or even touch each other's flesh, yet they were brought closer than they could be on any other occasion."

Of course the dance has long been a metaphor for sexual coupling, and not just the act itself but, in its elaborate rituals, its comings and goings, approaches and withdrawals, ins and outs, the prelude to the act (though of course at the time one doesn't quite know, one cannot be quite sure, that one is engaged in the prelude to anything).

Miss Austen was a great believer in what she calls "the felicities of rapid motion". The main purpose of the dance, of course, was to pair off, not just for the evening – still less for a quick snog round the back of the coachhouse – but for life. This Jane did not succeed in doing, but that was down to bad luck rather than any lack of inclination. Still, as she was to find, if you are not to be a full participant in the business of courting, and marrying, and mothering, there are always the pleasures of the observer, and some of them can be enjoyed at the ball too. The twenty-four-year-old Jane wrote thus to her sister Cassandra:

> I believe I drank too much wine last night at Hurstbourne; I know not how else to account for the shaking of my hand today ... There were only twelve dances, of which I danced nine, & was merely prevented from dancing the rest by the want of a partner ... There were very few Beauties, and such as there were, were not very handsome. Miss Iremonger did not look well, & Mrs Blount was the only one much admired. She appeared

exactly as she did in September, with the same broad face, diamond bandeau, white shoes, pink husband, & fat neck ... Mrs Warren, I was constrained to think a very fine young woman, which I regret. She has got rid of some part of her child, & danced away with great activity, looking by no means very large. Her husband is ugly enough; uglier even than his cousin John; but he does not look so very old. The Miss Maitlands are both prettyish ... with brown skins, large dark eyes, & a good deal of nose. – The General has got the Gout, and Mrs Maitland the Jaundice. Miss Debary, Susan & Sally ... made their appearance, & I was as civil to them as their bad breath would allow me.

Le Fanu's Dark Imagination | 2014

JOSEPH SHERIDAN LE FANU was born two hundred years ago today (August 28th) at 45 Lower Dominic Street in Dublin. He was author of at least fourteen novels, numerous short stories, poetry and one play. He also wrote a great many articles for the city's conservative press. Today, Le Fanu, whose family were originally Huguenot refugees and who counted Richard Brinsley Sheridan among his forebears, is mostly remembered for his Gothic and horror fiction. His imagination was dark, almost to the point of disorder. Here he describes the victim of a fire:

> The head and one arm and shoulder, as well as one knee, were thrust through the iron stanchions, and all was black and shrunk, the clothes burned entirely away, and the body roasted and shrivelled to a horrible tenuity; the lips dried up and drawn, so that the white teeth grinned and glittered in hideous mockery, and thus the whole form, arrested in the very attitude of frenzied and desperate exertion, showed more like the hideous blackened effigy of some grinning ape, than anything human.

Le Fanu, in this mode, might remind some readers of Stephen King. Certainly he could write sensational material very well, yet he never quite achieved his literary or commercial potential. His narratives seemed to turn in on themselves rather than advance towards the sort of orderly conclusions the Victorian reader had grown to expect. The indirection which marks his work ultimately derived from his ceaseless desire to imagine an Ireland in which Anglicans, like his own family, played a legitimate and honourable role. His elaborate narratives, which were frequently historical in setting, were ultimately allegorical and, at heart, tortured efforts to square the impossible circle of Ireland's past. If Le Fanu had been content to "just write stories" he might well have been an Irish Wilkie Collins – though he might have been less interesting as a result.

The family moved from Dominic Street when Joseph was two. His father was an Anglican minister and was appointed chaplain at the Royal Hibernian Military School in the Phoenix Park. The park, with its eighteen hundred acres of rolling grassland and various imperial institutions, was one of the few locations in the country where one might gain the impression of a well-ordered and harmonious society under a benevolent crown. Le Fanu spent about eleven years there and it seems they were untroubled and carefree. As WJ McCormack recounts in his biography of the writer, the young Joseph sometimes amused himself drawing pictures. One featured balloonists speeding towards the earth, having fallen from their basket. The picture was accompanied by the caption: "See the effects of trying to go to heaven." Perhaps he had heard of the Daedalus myth – or perhaps it was an early sign of his conservative instincts.

In 1826 Le Fanu's father, Thomas, having gained some remunerative clerical posts in rural Ireland, moved the family to a country parish in Co Limerick. The contrast with the well-ordered world of the Phoenix Park could hardly have been greater. In Limerick, the harsh realities of Irish life were unavoidable: it was an area which at that time – to use the term favoured by the authorities – was "disturbed". Beyond the modest walls of the glebe house the sullen Catholic masses were threatening. It was here that the young Le Fanu first encountered the Irish peasantry and their grievances. A part of him sympathised. He understood his relatively privileged status, and yet he couldn't have felt very privileged since his family was hard-pressed financially. The main reason the Le Fanus were short of money, and obliged to borrow from relatives, was that the Catholic peasantry was increasingly reluctant to pay the tithes tax to the Anglican church.

Le Fanu spent his teenage years in this troubling environment, which shaped his imaginative world and his political principles. His view of the world came to be characterised by two contending impulses: a deep sympathy with the fate of the "old Irish" and a firm commitment to the political interests of his caste. When he moved to Dublin to study law he gravitated towards conservative politics and spent many evenings attending meetings of the Metropolitan Conservative Society in Dawson Street. The meetings were held in the building which now houses the Royal Irish Academy. Yet one of his first pieces of writing from around that time reveals a pronounced sympathy for the rebels of 1798:

> But if you would ask me as I think it like,
> If in the rebellion I carried a pike,
> And fought for old Ireland from the first to the close,
> And shed the heart's blood of her bitterest foes,
> I answer you 'Yes' and I tell you again,
> Though I stand here to perish, it's my glory that then
> In her cause I was willing my veins should run dry,
> And that now for her sake I am ready to die.

It has been said that the character in the verse was based on a Co Limerick rebel named Kirby who was condemned to death for participating in the rebellion.

If Le Fanu had some popular sympathies he was also a virulent opponent of O'Connell and a staunch defender of the Protestant interest. He owned and contributed to *The Warder* and several other ultra-Protestant journals. But, it seems, he found no joy in this work and was driven more by wearisome duty than substantial emotional engagement. In the Gothic horror genre he found freedom from the oppressively factual, a freedom which allowed for literary exploration beyond the arid political rhetoric of the everyday. And in his historical fiction he could probe emotionally satisfying might-have-beens. Yet in both forms he found it impossible to imagine the desideratum of an Ireland where his alienation evaporated and both Anglican and Irish co-mingled in harmony. Fiction, even Gothic fiction, could only stray a certain distance from the actual.

An episode in *The Cock and Anchor*, an historical novel published in 1845, does offer the vision of an Irish unity but the unity discovered is not based on noble or generous impulses but rather on the basest of human instincts. The exhibition of a cock fight sees the coming together of all social classes but offers no hopeful augury for the future:

> ... all these gross and glaring contrarieties reconciled and bound together in one hellish sympathy. All sate locked in breathless suspense, every countenance fixed in the hard lines of intense, excited anxiety and vigilance; all leaned forward to gaze upon the combat whose crisis was on the point of being determined ... Every aperture in this living pile was occupied by some eager, haggard or ruffian face; and, in spite of all the pushing, and bustling, all were silent, as if the powers of voice and utterance were unknown among them.

Cruel Cruel,
Margaret Stackpoole | 2014

A PINCH of salt – medium to large – is required when considering the many miseries and oppressions that, in his own telling, befell the poet James Clarence Mangan. If things were bad at home – the wretched Pater! – conditions declined close to those of a galley slave when he was employed as an attorney's scrivener in York Street. Or did they? Some of those who worked with him describe conditions which were not especially bad.

Despite the tall tales, nobody seems to have had a bad word to say about Mangan. Undoubtedly, this is to do with his troubled life and soul. Yeats, Joyce and many others admired this larger than life figure who sacrificed his health and life for his aesthetic and embodied the romantic idea of the artist. His life was indeed rough; he died at the age of forty-nine, but the suspicion remains that he exaggerated its horrors.

One straw in the wind suggesting he may not have been exactly chained down in Hades is the reasonable social life enjoyed by the author of "Dark Rosaleen" in premises around D'Olier Street and Dame Street, mixing and drinking with contributors to various literary journals. He also seems to have been able, albeit in his somewhat dysfunctional manner, to attend to a matter of the heart.

The Stackpoole family lived on Mount Pleasant Square in the suburb of Ranelagh and it seems Mangan was on visiting terms. (Not bad going for a galley slave.) Indeed, it seems he took a particular shine to Margaret Stackpoole, a daughter of the house. According to Yeats, and by common assent, she was the prettiest of three daughters.

John Mitchel, of 1848, to hell with O'Connell, *Jail Journal* and there's nothing wrong with slavery fame, was quite pally with Mangan in his final years. Mangan had declared his support for Mitchel's form of nationalism in 1848. Those politics did not appeal to Joyce – a latter-day O'Connellite – and constituted his one criticism of Mangan.

In his account of Mangan's life, Mitchel seems surprised that the poet could have been on visiting terms at such a grand address and implies that he was out of his league. Of course Mitchel knew him in the later 1840s when Mangan was addicted to opium and wandered around Dublin with green tinted glasses, a massive cloak and large conical hat, frequently attracting the attention of disrespectful urchins, much like those who followed Leopold Bloom when he left the *Freeman* office some sixty years later.

Nevertheless, given the poet's meagre resources (according to Mangan's own account his family lived in an unspeakable hovel on Chancery Lane), it is probably safe to conclude that he was always wholly outside the realm of rational consideration for someone with Miss Stackpoole's position in society. The Stackpooles were a landowning Norman family transplanted to Clare in 1651, where they continued to hold land. In the eighteenth century they converted to Protestantism and continued to prosper as major landowners in the county. Some of the family moved to Dublin and they too were well got.

Mangan was probably accepted in Mount Pleasant Square – if it was Mount Pleasant Square (there are some anomalies) – as an interesting young poet with a knowledge of foreign languages and literatures, that is to say for purposes of entertainment. Once he plucked up the courage and made his feelings known he presumably got the Prufrock treatment – "That is not what I meant at all." – or perhaps Margaret employed the time-honoured and ever serviceable "as a friend but no more" formula. Nothing so unusual there; rejecting and being rejected is, after all, an everyday occurrence.

What is interesting is the afterlife of the whole business, which involved a fair bit of what might be termed literary misogyny. The agreed interpretation is that Margaret was a right b***h, that she led on the poor poet, encouraging his hopes only to dash them in the cruellest manner. Mangan's own self-focused view is reflected in the following lines from his autobiographical poem "The Nameless One", written over a decade after the episode:

> betrayed in friendship, befooled in love,
> with spirit shipwrecked, and young hopes blasted …

This is pretty much in line with the self-pitying way he interpreted virtually everything that happened in his life. DJ O'Donoghue, in his life of the poet, comments: "Mangan thenceforth looked upon the fair sex as essentially cruel and malicious and in one of his poems exclaims:

> Man at most is made of clay –
> Woman seems a block of granite!"

In his account of Mangan's life John Mitchel also takes an anti-Stackpoole line. This is probably the source of O'Donoghue's opinion, as his other main source of information on Mangan, Father Meehan, does not appear to have been aware of the Stackpoole affair. In Mitchel's version – which is his account of what an opium-addled Mangan told him some twenty years after the visits to Mountpleasant – some classic objections to female ways are introduced. One assumes they are Mitchel's own additions:

> He (Mangan) was on terms of visiting in a house where were three sisters; one of them was beautiful, *spirituelle*, and a coquette. The old story was here once more re-enacted in due order. Paradise opened before him; the imaginative and passionate soul of a devoted boy bended in homage before an enchantress. She received it, was pleased with it, and even encouraged and stimulated it, by various arts known to that class of persons, until she was fully and proudly conscious of her absolute power over one other gifted and noble nature – until she knew that she was the centre of the whole orbit of his being, and the light of his life; then, with a cold surprise, as wondering that he could be guilty of such a foolish presumption, she exercised her undoubted prerogative, and whistled him down the wind.

In the American poet Louise Imogen Guiney's account in 1892 there is no trace of gender solidarity but quite a bit of Mitchel's influence:

> His first love was given to a fair girl much 'above him,' according to our strange surveys. She encouraged his shy approaches; and he was tremblingly, perilously happy. For the pleasantest period of his life he was in frequent social contact with interesting people of station and breeding, with those who made for him his fitting environment. But at the moment when he feared nothing he was taken like a bird in the fowler's net, and cast scornfully away. Stunned and broken, he crept back as best he could to solitude.

Yeats, who also took an interest, seemed to think that he had made great discoveries regarding the poet's love. In his account, Mitchel's influence appears once more:

> This love affair is the first of my new facts. Mangan met – between his twentieth and twenty-fifth year apparently – a Miss Stackpoole, one of three sisters, who lived in Mount Pleasant Square. She was a fascinating coquette, who encouraged him, amused herself with his devotion, and then "whistled him down the wind" … She was a handsome girl, with a tint of red in her hair, a very fashionable colour in our day, whatever it was then.

Of course Yeats was no stranger to the torments of unrequited love. And yet, while the resulting verse can be impressive, a lingering question remains: What part of "she's just not that into you" do these intense poets find so hard to grasp?

A Sabbath Stroll | 2014

The Christian Examiner was an influential Dublin journal in the early part of the nineteenth century. Among other things the *Examiner* discovered and first published William Carleton, the peasant genius of nineteenth century Irish literature. Carleton was attractive to the editors, and in particular to

Caesar Otway, because he rejected the religion of his peasant forebears, offered a window onto the mores and culture of peasant Ireland and was in addition a talented writer.

In the later 1820s Dublin was transfixed by religious disputation, the ultimate (political) question being whether the poor would abandon their traditional religion in favour of a Bible-centred Protestantism. The stakes were high and involved nothing less than determining who would enjoy power in Ireland into the distant future.

Carleton was a convert to Protestantism, and if over time he drifted away from belief he never returned to the religion of his family and childhood. When he was dying in Ranelagh in 1869 a Jesuit came down from Milltown to see if he would consider departing the world in the religion of his forefathers. Presumably an entreaty of sorts was to be made and, in the manner of these set pieces, we can assume his ancestors and the welfare of his eternal soul would have been mentioned. However, when the inquiry was initiated the ailing Carleton responded by turning his face to the wall.

In September 1827 the *Examiner* published an article entitled "A Sabbath Stroll through Dublin". The author affects an apolitical tone, but in fact his writing groans beneath the political obsessions of the time, in particular the preoccupation with religion, the poor and the necessity to reform that reprehensible mass and direct them towards the light of pure religion.

The extract from "Sabbath Stroll" we reprint below tells us something of how life was lived around Thomas Street in Dublin during the 1820s. The depiction of the diminutive men of Connacht as "potato-fed pigmies" about to embark on a steam packet to England is unintentionally moving. The group was spotted standing together early on the Sunday morning in question with wallets of oaten cake strung behind them and carrying strong blackthorn sticks for the journey. The small band of adventurers was setting forth in search of seasonal employment on English farms, work that would enable their families to survive another year.

As he strolls, the author comments that "the professors of the Popish faith seem to have no moral sense in regard to the observance of the Lord's day". Shopkeepers, he noted, opened for business on Sunday mornings. He mentions, with a little irony, the practice of leaving up some wooden shutters on shop premises as a gesture towards the Sabbath. There was a high level of small-scale commercial activity in poorer areas on Sundays, as on other days, because of the exigencies of hand-to-mouth living, a fact which the disapproving author does not seem to take into consideration. (The partial shuttering of shops on Sunday was a long-lived custom and the present writer observed it in the streets around Thomas Street as late as the 1960s.)

Mention of news vendors is also made, suggesting an interest among the urban poor in political developments as the campaign for Catholic Emancipation intensified. There were no Sunday newspapers published in Dublin at the time but a few weeklies were published on Saturdays at various times throughout the 1820s. Newspapers were also hired out for set times by paper-sellers and it is also likely that in poorer areas second-hand copies of papers published some days earlier were also sold. If multiple news vendors were bawling their wares it suggests a reasonable level of literacy in the city's poorer quarters. Newspapers of the time bore the stamp of the political class's cultural values, which were literate, educated and middle class. While the poor were hugely interested in the doings of that world and aware of their importance, it was not entirely their world. Some signs of the urban poor's own culture are also to be found in "Sabbath Stroll".

The mention of storytellers on the streets suggests an autonomous culture in poorer areas and offers further evidence that oral culture was not only central to the lives of the rural poor but also to those who lived in the city. The prevalence of ballad singers, who were cultural institutions in Dublin and were last heard some time in the early 1930s, is also interesting. One of the functions of ballad singers was as cultural translators, redacting events from high politics into forms compatible with the norms and values of oral culture.

In addition to this interesting cultural and political mix the author also tells us of a boy bellowing out, amidst an immense crowd: "The Bible-men defeated, or the glorious victory of the Rev Father Maguire over the Protestant Pope". The shouting boy was selling a chapbook or pamphlet covering the great public debate on the relative merits of Roman Catholicism and reformation Protestantism which had recently taken place between the Reverend Richard Pope and the Reverend Father Maguire. In popular opinion Father Maguire had triumphed, a view perhaps endorsed by the series of articles which subsequently appeared in the *Examiner* pointing out where he had been in error – a series which would scarcely have been necessary had Mr Pope done the job of exposing Romish debasement properly.

It is telling that the young boy was surrounded by "an immense crowd". The poor knew which side they were on and if intellectuals such as Carleton saw Protestantism as the best option for the development and modernisation of the country most others of his class did not agree. The enthusiasts for a second reformation who conducted the *Examiner* were undoubtedly gratified by the collaboration of Carleton. However, the Protestant crusaders of the 1820s had taken on an immense challenge. The odds were stacked against them and they were met in the field by O'Connell, whose victory in 1829 confirmed to perceptive Protestant intellectuals that the great campaign to render Ireland Protestant had failed.

Entering then the south-western avenue to the city, and passing by the City Basin, once the resort and fashionable promenade of the nobility, gentry, and citizens, but now redolent with tan-pits and putrescency, I took my way through that broad thoroughfare, Thomas-street*, and so through Meath, and by Patrick-streets, into the centre of the city. And as I passed along I observed many of the shops were open and the shopmen here and there occupied in taking down half of the shutters – some panels left up in honour of the God of the Sabbath, others taken down for the service of the god of this world: content to sell in the dark, in courtesy to the fourth commandment – but resolved to sell by all means, as decided devotioners of Mammon. Look at yonder public-house disgorging and receiving crowds of dirty degraded creatures. See that sallow, unshaven tradesman, emerging from its gloomy and cavernous recesses, lit up still with the lurid light flickering from a gas-pipe – (and oh, what a record it would be, were the confession and indictment of that light taken against all the abominations of word, thought, and deed, upon which it shone!) See him reeling forth, and shewing, by his loitering step and brutalized countenance, that his wages and his night were spent amidst the orgies of this pot-house. Observe the slattern dress, the filthy face, the maudlin eye of that female just stealing in, unsatisfied with her MORNING (the cant phrase for a dram of whiskey), and still recklessly resolved to continue under the excitement of ardent spirits. A little farther on, I passed a carrier's inn, and saw tall, long-faced, high-shouldered Munster Carmen, loading their drays, and preparing to take the road – for Sunday is the lucky day on which it is PROSPEROUS to commence a journey. A little farther, in the middle of the street, stood a group of Connaught men, congregating like swallows before they commenced their harvest migration. These poor creatures were preparing to go on board the steam-packet – the dark brown clothing, the reaping-hook on the shoulder, the wallet full of oaten cake suspended from behind, a black thorn bludgeon in hand. These low-statured, light-limbed, sallow-skinned bogtrotters, the descendants and true likeness of the red-shanked kernes, described by Spenser and Stanihurst, three hundred years ago, these gaping Westerlings presented themselves in curious contrast to one of Guinness's draymen, who at the instant passed by; his immense height, his sinewy breadth of body, made more manifest by the frowzy quilted frock which he wore. The poor potato-fed pigmies stood indeed in ridiculous juxta-position beside this "stoute churle," who exhibited what bacon, porter, and comparative idleness can do in bloating gout and enlarging the human frame.

*If any of our English readers should desire, when they visit Dublin, to see that part of the city where true Irish characteristics can be best observed, we would recommend a walk to Thomas-street, on a Saturday evening in Summer. It is the great retail street for the lower classes – the great resort of carriers and countrymen from the South and West of the kingdom. Here flock the ballad-singers, the news-venders, and the story-tellers; here you observe a woman, with her hoarse, vice-degraded voice, singing to the praise of whiskey; a little further, a fellow detailing the barbarous murder of a whole Catholic family by the bloody Orangemen; and just at the corner of a street may be observed a boy bellowing out, amidst an immense crowd, "The Bible-men defeated, or the glorious victory of the Rev. Father Maguire over the Protestant Pope." This street must ever remain infamous in the annals of Dublin, for the cold-blooded slaughter of Lord Kilwarden, in the year 1803. There scarcely exists on record a murder more inhuman or wanton than that of this venerable and excellent Judge. In this street also was Lord Edward Fitzgerald arrested, after a sanguinary struggle in the year 1798.

In Love with Europe | 2014

"I LIKE Germany," says the Polish writer Andrzej Stasiuk, "it's a world that is the opposite of ours … I don't admire Germany. I just like to go there from time to time to see how matter is tamed and organised."

In truth, the Germans are no more efficient at organising and taming matter than are the French or the Dutch or the Swedes (which is to say, perhaps, that they are quite efficient). What impresses me as much as taming – speaking as someone who doesn't know his granite from his limestone, his bracken from his scrub – is naming. Indeed I'm all in favour of leaving quite a lot of matter untamed, but it would be nice to know what everything is called, what everything is made of. Here is Johann Wolfgang von Goethe, in Castelvetrano near Trapani in western Sicily, on April 21st, 1787. *He* knows.

From Alcamo up to Castelvetrano one approaches the limestone mountains over gravel hills. Between the steep barren mountains lie broad upland valleys – the ground is all cultivated, but there are scarcely any trees. The extensive alluvial deposits which form the gravel hills indicate by their alignment the course of the currents in the primeval ocean. The soil is well mixed and, owing to its sand content, more friable. Salemi lay to our right, an hour's ride away. We crossed hills where the limestone was overlaid with beds of gypsum, and the composition of the soil improved still further. The foreground was all hills; far away to the west we could see the sea. We came upon fig trees in bud and, to our delight, great masses of flowers, which had formed colonies on the broad road and kept repeating themselves, one large multicoloured patch following closely on the last. Beautiful bindweeds, hibisci, rose-mallows and a great variety of clovers predominated by turns, interspersed with allium and bushes of goat's rue. We wound our way back on horseback, crossing and recrossing narrow paths. Russet-coloured cattle grazed here and there, small but well-built and with small, graceful horns.

In a recent article in *Le Monde* (April 8th) German sociologist and philosopher Ulrich Beck sets out his views of the kind of Europe we need (we'll undoubtedly be getting a lot of this kind of thing fairly soon here too from our European Parliament candidates and their house intellectuals). The piece is titled "*Oui à l'Europe des citronniers!*" (Yes to the Europe of the lemon trees!), a reference to a poem (later set to music) by Goethe known as *Kennst du das Land?* which, full of longing (*Sehnsucht*), is a good example of Northern romanticisation of the perceived charms of the South. These charms still have their appeal, and are more immediately accessible today than they were for Goethe: from Klagenfurt in Austria to beautiful Grado on the Adriatic is a mere two-hour drive roaring down the fast lane of the motorway in one's Audi. The Austrians leave their houses, shivering just a little, after a good breakfast on a Friday morning and are sitting at an outside table on the Viale del Sole by one o'clock, sipping Friulian wine and gorging on the small fishes of the lagoon. The waiters are very polite.

> *Kennst du das Land, wo die Zitronen blühn,*
> *Im dunklen Laub die Gold-Orangen glühn,*
> *Ein sanfter Wind vom blauen Himmel weht,*
> *Die Myrte still und hoch der Lorbeer steht,*
> *Kennst du es wohl?*
> *Dahin! Dahin*
> *Möcht'ich mit dir, o mein Geliebter, zieh'n.*

Do you know the land where the lemon-trees grow,
In darkened leaves the gold-oranges glow,
A soft wind blows from the pure blue sky,
The myrtle stands mute, and the bay tree high?
Do you know it well?
It's there I'd be gone,
To be there with you, O, my beloved one!

Beck dreams of a new Europe, much different from the troubled and depressed place we seem to inhabit today, which will be healed by Mediterranean weather, beauty, wine, hope, joy, regionalism, *savoir vivre* and of course lemons. Did I say wine? Could this work? Who knows? One can say with some certainty that it has never been tried.

The obsession with debt which Beck finds to be sadly characteristic of his fellow Germans has been "a grey and detestable mask" on this joyful, cosmopolitan Europe. One might perhaps say that

> if the Germans had learned from the players of *pétanque* [bowls or *boules*] they would never have plunged the world into the Second World War. Or if Chancellor Angela Merkel had been a devotee of *pétanque* she would never have tried to convert the Mediterranean countries to the virtues of such a very Protestant health cure for their economies. And if Putin had been born on the shores of the Mediterranean and had played *pétanque* from childhood he would never have had the totally mad idea of annexing Ukraine!

One might indeed say any of these things but what connection would they have to the reality in which we live and which we must hope, in some manner – to borrow Andrzej Stasiuk's terms – to organise and tame? But then Professor Beck, politically it seems an ally of the idealistic but rather globalist European federalists (Delors, Cohn-Bendit, Verhofstadt etc) is introduced by *Le Monde* as a *sociologue* and *philosophe* – academic disciplines the point of whose prognoses I often have great difficulty in grasping. He is certainly not a *politologue*, and still less an *historien*.

I think it unlikely that Europe can be healed by the Mediterranean. First of all, for the reason that the Mediterranean might feel (does feel, to a considerable extent – the question of with what justification we will put aside for now) that it is Europe that has made it ill. Second, one can be intrigued and charmed by Europe's oldest cultures, their traditions and their considerable material relics. But that will not necessarily make us Europeans. Far from it. Remember that couple in the Piazza del Populo in Arezzo, she with her *Sunday Telegraph*, he with his perfectly pressed chinos, bickering over the price of the Chianti and braying loudly – in English of course – to the unfortunate waiter. Tuscany every year. But Europeans? I don't think so.

Love in the Afternoon | 2015

THE GRAFTON Cinema, formerly The Grafton Picture House, closed its doors at some stage in the 1970s. I was quite sad at the time, as it was a pleasant refuge for myself and my student pals on those sunny afternoons when the library seemed a grim antechamber to death.

The Grafton opened its doors on Easter Monday 1911. The building, especially its interior, which was designed by William Orpen's brother Richard, was impressive. A feeling of stepping away from the humdrum descended as one entered the cool and elegant hallway which led to the cinema theatre. Films and shorts of all sorts were continuously screened from midday. I saw *Don't Start the Revolution without Me*, starring Donald Sutherland and Gene Wilder, there. I have always been afraid to see it again just in case I don't still find it mindblowingly funny. The Grafton was perfect for anyone skiving off or wishing to have a secret rendezvous. There was always something on.

In the mid-1920s, The Grafton Picture House was well known to Rubin MacKenzie, a young man whose people were "well-to-do" Catholics. The family started out in Ardenza Terrace in Monkstown. Later they moved to Stradbrook in Blackrock and finally settled into a Shrewsbury Road mansion. The head of the family in the 1901 census was James MacKenzie, a shipbroker. Although wealthy, he was unlucky, and he died young a few years after that census. The religion of his wife, Frances, was given as Roman Catholic, while his was given as Presbyterian, as was that of his children who, at the time, were all male. A common agreement in "mixed" marriages was that the males would take the father's religion and the girls would follow that of the mother. It might be that after three sons Frances felt that in terms of the children's religious affiliation she had got the short end of the stick. But perhaps the listing under the father's denomination was more nominal than actual. In any event, by the time of the 1911 census Frances at forty years of age was head of the family and all her children were listed as Roman Catholic.

Simone Henry was also familiar with the Grafton and had, like Frances, entered into a religiously mixed marriage. Simone was French. Her father was a member of the Paris bourse and his daughter had been educated in France,

England and Germany. She was in Germany when the Great War broke out and returned home to join the Red Cross and drive an ambulance. She met her husband, WAD Henry – an Irish officer in the British army – at a dance at her father's house in Paris. The young pair were attracted to each other and a marriage was agreed before Lieutenant (later Captain) Henry returned to the front, where he unfortunately lost both his legs.

The planned marriage went ahead notwithstanding the disaster which had befallen the groom. The couple were married in a Paris registry office and also in the Anglican Church attached to the British embassy in Paris. Later, when they moved to Dublin, they were married once more in Harrington Street Church on the South Circular Road, Captain Henry having agreed to convert to Catholicism at his wife's request.

Simone was an energetic young woman in her twenties and found that she liked to leave her Fitzwilliam Square home and socialise in the evening. In the court case which eventually followed her involvement with Rubin MacKenzie, her husband said that he did not object to his wife going out alone, and that he was aware of and approved of her friendship with MacKenzie, a man with whom she dined regularly in the city's hotels and with whom she attended dances. Captain Henry, described as "a gentleman of considerable position in this country", may well have been telling the truth or it may be that he was, understandably, striving to avoid public shame – quite likely both.

Whatever the original purpose of her solo outings, Simone became very friendly with MacKenzie and it appears the pair fell in love. Back in the big house in Blackrock, Rubin's mother began to notice changes in his behaviour. Among other things he was staying out very late, and not only at weekends. In time she became concerned. According to his mother's evidence, he withdrew from his family's society and did not offer any explanation for his behaviour. This withdrawal from family life may have been due to distraction caused by an overwhelming emotional involvement. It seems also that he left Simone's letters lying around his bedroom, which was certainly indiscreet, if not the action of a man distracted by passion.

It was not so very long before Mrs MacKenzie picked up some of those letters and read them, with what degree of unease we can only surmise. The real horror may have followed only when she learned that Simone was "a married woman". We may assume she regarded Rubin's involvement with her as the potential ruination of a son she had struggled through widowhood to raise into social respectability. During the trial, Simone's counsel put it to Frances MacKenzie that her behaviour in reading Simone's letters was underhand. Frances rejected that suggestion, saying the letters were lying there in Rubin's wardrobe for anyone to read. This was hardly a convincing response but the court was not the place to explain that the prospect of a son's moral and social ruin would certainly allow a mother some flexibility in the area of his private business.

Whether acting on information gleaned from the letters or from another source, Mrs MacKenzie learned that her son was to visit the Grafton Picture House with Mrs Henry. One afternoon in the late summer of 1926, she pressed her – perhaps unwilling – daughter (also called Frances) into service and the pair made their way into town and slipped into the row behind the lovers in the cinema. The whole business might still have been dealt with privately were it not for what transpired outside the cinema.

Outside on Grafton Street Frances senior approached Simone and told her that if she didn't accompany her across the road and into South Anne Street she would call a policeman. Simone asked Rubin who the woman was, to which he replied "She is my Mother." Simone crossed with Frances, agreeing with Ruben that they would meet five minutes later in the Shelbourne Hotel. It was to be a long five minutes. In fact all four crossed the road, stopping at the third parked car.

It is interesting that Mrs MacKenzie confronted Simone rather than Rubin. A sense of unquestioning righteousness is reflected in her strange threat to "call a policeman". She could, figuratively speaking, have taken Rubin home by the ear and demanded an end to the relationship on pain of severe financial penalty. Indeed she could have done this at home, saving herself and her daughter the train journey. But she was aware that in Rubin's case it was more than an inappropriate dalliance which could be rationally challenged and that it was less a case of her son being bad than having fallen into the power of "a bad woman"; her Rubin had been bewitched by a Jezebel.

There were aspects of the whole business which Simone appears to have found mystifying. As she pointed out at the trial, Rubin was a grown man and presumably knew his own mind. No one cares to have their private business aired on the public street and this may have been behind Simone's suggestion that they converse in French. She perhaps also wished to use a language which was replete with terms adequate to discussing difficult questions pertaining to relationships and matters of sexual delicacy. Rubin's mother rejected this idea out of hand saying she would speak in "her own language" and it transpired that the English spoken in Dublin at the time was well able to encapsulate the full degrees of her hostility and outrage.

Mrs MacKenzie demanded that Simone tell her what "claim she had on her son" and allegedly said that Simone was "a respectable prostitute", that she was from the gutter, that she had "stopped a week" with a Mr Reddin, that she did not believe that she was married to "that man with no legs", and that she would throw her into a shop window and shoot her.

This was too much for Simone to endure. She told Frances that if it were not for her age she would slap her face. The self-confident *Parisienne*, confronted by a provincial matron, cannot have felt she had anything to apologise for. The son, as she said in court, was a grown man. Instead of slapping her face she brought Frances before the courts alleging slander. Too late did Frances learn she was not dealing with someone from "the gutter" who would cower before her social betters or someone who would melt away in the face of her moral perfidy being exposed; rather someone who could afford good lawyers and who would on principle bring her into court and see the whole business ventilated before a jury of ordinary Dubliners and reported in the press. It must have been an appalling vista for Frances, exacerbated, if possible, when Simone won the case and was awarded fifty pounds in damages.

During the case the lovers denied they were lovers. Rubin, when asked questions about the letters, repeatedly said he could not remember. Simone was asked about one letter in which she spoke of a joint visit to Paris. "How can I go to Paris without you my Rubin? I love you Rubin and you know it and will do so whatever happens." In her explanation Simone was economical with the truth. She said that this was merely an expression of friendship, that Mrs MacKenzie's counsel was bad-minded and that the French and Irish looked on these matters differently. Her husband, WAD Henry, made the same point about differing attitudes between the French and the Irish. The Irish press which covered the trial was fascinated by the idea of differences between French and Irish concepts of friendship.

At the distance of nearly a century, it is possible to see this in large measure as a clash of cultures, a conflict between the values of Parisian bourgeois culture and those of conservative middle class Dublin. Twentieth century Ireland never really had a European-style bourgeoisie. It did have a wealthy upper middle class, but that is a different thing altogether. The concepts of friendship were indeed different. It was difficult for 1920s Dublin to comprehend was that while the French bourgeoisie demanded discretion they did not make a tectonic fuss over adultery and that in certain circumstances it might well occur with a spouse's effective consent.

Communication between Ruben and Simone ceased. My guess is that Simone returned to Paris and that Rubin continued to be employed in the "office", from which it was said during the trial he might have had to resign. But who can be entirely sure what followed?

Orange Socks and Guacamole | 2015

THERE IS a well-known story that back in the 1990s Peter (now Lord) Mandelson dropped into a fish and chip shop while canvassing with local Labour Party members in his Hartlepool constituency and ordered haddock and chips; then, pointing to the mushy peas which are a favourite complement to that dish in the north of England, he is supposed to have added: "And I'll have some of that guacamole too."

The story is, of course, too good to be true, or at least too good to be true about Peter Mandelson. Apparently something of the kind did indeed happen to a young American intern working with the Labour Party around the same time and the story of her misapprehension came to the ears of Neil Kinnock, who found it highly amusing, could not resist retelling it and eventually had the bright idea of substituting as its protagonist his party colleague, a man whose cultural comfort zone was presumed to be strikingly at variance with those of his constituents in the safe northeastern seat that had been found for him after his successful stint as Labour's director of communications (a post to which Kinnock had appointed him).

On one level this is simply a story of political fun – somewhat spiteful fun perhaps, though at a fairly harmless level. But it also says something about how the British like to see themselves in relation to things culturally foreign, in this case particularly the British working class but arguably a broader swathe of society than that. In the Peter Morgan/Stephen Frears television film *The Deal* (2003), which revolves around the contest for the Labour leadership after the sudden death of John Smith, the wonderful Paul Rhys plays Mandelson as a softspoken, feline schemer, whose delicate transfer of his support from Brown to Blair proves to be decisive. Certainly Mandelson appears a strange fish to the hard-drinking Praetorian Guard of Scottish Labour MPs (remember Scottish Labour MPs?) surrounding Smith, who remarks with apparent shock that he seems to be wearing orange socks. Gordon Brown's chirpy cornerman Charlie Whelan meanwhile remarks: "That man smells of vanilla." It is of course far from irrelevant that this exotic intruder into the macho political world of Westminster is gay, and perhaps not completely irrelevant that his family background is partly Jewish.

There is a long tradition of associating "sophistication", particularly when that means a weakness for elegance or ostentation of dress or what is seen as a too refined or cosmopolitan taste in food or drink, with decadence, sexual licence, "effeminacy" and a decline in the homespun values (which of course have served us well). George Orwell, always a blowhard in such matters, routinely referred to some of the most accomplished poets of his era as "pansies". Some of them were indeed homosexual or bisexual but Orwell, whom it would be inaccurate to see as homophobic in the normal sense of the word, was thinking of many things other than sexual orientation. When he said that certain people (fashionable literary-political intellectuals) took their cookery from Paris and their opinions from Moscow, he was referring to what he saw as an unfortunate deviation from the natural, plain and decent, healthy and normal virtues – virtues he perhaps overvalued. Auden, one of Orwell's favourite targets, was, curiously enough, referring to much the same cultural gulf between the plain and the sophisticated in his oft-quoted lines "To the man-in-the-street who,

I'm sorry to say, / Is a keen observer of life, / The word intellectual suggests right away / A man who's untrue to his wife."

But how easy is it to establish what is plain and healthy and decent? Is an apparent lack of sophistication or intellectuality, a sturdy normality, an essentially English trait? Certainly it is one that can pay a political dividend: while poor Ed Miliband showed, to the satisfaction of many, through his inability to convincingly eat a bacon sandwich that he was not prime-ministerial material, Nigel Farage loves to be photographed with a pint of beer in his hand, and sometimes a cigar, just like a normal bloke. And the camera normally does not follow him into the restaurant, where it is said he has been known to polish off a bottle or two of Nuits-Saint-Georges.

Have the British, or the English, always been enthusiasts for plain "unmucked about with" food or is this merely a result of conditioning that derives from the introduction of mass-produced (highly spiced and salted) industrial branded grocery goods in the nineteenth and early twentieth centuries? One of the earliest English cookbooks, *A Boke of Cokery*, written about 1440, suggests that there may have been a considerable complexity and delicacy associated with English cuisine in the late medieval period, at least in the houses of the more prosperous. Here is a recipe for "custarde" – not custard as we know it, rather something like a meat quiche:

Take Vele (veal), and smyte hit in lituʰ peces, and wassh it clene; put hit into a faire potte with faire water, and lete hit boyle togidre; þeñ (then) take parcelly, Sauge (sage), Isoppe (hyssop), Sauerey (savoury), wassh hem, hewe hem, And cast hem into flessh whan hit boileth; theñ take powder of peper, canel (cinnamon), Clowes (cloves), Maces, Saffroñ, salt, and lete hem boyle togidre, and a goode dele of wyne with aʰ, And whañ the flessh is boyled, take it vppe fro þe (the) broth, And lete the broth kele. Whañ hit is colde, streyne yolkes and white of egges thorgh a streynour, and put hem (them) to the broth, so many that the broth be styff ynowe, And make faire cofyns (pie crusts), and couche iij. or iiij. (three or four) peces of the flessh in þe (the) Coffyns; then take Dates, prunes, and kutte hem; cast thereto powder of Gynger and a lituʰ Vergeous (verjuice), and put to the broth, and salt; theñ lete the coffyñ and the flessh bake a lituʰ; And þen put the broth in the coffyns, And lete hem bake till they be ynogh.

One of the main tropes of contemporary academic study (of almost anything in the humanities field, it seems) is the notion of "the other", the other being the people who are not like us, the uncivilised, the savage, the sinister, the threatening. For "Westerners", a wide category extending from ancient Greeks to modern Canadians, the other has over time included any number of peoples: the Persians, the Scythians, the Mongols, the Arabs, the Ottoman Turks, "native peoples" of many hues and body shapes, the Russians, the Arabs (or simply Muslims) again, the Russians again. And as well as real others there have been mythical ones, always lurking just beyond the known world: in Shakespeare's words "the Cannibals that each other eat, / The Anthropophagi, and men whose heads / Do grow beneath their shoulders". Of course it will usually be the case – and this seems to be less often emphasised in academic discourse – that those we consider to be other may very well look on us in the same way. Medieval travellers believed that the apparently well-attested race of dog-headed men lived somewhere in the Far East and when they first arrived there they asked where they might find them. But their hosts replied: "The dog-heads? We've heard of them of course. But we thought they lived among you, in the West."

The Greek geographer, traveller and historian Strabo (64/63 BC to AD 24) believed that a people's degree of civilisation could normally be measured by its degree of proximity to the Mediterranean (he himself was born nearer the Black Sea, in what is now Turkey). This said a lot about the Britons, but of course even more about the Irish, wilder yet, who according to Strabo ate their dead fathers and had sex with their mothers and sisters. And yet civilisation and its antithesis – savagery, uncouthness, or, seen in a somewhat different and more positive light, simplicity of manners – can be viewed in more than one way. Thus we can construe the Mandelson fable to suggest that a man who likes to wolf down a helping of mushy peas with his fish and chips is a man you can trust, while a man who mistakes it for some foreign muck he eats up in London is one you cannot. There can be virtue, it seems, in a lack of sophistication (or pretension), which should not of course be mistaken for a lack of intelligence: if a Yorkshireman tells you "I'm a plain man, me" that should not lead you to think that you are likely to best him in a financial transaction.

The historian Tacitus (AD 56 to c117) used his accounts of the military campaigns against the northern tribes and nations (Germans, Britons) to teach his Roman audiences some moral lessons: chiefly that their society was too decadent and soft and that if it wished to survive it might possibly have to learn something from the rude barbarians. Cassius Dio (AD 155 to 235), writing in the same vein, has the British warrior queen Boudica (Boadicea) encouraging her soldiers with reflections on the softness of their Roman enemies compared with their own sturdiness and adaptability: "They need bread and wine and oil, and if any of these things fails them, they die. For us, on the other hand, any grass or root serves as bread, the juice of any plant as oil, any water as wine." She may well be just a woman, she tells her troops, but the real woman, she insists (in Charlotte Higgins's translation), "is the emperor Nero, playing the lyre back in Rome, smeared in make-up. Free us from these Roman men, she begs – if they are men at all, with their warm-water bathing, their wine-imbibing, myrrh-perfumed homosexuality."

As the anti-European ultras, well-organised and likely to be supported by two or three major newspapers, gird up in their campaign to take Britain out of the EU we can expect to hear a lot more about the unique qualities of the island race, its toughness, resilience, independence, robust common sense and contempt for Jesuitical or bureaucratical scheming, not to mention wine sauces. Curiously, the modern Boudica, Mrs Thatcher, was a lot less isolationist than many of those who would now claim her as an inspiration might like to think. "Britain does not dream of some cosy, isolated existence on the fringes of the European Community. Our destiny is in Europe, as part of the Community," she told the College of Europe in Bruges in 1988.

Charlotte Higgins, in her wonderful study *Under Another Sky: Journeys in Roman Britain*, tells of the public reaction which flowed in 2011 from an article in *Antiquity* and subsequent coverage in the *Daily Mail* of the discovery in York of the skull of a young woman who became known as "the ivory bangle lady". Under the headline "Revealed: The African queen who called York home in the fourth century", the *Mail* quoted archaeologist Dr Hella Eckardt, who said: "We're looking at a population mix which is closer to contemporary Britain than previous historians had expected. In the case of York, the Roman population may have had more diverse origins than the city has now ... [The bangle lady's] case contradicts assumptions that may derive from more recent historical experience, namely that immigrants are low status and male and that African individuals are likely to have been slaves."

The readers of the *Mail*, or of its website, were not going to take this lying down. "More mult-cult propaganda and lies," wrote "Oppenheimer" from Dartford. "Derrick", in Nottingham, described the research as "insidious, neo-Marxist, multi-cultist propaganda". And while "David" from Nottinghamshire thought it was all a "desperate attempt to fool us into thinking we've always had a multi-racial society", "Ste" in Middlesbrough took some comfort from the thought that "if we were multicultural once and managed to reverse it, we can do it again".

There is a problem, however, in regarding the York find as a fake or as something insignificant freighted with too much meaning by academics with an agenda, for the evidence of the cosmopolitanism of Roman Britain – the thoroughgoing internationalism of its military and administrative machine – is lying about everywhere. In northwest Glasgow, Higgins, following the traces of the Antonine Wall, moves from New Kilpatrick Cemetery, full of the graves of Curries, Gillespies and Capaldis, to the prosperous suburb of Bearsden, where a set of Roman bathhouses can be found among the large gardens and adjacent to a 1970s block of flats. "When the archaeologists analysed sewage deposits from the Roman latrines," she writes, "they found that the soldiers had been eating raspberries, strawberries and figs, and poppy- and coriander-seed bread. As were, I suspected, the middle classes of today's Bearsden."

It is, of course, possible to shut one's mind to all of this cultural complexity and hybridity, to see Roman Britain as just a top layer, and Norman Britain another one, under which the unchanging life of the sturdy common people – first Britons, then Saxons – went on uninterrupted and largely unchanged throughout the centuries. For the island-race ultras this is a comforting theory, but theories can often be undermined by evidence.

For the people that made itself great and painted the globe pink on a plain diet of roast beef and ale, wine, one can affect to believe, was until very recently a drink for toffs only, while hummus, tapenade or guacamole were, and are, indulged in only by funny folk. But in 2011, excavations in the buried Roman town of Silchester in Hampshire reached down below the Roman stratum to the ancient British settlement underneath, dating back at the very least two thousand years. Perhaps the most remarkable object they found there was an olive stone. And thus the idea of Britain's "natural" cultural isolation from Europe seemed, yet again, to be compromised by a tiny piece of detritus half the size of a fingernail, casually tossed aside no doubt by some Iron Age metrosexual.

Pass the Palaver | 2016

JAMES JOYCE, who was born 135 years ago today (February 2nd), was, like most great artists, unusually observant. The mosaic of Dublin life, revealed throughout his work, is based on the behavioural minutiae of the city's population, behaviour which he registered aurally and visually like no one before or since. And despite the vast expanse which is Joycean studies, one suspects that not all from the great scope of his eye and ear has yet been fully noted or considered against the historical record of life in Edwardian Dublin.

The term sexual harassment, though unknown to Joyce, refers to something which is probably ancient but in any event certainly existed in early twentieth century Dublin. The phrase would have been immediately comprehensible to Joyce and, as with so many behaviours, reference to the phenomenon is found in his work.

Above any other category of women, those in service, that is to say household servants, women who would encounter tradesmen, delivery boys, male employers and their sons and who would be out and about on messages, were the ones most likely to encounter the problem. Women in service – and there were vast numbers in this category – were away from their own families, isolated, and often lonely, which compounded their vulnerability and susceptibility. Their situation facilitated a pattern of eroticisation in male consideration.

When Leopold Bloom goes shopping in search of a prized offal delicacy to consume for his breakfast he encounters the servant girl of his neighbour Woods and quickly finds himself engaged in an erotic fantasy. As he contemplates the servant's hips he imagines her swaying as she beats a carpet. (Poldy Bloom had for sure certain masochistic tendencies!) The reverie continues to address the girl's ideal terms of engagement: "no followers allowed". Better opportunities for engagement if the girl is isolated seems to be the underlying logic. Bloom, of course, is a decent cove and his erotic misdeeds are conducted in the privacy of his own imagination.

The main protagonist in Joyce's story "Two Gallants" is less gentlemanly, engaging as he does in the calculated exploitation of a servant girl's loneliness. The reader learns that the girl, who is a "slavey" in a Baggot Street house, has been sexually and emotionally exploited over a period by her supposed beau. The story focuses on a third and final piece of nastiness as the girl is cajoled into handing over the substantial sum of a half-sovereign, which will be spent, one assumes, by the gallants on drink.

But perhaps the most poignant reference occurs in Joyce's masterpiece novella "The Dead". It is generally recognised that things did not go well for its main character, Gabriel Conroy, on the night of the misses Morkans' annual Christmas party, held in their rooms above the cornfactor's premises on Usher's Island.

Some readers can't stand Gabriel but others, like the present writer, are sympathetic. There has been much acknowledgement over the years of Miss Ivors's cutting attack on him for preferring France to the West of Ireland and learning European languages instead of Irish, which culminated with the whispered insult "West Briton". (I wonder could Miss Ivors's attack could be construed as a form of sexual harassment.)

In the course of the evening Gabriel is assailed by self-doubt, apparently sparked by Miss Ivors's words. In the end, as snow falls across the country "on all the living and the dead", he realises his wife's feelings for him will never match those she holds for the dead boy Michael Furey, who stood outside her window in the cold and the rain wanting to die for love, not something one could easily imagine Gabriel undertaking, with or without his galoshes. All in all a pretty devastating evening for the *Daily Express*'s book reviewer.

It is less frequently observed that Gabriel's evening took on its bleak character from the moment he stepped into his aunts' house. As he handed his coat to the young housemaid, Lily, whom he had known over many years, he attempted pleasantries:

- Tell me Lily, he said in a friendly tone, do you still go to school?
- Oh no sir, she answered. I'm done schooling this year and more.
- O, then, said Gabriel gaily, I suppose we'll be going to your wedding one of these fine days with your young man, eh?

The girl glanced back at him over her shoulder and said with great bitterness:

- The men that is now is only all palaver and what they can get out of you.

Gabriel is quite thrown out of his stride. The author comments that he coloured as if he felt that he had made a mistake. Lily's sour note cuts the ground from under him and his forced jollity. It sets the tone for his evening.

Joyce, in touching slightly on this theme, was, as in so many aspects of his depiction of life in the dowdy city, reflecting a reality of its life. A letter written by a servant's employer to a newspaper would seem to confirm this. It was published on October 28th, 1915.

Much has been made of the low pay of women employed in factories in Dublin, the bad housing conditions under which the working classes live, and the drink evil ... Overlooked [is] the most important point of all, that is the deplorable fact that there are at present in Dublin a large number of men – if I can call them men – who set themselves out to lead unfortunate girls astray. The happy hunting ground of these gentlemen is not confined to the neighbourhood of the North Wall, Amiens Street or Marlborough Street; they also infest the suburbs and molest girls, mostly servant girls, in such quarters as Rathmines, Ranelagh, Ballsbridge and Sandymount. The prowlers ... are invariably well dressed and groomed ... A specimen of this class molested a most respectable young woman in my employment – the wife of a soldier fighting for his country ... Like all of his kind he was well dressed and in this particular instance sported white 'spats' ... A half-starved or silly woman found stealing is promptly sent to jail, but there seems to be no redress or remedy for what I have referred to.

Notes on Contributors

RACHEL ANDREWS is a writer and journalist. Her reportage has been published in literary journals including the *Dublin Review*, and her essay "A New Wilderness at the Maze", documenting the destruction of the Maze prison, was winner of the inaugural essay prize (2013) at the Centre for Documentary Studies, Duke University, North Carolina. Her essays and reviews have appeared in *Irish Theatre Magazine*, the *Dublin Review of Books* and the *Sunday Business Post*. She has contributed to RTÉ radio and BBC Radio 4.

DAVID BLAKE KNOX is a former director of production with RTÉ and executive editor with BBC Television. His independent production company, Blueprint Pictures, was founded in 2002, and has produced a range of TV programmes and films – including *Imagining Ulysses*, a feature documentary about James Joyce's novel. His book *Suddenly, While Abroad: Hitler's Irish Slaves* was published in 2012 by New Island Books.

FRANK CALLANAN is a senior counsel practising in Dublin and a historian. He has written *The Parnell Split* (1992) and *T.M. Healy* (1996). He is currently writing a book, to be entitled *The Shade of Parnell*, on the influence of Parnell and the Parnell split on James Joyce, and on Joyce's treatment of the Parnell myth.

MICHAEL CRONIN teaches at Dublin City University. He has published widely on aspects of language, culture, identity and translation. Among his works are *Time Tracks: Scenes from the Irish Everyday* (New Island, 2003) and *Translation in the Digital Age* (Routledge, 2013). He is a member of the Royal Irish Academy and the Academia Europeae.

CATRIONA CROWE is head of special projects at the National Archives of Ireland, and adjunct professor of history at the University of Limerick. She is a member of the Royal Irish Academy.

DENIS DONOGHUE's most recent book is *Metaphor*, published by Harvard University Press in 2014.

TERRY EAGLETON is professor of cultural theory at the National University of Ireland, Galway, professor of English literature at Lancaster University, and distinguished visiting professor of English literature at Notre Dame. His most recent book is *Culture* (Yale University Press, 2016).

MAURICE EARLS is a bookseller and joint editor of the *Dublin Review of Books*.

ROY FOSTER is Carroll Professor of Irish History at the University of Oxford and the author of many books on modern Irish history and culture, including *Modern Ireland 1600–1972* (1989), *Paddy and Mr Punch* (1993), *The Irish Story: telling tales and making it up in Ireland* (2001), *Luck and the Irish: a brief history of change, 1970–2000* (2007), *Words Alone: Yeats and his Inheritances* (2011) and the prizewinning two-volume biography of WB Yeats, *The Apprentice Mage, 1865–1914* (1997) and *The Arch Poet, 1915–1939* (2003). He has also written biographies of Charles Stewart Parnell (1977) and Lord Randolph Churchill (1981). His most recent book is *Vivid Faces: the revolutionary generation in Ireland, c 1890–1923* (2014). He is also a well-known cultural commentator, broadcaster and critic.

HUGH GOUGH is emeritus professor of history at University College Dublin. Born and educated in England, he did his undergraduate studies and doctoral research at Oxford, before joining the history department in UCD in 1968. He has published articles and books on different aspects of the French Revolution, including *The Newspaper Press in the French Revolution* (1988 & 2016), *The Terror in the French Revolution* (1998 & 2008). He has also edited and contributed to books on the Huguenots in Ireland, Ireland and the French Revolution, and Charles de Gaulle. He is currently completing a book on the history of the guillotine.

TIM GROENLAND teaches in the School of English at Trinity College, Dublin and in the School of English, Drama, and Film at University College Dublin. He recently completed a PhD at Trinity College on editing processes in the fiction of Raymond Carver and David Foster Wallace.

ADRIAN HARDIMAN was a judge in the Irish Supreme Court and a Joycean scholar. He died in 2016.

JOSEPH M HASSETT is an experienced trial lawyer and literary scholar living in Washington DC. He is a graduate of Harvard Law School and holds a PhD from University College Dublin. His book *W.B. Yeats and the Muses* was published by Oxford University Press in 2010 and his *The* Ulysses *Trials: Beauty and Truth Meet the Law* by Lilliput in 2016.

TOM HENNIGAN was born and raised in Dublin and has lived in South America since 2003. Currently based in São Paulo, he covers the region for *The Irish Times* among other publications.

JOHN HORGAN has been a journalist for many years, notwithstanding detours (some of them lengthy) into electoral politics, academia and media regulation. He is the author of a number of political biographies and of books on Irish media.

BENJAMIN KEATINGE is dean of the faculty of languages, cultures and communication and head of English at the South East European University, Macedonia. He is co-editor of *France and Ireland in the Public Imagination* (Peter Lang, 2014) and *Other Edens: The Life and Work of Brian Coffey* (Irish Academic Press, 2010) and author of several essays and reviews on Samuel Beckett.

CATHERINE MARSHALL is an art historian and joint editor of Volume V (The Twentieth Century) of the Royal Irish Academy's five-volume *Art and Architecture of Ireland*. She lectured in the history of art department of Trinity College Dublin and at the National College of Art and Design and is currently head of the visual arts steering committee for Bealtaine, the biggest, most inclusive arts festival in Ireland.

LARA MARLOWE has been a foreign correspondent for *The Irish Times* for the past twenty years. She currently lives in Paris.

CALISTA McRAE is an assistant professor in the humanities department at the New Jersey Institute of Technology in Newark, New Jersey. She received her PhD in English from Harvard University, where she specialised in lyric poetry. Her current book project, *Lyric as Comedy*, focuses on humour in twentieth and twenty-first century American poets.

PÁDRAIG MURPHY is a retired official of Ireland's Department of Foreign Affairs. He served as ambassador to the then Soviet Union from 1981 to 1985.

EILÉAN NÍ CHUILLEANÁIN is a poet and editor. Her latest collection is *The Boys of Bluehill*.

GEORGE O'BRIEN was born in Enniscorthy and reared in Lismore, Co Waterford. He is a professor emeritus of English at Georgetown University, Washington DC.

NIALL Ó CIOSÁIN is senior lecturer in the school of humanities at NUI, Galway. He is the author of *Ireland in Official Print Culture 1800–50* (2014) and *Print and Popular Culture in Ireland 1750–1850* (1997), and has published articles on the Great Famine and popular memory, book history and popular reading. He is currently writing a book about publishing and reading in the Celtic languages in the eighteenth and nineteenth centuries.

ÉAMON Ó CLÉIRIGH is a pen name used by the late Brian Earls.

ENDA O'DOHERTY worked first as a bookseller and then, from 1988 to 2016, as a journalist, first with the *Irish Press* and then *The Irish Times*. He is joint editor of the *Dublin Review of Books*.

FERGUS O'FERRALL is the author of the standard account of the struggle for Catholic Emancipation, *Catholic Emancipation: Daniel O'Connell and the Birth of Irish Democracy 1820–30* (Dublin, 1985). He has written a number of books and articles on Irish history and local history and has contributed articles and reviews to the *Dublin Review of Books*.

CORMAC Ó GRÁDA is professor emeritus of economics at University College Dublin. He has recently published papers on topics ranging from the European Little Ice Age and London's last plague epidemics to the origins of the Industrial Revolution and the welfare costs of antibiotic resistance. His best-known books are on Irish economic history, the socio-economic history of Irish Jewry, and the global history of famine.

SEAN O'HUIGINN retired from the Irish diplomatic service in 2009. His most recent foreign postings included service as Ireland's ambassador to Washington, Berlin and Rome. He also served in various capacities in the Department of Foreign Affairs in Dublin, including as head of the department's Anglo-Irish division during the formative stage of the Northern Ireland peace process between 1991 and 1997.

PHILIP O'LEARY teaches at Boston College. His most recent book is *Writing Beyond the Revival: Facing the Future in Gaelic Prose 1940–1951* (UCD Press) and he was co-editor, with Margaret Kelleher, of the *Cambridge History of Irish Literature*. He holds an honorary LLD from NUI Galway.

SEAMUS O'MAHONY has been a regular contributor to the *drb* since 2013. He is a consultant physician. His book *The Way We Die Now* was published by Head of Zeus in May 2016.

BARRA Ó SEAGHDHA has contributed essays, interviews and reviews in the fields of poetry, politics, cultural history and music to a wide variety of publications. Having worked in the EFL sector for many years, he has recently completed a doctorate on classical music in Irish cultural history.

SIOBHÁN PARKINSON is a novelist and children's writer and served as the inaugural Laureate na nÓg. She translates from German and is publisher of Little Island Books.

MATTHEW PARKINSON-BENNETT lives in Dublin and works as an editor and writer. He studied English and philosophy at UCD and completed his MPhil in medieval English at the University of Oxford in 2011.

DEREK SCALLY was born in Raheny in Dublin and studied at DCU and at Berlin's Humboldt University. Since 2000 he has lived in Berlin as the *Irish Times* correspondent, reporting on current affairs and cultural matters in Germany, Austria and Poland.

DEIRDRE SERJEANTSON is a lecturer in Renaissance literature at the University of Essex. Her research interests include the theory and practice of translation.

GERARD SMYTH has published eight collections of poetry, including *A Song of Elsewhere* (Dedalus Press 2015), and *The Fullness of Time: New and Selected Poems* (Dedalus Press, 2010). He is co-editor, with Pat Boran, of *If Ever You Go: A Map of Dublin in Poetry and Song* (Dedalus Press).

KEVIN STEVENS's books include the children's fantasy *The Powers*, which was a UNESCO Dublin Citywide Read in 2014, and *A Lonely Note*, a novel about a young Muslim man's challenges living in America. He also writes about jazz and literature and divides his time between Dublin and Cambridge, Massachusetts.

JOHN SWIFT retired from the Irish Department of Foreign Affairs in 2006. His last posts were as ambassador to Cyprus, ambassador to the Netherlands and permanent representative to the UN (Geneva).

CAROL TAAFFE is a researcher and writer based in Dublin. She has published a book on Flann O'Brien with Cork University Press, and is a contributor to the *Dublin Review of Books* and the *Dublin Review*.

JAMES WARD lectures in eighteenth century literature at Ulster University. He has published widely on this subject and is completing a book entitled *Memory and Enlightenment*.

PADRAIG YEATES is a journalist and author whose books include a quartet on Dublin in the decade of centenaries, *Lockout: Dublin 1913*, *A City in Wartime: Dublin 1914–1918*, *A City in Turmoil: Dublin 1919–1921* and *A City in Civil War: Dublin 1923*.